NOTES ON A COWARDLY LION

NOTES ON A COWARDLY LION

The Biography of Bert Lahr

John Lahr

Limelight Editions, New York

Library of Congress Cataloging in Publication Data

Lahr, John, 1941–
Notes on a cowardly lion.

Includes index.
1. Lahr, Bert, 1895–1967. 2. Entertainers—United
States—Biography. I. Title.

PN2287.L15L3   1984   791′.092′4 [B]   83-25134

Acknowledgment is gratefully extended to the following for
permission to reprint from copyrighted material:

Alfred A. Knopf, Inc.: *In Seach of Theatre*, by Eric Bentley. Copyright
1947, 1948, 1949, 1950, 1951, 1952, 1953 by Eric Bentley. *The Con-
fessions of Felix Krull*, by Thomas Mann. Copyright © 1955 by Alfred
A. Knopf, Inc. Atheneum Publishers: *Curtains*, by Kenneth Tynan.
Copyright © 1961 by Kenneth Tynan. "Baseball Sketch," by Abe Burrows, is reprinted by permission of the author from *Two on the Aisle*, a
revue by Betty Comden, Adolph Green, and Jule Styne. Directed by Abe
Burrows. Chandler Publishing Company: *Comedy: Meaning and Form*,
by Robert W. Corrigan. Chappell & Co.,Inc.: "But in the Morning No,"
copyright 1939 by Chappell & Co., Inc. Copyright renewed. "It Ain't
Etiquette," copyright © 1965 by Chappell & Co., Inc. "Friendship,"
copyright 1939 by Chappell & Co., Inc. Copyright renewed. "Dainty,
Quainty, Me," copyright © 1967 by John F. Wharton as Trustee of the
Cole Porter Musical and Literary Property Trust. An excerpt from an
interview with Alan Schneider in *Chelsea Review*, Autumn, 1958, is
reprinted by permission of Alan Schneider. Leo Feist Inc.: "If I Were
King of the Forest," from the M-G-M motion picture *The Wizard of Oz*
—lyrics by E. Y. Harburg, music by Harold Arlen. Copyright 1938 (renewed) Metro-Goldwyn-Mayer Inc. Copyright © 1968 Metro-Goldwyn-
Mayer Inc. Rights throughout the world controlled by Leo Feist Inc.
Used by permission. Grove Press, Inc.: *Waiting for Godot: Tragicomedy
in Two Acts*, by Samuel Beckett. Translated from the original French
text by the author. Copyright 1954 by Grove Press. *Embers: A Play
for Radio*, from *Krapp's Last Tape and Other Dramatic Pieces*, by
Samuel Beckett. Copyright © 1957 by Samuel Beckett. Copyright ©
1958, 1959, 1960 by Grove Press, Inc. *Proust*, by Samuel Beckett. All
rights reserved. "Hostility," a sketch by Arnold B. Horwitt and Aaron
Ruben, is reprinted by permission from the Broadway revue *The Girls
Against the Boys*, 1959. Directed by Aaron Ruben. The Macmillan
Company: introduction by Brooks Atkinson to *The American Musical
Theatre*, by Lehman Engel. Random House, Inc.: *Actors Talk About
Acting*, by Lewis Funke and John E. Booth. Copyright © 1961 by Lewis
Funke and John E. Booth. Simon & Schuster, Inc.: *The Beauty Part*,
by S. J. Perelman. Copyright © 1961 by S. J. Perelman. Warner Bros.–
Seven Arts Music: "Quartet Erotica" (Harburg-Gershwin-Arlen) is
used by permission of New World Music Corp. © 1969 by New World
Music Corp. International copyright secured. All rights reserved.
"Things" (Harburg-Gershwin-Arlen) is used by permission of New
World Music Corp. Copyright 1937 by New World Music Corp. in the
U.S.A. © 1969 by New World Music Corp. under Universal Copyright
Convention. International copyright secured. All rights reserved. "C'est
La Vie" (Harburg-Gershwin-Arlen) is used by permission of New
World Music Corp. © 1969 by New World Music Corp. International
copyright secured. All rights reserved.

Thanks are also due to Joan Blondell, Benedict Freedman, E. Y. Harburg, Ray Henderson, Herbert Lahr, Jack McGowan, Johnny Mercer,
David Merrick, Michael Myerberg, Joe Smith, and Mrs. Billy K. Wells
for graciously allowing me to draw upon private correspondence and
other material belonging to them.

For Anthea, who gave a new life to this book and to me

Take the clowns . . . those basically alien beings,
fun makers . . . their tumblings and falling over
everything, their mindless running to and fro . . .
the hideously unsuccessful efforts to imitate their
serious colleagues. . . . Are these ageless sons of
absurdity, are they human at all? Are they, I repeat,
human beings, men that could conceivably find a place
in everyday life? In my opinion, it is pure senti-
mentality to say that they are "human too," with
the sensibilities of human beings and perhaps
even with wives and children. I honour them and de-
fend them against ordinary bad taste when I say no,
they are not, they are exceptions, side splitting,
world renouncing monks of unreason, cavorting
hybrids, part human and part insane art.
                Thomas Mann, The Confessions of Felix Krull

Hamlet: *. . . Good my lord, will you see the players*
well bestowed? Do you hear, let them be well used,
for they are the abstracts and brief chronicles
of the time.
                                    (II, ii, 500–3)

PERSONAL ACKNOWLEDGMENTS

This book was written over a period of six years. In that time I learned that Bert Lahr meant many things to many people, especially his family: Mildred, Herbert, Jane, Mrs. Cele Levine, Georgeanna Motts. They all discussed their recollections generously. Each of them has a special story; this book is just one of them. I am especially grateful to my mother for advancing me money and keeping my father placated in her inimitable fashion when his "editorial suggestions" were not immediately taken up. Herbert Lahr discovered the invaluable film sequence of Lahr and Mercedes's vaudeville act.

I have been many thousands of miles in search of my father's past. Traveling the country, discovering old vaudevillians in sad boarding houses, witnessing the spectacle of clipping books brown with age hauled down from closets as carefully as memories—these images linger in the mind as powerfully as the kindness and enthusiasm of nearly everyone with whom I talked.

Mrs. Billy K. Wells has been especially helpful, allowing me to look at her husband's burlesque notebooks and to reproduce some of his sketches and songs. E. Y. Harburg and Harold Arlen have been continually encouraging and constructive, answering my many questions and talking with me at length about writing songs for my father.

There were many acquaintances of my father who disregarded my squeaking tape recorder and talked frankly with me. Some—Louis Shurr, Bert Wheeler, Charles Lahrheim, Emmett Callahan, Vinton Freedley—did not live to see the book. But there are still many to be loudly thanked: Sol Abrahams, Steven Aronson, Art and Pepper Arthur, Brooks Atkinson, Mrs. James Barton, Eve Bealey, Herbert Berghof, A. L. Berman, Nick Blair, Larry Blyden, Ray Bolger, Sam Berk, Abe Burrows, James Cagney, Carroll Carroll, Dave Chasen, Judy Cowen, Charlie Dale, Jean Dalrymple, Jack Dawn, Harry Delmar, Anna Delpino, Jeanie Drake, Alvin Epstein, Eddie Foy, Arthur Freed, Gale Garber, Luella Gear, Peter Glenville, Bert Gordon, Max Gordon, Bill Grady, Jack and Flo Haley, Margaret Hamilton, Ray Henderson, Angela Lansbury, Mervyn LeRoy, Beatrice Lillie, Leonard Lyons, Joe E. Marx, William McAffrey, A. J. McLain, Jack McGowan, Frank McHugh, Michael Myerberg, Jack Pearl, S. J. Perelman, Alan Schneider, Lester Shurr, Joe Smith, Noel Willman.

In acquiring original photographs, Richard Avedon has been as devoted to my father's memory as his pictures are pertinent to his craft. He made his entire collection of negatives of Bert Lahr available to me. Paul Himmel was also kind enough to dig up some of his famous studies of my father. Since the facts of Broadway theater are a labyrinth of misinformation, I was fortunate to have the guidance and help of Robert Kimball, Curator of the Yale Musical Comedy Collection, who not only read the manuscript but also allowed me to see the Cole Porter scrapbooks. Warren Lyons's chronology of American musicals was invaluable in checking facts; and Paul Myers, Dorothy Swerdlove, Avi Wortis, and the rest of the harassed staff of the theater section of the Lincoln Center Library for the Performing Arts never lost their good humor in answering interminable questions.

This book now seems like a Gothic cathedral, where everyone has had a hand in building it. Al Burt of the *Miami Herald* was the first to respond to my writing and suggested the idea for this book. Richard Solomon, then Assistant Professor of English at Yale University, read the first attempts and made helpful suggestions for future revisions. A great deal of care has gone into publishing this book. Phoebe Larmore and John Cushman have gone beyond the responsibilities of dutiful agents in their loyalty and incisive counseling. And many people at Alfred A. Knopf are also responsible: William A. Koshland, who encouraged me and asked the right questions about comedy; Suzi Arensberg, the Babe Ruth of copy editors, who nipped my ellipses in the bud, not to mention my misspellings; Janet Reder, who endured the retyping and my pestering with aplomb; and especially Michael Magzis, my editor, whose blue pencil is much more accurate than his jump shot.

Finally, what I owe to my wife, Anthea, is beyond words. She was there through it all—badgering, snooping, editing, criticizing, typing, indexing, making me laugh at myself until it was all over.

J. L.
New York
May 1969

A DRAMATIC CHRONOLOGY

1910   Enters show business
1916   Tours with "The Whirly Girly Musical Comedy Success":
        College Days
        Garden Belles
1917   *The Best Show in Town*
1919   *Folly Town* (summer-run burlesque)
1920   *Roseland Girls*
1921   *Keep Smiling*
        Tries out vaudeville act "What's the Idea?"
1922   Vaudeville
1925   The Palace
1927   *Harry Delmar's Revels*
1928   *Hold Everything*
1929   *Faint Heart* (Vita-Phone), first film
1930   *Flying High*
1931   *Flying High* (M-G-M)
1932   *Hot-Cha!*
        George White's Music Hall Varieties (1933)
        Radio
1934   *Life Begins at 8:40*
        Happy Landing (a Monograph film)
1935   *George White's Scandals* (1936)
1936   *The Show Is On*
1938   Hollywood: *Love and Hisses* (Twentieth Century-Fox)
                      Merry-Go-Round of 1938 (Universal)
                      Just Around the Corner (Twentieth Century-Fox)
                      Josette (Twentieth Century-Fox)
                      Zaza (Paramount), released in 1939
1939   *The Wizard of Oz* (M-G-M)
        Du Barry Was a Lady
1942   *Sing Your Worries Away* (RKO)
        Ship Ahoy (M-G-M)
1944   *Meet the People* (M-G-M)
        Seven Lively Arts
1945   *Harvey* (on tour)

1946 *Burlesque*
1948 *Make Mine Manhattan* (on tour)
1949 *Always Leave Them Laughing* (Warner Brothers)
1951 *Two on the Aisle*
      Mr. Universe (Eagle-Lion Productions)
1954 *Rose Marie* (M-G-M)
1956 *The Second Greatest Sex* (Universal)
      Waiting for Godot
      Androcles and the Lion (television)
      The School for Wives (television)
1957 *Hotel Paradiso*
      Visit to a Small Planet (summer stock)
1959 *The Girls Against the Boys*
      Romanoff and Juliet (on tour)
1960 *A Midsummer Night's Dream,* American Shakespeare Festival
      Receives Best Shakespearean Actor of the Year Award
1962 *The Beauty Part*
      Ten Girls Ago (unreleased film)
1964 *Foxy,* Wins Tony Award for Best Musical Actor
      The Fantasticks (Hallmark Hall of Fame)
1966 *The Birds* (Ypsilanti Greek Theater)
1967 *The Night They Raided Minsky's* (United Artists)

RECORDS

Two on the Aisle (Decca)
Waiting for Godot (Columbia)
The Wizard of Oz (M-G-M)
Great Moments from the Hallmark Hall of Fame

PREFACE TO THE NEW EDITION

Some years ago I saw Dad in a dream. I was having an argument with an actor about the comic character he'd invented. I stepped into the corridor to calm down, and there was Dad. He was wearing his blue sports coat with padded shoulders. His brown chukka boots were polished to a shine. I could see the liver marks on the outside of his hands. He smelled of cologne. We approached each other. He felt soft when I hugged him. "I love you, Dad," I said. I can't remember if he answered. I woke up sobbing.

When Dad died, I didn't need to mourn him. I had been mourning him over the many years it took to write *Notes on a Cowardly Lion*. But the dialogue with one's parents doesn't end at the grave. And when I saw him that night, there was—and is—so much to say. I wanted to tell Dad about our son, Christopher, who seems to have inherited his performing gene, and Jane's daughter Maya. I wanted him to see us—John and Jane, the punch-pressed "perfect children"—in adulthood as we coped with our inheritance of privilege and neglect. The family soon splintered after Dad died. Mother moved to midtown Manhattan, learning with hard-won grace how to take buses and be Mrs. Mildred Lahr. Jane married, became a publishing executive, and then divorced. I moved to London to convalesce from ambition. And Herbert Lahr, Dad's son by his first marriage, remained in Tucson, Arizona, where he is a successful lawyer and family man. Georgeanna Motts, our beloved friend who served the Lahrs for nearly forty years, lived into her late eighties, going first to an old age home and then to a pauper's grave. Georgeanna had also seen Dad in a dream. She said he was in heaven and thirty-five and very happy.

The manuscript of *Notes on a Cowardly Lion* was finished the week Dad died. He never read a word of it. A lot of thought had already gone into how to face him with the finished product. For a man so guilt-ridden about his past, who had once suggested I print his golf scores in the book, *Notes* would have come as something of a shock. He would have hated the book until the reviews came out. And when he'd read Harold Clurman on the front page of the *New York Times Book Review* or seen Brooks Atkinson's opinion, then he'd have relaxed and enjoyed the book's rousing success.

Dad was well-loved by the public. Wherever he went people waved at him from passing cars, accosted him on street corners, clutched his hand in gratitude for the fun he'd brought to American life over his half century of inspired performing. The spell such a star casts is powerful. Both the public and the performer are trapped by it. On talk shows promoting the book, and even in some reviews, people insisted that this was not the buoyant and genial Bert Lahr they knew. Bert Lahr belonged to them, and their vehement intimacy was not to be contradicted. But Bert Lahr is here on these pages being his grouchy and outrageous and vulnerable lost self. Somehow, even fifteen years after his death, I find this comforting.

Long after *Notes* was published, my wife pointed out that there had been at least one picture of Dad in every room of our New York apartment, including the kitchen. The observation startled me. (Now, in middle age, only Dad's bewildered mug as Estragon in *Waiting for Godot* still stares down at me in my study, but there's no other sign of him around the house.) The book helped me to get out from Dad's long shadow. I wanted so much to honor his memory; and once done, we were quits. I had to begin the hard job of unlearning the borrowed assumptions of a star's life. Much of my subsequent writing comes back to the price people pay for success.

Notes did its work in the world, remaining in print for a decade. Through it, I finally made contact with that stranger who called himself my father; and I began my writing career. This new edition brings Bert Lahr to a new generation of readers. The American clowns who flourished in the first half of the twentieth century were the purest and most profound metaphors of America's dynamism and panic. Very little first-hand information remains as a testament to their craft and their world. I am very grateful for this book, and for the fact that once upon a time long ago I said to Dad, "Tell me about the old days."

London
October, 1983

CONTENTS

Folios of illustrations appear
following pages 78, 174, 270, and 334

The first draft of this book was completed before my father's death. I have chosen to keep the tense in the present because his comedy and his conversation capitalized on immediacy.

J. L.

FROM THE WINGS: AN INTRODUCTION

The curse of the theatre's financial vice is that one tends to look back more in sorrow than in anger on the many stirring or bad plays that might be memorable if they had been permitted to plant themselves and flourish in a healthy system. . . . All in all, Bert Lahr was the most pitiable victim of the season for his play met the early fate of every other play that opened during the newspaper strike.

"The Beauty Part" showed him in the golden twilight of his preposterous maturity, the last and most marvellous of the American clowns cradled by burlesque. To see him on the Bench, a Justice Holmes from the Bronx wrinkling his anthropoid forehead . . . to hear his sparrow brain working over the great libertarian guarantees as they might affect a Los Angeles Hindu who made a human sacrifice . . . and then to hear the ruling: "I am here to presoive the right of every American to croke when they see fit, and not when some wog sets fire to 'm"—this was to be present at an historic exegesis of Western liberty, or Western hypocrisy, or something equally grand and fatuous.

Alistair Cooke, Manchester Guardian
June 13, 1963

BERT LAHR STANDS ALONE IN THE WINGS WAITING FOR HIS CUE. HE wears a smoking jacket with a shawl wrapped formally around his shoulders. A woolen beanie is pulled down to his eyebrows. It is damp in the backstage darkness; linoleum muffles every step. Bert Lahr seems to blend into the dusty shadows. There is nothing in his manner or in his worn face that indicates success. And yet, in that body, dwarfed beside the stage house, is a humor that has weathered five decades of drastic shifts in American comic taste.

He waits patiently, looking continually at his feet or the leathery, freckled skin of his hands. From the wings, the sense of isolation that surrounds his craft is unmistakable. The heads of the audience jutt out from their seats like bleached rock faces, detached from their bodies. The glare of the stage lights blurs their identities.

This is my father's world, and where he comes mysteriously alive. The scene is the creation of S. J. Perelman; but the character, Nelson

Smedley, aged ice-cream tycoon, becomes Lahr's unique invention. He can never be certain how the character evolved. "I just play in it; then it's almost intuitive."

His cue comes. He moves from the shadows into the white light of center stage, and the transformation is immediate and complete. His body finds new rhythms. His legs, pale and spindly at home, churn with furious energy. His fingers, delicate and langorous off stage, lash out, discovering the violence of senility.

"Get your paws off me! I can walk as good as the next man!" Nelson Smedley casts off his nurse, begins to take his first steps, and topples to the floor. The audience roars in response.

"Pushed me again, didn't you? Always pushing—push, push, push, puuuuuussssssh!"

To the audience, he is a slick professional—smooth, direct, with impeccable timing. They have always laughed at my father. They joke about his face—full of crags and mysterious angles, with a nose swollen like a gherkin. Even his eyes, penetrating and deep-set beads, can be manipulated into something outrageous. From the wings, his buffoonery, at sixty-eight, seems a much more personal and painful struggle than he allows anyone, even himself, to believe. If he rarely ventures outside his apartment, on stage he takes immense physical and emotional risks. He falls; his body unravels in flurries of contorted movement. The pratfall becomes the flesh's humiliation, and its redemption is laughter. The activity is hypnotic and strangely ugly; what is referred to so matter-of-factly at home as "business" becomes disciplined and controlled art. The gales of laughter that greet Nelson Smedley are not so much the product of the dialogue as of the gymnastics of his face, the bellowing and the slapstick antics that expand the words.

Lahr howls at the audience. The spittle from his slurred words sprays out against the darker background of the mezzanine. He has howled in his own way off and on the stage for many years. Gnashing his teeth, shivering in Smedley's paranoic rage, he crouches toward the audience, screaming. "Stop thief! Stop thieieieiefff!!" The noise is not rational. It leaps from his stomach like an animal's screech. Words are reduced to frequencies of fear. Like his theatrical trademark—"Gnong, gnong, gnong"—experience merges into a private language, a random conjunction of guttural expressions. This never happens at home. The effect on an audience is magnetic.

At the finale, Lahr moves off to a volley of applause. As he comes toward me his heavy make-up shines with sweat; his costume is gray with it.

"It went well tonight, Pop."

There is no answer. He passes me. It is not unusual for him to be silent after a performance. He is exhausted from play, and the transition between worlds is too fast.

Lahr stops in front of the bulletin board. A green placard is tacked next to the opening-night telegrams from two months before. He squints to read the print. He turns and climbs the iron staircase.

There is nothing special about the dressing room. It is small and cluttered. Dust cakes the only window and the labyrinth of unpainted pipes. It reeks of rubbing alcohol and mothballs. My mother, beautiful in her middle age, sits nervously at the edge of the room's only chair. She twists a lace handkerchief. The valet, a towering, slouch-shouldered ex-prizefighter, stands in the corner with a soft-drink bottle. He waits for the signal to uncap it.

"Hello, dear," Lahr says obliquely to Mildred. Then, looking at me, he mumbles a greeting. He wipes his face vigorously with a towel and drapes it around his neck. A single light above his dressing-table mirror covers the room with an annoying whiteness.

"I'll have a soda tonight, Earl." There is nothing but soda in the cooler. There hasn't been since the show opened.

"How did it go, Bert?"

She is on cue. This is the first question to her husband, now suddenly smaller and older in the cramped room than on stage. The phrase has been uttered in the same soft tones by the same woman for over twenty years. My mother has never questioned the formality or allowed it to dampen the care with which she surrounds her husband.

"We sold out," he says, taking a swig from the bottle and then hesitating to belch. "It wasn't a bad audience for a Saturday night . . . It's better than those goddam theater parties we've been playing to all week."

He drums the dressing table with his fingers and then looks away in thought.

"Did you see the notice, Mildred?"

"No. What notice?"

"It's posted on the board downstairs. I got a note from Ellis tonight. We close next Saturday." He fumbles on his table for the producer's letterhead. He can't find it. Although my father is never optimistic, he usually holds avenues open for new possibilities. Tonight, however, there is a finality in his voice.

Mildred paces a few short steps. "Well, Bert, *I* can't think for *you.* After all you've put into this show. It just makes me sick." She wipes the traces of dampness from her forehead and chin with the knotted handkerchief. When she speaks the word "sick," she closes her eyes. "This is a cheap show. The way they've been spending money, you'd think you were traveling with Ringling Brothers, Barnum, and Bailey . . ."

"Mildred, how many times do I have to explain that it's just economics. When I did *Du Barry* for Buddy DeSylva, he got off the nut in fourteen weeks. Today, a show costs between $350,000 and $400,000 to put on. De Sylva's show cost $85,000 in 1939; now it would probably run as high as $400,000. So if you're a hit, you've got to run a year before you get your money back. We grossed $19,000 this week, and we needed thirty-five grand to break even. It's economics . . . simple economics. It's just one of those things."

"How can you be so passive? How can a man of your talent and stature in show business let all these other people call the shots. This show is no lemon . . ." She is perspiring heavily now. "After all, Bert. you've got to assert yourself once in a while."

My father stops talking; he glances up at a series of publicity pictures on the wall. They are jaunty impersonations of Perelman's gargoyles. Hyacinth Beddoes Laffoon, the woman magazine editor, is his favorite. Dressed in a turban and ratty fur, Lahr captures her aggressive vulgarity. It is astonishing to look at the picture, and then down at the man gradually coming into focus not as Bert Lahr but as "Dad." It seems to bother him, too.

"I thought if a show got good notices, Dad—the axiom was that it would run?"

"Look, pal, don't ask me to explain it. I don't understand it either . . . This is probably the best material I've had since the forties. We opened at the Music Box, but Irving Berlin, who owns it, could only give us ten weeks there. We figured we could get another theater, but until the eighth week we didn't have one, so we couldn't sell tickets. We finally got the Plymouth, but as you can see, we can't build fast enough. Once a show loses momentum, it's difficult to re-build. There's not enough cash for an extensive advertising campaign to buck this newspaper strike—so we close. It confuses me, though. It's a lot of things, but the main thing is—well, it's such good material."

He taps the red-grained leather folder that contains the script. He anticipates my question. "We could go on the road, I suppose. But I'm getting too old to jump from town to town. It was easy in the burlesque days. I liked it then. But now, well, it just doesn't mean much. I waited for this one; and once we move off Broadway, something's missing."

Mother moves behind him and, taking a small hand towel, begins to wipe the make-up from the back of his neck. She kisses the top of his head. He says nothing, but stares straight ahead into the large dressing-table mirror. Taking the towel from her, he begins to dab cold cream around his eyes and mouth. He wipes it away. When he turns back to speak, only his lips and eyes have returned to their natural color. He looks like a panda. "I just can't understand it. Christ, I just can't. The play's good. I can feel it. You liked it, didn't you? I got good reviews, didn't I, John? And now something like this. What can we do?"

He stands up while Earl hands him his bathrobe. Lahr knots the black sash beneath his belly. In the cold light, his features are sharply detailed. A long scar on his forehead slopes from the top like a gently eroding hill. I know the gash came from colliding with a trolley car when he was ten years old. He alludes to it, but never talks about his past. His wrists are strange too. The left one is much larger than his right. It got that way, he says, from breaking falls in his burlesque and vaudeville days.

He rolls the cellophane from a pack of cigarettes between his fingers, saying, "You know something, Mildred, somebody must have put a jinx on me somewhere along the line."

"Be serious, Dad."

"I'm not kidding. Other shows have been the same. Sure. I've done O.K., but never as good as possible. That's why this one was so important. Because it was right for everybody. And now this. It's a hex."

There are two ways to defeat Fate. One is by performing, the other by adhering to certain theater superstitions. There is no whistling in his dressing room, or throwing of hats on beds at home.

Lahr's stage aggressiveness has evaporated. "Well, what else can you call it but a jinx. The last show closed despite good reviews. And what about *Godot?* The same thing. They like me, don't they? Before, I could never come up with a property I was completely sure about. Now that I have it, we're closing. You heard them laugh out there, John. You never heard laughs like that!"

My father's enjoyment lies in planning comic situations. He asks about the laughs after every performance, gauging his acceptance by the audience's response. Watching the audience from the wings, I understand the delicate balance of laughter. They laugh and are entertained, but their final expression is more than gratitude for an evening's entertainment. Their faces register a respect that is more than delight. It is the awe a physical feat inspires. On the stage he dares to fall and fail, turning his private inadequacies to public advantage.

Even the gratification at the audience's response has vanished from his conversation. He seems resigned.

"Bert, if we're going to Sardi's you'd better hurry. They're not going to hold our table forever . . ." Mildred moves toward the door. "I'll wait downstairs while you change. Don't dawdle."

Looking at me in the mirror, my father says, "An actor can do just so much, then he's got to be lucky. I've made it and hung on by myself. Nobody ever helped me, not really. The ones that tried to give me a push ended up slowing me down."

He gets up and goes to the wash basin. He lathers his face with soap. "One thing's for sure—I didn't make this mess."

The soap stings his eyes. He throws his head back with his eyes shut. With a childlike squeal he gropes for the towel. Earl rushes to him.

He is thinking to himself as he hurries into a clean shirt. I have watched him worry for many years. He worries about everything—his health, high places, small rooms, little cars, airplanes, onions, garlic, and his work. What is on his mind tonight is a fear deeper than the perfectionism of an old-timer wanting to make every performance live up to his reputation.

"Can't they raise money to keep the show going until after the strike?"

"Look, pal, I'm a realist. What can I do, for chrissake? I've done all I could, haven't I? I waited for this one. It fell through. I don't know what's coming, who does? Let's face it, this is all I know—all I can do . . . There'll be other jobs. Maybe they won't be as good as this one, but when you start getting old, you can't always expect the best scripts. I'm getting older, pal; but I can't stop working. I'll keep working even if I have to hustle bit parts."

Lahr looks at the ties the valet holds out. He glances at his suit and picks a blue silk one.

"Was it different in the early days, Pop?"

"That's another story, kid. Some other time, O.K.?"

A falsetto voice echoes up the stairwell. "C'mon boys, Mr. Sardi's not going to wait forever."

We start toward the door. "Hey, Pop, let's take a look at that Mondrian that turns into a bar."

He stops for a moment, glancing at me with tired eyes. "John, does a shopkeeper go back to the store after he's locked up?"

We move carefully down the iron stairs, which hum with the vibrations of a younger actor's footsteps. "Goodnight, Bert. See you Monday."

Downstairs, a stagehand is lugging a display board inside. It reads:

LAHR AND PERELMAN MAKE HAPPY MUSIC TOGETHER

Howard Taubman,
The New York Times

The marquee is dark; the names on it impossible to read. The street is nearly empty. Steam hisses from a manhole cover. Lahr lowers his head into the cold, tugging on his Scottish tweed cap. He walks ahead with Mother.

As we move toward Broadway, two middle-aged couples waiting for a taxi outside a bar recognize him.

"Hi, Bert! Hey, Bert, say something funny!" They laugh and point.

He continues on, pretending not to hear.

"Hey, Bert, say something funny."

"Not here," he says.

ROOTS

Interviewer: You're recognized as a pantomime artist, who without lines can reach people. What is it about you that people laugh at?
Lahr: I don't know. Maybe I'm funny looking, maybe my mannerisms are ludicrous, maybe over a period of years by practice and application I found that they'd laugh at this (rolling his eyes), and then when you do it or a movement or something. But those things haven't been planned or studied. Maybe some other fellas do, but I don't.

> Actors Talk About Acting, *arranged and edited by*
> *Lewis Funke and John E. Booth*

"God must have laughed when Bert Lahr was born."

> *Brooks Atkinson*

BERT LAHR WAS BORN IRVING LAHRHEIM ON AUGUST 13, 1895—A TIME when America was still warring against the Indians, before the car and airplane had given the world a new momentum. His first home was on the fourth floor of a five-story walk-up on First Avenue and Eighty-fourth Street in New York City; it took him half a century to move five blocks west to Fifth Avenue.

On the day of Lahr's birth, his father—Jacob Lahrheim—took a holiday from his upholstery shop on Eighty-eighth Street and Columbus Avenue where he worked thirteen hours a day for six days and brought home twelve dollars a week. His son, Irving, was the first fruition of his life in America. He would be the heir to Jacob's hard-won business, and a test to the family's frugality. Jacob provided the most efficient and economical medical treatment—a lodge doctor who, for a yearly fee, took care of the entire family. He had summoned the doctor early in the morning; the delivery had been prompt, almost pleasant, despite the fact that afterwards the doctor misspelled their name on the birth certificate—"Laurheim." The names of many of Jacob's friends had been changed at random by the Immigration Office when they entered the country; others had taken new identities later on to fit a new world, so Jacob was not concerned. The name was not as important as the ideas he would give his son—to be frugal, to be diligent, and to survive. From the earliest years, Lahr recalls his father slapping his pants pocket and saying joylessly, "A man's money is his best friend."

While Jacob's mother watched after Augusta, his wife, and the new baby, Jacob indulged himself and bought *two* newspapers to read on the roof—*The Staatszeitung* and *The New York Times*. It was a sunny day. The streets smelled fresh after the rains the night before, which the *Times* called "the most terrific thunderstorm of the year." Jacob felt comfortable in the summer air. To the east was the river, muddy and strangely turbulent, bringing the ice boats up to the Ninetieth Street pier, where they delivered to their horse-drawn trucks. Ferryboats taxied people to Astoria, where on Sundays they held dollar beer parties in the summer. To the west, Jacob could see the treetops of Central Park and imagine the spires of the regal châteaux of Seventy-ninth Street. The city was rimmed by a confident peacefulness. Beneath him, however, Jacob saw another world.

The storefronts on First Avenue, like his own apartment, were meticulous and sparse. Hunger and failure were belligerent shadows. But there was still a dream even if there was little time for dreaming— the papers carried gossip about six-course meals at the fine homes; but at Max's Busy Bee three cents bought a cup of coffee and a sandwich, twenty-five cents was enough for a pound of steak or two dozen eggs.

First Avenue, with carts rattling over cobblestones, and the smell of cabbage and dust in the hallways, was a bustling image of the city's contrasts. For Jacob, the struggle there was satisfying; he had come to America not, as some of his friends, to earn a grubstake to return to Germany, but to make it his home. He had arrived at the age of sixteen with his grandfather, also an upholsterer, and had begun then to carve a life from this recalcitrant city. Nothing numbed his dream, not the hard brown benches of the Immigration Office at Ellis Island nor the mass of bodies packed neatly like firewood into the cold building. Germany was far behind him, and with it, the memory of a father dead of pneumonia before he was seven, of land too overworked to yield sufficient livelihood. In his three-room apartment, a tintype picture of the small, white house with thatched roof where he had grown up reminded him of the barely fertile fields. On the second floor of that house, where the family had moved in order to take in boarders, he had seen his mother try to raise a family and keep food on the table. Now, in New York, there was promise, but also an undeniable threat. He saw it most conspicuously in the backyard gardens, in the leaves dingy with soot, deprived of light, languishing on the boughs. The city was crueler than the German countryside and less predictable. Jacob often talked about the fields around Meudt where the early morning light brought a warm, green luster to the earth. He would remember running with his brother, Charlie, five years his junior, to the orchard where they picked apples before the farmhands arrived. He talked about the freshness of the air in the morning, and the magical footprints that glistened in the dew.

But now Germany was only a romantic memory. He had apprenticed to his uncle, then set up his own shop, and married an American girl of good German stock who lived on the next block in Yorkville. His brother and mother had followed him to America a few years later. They had all lived together on Seventy-eighth Street in a nine-dollar-a-month apartment. The three rooms were cramped; and it was uncomfortable for the family to share the bathroom in the hall with other tenants. As his brother Charlie recalled, "When Jake got married he took mother with him. Gussie and mother were always fighting. Mother didn't want to stay with Gussie. She was very upset. First they sent for us, and then Jacob got married right away. He wasn't one hundred per cent clever; sometimes he told jokes that didn't come out right."

Jacob was interested in natural medicines, attending lectures on health foods and bringing home herbs and seeds to improve the diet of his family. When Charlie had arrived in America, Jacob made him join the local *tern-verein*—a German health club that sponsored intercity gymnastic competitions. Charlie wrestled; Jacob excelled on the parallel bars and long-distance runs. Together, they won many ribbons in their Sunday afternoon events. Jacob was wiry and short; his face was handsome, with a mustache etched over his upper lip. Both he and his brother had themselves photographed on a pedestal flexing like Sandow the Strong Man, with only a fig leaf on. Jacob could see the effects of his labor more quickly in his body than his business.

Jacob had no religion except work. He was given to damning all churches from his evening chair. "If religion can't create good will in the world, it is useless." Nevertheless, his son, Irving, followed German-Jewish tradition. He spoke German for the first six years of his life; Jacob stopped speaking German in the house at the beginning of World War I. The *Staatzeitung* gave way permanently to the *Times,* and his son Irving would adopt a neutral name—Bert.

Bert Lahr brought out of his childhood a dissatisfaction, an inarticulate yearning. The three most vivid memories of his childhood are presents—a bag of candy, a five-dollar sailor suit with an extra pair of pants, and a trip with his father to the *Schwartz Um Adler,* a German theater on Third Avenue. These were the only memories of family affection, the only tangible indication of his father's love. "I can remember one Christmas I put my stocking up, and when I came out the next morning there was nothing in it. I never got anything of consequence as a child or else it would be very vivid in my memory."

Yorkville was not as squalid as New York's Lower East Side. Few tubs hung out of back windows, and the streets were wider and less cluttered. The surface of life seemed quieter, more ordered, and hopeful. But Irving Lahrheim would never experience Yorkville like his parents, as a step up the social ladder. He came from a world where humble prosperity seemed just out of reach. He knew the street smells and the backyards where laundry flapped against the sky. If his friends remember him as flamboyant and energetic, Lahr's idea of his childhood has no gaiety and less innocence. "I was a lonely kid. I lived in an ordinary house in a coldwater flat." Even before a sister, Cele, was born in 1900 there was little family community. With a second child, there were no luxuries at all, no celebration of birthdays or holidays. "We were never taken out," recalls Cele. "Once we were supposed to go to the theater. Dad took out his pencil and paper and figured the expenses. We never went." Jacob usually settled back into a pensive silence after dinner. Sometimes he would not speak to his children for days. He kept many things from them. Augusta complained to her son about Jacob's growing indifference. Lahr can recall his mother crying when Jacob treated himself to a Thanksgiving dinner. "For that money," she said, "we all could have had a nice meal." In her teary confidences or the quarrels behind closed doors, the theme remained constant—money. In later years, Lahr would come to see the craftsman in his father, a man who was sensitive to fine objects, who liked to sketch and whose work with leather upholstery was careful and expressive. But to Lahr as a child, his father was an ominous figure, even if the boy used him as protection from the "Black Mariah" and other demons that Augusta's sisters had invoked to keep him obedient. "I was afraid of the dark. I used to sleep with my father in the double bed. If he'd leave the room, I'd wake up." The terror was real; Irving forced his father to sleep with him for three years between his sixth and ninth year.

Augusta's son knew her sadness and watched her patiently at work.

There was the house to clean, wood floors to polish, and, of course, the sewing. In the summer she would sometimes help Jacob at the store, working in the sweltering cellar, stuffing horsehair into chairs. It was grueling and, to Irving, sad. Cele could never understand her brother's reaction to the symbols of Augusta's bondage—scissors, hooks, and eyes. "Sometimes at dinner, I'd put mother's sewing kit with the hooks and eyes by his plate. He'd go into a tantrum. I remember him running around the table after me."

Lahr's mother perplexed him. He realized that she was a good woman. He recognized her hard work and sensed the frustrating silences that fell between her and Jacob. He knew that she had once saved a child's life in the apartment across the alley by sending money over on the clothesline to pay the doctor. He knew also that her personality could elicit a much stronger allegiance than his father showed her. When the family moved from Yorkville to the Bronx, Augusta's next-door neighbor and friend, Mrs. Harland, moved up to the area. Augusta made many sacrifices for her children, and, to her son, those moments were unforgettable. She would reach into the stein on top of the refrigerator for a few extra pennies for Lahr; she would indulge his pranks and small extravagances where Jacob would have none of it. But anxiety eroded her strength. Throughout his life, Lahr's filial impulse toward his mother was tempered with distrust. He disliked her whispered confidences about Jacob's insensitivity. Even if they were true, there was a betrayal of loyalty. He also came to suspect Augusta's spiritualism, which developed murkily as the years grew more difficult. And although she was a loving mother, Lahr could rarely be certain of her affection. He recalls playing a game with Augusta in which she would name an object in German and he would identify it in English. "She pointed to a volume on the table. I said 'book.' Then to one of the pieces of second-hand furniture. I said 'chair.' I remember pointing to her breasts, saying 'Was ist das?' And she hit me. She kept slapping me, 'Don't-you-ever-say-that-again!'" Augusta became an object of apprehension—she was assertive and complaining, religious yet capable of unexpected violence. From then on, her image always held a threat to Lahr.

Lahr understood the family's poverty early in his childhood. He delivered rolls at $1.50 a week, sold picture postcards, and once, at the age of nine, earned three dollars by renting boxes to spectators at the Hudson-Fulton Celebration Parade. He gave the money to his parents; but he yearned for a few possessions of his own. And he was often hungry. He began to steal. He remembers his thefts without emotion or guilt because there seemed to be no other choice. He was, by any standard, a fairly bad thief.

His first abortive effort to wangle money came when he was eight and Augusta denied his request for money to attend the nickelodeon. "We're poor people," she said. "We can't spend on little things like movies. Now bundle up and go outside." He tried to pay her back with the same threats that she and her sisters used to remind him to be a "good boy"—death. He went to the bathroom and dabbed iodine on the side of his mouth, letting it dribble down his chin. He lay down on the floor and waited for his mother to return. Cele was the first to discover him. She ran, hysterical, to the foot of the stairs to tell her mother. Augusta rushed to the bathroom. Her son was spread-eagled on the floor, breathing with careful heaves of his chest, his eyes shut. "You'll get no money, Irving. Go outside." That evening Lahr pelted his mother with a snowball, an act of rebellion that astounded his sister and amazed his friends.

"I remember running after my father who was boarding a trolley to work. I wanted some money. He just pushed me away." When Jacob gave his son a dollar to have a tooth extracted, Lahr saved fifty cents by having it done without an anesthetic. If his mother gave him a nickel for lunch, he would save three cents by purchasing a seeded roll and a banana for a penny apiece to make banana sandwiches. The petty thefts began out of desperation. He pilfered change from his father's pocket, school supplies from the neighborhood store, and then, finally, made a large vegetable cadge. Lahr and his friends on Eighty-eighth street (his family had moved there after Cele's birth) stole from local stores on the weekdays in order to resell the produce on Saturday mornings at the open markets cluttering First Avenue. Once Lahr stole a pumpkin from a policeman's garden, only to have the officer knock on his door minutes after the theft demanding the return of the vegetable, which was sitting on the fire escape.

He rarely recalls what gaiety there was in childhood: setting up high hurdles in the alley by his apartment and running them until the women complained in fear that their laundry would topple; swimming off the mossy pilings in the East River, where once he had to come home in a crate when someone stole his clothes. And there were Magic Lantern shows (a dime admission) where Tommy Lark would project slides on a sheet set up in the basement of his apartment, with Solly Abrahams beating a drum for musical accompaniment and Lahr taking the tickets. "He was a jokester, always kidding around," says Abrahams. "He was well liked. Even then he was doing that shuffle he still does today. He had motions—like he has today. He probably doesn't remember it. I recall it vividly."

Augusta worried about her son—often to his face. As Cele remembers, "Mother felt he couldn't elevate himself. She thought his friends were ordinary, far beneath him." Augusta was also confounded by her son's actions. He showed little interest in school, and acted impulsively, with a curious disregard for the family. Once, after Jacob had refused him money to have a tonsil operation, Lahr walked to Manhattan Eye, Ear, and Throat Hospital on East Sixty-fourth Street and had himself admitted for a free operation. His parents knew nothing about it until he walked home twenty-four hours later. (The operation had not been completely successful—a hemorrhaged tonsil kept him in the hospital overnight.) They were assuaged by the story of the experience, which Lahr could only vaguely articulate. "While I was in the hospital, it was crowded; they put me next to a man who was dying. He was going through the death rattle. I was right there. I watched him die. I was eleven."

Lahr remembers only his confusion. He had seen death; and he was surrounded by images of failure. He saw it in his father's hands, already cracked and dry, in his mother's taut face, in his own frayed clothes. "I used to ask myself—'What's going to become of you?'" There was never a satisfactory answer. In the summer, he sat with friends and watched criminals and drunkards, prostitutes and vagrants being arraigned at the Fifth Precinct Station across the street. He understood the warning in his father's eyes when he returned from work to find his son ogling at the offenders. To Lahr, the dank smells and spiritless labor of the upholstery business seemed only another repugnant but sadly plausible destiny.

He read voraciously, the only boy among his Yorkville friends to have a library card. His escape into fantasy was total. Cele recalls him reading quietly in the living room after dinner, and suddenly yelling, "Hit him! Knock him down!" to the printed page. And once she found him in tears when Frank Merriwell's life seemed doomed. But the Horatio Alger stories and the exciting tales in *Pluck 'n Luck* haunted him. Even his friends had glimpses of a despair Lahr usually camouflaged. Solly Abrahams, who looked down on Lahr's bedroom from the kitchen of his own apartment, remembers rushing to the window one night after he and Lahr had been treated to the movies. It was not unusual for them to holler to one another across the alley, but these were different noises. "He started to yell—or cry—I couldn't tell which. I thought he was having a bad dream. I screamed, 'Irv, shut up and go to sleep.' He was quiet for a while after that."

Lahr developed an enthusiasm for the theater that was as obsessive as his love of the penny dreadfuls. The quarter admission fee hampered his eclectic tastes for escape; but when he could afford a ticket, nothing offered greater pleasure. He walked to 107th Street and Third Avenue regularly to see the traveling melodramas. He was known to hitch a ride on the back of his cousin's horse-drawn express cart to Broadway, watch a vaudeville show from the balcony, and meet the wagon on its return trip uptown.

Jacob and Augusta rarely knew of their son's excursions—most of the time he traveled the city alone. He became increasingly moody and difficult to control. The teachers in his school complained about his lack of discipline, and worse, Augusta had discovered that he was smoking. Lahr would always savor his smoking adventures, amused at the names of the cigarettes he puffed so confidently and the thrill of a new-found "maturity." "A box of Helmars were classy. I was a real dude. You could go into a cigarette store, and they'd break open a pack for you. You could get one for a cent. They were a nickel a pack. They were called American Beauties."

Since Augusta suspected the neighborhood boys of leading her son astray, there was only one alternative—to move. They decided on a two-bedroom apartment on Wilkins Avenue in the Bronx. There, Irving would have his own room and Cele could sleep on the sofa in the living room. It was a forty-five minute subway ride uptown from Yorkville. But the Bronx was more spacious, and offered a completely new area where their son could breathe fresher air, make new friends. "It was semi-country. I remember there were very few apartment houses, and many acres of greenery. I can even remember chickens in the garden."

And Lahr did make friends on Wilkins Avenue. Joey Berado, the shoemaker's son, shared his enthusiasm for boxing, and Sam Berkowitz, the butcher's boy, frequented the same candy store. In 1907 there was already a list of famous Bronx personalities that Lahr watched in awe. Emile Mosbacher, who became the boy genius of Wall Street, walked home from his job at the Stock Exchange practicing the signals used on the floor. There were athletes, too, older and unapproachable. The most famous were the Zimmerman brothers—all nine of whom played professional baseball and one, Heine Zimmerman, who became one of the New York Giants' greatest third basemen. Other boys who seemed harmless and no different in their prospects from Lahr were to manufacture their own celebrity with reckless crimes. "Crazy Fat" would graduate to underworld immortality, only to be burned alive in the middle of Wilkins Avenue in 1921 by a rival mob.

Lahr's first inheritance from his Bronx environment was a new nickname. "Irving" was forgotten the day Lahr squared off against a burly Swede, cursing, "You Swedish son-of-a-bitch, I'll wipe the streets with you." From that moment, despite his nose and his unruly crop of curly black hair, he became known as "Swedish," and his ferocious bravado became a neighborhood joke. His cronies remember him for his prankish good nature and his dog, Fanny, a brown and white mongrel with a sagging belly: she was the strongest emotional attachment of Lahr's youth.

Wilkins Avenue was a change of location, but Lahr still teetered on delinquency. He recalls the fun of baiting policemen who patrolled on bicycles. The boys stood their ground against policemen, realizing that once an officer was off his bike they could easily outdistance him. Lahr remembers immobilizing policemen by sticking a shaft of wood through the spokes and running. There was a regular caper, known to his friends as "the Feinstein trick." It originated at a local restaurant whose owner, Arthur Feinstein, served the best kosher food in the area. When the boys needed a good meal, they went to the restaurant, and, after eating, staged an argument. The fight brought the aging proprietor from behind the counter to escort them bodily out the door. The tactic earned them a handful of free meals throughout the neighborhood.

Lahr discovered street singing in the Bronx. On Halloween he put on white gloves and blackened his face with burnt cork. He and a few friends proceeded into Wilkins Avenue to sing. The first outing was so profitable that Lahr tried it often. He and a friend borrowed two guitars, which neither of them played. They were careful not to sing too close to their own homes in case their parents should hear of their antics. Lahr had a strong baritone voice; his balladry and his aloofness earned him the reputation of a "character." He was never unaware of the group sentiment toward himself, and he allowed his friends to create a role for him. He liked to make them laugh, often revising popular songs for comic effect. The role brought an easy but satisfying security.

Lahr still found himself drawn to the theaters for excitement and escape. "We'd have to walk two miles to the McKinley Square Theater and the Boulevard Theater. On the other side of the park was the Crotona Theater and there I saw Willie Howard's brother, Sammy. The theater was over in the Jewish section, and it was a Jewish audience. He was with the Newsboy Trio, I think. They did an imitation. In those days, the dance craze was the 'Texas Tommy,' which was like the 'Frug' or the 'Monkey' today. They used to have troupes of 'Texas Tommy' dancers. The Newsboy Trio performed the dance as well as imitating the format of the amateur-night routine. At the finish, they'd have all the amateurs line up on the stage. If the prize was five or ten dollars, they'd put the money over the amateur's head. The audience would judge who was the best. Every time it came over a new head, the audience would applaud. When they put the money over Sammy Howard's head, he went down to the footlights and said, "Ich bin ein Yid." Naturally, he won. I screamed, the incongruity of it. I've remembered it all these years."

The Bronx did not change Lahr's life as Augusta and Jacob had hoped. He brought to his new home the same vacancy and irresolution. "I went alone a lot of the time. Always alone. Proctor's 125th, Proctor's 58th, Minor's 153rd . . . I'd go all over the city if I could get my hands on a quarter. I loved the theater, not for me to get into, but the acts. I was entranced by them. It was just entertainment for me. Barber shops in those days used to get free passes to the shows for displaying posters announcing the acts. Every time I'd see a billboard in a window, I'd go in and buy the passes from them. They'd sell for a dime or a nickel. I walked all over. In those days, you'd walk great distances to save a nickel."

Other incidents assured Lahr his reputation for eccentricity. "The Fairmont A.C. was down on 138th Street. My pal was Joey Berado, who liked to box, and I was his second. All I knew was I had to fan him with a towel. All the kids who wanted to box used to go down there and they'd give them fifty dollars worth of tickets. You'd sell the tickets to the boys (two dollars a ticket and you got half). One day when we were down there Eddie Glick came in. He was sort of a dull-witted guy and a plumber's helper. He said, 'I get six dollars a week, and I'm loosening toilets and radiators. I'd like to make a few bucks. I'd like to fight.' So we said, 'Sure. Go down and get the tickets and we'll train you.' He got the tickets and started training. I said, 'We got a new way of training. Eat cheesecake and beer and run around

Crotona Park.' He did. He could get cheesecake for a dime and beer we all drank. He'd run around Crotona Park. After four days, he came to us. 'I'm sick,' he says. 'That's what we want, it's getting the bad blood out of you.' We finally got him a fight against a little kid from Christ's Church. He's been doing this for a week but nobody's been teaching him how to box or anything. He came in the ring, and I went over to the opponent and said, 'This guy can't take it in the stomach.' The kid from Christ's Church comes out, feints him, and punches Glick in the belly. He threw up all over the ring."

His friends found Lahr's humorous incompetence often funnier than his calculated pranks. He rarely confided his family troubles to friends, but once he decided to run away from home. He got no further than the home of his next-door neighbor, "Butch" Berkowitz, who offered him a bed after hearing of his plight. He arranged for Lahr to sneak into the house around ten o'clock, just after Berkowitz's father had gone to sleep. His room was to the right of the front door, so there would be little noise to disturb the family. Berkowitz quietly fixed a bed for his friend, bringing a cot up from the cellar. In his small room the cot and regular bed consumed the width of the floor.

When Lahr arrived, he came complete with a pair of pajamas and a dime novel.

"What'ya bring that for?" said Berkowitz.

"I figured I'd read because I don't sleep good."

"We can't use the lights, dummy. It might attract attention. We'll just have to go to sleep. The cot's yours."

Finally, the chatter tapered off. Berkowitz was asleep.

Lahr tried to go to sleep, trying his mother's remedy of thinking happy thoughts. He remembered diving into the East River, the curious silence under water, cutting off the city noises, and then surfacing, to a world miraculously fresh. He thought of Frank Merriwell, and horses' hooves, a noise that captivated him on the riding paths of Central Park. He simulated the clip-clop with his tongue against the cavity of his cheek. He usually could lull himself to sleep, but not that night. He began to itch.

"Hey, Sammy—what's on the cot? C'mmon, Sammy, wake up!"

"Shut up, Swedish, I was almost asleep. You're dreamin' or somethin'."

"No kiddin' Sammy, what's wrong with this cot? I'm gonna scratch myself to death if you don't tell me. Put on the light, will you."

Sammy got up and reached for matches.

"This'll have to do," he said, holding the flame above the cot.

"Look at that!" Lahr stood up from the cot. "I told you I wasn't dreaming—bugs."

"Well, what are we going to do about it?"

"Look at the little things move. They're walking from my cot right over to your bed."

"So what's your idea?"

"Let's just pull the beds apart, and then the lice will break their necks when they fall between."

They swept away the lice and returned to bed. Lahr lay awake. He could hear the low whine of a dog. It persisted for several minutes. Berkowitz remembers Lahr yelling, "That's Fanny. That's Fanny. She's calling me." Lahr ran to the window and pushed it open, thrusting his chest far out of the window and scanning the alley.

"Here Fanny! Here Fanny!"

"Swedish, will you shut up for chrissake, it's nearly two o'clock."

"It's Fanny. I know it is. Listen. I'm sure it is. She misses me."

Lahr began to call again. When there was no answer, he grudgingly lay back on his cot.

"I hope you're satisfied, Lahrheim. You just woke up half the neighborhood with your yelling. Go to sleep and forget it."

"I'm tryin', I'm tryin'."

He imagined Fanny being left unfed or perhaps being given away for messing up the living room floor as his mother sometimes threatened. Finally, Lahr jumped from the cot and groped for his clothes.

"What'ya doin' now, Swedish?"

"Gettin' dressed."

"What the hell for?"

"I've got to get some sleep," he said. "I'm goin' home."

Besides his father's platitudes about idleness and the intimidation of the city he walked so often, school was the bane of Lahr's early years. He had never been a good student, but at P.S. 40 in the Bronx, he seemed to get worse. His parents were outraged by his curious inaction. He did not work; he would not even try. "I was like a caged animal in school," he says, remembering his teacher Miss Shea, who found his books tucked back in his desk after class and brought them home to Mrs. Lahrheim with stern admonitions about her son's behavior. Lahr had tacked her attendance book to the table, and had been called before the principal for throwing a book at her. He could not explain to his parents about the classroom—the anxiety over gray walls and long rows of wooden seats, the sadness of the winter stench of damp clothing and mothballs. In school, Miss Shea and others like her were watching, judging, ready to scold him for his obvious inadequacies. "I didn't feel free at school; it just didn't mean anything—nothing." The careless instruction in every lesson from mathematics to civics for an adult life in commerce upset him. "What do numbers mean, when you have nothing to count?" The only discipline Lahr enjoyed was penmanship. He had a fluid hand; he practiced writing out his name, spelling it in different styles, and always in dignified arabesques.

The only memorable event in Lahr's academic career was the Eighth Grade class show. It was the first time he had ever participated in a school activity. Although Lahr harmonized on summer evenings with friends on the benches of Crotona Park, he had never performed. The entertainment at P.S. 40 was a Kid Act, modeled on the popular Smith and Dale routines, which spoke not only to the boredom and rebelliousness subdued in school life, but also with the babble of familiar dialects. Lahr remembers the laughs he and his group of friends got on stage, mimicking the deeper, more outrageous accents of their parents, and wearing penciled mustaches like pint-sized adults.

He remembers how nervous he was waiting for that first cue and wondering if he could growl the broad "Dutch" dialect with the panting "h" and the rolled "r" like his father. But on stage, the words seemed to speak themselves. Gestures happened smoothly, impelled by a laughing audience. Lahr liked other people laughing at him. He was amazed at the effect of even the ordinary words he spoke. These same words which had seemed so matter-of-fact when he had memorized them now moved people to laughter. He found himself making up new movements that had nothing to do with the script. When the boys rushed off the stage after their final gag, the audience applauded until they had to hurry back for a bow. Lahr recalls how the experience filled him with a satisfaction. He felt completely in control on stage, proud and curiously powerful. He had enjoyed it all—the make-up, the clowning, the noisy laughter. As he left for home after the performance, his teacher stopped him at the door. "Well, Mr. Lahrheim," she said, "if you don't go on the stage, you'll probably go to jail." Lahr was astonished that Miss Shea talked to him about anything except his laziness. "All I could think to say was—'thank you.'"

The weeks that followed his performance were more exciting than he had ever known. His friends and even vague acquaintances greeted him with the "Dutch" dialect he had bellowed. Sometimes they threw up their arms in the same wild rhythm. They knew him and showed they understood more about him. They challenged his reticence; and he basked in this new recognition. "He was such a success," recalls his sister, "that Gus Edwards heard about him and wanted to put him in a school act. Mother and Dad wouldn't hear of it. But after that performance I remember a teacher said he was the clown of the class and they couldn't do anything with him."

Lahr himself never quite feared the life of delinquency his parents kept predicting for him. Yet, when he failed his eighth-grade year and was ordered to repeat it, the question that plagued him was hammered into his mind by Jacob. "What's going to become of you?" Jacob wanted his son to have an education; but Lahr was not interested. If he did not attempt anything, he could not fail. The upholstery business was the alternative. His hands were not those of an upholsterer but long for their size and, like a woman's, thin and brittle. They were, as he said himself, clumsy and groping, unable to master the intricate maneuvers of tools and thread. He tried those things to please his father. The results had been disastrous because he could never concentrate. Without a trade and without an education, his possibilities seemed as bleak as the streets he was born to. There was never an answer to the question he asked himself: "What's going to become of you?" He was only conscious of his immobility and a vague, undirected energy.

Although Lahr would become P.S. 40's most famous alumnus, he never graduated. The idea of repeating the eighth grade was oppressive, and Lahr had a scheme for avoiding that humiliation. The plan lay in the very hands he looked upon with such ironic bewilderment. At fourteen, he could get a working permit, so each day he read the papers and the list of available jobs. He would write a letter to his teacher explaining that it was necessary for him to leave school to work in his father's shop, not an unusual request; many of his friends had been taken from school by a poor parent. It took him two minutes to compose the note and another minute to copy Jacob's signature. He hesitated a week before handing it in; but when he did, the teacher excused him without further questions.

For a week following his withdrawal, he did not tell his parents, preferring to rise with his family and set off as if he were heading up Prospect Hill to P.S. 40, two blocks away. In fact, he had composed letters of application in his finest script and was awaiting the results. "I was certain that with my good penmanship, I could get a job."

"On my first letter, I got a job with Wetzel the Tailor. I was a lazy kid, I didn't know where I was going. Now, here's a complete metamorphosis. Wetzel paid me $4.50 a week, and this year [1966] my agent gave me a Christmas present from Wetzel the Tailor—just a sports coat cost $250. I worked in the vest department, delivering vests up and down. I don't know how I lost that job, but after that I worked in Rogers Peet, downstairs, on Thirteenth Street. I tried to install the Wetzel System. I was a stock clerk and delivery boy. It was all wrong. They had charts of how things should be done. I loused that up too. Once I had to deliver a suit way up on Broadway. You could get a transfer and travel all over the city for a nickel in those days. It was a long way uptown and getting dark. When I got to the address, I realized it was a cemetery. The caretaker evidently bought a suit and he lived right in the middle of the grounds. Brother, this was really something, because when I was a kid I used to be afraid to sleep alone. I remember running back, running through those graves. I didn't quit that job, I must have been fired. But there was this fellow in the stock room who belonged to the Boys' Club on Tenth Street and Avenue A. They spawned a lot of fighters like Knockout Brown, who was cross-eyed and his opponents didn't know which way he was going to punch. My friends and I used to fool around boxing behind the clothes rack. We were always knocking down the coats."

In six months after leaving school, Lahr held and lost fourteen jobs. His optimism was gone, his sense of failure multiplied by his parents' disgust at his aimlessness. The routine of finding work was as habitual as ways of coping. "You'd earn $4.50 a week and you'd bring it home to your mother. I used to get twenty-five cents a day, a nickel on the subway and fifteen cents for lunch. One time all I ate for four days was banana sandwiches. I broke out in the damndest rash and had stomach aches. I remember that."

His fifteenth job was his last ordinary employment and his shortest tenure. Jacob had arranged a job for his son as a delivery boy with L. & M. Friedlander on Wilkins Avenue, who ran a prospering hardware store. His duties were easy enough—to deliver merchandise and help around the store. It was the first time, however, that he had been invested with the responsibility of buying merchandise for the store. The proprietor gave him five dollars to buy brooms at a local warehouse. On the way back from the assignment, Lahr erased the wholesale prices, marking higher ones in their place. He pocketed the difference. His sleight of hand was uncovered that same afternoon. He was fired immediately, and Mr. Friedlander sent a note to Jacob about his son's actions.

The family was mortified. This was the first either Jacob or Augusta knew of his thefts. Lahr found himself being judged suddenly as an adult. There had been no respite after childhood, no bridge to responsibility. "I never stole a thing after I got caught at the hardware store. I made up my mind—voom, just like that, when I saw Mom crying in her apron. It was over. Finished."

Lahr never dreamed of becoming a professional performer or regarded the theater as more than a convenient, gaudy escape. While he was floundering from job to job, many of his friends were trying to forge careers in show business. This took a conviction, an optimism that he lacked. Convinced of his own worthlessness, driven between the demands of his parents and his own intense dissatisfactions, he was stymied. The family's growing hostility and his own list of failures, too long for a boy of fifteen, cowed him. But it also made choices easier. So, when Charlie Berado, the older brother of his boxing friend, asked him to be part of a school act for a professional tryout, he did not hesitate, disregarding his parents' disdain for other children who had gone, against their family's wishes, into the theater world's frivolous good times and make-believe. The tryout at Loew's 145th Street was held once a week, as a service to both an eager public that craved new entertainment and the plethora of young performers who would work for nothing in the hope of getting bookings on the Loew's circuit. Lahr was buoyed up by the memory of his eighth-grade performance; but now he faced a more disparate audience.

Some of the same friends who had seen him on the school stage were there to watch him on a "real" one. They were tougher now, more cynical toward Lahr's aspirations.

Lahr cannot remember their act or the preceding scenes that he watched eagerly from the wings. The song, however, never left him. In the middle of the school act, he turned to the audience and sang:

> My parents always tell me I'm the apple of their eye
> But my friends just look at me and joke.
> I gaze into the mirror and then I start to cry
> Am I descended from an apple tree or just a poison oak.

"You said it—Swedish!" yelled one of Lahr's friends sitting with a block of Wilkins Avenue cronies. Lahr was bewildered: the laughter was not the same affectionate kind he had known at P.S. 40. He tried to relax and continued.

> They say my face is like a mangy dog's.
> They don't let monkeys into synagogues.

"I would've been your father," came a faceless voice from the stalls, "but a bulldog beat me down the alley."

> So what's a guy to do?
> Join the circus or the zoo.

When the song ended, the neighborhood kids exploded with applause and cheers for Lahr. He didn't hear it. "We were pretty bad; the act wasn't too good, and nothing came of the Loew's tryout."

After the performance, he removed his make-up, washed quickly, and wrapped his damp costume in the towel he had brought with him. As he stepped outside the stage door, he saw his friends huddled in the shadows of the fire escape waiting to greet him. They clamored together, chuckling about their friend who stood there, half smiling, half terrified at their presence. A friend sounded a note on his harmonica, as they did at Crotona Park.

> Hooray for Swedish
> Hooray at last
> Hooray for Swedish
> He's a horse's ass . . .

"I'll throw pennies at you bastards one day." The rest of the words could not be forced through his anger. They were laughing at his performance and his vague hopes. He threw his towel at them. It flopped under the fire escape. He pushed his way past the boys and stalked alone into the streets.

Lahr's anger dwindled quickly. His moment on stage—and watching the other performances from the wings—was so much more vivid than the blurred memory of jobs not four weeks in his past. When Berado approached Lahr to be part of a full-time professional act called "The Seven Frolics," he had no second thoughts. He did not know what kind of performer he could be. He had a loud voice, which qualified him as a singer; his athletic agility could have made him an acrobat; and, of course, there was the clowning. The thought of becoming a "Dutch" comic and using the familar German-American dialect appealed to him most. "I don't know if I was impressed with the idea of the stage or not. You know, when you're a kid your thoughts are on women. What attracted me more than anything else on stage was that you'd see the comedian holding the women around the waist and walking them across the stage. And I said to myself, 'Wouldn't it be wonderful if I could do it.' Just to be around the women, that impressed me more than anything."

Lahr, with his wild shock of black hair and his jagged nose, was no more convinced of his attractiveness than of his talent. The theater brought response and a special kind of excitement, but he never romanticized its appeal. The theater was a practical concern. "I liked it the minute I got into it because performing was easy, and I was doing something I liked. Any job I ever had, I lost. I was lackadaisical. I was all mixed up. I had no ambition *to be* anything. My idols were the Dutch comedians—Solly Ward and Sam Bernard—because I was born in a German neighborhood and knew the accents. I copied Solly a lot when I was a German comedian. In those days, I couldn't wait until I got on. I would have done twenty shows a day. It was like a shot of— dope? adrenalin? . . . When I began to work steadily and travel, I found I liked living alone. I didn't have anybody waking me up with the words 'Get up and go to work.' I just wanted to get away. I wasn't worried whether my parents loved me or not. I wanted to make some money and get away from that type of life. I wasn't happy at home."

Lahr and The Seven Frolics could not have picked a better year than 1910 for their initiation into the entertainment world. The year climaxed a decade of extensive urban development. Between 1900 and 1914, thirteen million immigrants, accounting for forty per cent of the urban population, would make their way from Europe; eighty per cent of this number would be engaged in industrial and commercial jobs. The economy mushroomed in the decade between seventy-five and eighty per cent, although the workers' wages did not increase in proportion to the mammoth profits. The new wealth created leisure and a demand for entertainment among the middle classes, while the lower classes, as Lahr knew so well, sought the relaxation of the theater after the ennervating demands of a day's work. From honky-tonks to side shows, men with a sense of public demand and a flare for publicity made fortunes in packing the harried, entertainment-hungry public into theaters. New York had over two hundred theaters by 1910. Lahr and his friends did not know the figures, but they caught the spirit of possibility that filled the theater world. "Anybody could get on. There were even people who made a living getting the hook. Almost anybody could get a professional tryout. When I started, things were pretty bad, even when I did get work." It was a seller's market; and that knowledge gave every performer, no matter how mediocre, hope.

Lahr entered show business in the salad days of burlesque. After the somber nineties, burlesque rallied until, in January 1910, it reached the pinnacle of its popular acceptance with the opening of the Columbia Theater in New York. The theater represented a decade of building by Sam Scribner and symbolized a theatrical circuit of about forty theaters extending throughout America's largest cities. They provided the highest quality of burlesque entertainment. Many followed Scribner's example and established chains of theaters. Lahr had seen the names of these circuits on billboards—the Western Circuit, the Gus Sun Time, the Mutual Wheel—vague, awesome terms. Each handled its own performers and booked its own acts. There seemed to be so many outlets for entertainment that Lahr was sure The Seven Frolics would succeed.

The tedium of waiting for bookings around the Fitzgerald Building on Forty-second Street was alleviated by the rumors of sudden success that came to performers with less talent, but more luck, than The Seven Frolics. Lahr was always ready to believe the stories. Berado needed only to mention William Hammerstein and his low-brow variety "Nut-Houses" to keep his troupe pacified when jobs were scarce. Hammerstein had proved that while talent was an important theatrical commodity, it was not always necessary. He made show business headlines by booking Conrad and Graham, the two girls who shot W. E. B. Stokes in the Ansonia Hotel. The figure Berado quoted to his troupe was correct; the girls, with absolutely no experience, headlined at three hundred dollars a week, billed as "The Shooting Stars." Hammerstein also featured freaks like "Sober Sue" and offered a thousand-dollar reward to anyone who could make her laugh. The best comics of the day tried. Not even Sam Bernard or Eddie Leonard could bring a smile to her face, which was understandable, since, unknown to the audience, her facial muscles were paralyzed. Occasionally famous athletes like Jack Johnson the boxer or the Olympic marathon champion, Dorando, were booked into the Nut House entertainments.

The luster of these stories and the flamboyance of Broadway characters filled Lahr's imagination. He and his friends spied on the Lobster

Palace Society, which made the famous Rector's its meeting place. Each immigrant group had its own heroes, but Lahr admired them all—Diamond Jim Brady, whose thirty sets of diamonds were a glittering indication of Broadway's prosperity; Adolph Zukor and Marcus Loew, factory workers from his neighborhood who set up a chain of nickel-odeons and went on to fabulous adventures and fortunes in the film industry. The possibilities were exciting; they filled him with a voluptuary's dreams, unspeakable fantasies of wealth and leisure.

Lahr had no idea at fifteen what his comic image was or would be. "I guess I did copy Solly Ward. All German comedians copied someone when they were young. I learned ways of working and delivery. Maybe I copied a few of their mannerisms, not to a great extent, though. I copied ways of carrying the body, maybe a catch line here and there. Finally, I found my own method and threw all those other mannerisms away." In 1910, the theater *was* comedians. People wanted to be amused and, at no other time in the history of the American stage were there so many experts at making them forget or, at least, laugh at the gross inequities of the age. Ed Wynn, Hal Skelly, Ben Welch, Clark and McCullough, W. C. Fields, and Weber and Fields were among the many who reaffirmed Lahr's decision to become a comic. His body, with its wiry, ungainly humor, his protean face, his need for affection made the decision for him.

"My appeal has been that people identify me with the common man." Lahr did not analyze it like that in 1910. The comic milieu that spawned him and the rest of America's great comedians dealt immediately with the elemental emotions—lust, fear, appetite, greed, misery. These spoke to Lahr's experience; he found a satisfaction in laughing at things that had been painful for so long.

The humor of the first decade of the twentieth century cut deep into the paradoxical fabric of the New World. It was at once a criticism and an acceptance of America's ideals. Lahr remembers seeing Ed Wynn perform and watching him jibe at the rich who could afford the luxury of private education. "Rah! Rah! Rah! Who pays the bills. Pa and Ma." Although Solly Ward was the one important influence on his early comic identity, Lahr watched a great many comedians, all of whom had something to teach him. Tramp acts were successful in these early years, introducing some of the theater's brightest stars —W. C. Fields, Lew Bloom, Nat Wills. These acts laughed at the inefficiency of government and the paradoxes facing an unsophisticated immigrant populace. Lahr recalls Ben Welch, the finest of the early

Jewish comedians, whose mangled monologues dramatized the immense difficulty that foreigners had in adapting to a new idiom. American society could match its optimism with unexpected terrors. Lahr saw something intrinsically funny in the malaprop, in the same way that random violence on stage took on a ridiculous perspective it didn't have in real life.

In its passion to be entertained, the American public encouraged every form of entertainment. Young people like Berado and Lahr could go on the stage without experience or polished material. The most accessible formula was the kid act, satirizing life in the classroom. The young performers could write their own material or crib it from various acts, supplementing their skits from the plethora of material in "business" books like Joe Miller's *Joke Book*. If they sometimes lacked the words, they knew well the tedium of overcrowded classrooms and bad teaching and were able to improvise. There was a challenge in this kind of formula routine; its proximity to the adolescent world made it an exciting vehicle for Lahr and his friends. Many entertainers who would become important to America's theatrical history began in these raucous, simple skits. Jack Pearl, the Marx Brothers, Mae West, Eddie Cantor, George Jessel, Bert Gordon (the Mad Russian) and Lahr were among many who first discovered the theater through these routines.

The Seven Frolics, conceived in urgency and propelled by hunger, got only sporadic work. "We were playing Keeney's Third Avenue (Thirty-third and Third Avenue), the smallest of the small time," Lahr recalls, "when a fellow came up to our manager and asked if we'd like a job in a circus sideshow. That was a great break. We had no money for a truckman to get our gear to the railroad station. So we bought penny wheels and penny axles and carted it to the station ourselves. We went to Pittsfield, Massachusetts, where we joined Harry Six's Greater New England Carnival. Our show was called 'The Little Red School House.' The man who approached us in New York was also the pitchman for the sideshow. He'd go out in front and say, 'See The Little Red Schoolhouse. Remember when you were a child. See the eccentric teacher, and all the boys. Have fun in the schoolhouse . . .' We also shilled. We'd stand in front of a sideshow and buy tickets for the games throwing the balls against the bottles or shooting. It was sort of a come-on. The Saturday after we arrived, we went to collect our pay from the pitchman who had gotten us the job. He wasn't there; he'd run off with our money. It wasn't very much, but we were stranded. All the carnival people—I think they were the kindest people I ever met in my life—got together and helped us. They helped us, kid. They gave us a mess book—a $2.50 meal ticket so we could eat. I remember sitting on a wall in front of a city hall. One of the carnival people came along. He said, 'Have you eaten, kid?' I said, 'No.' He gave me a quarter. They even bought us a ticket back home. It was a great experience! It gave me an insight into the real camaraderie among people who are supposed to be the lowest in show business."

Theater meant community; and despite the hard times, Lahr found the unity of aspiration and the fellowship exciting. He daubed make-up on his collar (even when he was out of work) so that people could see he was a performer. With the theater he not only inherited a profession, but also a place in the geography of Manhattan that was the focus for his enterprises. The Fitzgerald Building, an ugly sand-brown edifice whose hallways reeked with cigar smoke and dust, was the center for small-time booking agents and theater-chain managers looking for cheap new talent for their low-priced emporiums. There were other buildings where the big stars and famous theatrical magnates like Keith and William Morris operated their multimillion-dollar entertainment ventures.

Lahr rarely had the full round-trip fare to the Fitzgerald Building and back to Wilkins Avenue. The bus or the subway was five cents one way; Lahr often set out with only enough to get him downtown, trusting to the generosity of a more recently employed entertainer to get him home. Everyone congregated on Forty-second Street. The waiting was never lonely. Berado was there, and other young hopefuls like the aggressive, cocky Joe E. Marx, and a quiet, good-looking boy who came from his Harlem home every day, Jack Pearlman. The organizers of the theatrical groups were no more than eighteen, with only a few years of sporadic experience.

The meeting place was the Automat across the street from the Fitzgerald Building. There, deals were made, dreams plotted, acts revised. It was there that Pearlman decided to change his name to Pearl, and Irving Lahrheim became Bert Lahr. "We had no money," recalls Pearl. "We had nothing, just little kids trying to make a reputation in show business. Bert and I were both in kid acts. I went up to his house. I used to say to him, 'Cut off your name, I'll cut off mine.' Everybody said, 'Watch this kid, watch this Lahr.' We used to compete. Whoever made the funniest face would win. Well, Bert won, and he never made a face."

The Automat was an appealing hangout. It represented an unlimited source of food. Occasionally an actor who had found work doled out enough nickels so the group could enjoy coffee and sandwiches. When there was no benefactor Lahr had to rely on his own ingenuity. Investing a nickel for a ham and cheese sandwich, he would wedge a piece of gum in the corner of the small glass door so that it did not close completely but gave the appearance of being shut. After that, it was every man for himself.

Pearl called Lahr "Dog-face." Their prankish association lasted a lifetime, with Lahr receiving phone calls in the thick German dialect of Pearl's Baron von Munschausen. Pearl recalls the tenor of Broadway life from the bottom. "Those jobs weren't there all the time for you. And when you did get one, you'd bargain. I'd say, 'Can you make it $37.50 instead of $35?' The manager would say, 'Take it or leave it.' So you took a $35-a-week job. Bert and I were very close. He never played any tricks on me, but the fellahs were always trying to make a little jealousy between Bert and myself. They'd say, 'He's doing better than you are.' But we were such good friends we didn't care."

Pearl's superstitions made him the brunt of many of Lahr's schemes. Pearl believed that if he was touched on the ear it was bad luck, and that he had to touch a person back to neutralize the curse. He once chased Lahr ten blocks up Broadway to break a "spell." Another time Pearl and Lahr convinced a crony that a bowl of fruit would buy him an evening with a beautiful Indian. The boy bought the fruit; but when he arrived at the appointed place, he was chagrined to find an Indian of the wooden cigar-store variety. Lahr and Pearl shared the food and a good laugh.

The jokes and reminiscences overlook the hunger. Pearl used to line his shoes with cardboard to prevent the soles from wearing out; Lahr remembers the humiliation of his threadbare pants. He camouflaged the holes by walking casually with a newspaper behind his back.

In the evenings, if he had enough money, Lahr would leave the warmth of the Automat and set out for a theater where a favorite entertainer was playing. One November evening, while he stood gazing at a poster of Sam Bernard, his newspaper in its usual position behind his pants, a man approached him. Lahr remembers his careful diction. The man asked if he was a performer; when Lahr said that his specialty was Dutch comedy in a school act, the man expressed still keener interest. "He said he'd like to help me. He could see by my pants and by how I talked that things weren't going so well. He offered to pay me five dollars to show him my act. 'Professional services' he said."

Lahr found himself accompanying the gentleman to his hotel. "He told me that he'd play the school kid."

Using the man's walking cane as a ruler, Lahr went into his routine; the man sat silently, watching Lahr's movements. "I remember how he looked up at me and said, quietly, 'Hit me with the stick.' I was confused. 'You're some kind of fruit!' I said to him." The man persisted, putting two more five-dollar bills on the table. "I didn't know what to do. I told him I'd call the cops. He kept saying, 'That's not very theatrical—Bert. Preserve the illusion. Preserve the illusion.' When I tried to run past him he pushed me back. I'll never forget it. He said, 'Remember, my friend, you are an entertainer. You are owned— by managers, by agents, by the public, by me. Hit . . .'" Lahr was ready to swing at the man, when, instead, he suddenly kicked at the man's groin. He vaulted the table and made for the door. He ran downstairs into the street, his throat dry, his head feverish. He went back to the Automat, and waited in the yellow light alone, until the last customer had left. "Sometimes in those first two years, I didn't come home at night because I was afraid to tell my mother I wasn't working."

There were other humiliations. "A young comedian called Sid Gold and myself tried out at the Amphium Theater in Brooklyn. We did a two-act. The Seven Frolics had split up, and there wasn't much work around for me. When I got to the theater, I had a stomach ache. One of the performers told me that cherry brandy soothed the spasms. I went around to a bar and had two before the show. I went back to the theater to put on my make-up. In those days you didn't put on pancake, you put on all kinds and blended them in. We used what they called "flesh color" and put on a little rouge. When I touched my cheek, my skin seemed to hang apart from my face. Gold asked me how I felt. I said 'Fine.' We got ready to go on. I remember hearing our cue and coming out on stage. I got out there and the lights and the people blurred in front of me. I couldn't say anything. Gold kept ad-libbing. I tried to speak, but what came out was incoherent. I could hear the audience laughing and coughing but I couldn't see them. It was the first time I couldn't see them. The manager yelled at us from the wings, 'Get off the stage, you punks.' We tried to keep from going. He brought the curtain down on us and pushed us off the stage. I remember what he said when I tried to explain. 'Don't waste your breath on me, kid. You'll never work the Amphium again. Get your things and get the hell out of here.'"

Two weeks after that disastrous performance, Lahr was approached by the diminutive Joe E. Marx to play the Dutch comedian in a kid act. Marx, a veteran of five years of school acts, had wangled a big booking at the Hippodrome Theater in Chicago. The Seven Frolics, Lahr recalled, averaged ten dollars each. "You could live in a boarding house for five dollars a week, then they'd give you 'night-lunch.' " But Marx's offer was more promising than any Lahr had ever received. The Hippodrome was a well-known vaudeville establishment with continuous performances from one o'clock in the afternoon on. Lahr had played the cheapest of vaudeville theaters, where three acts were interspersed with a nickelodeon show. "You could get in for a dime; and we'd get three or four dollars a day." The Hippodrome was outstanding in comparison, despite a grueling five shows a day. Lahr had worked harder. "When I worked Jersey City with The Seven Frolics, we played two theaters in the same town. Four shows a day in each theater. We'd go from one theater to the other in horse-drawn carriages. We got a meager sum, and we dressed in the boiler room." Vaudeville theaters were notorious among the performers for their bad conditions and the cruel pragmatism of the management. The Hippodrome was a big city theater; and the Marx's troupe could expect a better stint. The price was $350 for nine players with the cost of scenery, costumes, and travel coming out of the wages. In order to defer traveling expenses and break up the trek to Chicago, Marx booked a week at Gluck's New Castle Theater, in New Castle, Pennsylvania.

When the troupe arrived at New Castle, they were tired and inadequately rehearsed. The act did not go over well. After the performance, the manager called Marx into his office and informed him that all he could offer was three hundred dollars. Marx took the fifty-dollar cut in salary. This was not unusual theater practice. "There used to be a saying in vaudeville—'Don't send out your laundry till after the first performance.' In those days, the manager could come backstage and hand you your publicity pictures, and say, 'You're canceled.' If the manager was a kind man, he'd give you your fare back to New York. If he wasn't, he was not obligated. There were no dressing rooms in many of the theaters; you had no protection." Marx was forced to play Gluck's New Castle for two weeks in order to make enough to continue to Chicago. In that time, Lahr was not so much obsessed with the exploitation of the performers as with one of the girls in the act, a pert blonde called Dixie Dunbar. She encouraged him, but Marx had laid down strict rules about dating. Nevertheless, Lahr persisted, much to the annoyance of Marx, who finally confronted him in the hotel lobby.

"I said there was no sketching! I'm fining you a buck." Lahr talked back, but before he could finish a sentence, Marx punched him. The fight lasted less than a minute, with Lahr at the bottom of the skirmish. The battle didn't diminish his affection for Dixie. Lahr recalls watching her from the wings. "An acrobat who was also on the bill came up to me, and asked what I thought of her. I told him how she kept quiet when you talked to her and how kind she was. The guy followed us to Chicago and ended up marrying her!"

When the troupe arrived in Chicago, news of their performance at New Castle preceded them. The Hippodrome had canceled their booking. Marx, who also did a single act, got work at seven dollars a day. The wages fed the others.

Lahr and a friend took a room in a sleazy Southside hotel. After two days, their money ran out. They confided their despair to a lady who lived next to them on the third floor. Janet was her name; Lahr remembers her tattoo, the money she kept wedged in her stocking, which peeked out of a kimono smelling of perfume and cheap silk. The night Lahr and his friend confessed their dilemma Janet was drunk. She asked them to bring their luggage into her room and talk about it. Finally, after a few drinks, she made a suitable proposal. "Why don't you boys sleep with me!" Lahr tried not to smile. "I thought to myself 'the guys are never going to believe this.' But she was plastered and pulled us down on the bed beside her. Anyway, she was bigger than me. Then she passed out. I looked at my friend. He looked at me. We got undressed, put our clothes over our valises, and went to bed."

Lahr did not get much sleep. Janet tossed on the bed, her body slipped close to him. He lay awake. "I was thinking about the job. I'd been stranded in Massachusetts, in Albany, and now Chicago. It wasn't funny. I was thinking about Wilkins Avenue . . . and how my mother cried that time. Every once in a while Janet would toss from one side of the bed to the other. I could hear my friend snoring, then I felt the money, like a knot of wood, against her leg. I was very quiet; I slid my hand over her thigh. I reached for the money. I felt a hand—a hairy one. I looked up. My friend was trying to do the same thing. He grabbed the money; and we jumped out of bed. I was laughing too hard to get dressed. My friend whispered, 'What are we going to do with the bags? They'll make us pay downstairs.' So we opened our trunks and put everything on. I had two pairs of pants and four shirts on. My toothbrush was in my pocket; I stuffed my second pair of shoes under my belt. The noise woke Janet. She was still drunk but she knew something was wrong. We ran downstairs. I dropped a shoe. I wanted to go back for it, but I could hear her screaming down the hall for the manager."

Outside they counted the money—seven dollars. The next morning Lahr swallowed his pride and wired his mother for ten dollars. When it arrived the following day, he borrowed another ten from a friend and bought a ticket home.

Lahr's failure in Chicago convinced Jacob that his worst paternal suspicions were correct. "I want a son I can be proud of. I want you in the business." Lahr had no successes with which to rebut his father's claims, no tangible accomplishments to justify three years of perseverance. Nearly seventeen, Lahr nurtured private memories more thrilling and deliciously vulgar than he could express. It made him at once ashamed of show business and eager for a stage career.

But Lahr's reputation among performers around the Fitzgerald Building mounted. Five months after his return from Chicago, Bert Gordon asked him to join an act he was framing for one of the more successful kid-act entrepreneurs, Joe Wood. Gordon, another product of Wilkins Avenue but a few years older than Lahr, would go on to win national burlesque notoriety as the Mad Russian. He had originally cast Jack Pearl as the school teacher in "The Nine Crazy Kids." Pearl's delivery was not eccentric enough; his voice lacked the strength to carry over the laughs and mayhem generated on stage. Gordon explained the problem to Wood, who suggested a wild, outrageous youngster named Lahr. The association that followed with Gordon was brief, but important.

Lahr may have still had many faults as a performer, but he was blessed with a voice that could carry to the farthest seat in any house. Gordon emphasized what Lahr as a performer was just beginning to realize—how to build a laugh. Gordon, a seasoned veteran of burlesque at nineteen, recalls the ideas he stressed to an eager, untrained comedian. "You can't let the audience fall back for a minute, Bert. Every time you get a laugh, you've got to top it with another one or you lose your pace. That means you've got to use your voice to get *over* the laughs, to keep it going."

The tactics of comedy, in the beginning, were not elaborate. Lahr studied his audiences; and it was to their needs and their instincts that he adapted his comic spirit. Although Lahr never formulated any axioms for comedy ("I was always instinctive"), the rules that the frizzy-haired Gordon stressed worked surprisingly well. The Nine Crazy Kids were professional enough to play many of the RKO theaters in New York as well as the larger cities on the Eastern seaboard. They made one big-time appearance at the Union Square Theater on Fourteenth Street. Although the "Crazy Kids" was not unanimously well received, Lahr could assure himself that a momentum was building, that his career, like his life, was taking shape.

The act (see Appendix 1) itself was a standard kid act of the day, cribbed, by Lahr's own admission, from the successful comedy formula developed by the Avon Comedy Four (which starred two comedians who would headline for decades as Smith and Dale). It included the standard social stereotypes, as reflected in the names of the characters —Isador Fitzpatrick, John L. Fitzcorbett, Sharkey, Reginald Redstockings. Also included was the boisterous teacher, who entered brandishing his wild Dutch dialect like a ruler.

The act was never written down, but Gordon still remembers the introductory song:

> Nine o'clock, nine o'clock, don't be late for school,
> Don't be late, don't be late, or else you'll get the rule.
>
> Ring the bell, ring the bell, c'mmon hurry, let's run,
> Nine o'clock, nine o'clock, strict attention's soon begun.

Lahr entered wearing a Prussian mustache and a putty nose.

> I heve some very sed, sed news that I have come to say,
> Your poor, dear teacher's very sick and cannot come today.
> *Chorus:* Hip, hip, hooray, hip, hip, hooray, and we have come to stay,
> For our poor teacher's very sick and cannot come today.
> *Lahr:* But I'm to be your teacher because he is not here.
> You will be expelled if you act wrong, never fear.
> *Chorus:* Oh Fudge!
> Oh, kids, let's go home, let's go have some fun.
> Playing ball, skating's fine too,
> We'll fool around, that's what we'll do . . .

And Lahr remembers himself playing with words. They must have called on strange recesses of his experience.

> *Teacher:* Gladys, vot is de opposite of misery?
> *Gladys:* Happiness.
> *Teacher:* Dot's right. Now, Abby, vot is de opposite of woe?
> *Abby:* Giddyap.

His final job with this brand of entertainment was by far the most lucrative and the longest. Once again he signed to replace his friend Jack Pearl, who had graduated to burlesque in Joe Wood's variety act, *College Days*. Lahr was to meet the troupe in Seattle and continue with it on the Western circuit. En route, the train stopped for half an hour in Portland, and Lahr got off. As he strolled down Portland's main avenue he heard a familiar voice.

"Hey Dog-face!"

When he turned, he was standing face to face with Pearl, whom he was supposed to meet in Seattle. The show had closed in Washington and was now on its way to California. Lahr had confused the dates; he would have missed his first important booking.

The tour was successful. He earned eighteen dollars a week, playing to four audiences a day. He sent ten dollars home each week. He had forty week's work on the tour. What pleased him was not the money, but the exposure. He was learning about audiences and struggling with them. "Comedy is sympathy," he would say later. In this Western tour he was learning how to modulate his image and create this sympathy before audiences whose tastes were as varied as the countryside. He did not wear the outrageous comedy clothes that many other comedians did. When he won over his audience, it was with his body and his voice. He worked with a fierce energy on stage. The eyes that rolled as frantically as a hunted deer's were real and their panic honest. He became aware that his face could win more laughs in its contorted movements than written lines or wild costumes.

By 1916 it was apparent to Lahr that he was already too old to continue with the kid acts. When he returned to New York, he teamed with a man and woman to form Hardy, Lahr, and Usher. They did not get much work, but even in this shabby act, Lahr's rough talent attracted attention. After their final performance in Brooklyn, Lahr was sitting in his dressing room, pondering the trio's tepid reception. A performer on the same bill came in and introduced himself.

"I remember Billy K. Wells was a very natty fellow, small, always well dressed. He was a monologist. He said to me 'I've been watching you work. You've got talent.' "

Lahr and Wells chatted: finally Wells handed him his card. "I'm a writer for Blutch Cooper, ever heard of him?" Lahr knew the name. His friend Jack Pearl had signed onto the quality burlesque Columbia Wheel and Cooper had produced Pearl's show.

Wells did not waste words. "He told me he'd be in touch. He said they could use young kids with talent. He said this was no gag. Then he left. I remember sitting there, amazed. More than five years in the business and now a shot at burlesque. I wondered if I was ready."

BURLESQUE

I'll never forget him. He was only nineteen or twenty and that's in-
fancy for a comedian, but he was completely at home on the stage. He
already had that crazy stiff-arm gesture of his, and he was doing the
gnong, gnong, gnong business. I signed him up for burlesque right
away. He got thirty-five dollars a week the first season. Then, he was
raised to fifty dollars, and the third year, I think, he got one hundred
dollars. He was known as the boy wonder of the Columbia Circuit.

Billy K. Wells on Bert Lahr, Theater Arts Magazine

B ILLY K. WELLS DIED IN 1956. AMONG THE THEATRICAL MEMENTOS
that hung on his wall was an autographed picture of Bert Lahr.
In it Lahr is lean and smooth. His hair is full. He can be no older than
thirty. The dedication reads:

To My Pal Billy,
    Who is responsible for what little success I have attained.

This is not hyperbole; Lahr was too careful and self-conscious with
words to waste them. Nothing he ever again wrote would approach the
frankness and gratitude of that inscription.

Lahr would probably have become a star without Billy K. Wells
—even at nineteen he possessed energy and an individuality of style.
But the road to comic expertise would have been longer and more confusing alone. Wells provided not only much imaginative material on
which Lahr could embellish, but also an entree into the most important
burlesque circuit—the Columbia Wheel. Because of Wells, Lahr was
exposed to the best burlesque comedians and the most critical audiences. The competition and the pressure matured his comic sensibilities
faster than they otherwise would have developed.

Wells had turned to writing as a sideline after his wife died, in
an effort to support his children. He was a good performer; as a
writer he created jokes and sketches for burlesque, and gradually expanded into vaudeville, theatrical, and, finally, movie writing. He

wrote for many of America's famous comedians—among them Jack Pearl (for whom he created Baron von Munschausen), Eugene and Willie Howard, Amos 'n Andy, Jack Benny, and Weber and Fields. He also contributed to *George White's Scandals* and the *Greenwich Village Follies*.

Sitting at his cluttered mahogany desk, Wells draped a string from one side to the other, and, in a clothesline effect, pinned the various jokes and "bits of business" on the line, rearranging them as he built the scene. He kept a detailed account of the number of jokes he wrote; he tabulated the laughs per minute of every sketch. Even the malapropisms that salted his comic dialogue were uncovered in the same methodical manner. Wells would take a word and write it on one side of a file card and on the other side list similar sounding words, testing each for its comic possibility. With this businesslike procedure of comic creation, he brought to burlesque the instinct for social criticism that gave his comedy a depth approaching the English burlesque from another century. His fey imagination was able to ferret out fresh humor from old forms.

During the eighteenth century, the term "burlesque" had been synonymous with parody. (Henry Fielding and Richard Sheridan were among those who contributed to the tradition of English burlesque.) The twentieth century changed the meaning of the term and the nature of the entertainment. Burlesque became a much less cerebral, more robust low comedy that lacked the fundamental impulse for social parody. The American interpretation of the term began in 1865 when Michael Bennett Leavitt, a theatrical manager, decided to combine a variety of individual entertainments into one evening's fare. American burlesque was conceived as "consisting of three parts—minstrel, vaudeville, and burlesque—the latter being the real feature." The format would evolve into a miniature comedy that differed from vaudeville in its consistent form and story line. Because of the caliber and variety of entertainments in burlesque, the form demanded a long and versatile apprenticeship. Those who claimed to *write* for burlesque mainly wrote bits or monologues. Most of the classic American humor evolved from the comedians themselves, who knew their audiences and the format of this type of entertainment. Since burlesque made no pretensions at communicating ideas, the actors and those who wrote for it relied heavily on formula scenes passed down from season to season and on material revised from humor magazines. Wells was an exception. Still, Lahr was attracted to burlesque neither by Wells' competence nor by the stars on the circuit, but by the thought of working steadily. It meant that he could pacify his parents by sending home a good percentage of his earnings. He did not realize that his father would never spend the money he sent, fearing that his son would need something with which to start a new life once his fling in show business had lost its luster.

Lahr was the last of America's great comedians to graduate from burlesque, leaving it late in 1922, just as burlesque was beginning to lose the *brio* that sparked its growth during the previous two decades. The theatrical revue, along with the silent film, was absorbing the best of the burlesque "bits" and specialty numbers. The stunning Broadway chorus lines extended the leg-show aspect of burlesque to a new titillating pinnacle. As early as 1923, while burlesque performers were still in tights, the Shuberts brought nudity to Broadway revues. (Lahr never participated in the bastardized burlesque.) He knew burlesque when it was fresh and vital, exploring the truths of the working classes and the struggles of the minorities to make their way in America. What burlesque had to say, it said not with bitterness but with gay irreverence. The springboard for many creative entertainers and a multitude of "classic" sketches gave way to spectacle with nothing to offer but a peep show.

Wells made his offer to Lahr at the Olympia Theater in February of 1916, but Lahr could not make his debut on the Columbia Circuit until September of 1917. He would have accepted Wells's proposal immediately, but he was already under contract to Charles Feldman to tour with a show called *Garden Belles*. He begged Feldman to release him, but to no avail. A letter from Blutch Cooper, one of the biggest burlesque producers of his day and the son-in-law of Sam Scribner, the founder of the Wheel, explains the situation and indicates the excitement Lahr's talent generated in Wells and the portly, tight-lipped entrepreneur. It is an important document for Lahr, pasted on the first page of his makeshift scrapbook. The date is March 10, 1917. Cooper's letter represented the first tangible indication that Lahr's talent lived not only in his own mind, but in the imagination of others as well.

Dear Bert,

I just received your letter and I note where you say you humbly beg my pardon for the Feldman mix-up, you don't have to beg my pardon. It was just a good opportunity that you have let slip through your fingers, and I don't hold it against you, as I told you the other day when you came to see me. I wouldn't have admired you jumping out of any show whether he is a big fish or a small fish. I gave Mr. Feldman ample time to get another man, and I hustled around and got him a man and was willing to give him $5 a week toward the new man, but he stalled me and lied until it was practically too late for me to send another man up. . . .

You don't have to write me about your lack of business ability by not grabbing the opportunity that we offered you, but those things has to come to every man in life. It is an old and true saying, "Experience is the best teacher." There isn't a successful man in the world who doesn't make mistakes. You are just a flower starting to bloom and your friend Mr. Feldman was there with a knife to nip the bud, but he is not good enough to kill the flower that has a wonderful chance to enjoy the sunshine that's coming to him. My feelings toward you are not hurt to that extent to try and kill your future. I will endeavor to do my utmost next season to make you briter [sic] than any spotlight we have on the circuit. This is not any salve, but its right from the heart as you know from business dealings with me that I am not a mushy sort.

With best wishes for your future success, I remain yours sincerely

Blutch Cooper

Cooper was, indeed, not a "mushy sort." He would never again be so overt in his praise of Lahr. He would nurture Lahr. In June of 1917 he made good his promise, signing Lahr onto the professional circuit as the third comedian in *The Best Show in Town*, featuring the Italian comic Frankie Hunter. A squib in the *Burlesque News*, heralding the transaction, spells Lahr's name wrong in his first publicity clipping.

Wells Lands a "Find"

Billy K. Wells, producer of "Blutch" Cooper productions has, in his estimation, landed a "find" of a Dutch comedian for one of the Cooper shows on the Columbia Wheel for next season.

The new addition is Bert Lehr and was plucked from the "bushes" during one of Wells' recent scouting tours. He has been signed to a three year contract under "Blutch."

The show opened in Cleveland in September. After the first performance, Lahr was made second comedian. In assigning Lahr the heavy responsibility of the second comedy slot, it was clear that Cooper expected results; it was also apparent that he would get them.

"You can't learn to be a comedian," Lahr once told a reporter. "You're either funny or you're not. Let the audience tell you." As early as 1917, the burlesque audience was communicating its approval of his broad "Dutch" comedy. But while his delivery was fresh and funny, his performance was far from polished.

Lahr made his entrance wearing a tight-fitting Palm Beach suit whose conservative checkered weave was marred by conspicuous spots. He wore no wig, but, instead, combed his thick black hair high on his head and matched it with a small brush mustache which curled up at the edge of his nostrils. His face was streaked with heavy pencil marks to indicate wrinkles. The pencil accentuated the pouches beneath his eyes, making them look like poached eggs, and outlined his mouth before time and continual smiling wore these contours deep into his face.

The final touch to his make-up was a large, bulbous putty nose, completing the German-Jewish stereotype. It transmitted, in its obvious falseness and inflexibility, a benevolent urgency and sympathy in his character to the audience. Whether intended or not, urgency was the primary emotional state that Lahr felt in this first circuit tour and in the remaining years of burlesque. In the glossy picture used for lobby displays, Lahr was pigeon-toed, his left hand drawn tight to make a fist. He was the self-conscious funny-man. If nothing else, these pictures show the approach he would take toward his audience. Young and inexperienced, Lahr would grapple with the people over the footlights. His tactic was as straightforward and unrelenting as his pose indicated. His job was simply to *make* them laugh and, if they laughed, if he could make them snicker or guffaw, then he was doing his work and insuring his survival with the Cooper shows. From his first success in Cleveland, burlesque meant steady employment and security.

> *Interviewer:* What was the best teacher in burlesque—the other comedians, or the audience or what?
>
> *Lahr:* Observance. Observance. A capacity to pick it up and a capacity to edit yourself. You could learn to be an acrobat if you were strong enough; You could learn to take falls. Or if you wanted to be a comedy acrobat, you'd put on funny clothes and have gags, pull wigs up and down, which the audience would laugh at.
>
> *Actors Talk About Acting*

It is hard to imagine *the laugh* as an absolute value. However, it has been the one absolute in my father's life, the focus of his imagination. Laughter is more than a serious business; it is an obsession. "It's the hardest thing in the world to get a laugh, and the easiest thing to kill it," he maintains. Burlesque was a good teacher not only because it offered Lahr a showcase in which to experiment with his audience and learn to build comic moments, but also because he learned to protect the laughs.

The Best Show in Town (1917) opened with the mellifluous chorus belting out a call to fun and festival.

> . . . The plot is a lot of rot.
> What's the use I'd like to know
> So long as there's girls
> And comedy whirls
> Who cares about the plot of the show.

The finale, in which Lahr sang with the girls, may not have had the eloquence of a Shakespearean epilogue, but the functions of the players and the stage had not changed.

> There's been no rhyme or reason
> In anything we did.
> All we did was kid.

On stage, Lahr was the most frivolous of all, the loudest howler, the wildest acrobat, the merriest Merry Andrew. He worked hard on stage, trying out many different comedy gestures, eliminating the ones that did not get good laughs or which, in certain situations, killed a bigger one to come. He had already acquired, along with his distinctive delivery, a catch phrase. All the great comedians used some such phrase or action not only as a trademark but also as a psychological gimmick to elicit the audience's response at the right moment. Will Rogers lowered his head and twirled his lariat after he told a joke. George M. Cohan glanced sideways toward the boxes and pretended he was cleaning his molars. Lahr did a double take toward the audience after the punch line and then growled his "gnong, gnong, gnong." The audience was led to the joke, cued to laugh, and then, with an effective comic phrase, the basic joke was expanded far beyond its original proportions.

As Lahr learned to lure his audience and wrench from his material every possible laugh, he also became aware of how every technique could be employed against him on stage. With four comedians in a burlesque show, the competition was grueling. It was a struggle not only for the extra laughs, but also for the audience's attention, for personal pride, and sometimes even for private dislikes. In those first months, Hunter would purposely kill some of Lahr's laughs by making him seem the antagonist and flinching from him in mock fear. Lahr had to learn fast. "Never move on a joke. I can kill any joke by movement. It's disastrous." It is the one stage tactic that infuriates him to this day. The audience must focus on the person telling the joke; the slightest movement shifts this concentration and the action loses its impact with the switch of interest.

Hunter liked to toss his head just as Lahr was delivering a laugh. He was not the only culprit; Lahr himself could fight ruthlessly for an audience's attention. If he had found a new faith in his comic delivery, he also had developed an occupational suspicion of other performers. "I've worked with very few men that I've ever had trouble with. I have a funny face, and whoever wants to make it a contest has two strikes against him."

Women posed even more of a threat. Beatrice Lillie and Nancy Walker are the only two comediennes he admires. He claims that they "played theater." "Play" has always been a key word for Lahr because, from the beginning, his comedy and success involved his ability to build scenes and situations rather than simply to tell jokes. Although no antifeminist, Lahr's attitudes toward the majority of comediennes is adamant, and always skeptical. "Beware of the woman who gets the first laugh." He says this wryly and with a smile, but experience has left him no other judgment. A woman on stage brought with her an immediate sympathy and appeal. Even if she behaved badly, the slightest sarcasm from Lahr dampened the audience's sympathy toward him and shifted the delicate mechanism of the laughter.

He cites an example, a scene in *Two on the Aisle* that he knew was good material even though the audiences weren't laughing. The sensation never changed. It was not so much a feeling of frustration as a sense of panic. Had the plotting and playing been wasted? Was the joke worthless? Was he himself worthless? Couldn't he *make* them laugh?

During one performance he turned by chance to the woman playing the scene with him. She was tinkling a champagne glass just as he was about to deliver the punch line. He was livid; at the same time he knew he couldn't let the audience see his fury. He spat out his line, changing its rhythm, surprising the actress, who understood that she had been caught.

She blushed, and then, in her embarrassment, forgot her lines. "What do I do now, Bert; what do I do?" she whispered.

"You got yourself into this, baby—now get yourself out."

He waited on stage without moving or saying a word until finally someone from the wings gave her the lines.

Sympathy was also the emotion he longed for off the stage. Lahr knew many of the tricks to create it on stage; but it has taken him fifty years to learn how to express his knowledge in words.

Interviewer: Is it harder to make people laugh than to make them cry?

Lahr: Well, you're equipped for both. Let's put it this way, if you're equipped for both, they're both easy. But you will find that a comedian—a good comedian—has to be a good actor. And the reason for a comedian being a good comedian, he creates sympathy. He immediately creates a warmth in his audience, so once you do that, and the audience roots for you, it's a very simple matter to make them cry. I think you laugh at a great comedian because you want to cry. Laughter is never too far from tears.

Interviewer: What is your secret of getting sympathy from an audience?

Lahr: I think it's a physical and chemical thing, the same as if you go to a party and somebody comes in a room and immediately attracts you. So a person comes out with a manner on stage that makes you say "Aah, he's a sweet guy"—do you see? Which I don't think you can acquire, and I don't think you can acquire good taste—I think you've got to be born with that. I know what not to say, what not to do. I think it's his manner, his general attitude, a humbleness.

Interviewer: You must have done something to cultivate this. Let's start with the fact that you have the basic equipment.

Lahr: It isn't a question of cultivating. You cannot cultivate humbleness, it becomes phoney. He's either a humble fella or a brash fella . . .

Actors Talk About Acting

Lahr learned quickly that the audience responded to individuality and that the imitator's staying power in burlesque was short. Critical reaction reinforced his theatrical eccentricity. He was noticed immediately by reviewers.

[Lahr performs] in a most pleasing and different way than is usually seen . . . He is a newcomer to burlesque and a welcome one.

New York *Clipper* on *The Best Show in Town*

As a low "Dutch" comic, much of his spoken humor came from malapropisms. He had grown up with this aspect of dialect humor; few had a keener ear for the funny sound or the ludicrous innuendoes of words. Lahr and Wells would discuss various elaborate word plays, with Lahr improvising on Wells's script. Wells, perhaps more than any other writer besides S. J. Perelman and Damon Runyon, was a master of the mangled phrase.

Lahr's singing was another source of comedy. His voice could never be trained to stay on key. He had never tested the real possibility of the comedy song in the school-act days. *The Best Show in Town* brought the comedy song into his act. Sometimes it would be a rendition of a popular ballad complete with malapropisms and thick Dutch dialect such as he had used on Wilkins Avenue. Later in his career he found that he could create more laughter with his voice when he tried to sing seriously than when he launched into a wildly athletic and raucous spoof (as he did in *The Best Show in Town*). There is no better example of the burlesque malaprop song than the one he did in *The Best Show in Town,* a number introduced a few years earlier by Sam Bernard. Frederick Morton wrote, on hearing Lahr's version years later, that the sound "was indescribable. Perhaps a Wagnerian tenor could achieve it, if in the midst of wooing Kriemhild, he were given a hotfoot."

Lahr's delivery was fast, his hands froze at the peak of their excitement to emphasize the delight of each statement in the song.

Ououououououoouch—how dot voman could cook!

His eyes rolled in dumbfounded ferocity. His voice strained in its passion so that the veins around his temples swelled perceptibly.

Her zoop had a flavor like—like bitches and cream
Her pancakes—ah!—Vhat a bootiful dreaeaeaeammm!

His hands suddenly shot out in front of him as if he was feeling his way along an imaginary wall. They trembled. He closed his eyes as he spoke; his nostrils dilated until they became the fulcrum of his face, teetering between delight and disgust.

And her oyshters and fishes
Were simply . . . (he pauses in sensuous reverie) . . . malicious.
Ach, Gott, How Dot Voman Could Cook, Jawohl.

This was a subtle version of the word-murdering potential of his comedy. A year earlier, before he had signed on to the Cooper shows, Lahr did a stint with Joe Woods's *College Days,* once again replacing his friend Jack Pearl.

The program of the performance, featuring such characters as Heinrich Hasenfeffer, manufacturer of excited oats, Charlie Horsely, and Ivy Green, gives an indication of the playful simplicity of the humor. The song Lahr performed in this two-act farce was less sophisticated than his later misuse of the language.

> Ve're two ignorant Germans just arrived from College,
> And our geographical language is just supreme.
> Ve have learnt to speaking English in a bar room
> And that is vhy ve don't know whose the reason . . .

He is embarrassed now at the nonsensical, hokey quality of the humor; but in 1916 it was a big success.

After *College Days,* Lahr had worked himself up to burlesque and *The Best Show in Town,* which became one of the season's choicest burlesque offerings. It played to rave reviews and packed houses for its full forty-week tour. After the fourth month, the program for the show ran an advertisement announcing that "Bert Lahr, eccentric Dutch [was signed] three years more with Blutch Cooper."

The gaiety of this time is reflected in a picture of Lahr in his tattered first scrapbook. It shows him and Frank Hunter mugging with the soubrette of the show. They are dressed in children's clothes complete with pillows for paunch and little skullcaps. They are being embraced by a *zoftig* beauty wearing a rhinestone star in the middle of her forehead. It is the only picture he has kept that depicts him clowning off stage.

During the run of *The Best Show in Town* there was little leisure time. Performers worked two shows a day, seven days a week in the towns west of Chicago. When they were in the East, Sunday was a day of rest, but any free time was spent sleeping or planning new material. At every circuit theater, rehearsals would be held at 9:30 each morning and the chorus and routines overhauled.

Lahr thrived on the work. He did not waste time at rehearsals. His earnestness made him the brunt of much good-natured joking. During the first tour he incorporated new kinds of comic movements into his performance, adopting many of the antics of the acrobats, who fascinated him. He developed a neck fall and a backward flip that he worked into the memorable Flugel Street Union scene (see Appendix 2) he did with Hunter.

Wells's burlesque was high-level entertainment. The audiences appreciated his skill. In cities like Detroit and Cincinnati, the local theater buffs announced that it was the best burlesque to come their way in a long time. Cincinnati offices reported that *The Best Show in Town* was "the most successful season of burlesque in the city." And Dayton, where burlesque houses had been languishing because of a dearth of talent and suitable material, saw Wells's show as heralding a new type of burlesque. One critic was outspoken on the subject:

> By this time, Dayton has learned that burlesque is not so black as it is painted. It has been pretty well cleaned up. Rot and coarseness, the solid foundations upon which the old burlesque was built, have been amputated and what remains is no worse than that which is found in almost any musical comedy. To be sure it is no show for babes in arms . . . But then the average man or woman can see it without being any the worse for the experience. It is spectacular and diverting and musical and its principal exponents comprise some of the cleverest people on the stage.

Lahr's reviews continued to be outstanding. He was "a coming Teuton" in almost every critical appraisal. He pasted each clipping in his book.

Now the scraps of paper are brown with age. Many of them disintegrate at the touch. They tell little of the enthusiasm of those performances, but they include a few random entries that are not about him. These are mysterious and touching inclusions in a book that represents so much of his early dream and the beginning of his future. One clipping from a Charleston paper is about a show called *Katinka* (1916). A paragraph in that review is marked with a thin red line of lipstick:

> *Katinka* brought a large and capable cast to Charleston and yes— one really pretty girl; the petite little brunette, and there was only

one. Too bad she was in the chorus, because there are better things ahead of her, much better things.

A few pages later in the book there is another mention of someone other than Lahr:

The chorus is both beautiful and energetic. Even a sober-faced young woman who is a good chorus girl "because she is so different" won applause from the enthusiastic Sunday crowd.

These clippings are the only indication that someone shared his theatrical dreams. Nameless in these notices, she used many aliases. She may have been looking for the right stage name, or perhaps the right personality. Mercedes La Foy, Elizabeth La Fay, Mercedes del Pino. Her real name was Delpino.

My father had seen her at rehearsals, but he was ashamed of his shabby clothes, fearful of his unattractiveness, and he did not dare speak to her. The first words that passed between them were in Philadelphia, at a candy store across from the theater. He offered her some candy and began to talk about the show. As he talked, he kept looking down at his pants. He had a large hole on the side of his trousers.

"Oh, don't worry about it, Bert," she said, "I have those too." She lifted up her long skirt and showed her stockings—they were ripped. She smiled at him. They laughed, and Lahr forgot his feelings of awkwardness.

Their meetings had been infrequent, although Lahr thought of her often on the road. When he met Pearl in Portland for *College Days* (1916), Lahr asked about her. Pearl, who knew Mercedes from other kid acts, mentioned that she was going into a show called *Katinka*. It was not until the end of the summer that they met again in New York. Pearl recalls her. "She was the most beautiful Spanish woman you have ever seen in your life. Beautiful, beautiful, God . . ."

She never spoke of her past, although Lahr talked about his family affectionately and puffed up his cheeks to imitate his father when he was in a rage. She spoke modestly about her dancing, which was the only thing that elicited her excitement. When she talked about it, her eyes, beautiful against the rich olive smoothness of her skin, would widen with intensity. Her hands, which usually lay placidly on her lap, became animated; and she continually raised them to smooth back her hair. He was amazed at how passionate she became about the theater. She was usually so quiet and unassuming, but when she spoke about herself and her work she took on a strange aggressiveness. It was unexpected. It made her mysterious.

When Lahr went into *The Best Show in Town* Mercedes auditioned and got a job easily. She was very popular with the girls in the troupe. They called her "Babe" and flattered her. Although she was the most attractive of the girls, they did not look on her as a competitor. She showed little interest in men except for Lahr. She did not respond to the camaraderie of the cast, but she was friendly and never rude about the wisecracks they made. She took care of her body; her hair was always carefully combed and her lips painstakingly drawn. But in her clothes she showed a curious lack of imagination. The girls always had to remind her that her clothes did not match and that red and yellow —her favorite colors—did not go well together. It was as though she could concentrate only on one part of her body at a time, and could never see herself as a unity.

At rehearsals Mercedes worked with the same ferocious energy in her dancing that Lahr put into his comedy. She practiced her new steps in the shadows of the large stage, working late on routines until her body responded without effort to the tempo of the music. (Her success had won her the unofficial title of "Miss Pep" from the performers and the press.) She was proud of her gracefulness. She knew how her legs tightened and relaxed when she beat out a rhythm on the stage. And when she was working well, she had the wonderful sensation of being apart from her legs and admiring them for their supple strength and smoothness. She always said she had beautiful legs. When she mentioned this in public people glanced down at them in amazement, because her face and raven hair usually captured their complete attention. Occasionally, Lahr wandered out on the stage while she was rehearsing. She would smile at him, but when he tried to talk with her, she would cut him short, saying, "Can't you see I'm working?" She never lost a step.

When *The Best Show in Town* went on holiday in the last week of May, Lahr and Mercedes pooled their savings (four hundred dollars) and headed for Lake Hopatcong, a New Jersey vacation haven for burlesque performers. With Lahr making forty-five dollars and Mercedes sixteen as a chorus girl, the sum represented a rigorous and dreary struggle to economize. The hotels they chose had been the dingiest; they limited their meals to one a day. As a result, Lahr often complained about his legs aching. "I didn't know it then," he explains now, "but I was suffering from malnutrition." However, with the savings and a three-year contract on the Wheel, life was exhilarating. Looking back at it now, my father pauses in his speech to make sure he's telling the truth, but finally maintains, "I think those were the happiest days of my life. I felt secure in my business. I knew I could always get a job . . ."

Lahr, Mercedes, and a few of their friends from *The Best Show in Town* found bungalows in a village called Northwood, along the lake. Many other famous burlesquers, such as Joe Cook, Jim and Betty Morgan, and Rose Seidel spent their holidays there too.

Lahr and Mercedes lived in a two-room shack, which he describes as "just four walls and a bed." There was no electricity, and their cooking was done either on sterno stoves or at a stone fireplace overlooking the lake. The closest telephone was a half mile away, and the greatest novelty of all was lugging provisions by boat to the house. Whereas the months in burlesque had been hectic, limited to one dressing room after another, Lake Hopatcong offered an exotic adventure that they explored with childlike curiosity. It only cost them a dollar a day, which made it an even happier time.

Lahr's first acquisition was a boat. He dubbed it the "Flying Leopold" because its engine was always sputtering to a standstill. It provided them with a great deal of fun. It was this boat in which he took his first fishing trip, setting out with a few friends to still-fish for bass and grass pickerel. They spent the day with feet jutting over the sides, drinking and swapping stories. Sometimes they caught a fish. Lahr often found himself seeking the solitude of the boat. He liked sitting on the water and being rocked in the silence of the waves. Occasionally Mercedes came along as pilot, but she never fished. Often she was content to stay at home and sun herself or comb her hair. She found a small dog on which she lavished elaborate affections while Lahr was away. She seemed content.

Mercedes and Lahr rarely ventured beyond their group of burlesque friends. Mercedes was beautiful, and people responded well to her. She complemented him and did not try to criticize his work or his eccentricities. Sometimes during these summer months, with homemade beer and a packed lunch, they would set off down the lake in the Flying Leopold. It was different seeing Mercedes alone. It seemed more difficult to judge her, and yet, her beauty and sweetness were as real in these private moments as they seemed in public.

Together they explored the coastline of the lake, leaving their boat on the shore and sitting on the mat of rust-brown pine needles that began a few feet from the water. They liked staring up at the vast blue sky and then down at the last row of bungalows. They savored the isolation.

Once, while they lay half covered in water, he asked her about the amulet she always wore around her neck. It was a picture of a young girl enclosed in a delicate Florentine gold frame.

"Some people carry St. Christopher for good luck. This is my St. Christopher. It's a picture of my mother," she said. "Her father had it made when she played for the King of Spain. She gave it to me a few years ago. I remember, because Anna, my sister, was very jealous and wanted to wear it. I hid it from her and wouldn't let her have it because it was special from Mother to me. Mother always liked me best. I feel very sorry for her now. She always thought I was the prettiest."

"What did she play?"

"She and her sister—they were sixteen then—played the piano for the King. They learned music at the Convent of St. Alphonso. They were the most beautiful and talented young ladies in Madrid. My grandmother was very rich, and Mother told me often about how lovely it was walking in the court with royalty—their fine silks, the long halls which smelled of scent and the fresh spray of water from the fountains, the cool marble floors with their beautiful patterns, and the fine paintings all cracked and old. She told me about all that, and their soft hands. Sometimes she would cry. I couldn't stand it, but I had to sit in her room and help until she stopped. It was a big change for her, Bert—much bigger than I understood when she first told me about her early life. That's why she gave me this. She didn't want any memories after my father died. She didn't want to be reminded about her wealth and that life. She is too poor now for those memories. She wants only the best for *us* . . . and that's all."

He wanted her to continue, but she stopped abruptly. He remembers returning in the boat and watching Mercedes lean over the stern concentrating on the boat's wake. They would share other quiet moments, but he would never be able to recall everything she revealed about her family and herself.

The summer was a happy one. There were cookouts almost every night, and during the day there was fishing and swimming. Lahr and his friends would often get a barge and paddle it across the lake to buy applejack. The attitude of the performers at the lake is epitomized in the estate Joe Cook owned there. His dining room was like a Coney Island fun house; there were chairs wired with an electric shock and vents in the room shooting jets of air up the women's skirts. He built a one-hole golf course that was designed so that anyone reaching the green would shoot a hole-in-one.

Lahr remembers scheming to annoy a burlesque straightman called Ned "Clothes" Norton, who slept on the porch of Lahr's next-door neighbor. While Norton was asleep they tied a bell to one of the pine trees with fishing line and walked fifty yards away to where they could watch him. They would ring the bell every ten minutes. Norton would shake himself awake, look around, and then try to go back to sleep. Finally, resolving to find the bell, he spent the early morning hours trying to climb every tree in search of it.

A postcard from one of the burlesquers at the lake indicates the changes taking place in Lahr's life as the summer neared its end. The card is from Frank "Rags" Murphy, a tramp comedian, and it contains pictures of Murphy in various comedy poses. It reads simply:

> Lake Hopatcong, same summer: To My Pals Bert and Babe, here's luck to you both and wish you God speed as a sailor . . .

The good wishes were not for the skipper of the Flying Leopold, but for the new member of the Naval Reserve. Lahr had enlisted soon after he had been informed by his mother that he would be drafted in October. Lahr was not a fighting man; he was a performer. The Naval Reserve would interrupt his career and change his life for a while, but it was safer than the trenches.

Lahr's life, even without him actively willing it, had changed in other ways. He and Babe were inseparable. Friends, like Murphy, assumed they were married. Mercedes wore a small gold ring on her left hand, and no one asked any questions. It was not unusual for burlesquers to marry each other after a year of constant association, and it was even more ordinary for them to enjoy the benefits of married life without the legal responsibilities. Lahr had given her the ring at the beginning of the summer, but she never mentioned marriage to him. When asked why he didn't make the marriage legal, my father answers in quiet befuddlement, "I guess we never thought of it." Their life was their work. Marriage represented a stasis that neither could imagine for themselves.

Lahr remembers coming home from Lake Hopatcong with Mercedes and going to the Naval Reserve Induction Center to begin his "hitch." Just as he was about to board the bus to take him to training camp, Mercedes threw her arms around him and began to cry. She cried after he was on the bus, and, as the bus turned the corner, he could still see her standing in the same spot. That moment is still vivid in his mind. "I guess that was the only time she showed real emotion for me," he says now, adding cryptically, "Funny, isn't it."

He was stationed at Pelham Bay. His time in the Naval Reserve was hopelessly unheroic. (In later years, he would elaborate on those days for me and my sister, explaining that he was a chef and making it sound as romantic as a Conrad novel. Once, in order to show his credentials as a full-fledged cook, he baked some brownies for us, "The kind I used to serve the men." Exuberant over his creation, he tossed a piece high in the air. He miscalculated, and the fresh brownie fell on the floor. It didn't break.) He joined the Naval Reserve through the influence of a burlesque friend, Johnny Walker, who later became a movie star. The commodore of the unit was the famous theatrical agent M. S. Bentham, who would later handle Lahr in vaudeville. The unit had many performers in it, including Brian Foy, of the famous Seven Foys, the Callaghan Brothers, and Bill Gaxton. Since it was only Lahr's first year on the professional circuit, none of the veteran performers knew him as an entertainer. He could not arrange the extended leaves other better-known performers were allowed in order to play an occasional engagement.

Lahr became a politician, making curious connections. His friendship with a bouncer at the Ziegfield Roof was an important maneuvering point. Through his bouncer friend, he was detailed to the mess hall. It meant that he could have a bed, instead of a sleep-defying hammock, and also that the tedium of drilling and odd assignments were eliminated.

While he couldn't get leave to perform, his rating as a chef's assistant proved profitable. He gave the guards on the base extra food. They in turn gave him extra leave without reporting his absence. When he wasn't mixing the soup and preparing the meats by formula, Lahr was detailed to other jobs. For a time, he was made storekeeper, a task he also turned to his advantage, managing to filch cans of apple butter to take to his mother on weekends. Also, since he had to check in the large amounts of meat that arrived every few days, he would slice off the tenderloins for his friends and himself. "We ate very well up there."

Lahr the sailor never got farther than a few forays up the Long Island Sound. After nine months he was discharged, in time to highlight the summer-run burlesque show *Folly Town* (1919), which brought the cream of the Columbia Circuit to Broadway for two months. It was an honor for the performers, a chance for them to be seen by the big-time theatrical managers and producers. Lahr was second comedian, with Frankie Hunter again in the first comedy slot, and his friend from the Navy, Johnny Walker, the "third banana."

Lahr cannot remember his boisterous enthusiasm at the first rehearsal, but others, who worked with him, can. Blutch Cooper was on stage, his hulking 250-pound frame towering above the performers. Wells was there also with a handsome young singer whom he had induced to come down from Boston to play the light comedy parts in the show. When the youth walked on the stage and saw the three seasoned comedians it was apparent that he would have to settle for his usual juvenile or straightman role. He was talking with Frankie Hunter when Lahr came up to them and with unusual brashness asked, "Have you ever been in burlesque before?" When the boy answered that he had not, Lahr turned to Hunter, exclaiming, "Will *we* put sand in *his* make-up!"

The boy was Jack Haley, and the immediate dislike he felt for Bert Lahr was soon erased when he realized that the high-spirited comedian was only a one-year veteran himself. They became close friends. Haley's shrewdness and his aloofness gave him time to assess his new associates. Two things impressed him about Lahr: his body and his love of the stage. He often kidded Lahr about his "washboard chest" after watching him box with friends on the stage each morning before rehearsal. Lahr could not stay away from the theater even for exercise.

After the show opened, Lahr's immediate success won him the first-comic rung. Hunter was dropped to second comedian. But Haley recalls Blutch Cooper stopping a rehearsal in the second week of the Broadway run to reproach Lahr in front of the entire cast. "It was an empty theater, after the show had opened. Cooper tore him apart with horrible insults. I could sense it was to mollify the feelings of the top comedian. Lahr just stood there. I was never sure that Bert didn't know Cooper's motives and kept silent to help Cooper make his point to Hunter. This is the sly facet of Bert's personality, one moment he's brilliant and the next rather dull."

After the summer run of *Folly Town* Lahr moved directly into the *Roseland Girls* (1920–1921), another Wells concoction. He was first comedian, and his new salary was an amazing sixty-five dollars a week.

As first comedian Lahr began to take on certain production responsibilities. Since no general manager traveled with the show, the first comedian was in charge. He kept the cast in line and the sketches tight, not a difficult task for Lahr because he was so engrossed and successful in his work. The reviews emphasized his importance in carrying the show, and the troupe, whether they liked him or not, preferred to eat regularly rather than complain. Sometimes, however, they could make it difficult. When they played near New York, Lahr took trips to the city to see his family. The members of the cast suspected him of informing on them to Blutch Cooper. He returned a few times to cold shoulders, and finally had to call the cast together to assure them that his business in New York was strictly personal.

The performers held to a code of etiquette that reflected a communal dependence lost in the modern theater. Lahr considered himself a professional and carried himself accordingly. To be considered "professional" meant following the code of the burlesque performer, thus being able to exist for long periods of time with the same people. It fostered independence and selfishness; but it kept friction to a minimum. The most damning thing that could be said to another performer was that he "was not professional."

A professional never borrowed anything. If he needed anything, he would either buy it or go without rather than ask a cohort. The actor might have given him what he wanted. However, to ask was considered "unprofessional" and an invasion of privacy. Sometimes Lahr carried Mercedes's bags, but often she would not allow it, for a burlesquer was responsible for catching trains on time and carrying his own baggage. The burlesque life was hard, and any extra effort in the tedious process of going from town to town was kept to a minimum. The ethic of independence has had its effect on Lahr. He still believes in every possession being in its place, and untouched except by the owner.

Lahr and Mercedes existed very easily with this independence of spirit. From the beginning, he could come and go as he pleased. Often he would ask her to come out with him and some of the cast, but she would refuse, preferring to sit alone and read.

As first comedian, Lahr was able to spend more time working with Mercedes, improving her dance numbers and teaching her a few comedy tactics of her own. "She looked beautiful out there," he says now. He speaks slowly, trying to fill out the image of that jaunty body as it swung into her solo dance routine in the *Roseland Girls*. In December, their efforts were rewarded. A clipping from the New York *Telegraph* announced the results:

> Babe Lahr, wife of the featured comedian Bert Lahr has been promoted from the chorus to a real second soubrette principal this season, and it is now Mercedes La Fay she is soubretting under, if you please. Boss Blutch Cooper likes the work of Mercedes so well that he is going to present her as a first soubrette next season. Looks like another Flo Davis, Stella Ward, and Babe LaTour, all in one.

During the New York run of the *Roseland Girls,* Mercedes took Lahr home to meet her family. It had taken a long time to engineer this meeting. Lahr purchased a new Palm Beach suit, which, unlike the one he wore on stage, fitted well. He can remember only the mother's white hair and the tenderness with which she held her daughter's hand as they talked. Mercedes had spoken often to her about Lahr. Her mother's replies were always ambiguous; a good Catholic, she viewed her daughter's affection for a Jewish boy with silent skepticism. Isabel Delpino assumed a stoic pose for her family. She accepted the fate the Lord had dealt her in claiming her husband Roberto when she was thirty-five. Everything—Roberto's death, her arthritis, Mercedes's new boyfriend—became part of His design. When Mercedes announced that she and Lahr had been married, producing the gold band to prove it, Isabel exclaimed, "Holy Mary, Mother of God, protect us."

But by the end of their first and only meeting, Lahr had won over Mercedes's mother. They sat for more than two hours in the parlor of her apartment chatting over tea about the stage. Lahr took great pains to elaborate Mercedes's success. Isabel would often interrupt, adding, "She does have a beautiful figure, doesn't she. A beautiful figure." She would look at Mercedes and squeeze her hand.

Leaving the apartment, Mercedes confided, "She liked you very much." There was no more talk of family sentiments. Lahr remembers feeling proud, amazed that Mercedes, with her reticence, shared such a small privacy with him.

In *Roseland Girls,* Lahr performed the "Lord Onion" sketch, among the funniest of his burlesque scenes and one of his favorites. The scene depicts an anxious lover (Lahr) trying to outwit his mistress's husband by convincing the cuckold that they are rehearsing a dramatic scene in which he uncovers them embracing. The husband agrees. He enters to find them in passionate embrace. They stop, drink to his health, and send him out to run the scene again. Lahr gets progressively drunker. With Prussian mustache and powdered wig, Lahr lampooned Prohibition strictures as well as his idea of aristocracy. He also discovered a sodden rendition of "Peggy O'Neill," a sprawling, outrageous sound that he later fitted into his vaudeville cop act.

During *Roseland Girls*, Lahr began a quiet program of self-improvement. Dreaming of a time beyond burlesque, he worried about his Bronx inflection and his limited vocabulary. He began to work crossword puzzles; he read the classics, focusing on Dickens and comic situations he knew intuitively from the stage. In Albany, he underwent his first press interview, a document whose formal colloquialism and self-consciousness attests to the ponderous weight of Lahr's new learning. When the reporter asked him if it was easier to make people laugh since Prohibition, Lahr salted his reply with clinical observations on the burlesque audience of the twenties.

> . . . Their smartness sometimes ran to kidding the players and their remarks *sub rosa* disturbed others near them.
> There were some who became dull and did not get the jokes quick enough. They'd start laughing a few seconds after the line went over and put the whole audience out of gear. Sometimes the whole audience would get to laughing at them and pay no attention to the stage. It's different today. Their coming is not part of an impulse born of a good time down town. They want to be entertained. . . . If you have the stuff, they'll get it before it goes over the lights.

A few weeks later in Montreal, a drunk interrupted Wells's famous "Lord Onion" sketch. When Lahr began the scene, he noticed a man in the first row sitting, exposed, in his seat. The man next to him took a newspaper and covered his lap. They began to argue. The audience guffawed as the drunk got up and began urinating in the aisles. Lahr muttered to his actors, "Keep mumbling dialogue." He did not have to whisper instructions; the audience's laughter drowned out every furtive word. The police were called; but in their anxiety to get the drunk out of the theater, they faced him toward the audience, compounding the ruckus. The man was finally removed; the scene began again.

Soon after the performance resumed, the police returned to scour the aisle with cleaner fluid. The actors waited three minutes on stage before the policemen let them complete the sketch.

In *Keep Smiling* (1921-2), Lahr achieved his greatest burlesque success. He confided to a reporter that year, "When I was a boy, my aim in life was to be a burlesque comic; now that I have attained that, I am the happiest man in the country." Lahr very rarely talked about happiness, especially in relation to his comedy. But his burlesque notoriety gave him an inkling of maturity. His performance changed with self-confidence. "I was a scene stealer," he admits now. "If the scene wasn't written my way, I'd find ways of turning the attention to me and improving my part." His urgency to please became a theatrical joke. Lahr, who claims to have coined the term in his burlesque days, performed under a continual "flop sweat." He worked his fellow performers and himself tirelessly. Sometimes his friends took advantage of his seriousness. Once, they kept him playing pool until five minutes before opening curtain. When he went to apply his stick of greasepaint, it wouldn't go onto his face. He went on stage with no make-up. He discovered afterwards that his friends had wrapped a transparent condom around it.

Lahr sometimes had an easier time controlling his audiences than headstrong members of the cast. In *Keep Smiling*, his direction of the comedy scenes could not cope with the eccentricities of a certain Broadway performer who had moved back to burlesque. Her style and comic ability once earned her jobs with George M. Cohan. However, her Broadway days came to a disastrous conclusion when, cast as a queen in one of Cohan's productions, she fell off the throne drunk. The burlesque wheel was more relaxed; even if drinking was strictly prohibited, the stakes were not as high.

In *Keep Smiling* she and Lahr did a vampire skit, burlesquing the fashion for horror films that catapulted Theda Bara to stardom. In the sketch, Lahr is lured away from his fiancée by the actress and convinced by her to steal money and then flee with her to the Riviera.

In Milwaukee, Lahr spoke his lines about a getaway to the Riviera and looked to the wings. There was no response to the cue. When the actress finally staggered on stage, she stood with her back to the audience, muttering, "Take the revolver to the Riveera" and "To the Riveera take the revolver."

Lahr ad-libbed an exit and went off stage to cue the musicians to go into the soubrette's number, which was next on the schedule. In the meantime, he brought his inebriated co-star back to her dressing room. The house manager was waiting backstage. He wanted to fire her on the spot and threatened to report the incident to the Scribner office.

The show went on as usual. At intermission, she seemed fine, a nap having sobered her. Lahr went to the manager and urged him to allow her to continue the show because of the important finale number, "Greenwich Village." He agreed.

"Greenwich Village" was highlighted by a song and dance to the tune of "Ballin' the Jack." The woman sang; Lahr worked up the song with comedy dances. It was a show-stopper, a routine they interpolated for five or six encores. However, between intermission and the finale number, she found a bottle. When she came on stage, she was drunker than before.

They began the song, with Lahr singing the lyrics and the actress pantomiming the actions. She raised her skirt and brought her shapely legs close together. With that, she tried to swing her legs, now close together, and fell on her face. The manager brought down the curtain. The performance was not allowed to continue.

The comedian's responsibility for the troupe was important to Lahr's sense of theater; it also bred revenge. When he caught a chorus girl parodying his gestures in drunken irreverence, he told her to leave the show and go home for the day. She cursed him, but obeyed. The show went on until the "Operating Room" sketch at the end of the first act, a sketch featuring Lahr examining painted ropes as veins and sweeping arms and legs out from under the operating room table.

In the middle of the scene, Lahr heard a Bronx cheer from the boxes. He looked up to see the banished chorus girl whistling and yelling, "You stink, Bert. You stink."

Whatever the performers' private feelings, the audience and critics were pleased. The pranks or the catcalls could not deny Lahr's enormous appeal in *Keep Smiling*. His success fed his ambition. He imagined himself in vaudeville, films, Broadway. He had never entertained those thoughts in the first years of burlesque, happy to ride the Columbia Wheel as far as it took him. But the ride had been so fast. His experience, the "bits of business" for which audiences clamored, spun gaudier dreams. A decade earlier, he had sat with Jack Pearl imagining what life at the top would be like with a hundred dollars a week. Now he could go higher and the distance would still be measured in dollars and cents. He talked of his visions to no one, not even Mercedes, for a while. His contract in burlesque was renewable after 1923. With Wells providing the material, he could continue to play packed burlesque houses. But after a three-year apprenticeship on the Columbia Wheel, it was apparent to Lahr and to the critics that he was ready for a new challenge. His comedy had found its focus; his energy, even when filtered through a German dialect, captured something real and hilarious in life. *Variety*, the arbiter of burlesque opinion, summed up his achievement in *Keep Smiling*, a testament to his polish and growth:

> . . . Mr. Lahr has a real sense of *travesty*—something which can hardly be said of more than one burlesque comic. He knows how to handle the ins and outs of dialogue and situation perfectly. He's clean, inclined to be a bit boisterous at times, and works like a Trojan always, but he never gives the appearance of straining for effect in the slightest degree. With all the facility of expression of the experienced burlesquer at his command, Lahr combines this practiced touch with the life and spirit that springs from the temperament of youth. He knows the business from the ground up.

VAUDEVILLE:
LAHR AND MERCEDES

Comedy is always close to sadness. There was a vaudeville actor, Harry Rose. He used to make his entrance saying, "Here's Harry," with a high tenor voice. He was playing a Loew's theater in Brooklyn where the orchestra would rise up out of the pit and they also had a platform where some actors would go out and entertain the audience. This day, Rose came out, said, "Here's Harry," and the platform didn't come out. He fell down into the pit and broke both his legs. The audience screamed with laughter. That's funny, but it's tragic. There was a certain actor when we were kids, a big shot called Herman Timberg. Herman couldn't see very well. In later years, his eyes got pretty bad. I was headlining the Palace and there was a knock on my dressing room door. It was Herman. I said, "Come in Herman." He followed the sound of my voice. "Isn't it wonderful, Bert, you've reached these heights. Remember when we were kids." (He was on the same bill.) I said, "How do you feel, Herman?" "I've never felt better," he said. "I'm in Christian Science and I can read and write with no trouble." I said, "Sit down." So he sat on the floor.

Lahr in conversation, 1967

"TELL ME ABOUT MERCEDES, DAD."

"She was a very sweet girl, very quiet and sweet," he says, tapping a pencil on the side of his desk.

"Well, do you remember much about her? What did she wear? Did she have any special phrases? Did you discuss your ambitions together?"

"Oh, it's so long ago, John—we were just kids. Of course, we discussed our plans together. We were a team."

"What was it like working as a team?"

"It was hard work. You had two shows a day, and you always wanted to do your best out there. I was very ambitious—I wouldn't let anything get in my way. You know there are things in my life that I'm not very proud about—things that would make me seem a heavy."

"What do you mean?"

"I just don't think I can talk about them because they might hurt someone. For years people have wanted to write books about me, but I turned them down because they would involve incidents which I just don't think would do anybody any good."

He continues as if he never intended to stop.

"You understand, John, I was very ambitious, and I just didn't see anything but my plans. We were very young."

As he talks, he looks in the mirror and feels the sagging flesh around his cheeks. I know what he is thinking. "How many years?" His skin is leathery, the pouches beneath his eyes are cracked in a labyrinth of lines. He looks like an old turtle this morning. If there were a shell on his back, he could jut beneath it, cutting off the past and the world. But he cannot.

My mother comes into the room and hunts in one of the bureaus for the laundress's check. She stays too long, hoping to hear about Mercedes. My father stops talking and waits until she leaves.

There is a picture of Mercedes in his drawer. It is buried among the golf balls, screwdrivers, and tobacco. It shows her at the lake with her little dog. She is smiling.

He does not know about her the way I do. He does not know about the quietness of the Arizona night and the loneliness of the small house where she lived with her sister and her son. He cannot imagine the night sounds, the restless sand shifting in the wind, the debris rattling over the barren plains. Sometimes you could hear her, as her son and sister did, shuffling her feet on the uncarpeted floor of her room. She was trying out a dance step, and mumbling the lyrics to one of her old songs. He does not know that in her mind she was still married to him or that in 1930 and 1940 and 1950 she still hoped to get back on the stage.

Her face, like her body, has grown formless and flaccid. She sat in her room in a drab shift, only induced to change her clothes if assured Bert Lahr had picked them out. He cannot visualize the catatonic stupor in which she sat listening to the radio or the television, staring out of her window at the bleached landscape. She rarely saw people. Once when my father's lawyer dropped in for a visit, she came away from her radio. After a few minutes, she stopped talking. "You have to excuse me," she said, "I have to go on."

When Mercedes died in 1965, my father sat up for three nights. He refused to talk.

There is a film of their act that lay unopened in Mercedes's closet for nearly three decades. It is only one minute long, taken against a cheap backdrop at a Pittsburgh vaudeville house while they were rehearsing. My father never wanted to replay it—the last remaining image of their partnership. In the film he leaps from the wings directly into Mercedes's path. She has been doing her hootchy-kootchy dance. When Lahr accosts her, she pushes him back and knocks his hat over his eyes. Even without words, the movements are hilarious. Everything in this rehearsal seems perfectly organized. His hat falls effortlessly over his eyes. His policeman's nightstick bounces on the floor and miraculously rebounds back into his hands.

The performance they give is intimate in its comic turns, filled with the charm of two performers instinctively responsive to each other. The daily ritual of those actions must have formed a deep bond. Mercedes's body is wonderfully alive. She dances energetically; her movements are supple and graceful. When she reacts to Lahr, it is humorous and natural. Her eyes glisten with understanding, and she laughs at him in her glow. She likes the humor. She stares at him as if some gaudy, harmless leprechaun were cavorting around her. He runs, he waddles, he falls on his face. At one instant he is singing the refrain from "Peggy O'Neill," at the next, getting hopelessly caught up with his policeman's stick, which resists his efforts to control it. Gestures raise the comedy beyond entertainment to statement. Suddenly, the act stops in midstream; the photographer moves in for a close-up. Like amateurs, they are talking to the camera, and laughing. Lahr is mugging and sticking his tongue out. Mercedes looks at him and smiles. She stands there making her hair smooth and neat. She wears a mantilla. He reaches over and kisses her on the cheek. She puts her hands on his shoulders and pushes him away. She is embarrassed. He tries again. Finally, Lahr resorts to clowning. He inflates his cheeks like a bloater fish and crosses his eyes. They move off the stage. His arm is around her.

"It was a mystery." He waits, and, almost to himself, adds, "I just didn't see. I didn't know what was happening."

He looks at me and his eyes widen in glazed emphasis. He shrugs his shoulders, and then sits back.

"Did you love her, Pop?"

"Of course," he says, looking away.

"Did she love you?"
"I guess so." His words are lifeless. He turns back to me; and he is crying.

Although theater historians gloss the fact, Bert Lahr spent as much time in vaudeville as he did on the burlesque wheel. The vaudeville experience was more lucrative, but at the same time, limited the scope of his performing. In the four years he put into the Orpheum Time, the nation's highest-quality vaudeville circuit, he performed only one act. He often tried to talk managers into taking another sketch, but they, like their audiences, demanded the brand-name product. In New York alone, he estimates that "Lahr and Mercedes" could have played vaudeville for two and a half years without repeating a single theater.

Lahr had conceived the sketch. Wells had framed it, amalgamating most of the big laugh sequences and "bits of business" from Lahr's burlesque days. The act was known by various titles: "What's the Idea," "The Limp and the Law," and "The Limb of the Law." The sketch remains one of the vaudeville classics. Since vaudeville offered a variety of acts with no attempt at plot or cohesive musical format, each performance was spotted at that point in the bill where it would function best. The New York papers, for instance, rated the acts in the same way as they touted the nags:

Entries	Pos.	Co.	Songs	Start	Finish	Bow	Ran
Bert Lahr	8	2	2	Fair	Big	7	1st

Lahr contemplated the leap into vaudeville as early as the summer of 1921. With his characteristic sense of insecurity, he felt that he did not have the material to make the switch despite the fact that vaudeville agents and the press were already beginning to suggest what he had envisioned:

Bert Lahr, the principal comedian and star, is not likely to stay long in burlesque, or we are no judges, but will follow James Barton, Bobby Clark, Tommy K. Morton, and many others into the musical comedy field. This is if musical comedy managers have their eyes open. Lahr "has everything" and will go far . . .

Lahr's sense of comic contrast and caricature had been carefully nurtured in burlesque. The idea that produced "What's the Idea" was not so much a routine as a picture in his mind of Mercedes with a gorgeous comb in her tightly drawn hair, wearing an exotic sequined dress. He saw her entrance, and judged the laughs, plotting the comic complications even before the scene was on paper. The beautiful, sensual woman versus the groping, inarticulate cop. The entrance, the songs, the dances were his own suggestions and improvisations. During the layoff between burlesque seasons, he tried the act out at the Amphium Theater in Brooklyn, the sleazy break-in house where he had been banned for being drunk on stage. "When I played it with Mercedes—the first theater we ever played together—we stopped the show. It was a meager house, but they wouldn't let us off the stage. We really stopped them cold. The stage hands kept saying, 'Go on, go on!' I said 'We haven't any more.' 'Say thank you.' You understand, John, I finally had to make a speech."

That summer Lahr and Mercedes played the New York area on "split weeks," performing four days at one theater and three in another. They received $250 a week. Mercedes gave Lahr a "boodle bag," a chamois sack that she sewed for him, to carry their money. It was an old vaudeville custom, a sign of good luck, and more than that, a symbol of their dream. Lahr wore the bag around his neck even while performing for the next four years. Only after his first Broadway appearance would he open a bank account.

The sketch became such a favorite with vaudeville audiences that it was included in Lahr's first Broadway show, *Harry Delmar's Revels* (1927) and also in *Burlesque* (1946). The act not only created a humorous situation with some well-tested lines, but was built on a format that enhanced the comedy through sudden surprise. Mercedes, for instance, came on stage singing "La Soldata" in Spanish and doing a flamenco dance, which quickly degenerated into a "bump and grind." Her song and dance lasted a full minute. When Lahr bolted on stage in his misfit policeman's outfit, with his hat askew, the contrast was hilarious. The act highlighted the dominant aspects of his comic personality—his physical grotesqueness, his wild, carnival spirit, his instinct for anarchy, and his resilience. The performance lasted fifteen minutes. He and Mercedes experimented with every joke, shifting the stage "business" until they could adapt their sketch to fill a ten-minute time slot or extend it to twenty if there were encores.

At the end of *Keep Smiling* in 1922, when their burlesque contracts expired, they shifted to vaudeville with remarkable ease. Lahr remembers waiting outside the Seigel Building, where the Keith-Albee bookers and vaudeville agents worked, waiting to see his own agent,

Charlie Allen of the M. S. Bentham Agency. Another agent stopped Lahr in the hallway. "Listen kid, you don't know me, but they're talking about you at the office. You can get five hundred a week. Don't take less." When Lahr confronted Allen a few minutes later and asked for that astounding amount the agent didn't even blink. "I'm not sure I can get it for you, Bert, but I'll try." They met a few hours later. Allen looked dejected. "I couldn't get it, Bert. The closest I could come was $475—what do you say?" Lahr was astounded. He would have taken his summer-run salary.

Vaudeville represented not only a substantial increase in salary, but also a work day that was cut to an unbelievable thirty minutes. "I was ashamed to take the money, the work was so easy," he says now.

The new leisure did not bring peace of mind. Lahr went back to reading. Improbably, he read books like *Pepys' Diary*, Boswell's *Life of Johnson*. The archaic and high-flown diction amused him, and he found he could work them into his speech both off and on the stage. He enjoyed the burlesque in the real life of these English men of letters as much as he did on the stage of the Columbia Theater. He also took up golf. But with his livelihood resting on one short sketch, Lahr would never believe that the act was as good as it should be. He brooded over the gags and his delivery in every hotel room and vaudeville house on the circuit. With more time to think about his comedy, he became even more self-conscious and obsessed with his craft. He would wake Mercedes in the middle of the night to improvise a line.

Lahr remembers fetching Wells's typed sketch from his valise and placing it by the night table, sitting up in his pajamas while Mercedes slept in the opposite bed. The comic taste he would acquire in time was then not always pertinent. He would ad-lib a line like "Oh, Mama, sock me in the puss with a wet sock." Wells wanted him to take it out, but Lahr refused because he got a laugh. Looking back on it, he is amazed at the lack of subtlety. "It's the kind of line that, if you did it on Broadway, the audience would freeze up on you." But without such considerations to bother him, he plowed into the script, trying to wring out every chuckle. The copy still exists. My father's continual experiments with the sketch can be seen scrawled on every page. He would write in the margins, in his slow, florid hand, talking to Mercedes without raising his eyes from the script.

"Babe, listen to this . . . Hey, Babe, wake up. I think this is much better for the finish."

"Bert, can't we do it tomorrow?"

"Let's run through it, and see what it sounds like."

"Bert, please."

"Let's run through it now. C'mon, Babe."

"Where should we start?"

"Start from where I say, 'It was July. I was patrolling my vegetable.'"

"Vegetable?"

"I mean patrolling my beat."

He tries to read his own writing.

"When suddenly I heard a woman scream. Did she scream loud! She screamed so loud she woke me up. Without a second's delay I rushed upstairs. When I reached the first floor, the yelling was louder; when I reached the second floor, it was still louder, and when I reached the third floor it was still louder. Then I stopped . . ."

He points to the line he wrote for Mercedes to speak.

"To get your gun?"

"No, I was in the wrong building. I rushed down again. Up the right building. Busted in a door. There was a man. In his hand he had a gun. He was going to shoot his wife with it. I said, 'Stop!' He turned around, looked at me and laughed. Oh what a dirty laugh! Then he started to sneak toward me with fire in his eyes. Nearer and nearer he came with fire in his eyes. Four feet. Three feet. Two feet. He came with fire in his eyes. One step nearer he came, the laughter in his face, the gun in his eye . . ."

"Well, what did you do?"

"I sang 'Peggy O'Neill' and he shot himself."

He stopped reading. "Well, what do you think? I don't see why we can't get off with our song at the end of that bit."

"Whatever you think, Bert—you're the funny-man. I just want to go back to sleep."

"Do you like it?"

"Sure."

"Let's get to the theater early and try it out?"

"Goodnight, Bert."

She would lie back in her bed, and he would continue reading his lines in the shadows of his bed lamp, working out intonation and plotting added movements.

His comedy evolved through trial and error just as it had done in burlesque. This particular bit was tried and cut from the final version. They also eliminated their singing exit in favor of a much more elaborate stage joke. After Mercedes's opening number, Lahr came on stage rapping his club on the ground and blustering: "Stop. In the name of the station house, stooooop!! What's the idea? What's the idea? What's the idea of massaging the atmosphere?"

Mercedes: (looking haughtily at him) Are you speaking to me?

Lahr: Yeah to you. (And looking at her breasts) and to you too.

Mercedes: Well, what was I doing?

Lahr: You was violating the law.

Mercedes: Law? What law?

Lahr: Nineteenth Amendment, Section Six, Upper 7, which says it's a public nonsense to shimmy or vibrate any part of the human astronomy. And it's punishable by a fine of one year or imprisonment for two years of E pluribus Aluminum.

Mercedes: But what was I doing? I wasn't doing anything wrong.

Lahr: You wasn't doing anything wrong? Gnong, gnong, gnong! I saw you. I was standing right down there, and the second I saw you I said to myself, "This has got to stop at once." So I watched you for ten minutes.

Mercedes: (wide-eyed) But what was I doing?

Lahr: Well, if you was wearing license plates, the numbers would be all wiped off. Come on to the station house.
(He reaches out to grab her arm, but she pushes him. His hat falls over his eyes. Lahr pushes the hat up on his head and looks at her, puffing his cheeks and swaggering around her in his crouch. He passes his nightstick from hand to hand, and then makes a few flourishes with it, like a baton twirler with broken wrists. He tries to throw it up from under his leg. He cannot do it; the club and his hand get lost somewhere in the back of his knee. He staggers and turns back to her in a huff. He holds the cuffs of his jacket with his hands.)

Mercedes: Don't touch me! (She pushes him again.)

Lahr: Here, stop pushing the City Hall around. Where do you get that stuuuuuuuuuffffff? Where do you get that stuuuuuuuuuufffffffff?

Mercedes: I believe you're intoxicated.

Lahr: Well, if I ain't, I'm out seven bucks.

Mercedes: Now see here, if you don't stop annoying me, I'm going to call the station house and tell the captain you're drunk. Understand me? Tell the captain you're drunk!

Lahr: Go ahead. What do I care? Do you want to know something? The captain's drunker than I am. Besides, the captain has my seven bucks. I think I'd better get the petroleum wagon.

(He stands sideways, pouting. His arms are crossed. He cradles the club in his arms. Mercedes comes up to him and pulls his coattails. He jumps away as if he'd been pinched.)

Mercedes: (pulling his coat) Now look here!

Lahr: What's the idea? What's the idea? Don't get so personal. Was we properly introduced? You know you're fooling with the government?

(He breathes heavily. He points to his breast pocket and looks down at his badge. It's not there. He feels the periphery of his pockets and checks his cuffs, and then looks back at her perplexed, exclaiming) Lost the government.

Mercedes: Now see here! (She pulls him again by the coat.)

Lahr: What do you think this is—ecclesiastic? (He picks up the bottom of his jacket and examines it.) Why this is genuine fluff. Why it's imported. Smell the ocean. (He holds it up to his nose.) No that's lobster bisque—here's the ocean. I think I'd better serve you with a subpeanuts. What's your name?

Mercedes: In English, my name is Nellie Bean.

Lahr: Nellie Bean. And your mama's name is Lima Bean?

Mercedes: Yes.

Lahr: And your papa's name is String Bean?

Mercedes: Yes.

Lahr: Nellie, look at me. I'm your Uncle Succotash. (They embrace.) I'm glad to see you, Nellie. I didn't saw you since your infantry. My goodness how time flitters! Tell me, Nellie, what are you doing now?

Mercedes: I'm an actress.

Lahr: Oh sure you're an actress. Ain't I the dumb bell? Why it's in the blood. Your mama, she was an actress. Your papa, he was an actress too. And say, I wasn't such a bad actress myself. Want to hear something?

Mercedes: Yes.

(Lahr drops down to a duck crawl and screams out) 's Peggy O'Neill. (Turning to her he asks) Pretty good, isn't it.

Mercedes: Wonderful. Is your voice trained?

Lahr: No, it's still running wild. It took me two days to learn that song.

Mercedes: What's the name of it?

Lahr: "Peggy O'Neill." Do you like it?

Mercedes: Yes, indeed.

          (Lahr sings the song again. This time he sings louder, and flaps his arms as he exaggerates his duck walk.)

Lahr: Sure, every night from station P-U-N-K, and I get letters from the people who listen, see. (He takes several letters out of his pocket and begins to read.) This is from a hospital. "Dear Sir, last night five of our patients who were at death's door heard you on the radio. Your singing pulled them through!" . . . Here's another. "My dear friend, last night I heard you sing. Something tells me, I'll meet you in the near future." Signed John Nutt, Superintendent of the State Insane Asylum.

Mercedes: Wonderful. I wish I could sing like you.

Lahr: Try it. I'll help you out.

          (Mercedes sings "La Soldata." Lahr watches her for a moment, and then throws his hand behind his head and starts a gyrating parody of her movements. He dances with his elbows pointed out at his waist and moves in his baggy-pants crouch. He does a very simple time step, but looks at his feet with the confident arrogance of a tightrope walker. As he does the simplified step, he takes a hand from his hips, yelling proudly) One hand. One hand!

Mercedes: (stopping the orchestra) Just a moment.

          (Lahr is carried away with his performance. He begins to sing "Peggy O'Neill," and in his effort to put more punch into the number begins boxing with his back to Mercedes.)

Mercedes: In a forest you'd be considered a marvelous tree.

Lahr: (turning to her) Why?

Mercedes: Because you're one hundred percent sap.

Lahr: Thank you, I—come to the Station House.

Mercedes: Ah—you wouldn't arrest me, would you?

Lahr: Yesatively! Come on!

          (Lahr tries to arrest her, but Mercedes vamps him, dancing around him and touching him seductively around the ears. He cringes in delight, pursing his lips and swaying his shoulders. He grips the cuffs of his oversized coat to control himself. Finally she says)

Mercedes: You wouldn't arrest me, would you?

Lahr: Certainly not, who made that crack?

Mercedes: Oh, you're just the grandest thing.

Lahr: And you're the granderest girl!

(A sergeant enters from the right and strolls across the stage.)

Lahr: Cheese it, Nellie here comes the sarge. I'll see you around the poolroom. (He taps her on her buttocks. She exits.) Hi ya Sargie. How's everything down at the station house? (Lahr starts to pass his nightstick between his hands, but on the second fillip he misses his hand completely. The club shoots across the stage, with Lahr fanning the air, thinking he's manipulating it. He does a double-take and retrieves the club.)

Sergeant: Don't try to get yourself out of this. What were you doing with your arms around that woman?

Lahr: I was frisking her. She's a very dangerous character.

Sergeant: Why didn't you pinch her?

Lahr: I did! I mean, I gave her a ticket.

Sergeant: Speaking of tickets, officer—did you sell your dozen tickets for the Policeman's Ball?

Lahr: I always go to the Policeman's Ball. I never miss the Policeman's Ball.

(Enter a woman, right, and a man and woman, left.)

Marie: Pierre!

Pierre: Marie, you!

Marie: Yes.

Pierre: (speaking to the girl holding his arm) Come my dear.

Marie: Wait! So this is the woman who has taken my place in your heart. You did forsake me for her—me who worked and slaved for you. Oh, Pierre, think of the past. Think what I've been to you. He belongs to me. You must give him up. I love him. I love him.

Dorothy: And so do I! He doesn't love you, and he never would. You cannot take him from me.

Marie: Very well then, I'll take *you* from *him*. (She draws a revolver from her fur coat and shoots the other woman.)

Pierre: You fiend. You've killed her. (Marie shoots Pierre.)

Marie: Oh what have I done? I've killed him! My Pierre. There's nothing left to live for. (She shoots herself.)

(Lahr and the sergeant look at the carnage that lies at their feet. Lahr turns to the sergeant, and taking his arm says:)

Lahr: Were you at the Policeman's Ball last year? (They walk off stage.)

(Blackout)

When he came out on stage to take his bows, Lahr would defy the audience, slapping his club on the ground and yelling out at their approval, "What's the idea? What's the ideeeeaa?"

No matter how successful burlesque performers had been on the Wheel, there was no guarantee of immediate or similar success in vaudeville. The act had to prove itself. It meant adapting to a different format of entertainment and caliber of audience. The sketch usually went well, but in a nation whose tastes had not yet been made uniform by television, Lahr's raucous fooling sometimes infuriated local taste. His comic stance could make the self-conscious middle class bristle.

> Comedy of a slightly lower type is offered by Lahr and Mercedes . . . The act is designed to appeal to the masses, but the classes can find plenty of things to be amused at. . . .
>
> Los Angeles

Occasionally, Lahr's mugging left the vaudeville audiences puzzled. In Chicago, a city accustomed to sophisticated entertainment and a wide variety of performers, one vaudeville reporter observed:

> The audience was slow in getting the humor Bert Lahr tried to put across. . . . By the finale, however, the former burlesque comic held the audience in a fit of laughter.

The act completely eluded Texans when he played the Interstate Circuit there. He has no clippings from those bookings, and with good reason. "We did so bad," he says, smiling, "they hissed us on the street." The audience was confounded by the polyglot inflections and urban eccentricities of the act. My father refers to those nights when he had to milk a single curtain call, as "laying a cake—twelve eggs."

The manager of the Houston theater had spotted Lahr and Mercedes after another comedy act, the "Hickey Brothers." "I got finished putting on my make-up and I heard tremendous laughs from out front, but I didn't know enough about vaudeville then to realize that one comedy act right after another always hurts the later act. So I said to Mercedes, 'Gee, that's a great audience.' Now I was made up in a putty nose and misfit clothes. I went upstairs to the wings. On the stage were two comedians, one was hitting the other over the head with a steel tray. They were wearing steel-plated wigs; their teeth were blacked out, and they had boards in their back to give them broad shoulders. I looked like a straightman compared to them. They were a riot."

When Lahr's turn came, the situation changed immediately. His sure-fire opening drew absolutely no response from the audience. "I said, 'Stop in the name of the station house, stoooooooopppppp!' Nothing happened. I said it again. I couldn't imagine anybody not laughing at this."

But the audience remained tight-lipped. Lahr worked hard, pressing for laughs, taking a few more pratfalls than the situation demanded. "Half way through the act it was almost like clairvoyance—I realized that somebody hated me. It's hypnotic. When they hate you, somehow you find them out. I looked up in a box and there is this girl with this man. She's pointing down at me. I imagine she was saying 'This guy is awful.' Nothing was happening. I'd look up to those boxes, and there she was—incensed. When I sang 'Peggy O'Neill' I'd crawl around and do it with the vibrato and everything. I did it a second time during the act. When I did it again, the woman stood up in the box and yelled, 'You can't sing either!' "

Talent was not the only prerequisite for laughter; the environment was also important. "Sometimes climatic conditions could hurt comedy; if the people in the audience weren't comfortable. I loved to follow a big hit singer in vaudeville. The audience was set up for me. Once, I played the Hippodrome. It used to have extravaganzas. Animals would be paraded on the stage; you could see girls swimming in transparent tanks. We had to fill three to four thousand seats without microphones. I followed Houdini, and I didn't get on until six o'clock in the evening. After Houdini, everyone wanted to go home for dinner. When I came out, all I could see were backs."

Lahr's most stringent critic was his father, who came to see him at the Hippodrome. "I said, 'Pop, how'd you like it?' He said, 'The horses were good.' He didn't get my humor. Later, when I did more of the vibrato, he'd take me aside and say, 'Why don't you stop that gnong, gnong, gnong—it's undignified.' " But despite such criticism, the first year was successful. Vaudeville audiences and critics were taken by surprise:

Bert Lahr and Mercedes are the real hit of the bill. Their coming was not heralded by the program and their sudden descent upon the unwary audience was somewhat of a surprise. The title of their act is "What's the Idea," which is just about what the audience thought when they began their nonsense . . . Lahr as a comedy cop proves himself one of the most amusing comedians in vaudeville. . . .

Cincinnati

The act was so successful that bookers were asking them to play more than their forty-week circuit. They were popular enough to work every week of the year, and for their first two seasons on the Orpheum Time they nearly did. Yet, with each successful review, Lahr's passion for perfecting his performance and his dream became stronger.

"If anything went wrong in the act with Mercedes and myself, I never blamed myself, I always blamed her."

This is his guilt and his burden. He never talks about it.

As he speaks about Mercedes now, he is eating a dinner that my mother prepared. He loves her and knows the care she takes to feed him. It is her pleasure, and she does it well. He takes a bite. "The meat's tough." Mother looks up in nervous disgust. "Well, Bert, *mine's* all right." He chews another piece. "I just got a tender one." His face lights up; and he talks with his mouth full until he drips something on his pants. He has hurt Mildred in the same unthinking way he must have hurt Mercedes. He screws up his face to express his sudden pleasure. It is humorous, but also disconcerting. He can perceive a situation with chilling accuracy, and yet with those closest to him he often acts as if the person were simply an appendage of himself, responding to the same drives and demands. He shared his dream only once, and that was with Mercedes. In time, it destroyed her. This is the torment of his vision; it is totally his and no one—no matter how intimate—can ever share it again.

He still cannot assess the nature of his relationship with Mercedes.

"Did you get along, Dad?"

"I guess so. I mean, we had our fights, but we were a team. We were together nearly twenty-four hours of the day." This is as much as he will volunteer. I try to cue him. "I never saw it. I never saw it," is all he will add.

Their friends, however, have different recollections. Haley remembers meeting Lahr in Montreal at two in the morning. Lahr had a suitcase in hand. "Where are you going at this hour, Bert?"

"Babe and I just had a fight. I'm going to a hotel." Haley laughs at the memory of Lahr in such a rage that he didn't even bother to take another room in the same hotel.

Jean Dalrymple, now the general director of the New York City Center, appeared one week with Lahr and Mercedes in Minneapolis during the 1924 season. Lahr's sketch followed her one-act play. She recalls standing in the wings and watching the act. "I felt I could learn something from him. He was rather taciturn even then. His mind was on the act. I know that I told him how much I admired him and how great I thought the act was and how amusing it was. He never was particularly ebullient about it."

Miss Dalrymple remembers that week because the ten-foot snow-drifts kept people from the Christmas Eve show, and the cast had to have their dinner sent into the theater. They ate on stage. Mercedes did not eat with everyone else. Lahr brought her food to the dressing room. They had been arguing about the act. Their relationship made an impression on Miss Dalrymple. "They had a hard time getting along. I didn't really hear them quarrel, except for a few gruff words. It was mostly about her performance or his performance. I remember the people on the bill said they quarreled like cats and dogs."

"I guess I was too demanding" is the only explanation my father gives for his disagreements with Mercedes. "We never fought about anything but the act." However, since the act encompassed almost all of their experience, Lahr found himself not only monitoring her performances, but also taking charge of her wardrobe and appearance. He accompanied her to buy clothes and make sure she did not indulge her inclination for steaks and chops.

Later, her fantasies would try and reshape the pressures.

Sept. 15, 1933

Mrs. Lahrheim is naturally fond of jewelry and fine clothes. At present, however, she is wearing only a diamond ring on the third finger of the left hand. She says she has always liked to spend money for clothing, and when in the RKO and Keith-Albee Circuits frequently spent $20 for a pair of shoes, and bought sable fur and coats.

Despite their problems, in less than a year Lahr and Mercedes vaulted into the vaudeville limelight. By June of 1925 they were listed among the Keith-Albee All-Star acts. When they played the Palace in New York, the supreme test for every vaudeville performer, the critics

Jacob Lahrheim

Augusta Lahrheim

At age six

The Nine Crazy Kids (c. 1913) . Lahr second from left

Overleaf
In *The Best Show in Town* (1917)

In *Garden Belles* (1917)

Stranded in New Castle, Pennsylvania. Lahr top left (c. 1914)

Seated in center. From *The Best Show in Town* (1917)

In *The Best Show in Town*

In *Roseland Girls* (1920)

At Lake Hopatcong (c. 1922)

Vaudeville Christmas card (1923)

With Mercedes in
"What's the Idea"
(1924)

With Frank Fay (left) and Harry Delmar (center)
in *Harry Delmar's Revels* (1927)

With Mercedes backstage (1927)

knew that the act had found its pace and maturity. Lahr played the Palace for five hundred dollars a week; five years later he played it three times in one year for five thousand dollars a performance. The effect of his first Palace appearance was hard to misread.

"What's the Idea" created sensational moments of comedy. Lahr drawing some of the most deep-seated laughs imaginable . . . This is their first appearance at this house, and they surely showed 'em something.

With his growing stature, Lahr began to move outside the chrysalis of his work. He joined the Friars Club and spent much of his free time with comedians whose friendship he had never had time to indulge on the road: Bert Wheeler, Eddie Foy, James Barton, and Jay C. Flippen.

Foy, who is known to make his exit from parties doing a "buck and wing" is still as irrepressibly gay as he was when he first met my father. He wears a jaunty colored cap and talks about the time he nailed every piece of his wife's clothing to the floor when she left him.

Foy recalls having drinks with Lahr at the Friars Club, just after he had been accepted as a member. Foy, Jay C. Flippen, and Joe Frisco were sitting at the table when Lahr entered. Frisco had never met Lahr, and when they sat down to the table the first topic of conversation was business. Lahr was excited about his reception in Kansas City, a notoriously difficult vaudeville town.

"I went over big," he said. "Five curtain calls."

The men were amazed, and said so. Frisco, however, could not believe it. "Tha—that's very s-strange, I couldn't get arrested when I p-played there."

Lahr offered to buy drinks. "What would you like?"

Foy and Flippen asked for beer. When he turned to Frisco, the comedian looked up without a trace of emotion on his face, "I-I'd like to see your act, you bastard!"

The year was filled with good times. Mercedes and Lahr spent the money they earned lavishly. In New York, they stayed at the Forrest Hotel. If they were not registered, friends knew they were on the road. The company at the hotel off Broadway and Forty-ninth Street was always interesting—Damon Runyon, Jack and Mary Benny, Fred Allen, George Burns and Gracie Allen, the Haleys. The excitement of that time is typified by Lahr's trip to Canada with Bert Wheeler in search of sparkling burgundy. The comedians and their women conceived this craving one Friday evening and traveled to Canada the next day to quench their thirst. There they filled their hotel bathtub with the wine and drank until it was empty. They returned on Monday.

And there was Lake Hopatcong, with long hours of fishing and golf. Lahr remembers Mercedes around the campfire, shading her eyes from the smoke as she watched over the barbecue. She delighted in these cookouts; her food and the exuberance she had for these summer evenings earned her the nickname "Mom."

Lahr had invited the dance team of Donald Kerr and Ephie Weston to spend a few weeks with them on the lake. Lahr and Mercedes had met them while playing many of the same bills during the year. Kerr and Weston, who were married, were a comedian's delight. Lahr enjoyed their private idiosyncrasies. When they tried to use the English language in a manner commensurate with their $750-a-week vaudeville pay, they inevitably got lost in the words. Many of the gags my father used around the house are derived from their search for the *mot juste*. "Pass the salt if I'm not too inquisitive." "Get in my car and I'll drive you to your destitution." Once when Kerr was touting his wife's dancing ability, he confided to my father, "She can kick the chanticleer."

With Weston and Kerr in the next room, Lahr and Mercedes were treated to some unusual antics. After one night of drinking, Lahr heard Ephie proclaiming loudly to her husband, "Donald Kerr, you beast! You let me sleep with my clothes on, but my drawers are off!!"

Lahr had purchased a Hupmobile. He recalls a summer excursion with James Barton to Coney Island. "On our way, the car hit a steel hoop and began losing gas. The gas station attendant told me we'd have to have the gas line soldered. I said, 'Well, I got an idea.' We went to a drugstore—they carried theatrical supplies in those days. Neighborhood theaters were in all sections of the city. Now nose putty is a product made of wax. You can mold it and put it on your nose. The body heat makes it stick. We used to wear it a lot in burlesque. I bought some and stuck it in the puncture. It held the gas. The car still wouldn't go because rust had somehow gotten through the gas line and clogged the carburetor. There was only one way to do it, bypass the filter and get gas immediately into the carburetor. I had another idea. We went back to the drugstore and bought a douche bag and cans of cleaning gasoline. We drove to Coney Island and back with Jim Barton holding the douche bag and pouring gasoline."

The giddy profusion of that year is reduced to snatches of dialogue and fragments of experience. After so many years of skimping, extravagance and waste suddenly held a childish appeal. Lahr's name was becoming better known, but vaudeville reputations were mercurial. He was conscious of friends moving into Broadway revues: Bert Gordon had performed in *George White's Scandals* (1921); Joe Cook had steady work with the *Earl Carroll Vanities;* and Jim Barton was scheduled for *Ziegfeld's Palm Beach Nights* (1926). Lahr brooded about his career and an elusive big-time reputation. As his act became more amusing with each technical "bit" honed for laughter, the nature of his humor escaped his own understanding. The reasons for performing were private and inscrutable; he felt vulnerable when he or others questioned it. When asked to analyze his craft, he sidestepped the personal aspect of laughter with commonplaces. He was handing out this kind of statement to reporters in 1926:

> Laugh and the world laughs with you, is the truest saying in the world. . . . There's a lot of comedy in humanity, in life, everywhere. . . . Look around as you ride on the trolleys or as you walk along the street. There's a funny character here, and something funny there, and lots to amuse you.

His enthusiasm for making laughter is not conveyed in such statements, yet his spontaneity toward life is grossly overstated. He is talking to fit the image of the public while refusing to speak about his own image of himself.

Lahr and Mercedes became headliners on the Orpheum Time toward the end of 1925. As one of the strongest comedy acts on the vaudeville circuit, Lahr took on added comic responsibilities. The circuit was grueling:

1926: Orpheum Time

August	23–29	Orpheum, St. Louis, Mo.
	30–5	Palace, Chicago, Ill.
September	6–12	Orpheum, Minneapolis, Minn.
	13–17	Orpheum, Winnipeg, Canada
	20–26	Orpheum, Vancouver, B.C.
	27–3	Orpheum, Seattle, Wash.
October	4–10	Orpheum, Portland, Ore.

	11–16	Orpheum, San Francisco, Cal.
	18–24	Orpheum, Los Angeles, Cal.
	25–30	Orpheum, American, San José, Cal.
November	8–14	Orpheum, Oakland, Cal.
	15–21	Golden Gate, San Francisco, Cal.
	22–28	Hill Street, Los Angeles, Cal.
	29–4	Orpheum, Denver, Col.
December	5–11	Orpheum, Kansas City, Kan.
	12–18	St. Louis, St. Louis, Mo.
	19–21	Orpheum, Chicago, Ill.
	22–25	Diversey, Chicago, Ill.
	26–1	Orpheum, Des Moines, Iowa
1927:		
January	2–8	Orpheum, Davenport, Iowa
	9–15	Orpheum, Chicago, Ill.
	16–22	Palace, Cleveland, Ohio
	23–29	Keith's, Toledo, Ohio
	30–5	Temple, Detroit, Mich.
February	6–12	Keith's, Indianapolis, Ind.
	14–20	Keith's, Cincinnati, Ohio
	21–27	Keith's, Dayton, Ohio
	28–5	Keith's, Louisville, Ky.
March	6–8	Keith's, Columbus, Ohio
	8–10	Keith's, Canton, Ohio
	11–12	Palace, Akron, Ohio
	13	Palace, Youngstown, Ohio
	14–20	Perry, Erie, Pa.
	21–27	Keith's, Syracuse, N.Y.
	28–4	Temple, Rochester, N.Y.
April	5–10	Keith's, Ottawa, Canada
	11–17	Imperial, Montreal, Canada
	18–24	Keith-Albee, Providence, R.I.
	25–1	Keith's, Boston, Mass.
May	2–8	Hippodrome, New York City
	9–15	Keith's, Philadelphia, Pa.
	16–21	Keith's, Baltimore, Md.
	22–28	Keith's, Washington, D.C.
	30–5	Fordham, Bronx, N.Y.
June	6–12	Keith-Albee, Brooklyn, N.Y.
	13–19	Proctor's, Newark, N.J.
	20–23	Proctor's, Mt. Vernon, N.Y.

24–26   Keith's, Patterson, N.J.
27–3   Riverside, Ninety-sixth Street, N.Y.

July   End of Tour

Lahr teamed up with "the world's tiniest star," a midget named Jeanie, to do an afterpiece (see Appendix 3). The sketch, "Beach Babies," incorporated Lahr's fumbling braggadocio with Jeanie's pranks. The skit challenged his ability to be at once gruff and beleaguered, and yet to maintain the sympathy of an audience that saw Jeanie as a child. There was a special finesse in this kind of comedy that Lahr always appreciated. "Take W. C. Fields, who was a real horror off stage. On screen he always had a wife who was a dragon. If he did anything with a child, the kid was a brat and the audience wanted to stab him too. So you forgave Fields's rascality. He always got a form of empathy from an audience. Every comedian finds tricks. I found gutteral noises, ways of moving, doubletakes."

Jeanie was an engaging performer, and although she was only thirty-eight inches high, she was in her late teens. Lahr and Mercedes would get her on the trains for half price, claiming that she was their child. Jeanie, who enjoyed the fraud, would skip or talk childishly for the occasion. Once, on their way to Pittsburgh, the conductor confronted Lahr. "Is that your little girl in the next compartment?" Lahr said "Yes."

"Well, she's drunk and telling snappy stories." He had to pay full fare.

When they were playing Chicago, a telegram arrived for Mercedes from her sister announcing that her son—Mercedes's nephew—had died of rheumatic fever. Anna Delpino was a few years older than Mercedes. They had both been in the *College Days* chorus line when Lahr first met Mercedes. Although Mercedes rarely confided in her sister, Anna was a good friend. She became, in time, Mercedes's only link with the past.

Anna talks now about those harrowing days as if they were a dream. "I had a boy twelve who died, and when Mercedes came home for the funeral that's when we first noticed something strange. She was nervous then. She acted nervously. She didn't realize what was going on, I suppose."

She remembers that Mercedes sat rigid, refusing to look at the boy.

She didn't cry at the funeral, in marked contrast to her mother, who was inconsolable at Sonny's death. It is conjecture, of course, but perhaps Mercedes was silently taking her mother's grief on herself. The boy, who lived with his grandmother while Anna pursued her career, had been her mother's great hope, a hope held out against a world that had proved itself indifferent to her prayers and her rosaries. Mercedes herself had contributed to her mother's sorrow. She had first married at sixteen (a fiasco of a marriage, to a middle-aged booking agent, whom she left the day of the ceremony) to legitimize her escape from her mother's house and to ease her mother's fear about a career on the stage for "the joy of her life." Anything, Mercedes had thought then, would do if she could earn some money for the family. Now, she must have wondered, what solace could her stage gaiety offer to replace the humiliations her mother had suffered? And what were the reasons for those continuing sorrows? Wasn't she herself guilty of causing her mother pain?

"The why and the wherefore." Later, walking down sanitarium corridors, in her Arizona room, Mercedes would repeat these words. She would say them cryptically to doctors and nurses, to inanimate objects, to her dogs. *The why and the wherefore.* She would repeat them to the picture of Lahr and herself that she kept—the same one they used on their vaudeville Christmas card.

Lahr, who reluctantly attended Sonny's funeral, did not find his wife's behavior peculiar. She had always been a quiet girl. She loved her sister's son and was absorbed in her mother's welfare. He put her silence down to natural grief. "I was so naïve," he says now. "I didn't know about those things. I was so young, you know what I mean. I couldn't distinguish. I didn't know what was wrong with her."

If she continued to be self-absorbed off stage, her performances, once they returned to the Orpheum Time, were as professional as ever. On stage she was vivacious, playing as she had before Sonny's death. And there were other things for Lahr to think about.

Harry Delmar had approached Lahr about working in a high-powered revue on Broadway. Delmar first saw Lahr perform in Newark. He went on the recommendation of Charlie Allen, the agent, and what he saw pleased him. If Lahr and Mercedes could make people laugh like that for fifty cents, they could wreak the same kind of havoc for $5.50 on Broadway. Allen was certain of the talent he represented. "Harry, this Lahr is star material—keep your eyes on him." Delmar was only twenty-seven, and though a successful vaudeville "hoofer," his aspiration was producing. He conceived the idea of an all-star revue and clung to it tenaciously. He saw himself being catapulted by one show, like George White, to the zenith of the theater world. He was staking all his money and his dreams on this one idea, and he needed attractions that would draw big money.

Delmar did not meet Lahr until 1926, four months after Sonny had died. They met in Washington, where they were both featured at the Keith Theater, and had adjacent dressing rooms. Lahr was well received in Washington, and Delmar was impressed. "After all," he explains, "if a low comic could make the predominantly middle-class audience of Washington laugh and not blush at the coarseness of the material, then the New York stage was not far behind."

Delmar remembers their first conversation vividly because the show, which would eventually bear his name, *Harry Delmar's Revels,* became one of the highlights of his career. Lahr, however, had remained cynically aloof to his proposal. Many important producers had watched him perform. Even before he played the Palace in New York, the Shuberts had put him under contract, then let it expire. Florenz Ziegfeld had laughed at his antics at the Palace, intending to find a place for Lahr in one of his extravaganzas, but he never approached him with a contract. So, when Delmar made his opening offer, Lahr was understandably skeptical.

"You let me know, Harry, when you get everything set up." Delmar remembers those words with relish because, to the astonishment of everyone but himself, his dream was close to reality. He was to sign some of the biggest vaudeville attractions of the decade—Frank Fay, Winnie Lightner, Blossom Seeley. One star seemed to assure another, and his cast fell into place.

Nobody had suggested Broadway to Lahr before. The thought fascinated him. On his dressing table was a review from the Washington *Daily News.* Never before had he allowed himself to be overwhelmed by what the critics said.

> I have reviewed Bert Lahr's act week in and week out. He had meant nothing in particular. He had just played.
>
> Now Lahr, in his present act, comes out as one of the leading comedians of vaudeville. His new act is a Dutch, done first with a very handsome girl [Mercedes] and second with a child named "Jeanie" who is smart and adept.
>
> Lahr, as I say, has loomed. He is now a headline comic. He has ease, poise, smash. He is a new Mahoney, a new Dr. Rockwell.

May Mr. Albee do right by this lad, and not starve and annoy him while he leaps. A new performer, my friends. If you have never seen this lad, now is the chance. He is the big time's new comedian.

He read the review over many times to himself and then to Mercedes. How hard they had worked for those words! In Washington, Lahr had to correct Mercedes's movements. He had to keep polishing; there was too much activity on his lines; it was cutting the laughs; they were not as big as they had been the opening night. He was worried about Mercedes's figure, too. She looked lovely in costume, but now she was putting on weight. Spanish women, he kept reminding himself, had a tendency to gain. "She had to look sexy and nice out there as the straight for my jokes." He reiterated his worry to her daily. She listened, as she usually did, without argument. Every night there was some gesture, some laugh that could have been funnier. Once she threw a hairbrush at him in frustration. "She had a hot little temper, but it took a long while to come to the surface," but usually, he thought, she took the criticism quietly, like a real professional.

Whatever daydreams the reviews and the possibility of working on Broadway may have inspired, they were suddenly forgotten in Washington when Anna wired Mercedes to return to New York at once—their mother was dying. Mercedes traveled alone to New York; Lahr finished the engagement in Washington and moved on to New York to their next booking at the Fordham Theater in the Bronx. Only five miles apart in the city, they made no plans to rendezvous. Mercedes did not seem to care whether Lahr was with her or not. Another girl in the show would take her place, and she would join him as soon as she could. Secretly, he preferred it that way because he hated funerals, and the thought of having to undergo another ordeal like Sonny's wake was abhorrent. Mercedes had packed only an overnight bag. She kissed him goodbye at the station absentmindedly. She seemed nervous, but he recalls that she did not cry. She was wearing the amulet she had worn at Lake Hopatcong. It was depressing, but Mercedes, Lahr thought, was a good trouper, a strong girl. When she returned her worry about her mother would finally be resolved. The act could continue.

Mercedes arrived home an hour after her mother died. Isabel was laid at rest in her bed. Mercedes stared at her mother for a long time. The other people in the room, weeping and praying in loud whispers, became shadows to her. She saw only the bed and her mother. She began to sweat profusely. Anna came over. Mercedes stared blankly ahead of her. "What's wrong, Babe?"

"I don't know, Anna," she said, "I don't know."

As she would relate to doctors later, everything was spinning. She was moving farther away from the people in the room and farther into herself.

Isabel had understood her daughter in a way Lahr could not. She had dwelt on her beauty and cared for her with a concern that was absolute. Bert was different. It was always the act, always the same words, which never reflected that personal insight. With her mother dead, Mercedes's whole framework of identity slipped away. Nurses would overhear her joking with herself about her name. She would laugh at her many faces. "Mercedes Delpino, Mercedes del Beano."

Present Illness

About four years ago when her mother was ill, she began to worry a great deal. When doing her act on the road she would become almost hysterical, and it was necessary for her husband to be very stern with her. Her sister states that she began to have peculiar spells in which she would tremble and become faint and stiff. She also had attacks of uncontrollable laughter and crying. On one occasion she smashed everything in her dressing room and also complained of someone peeking at her. Her husband observed that her pupils were widely dilated.

The case record runs from 1931 to 1936. Lahr never read it thoroughly. If he had, perhaps, the late months of 1926 and the following year would have been more comprehensible. As it was, there was a kind of theatricality about Mercedes's actions, a stubbornness that perplexed and angered him. A month after the death of her mother, she smashed their dressing-room mirror during a performance in Los Angeles. Lahr returned to the sound of crashing glass. Mercedes sat slumped in her chair. She was holding her hairbrush in her hand. But she did not speak.

Lahr grabbed her and brought her face up to his. It registered no emotion. "What happened, Babe?"

"Nothing."

"You broke the mirror. What happened?"

"Nothing."

"Why did you do that?"

"Forget it. I don't know. It just happened."

"Is something wrong with you? We'll get a doctor. Do you hurt any place? Do you want me to get something? What's wrong, for chrissake?"

He could never get an answer. She just looked at him and stared. Although a better educated man might have seen mental disturbance in these incidents and sought a way of dealing with them Lahr viewed them simply as an expression of grief about her mother and Sonny. He believed the purpose of the team was to perform, and Mercedes loved the theater no less than she had before the deaths. She was fine in front of an audience, so he could overlook the curious off-stage behavior. "She always acted peculiar, but I didn't help matters any, I guess." He is more compassionate now than he was then. He loved her, but his lack of understanding bred contempt and frustration. Why could she not talk about what was bothering her?

Lahr was a victim of his own energy and resilience. He could not conceive how personal sadness combined with constant performing could force such a change. Mercedes shared his dream; and, in his mind, she shared his stamina. Each new town was a challenge, a step closer to their goal. Doctors assured Lahr that Mercedes's actions were the logical effects of depression, nothing more. She had been lucid prior to 1926, when they began the Orpheum tour. Now the schedule was more difficult and demanding than Lahr would ever acknowledge. The stage, which held his only hope, was offering its first bitter fruit.

In New York, two weeks after the conclusion of the circuit, Lahr returned to his hotel room to find Mercedes in front of her dressing table, her beautiful black hair sheared from her head. She looked like a monk. "Why, Babe?" was all he could say. She looked at him in the mirror. She said nothing.

Harry Delmar got in touch with Lahr again at the end of his tour. He had raised the money and assembled a sparkling cast. Lahr was impressed, but worried. He could not see where his talents fit into such a bill. Delmar assuaged his fears. Lahr was especially impressed when he learned that Billy K. Wells had been commissioned to write the comedy scenes. Lahr along with Mercedes was signed as the "unknown quantity" to a two-week contract, while the others players had run-of-the-play agreements.

Harry Delmar's Revels was scheduled to open in the first week of November 1927. After the first few tryouts in Hartford, nothing, not even the four hundred-dollar-a-week paycheck, could keep Lahr from wanting to quit. "Harry, I'm telling you this material just isn't funny enough." Delmar countered every argument and prevailed upon him to stay with the show. Lahr finally agreed when Delmar promised to provide some new sketches for him.

Besides his anxiety about his part, there were other minor annoyances that the Broadway show created. Frank Fay, who was one of the nation's finest stand-up comedians and whose style was later adopted by such favorites as Bob Hope and Jack Benny, was suave, handsome, and monumentally egocentric. He did not like Lahr's brand of comedy or the energy and intensity with which he roamed the stage.

Fay, who was, in comparison to Lahr, glib and sophisticated, would unnerve Lahr at the theater, greeting him with "Well, what's the low comedian doing today?" Once, when they played a benefit at Madison Square Garden, he introduced Lahr saying, "Ladies and Gentlemen, I'm going to introduce you to one of the funniest persons on the stage. A man who will keep you in stitches for forty-five minutes. Bert Lahr."

"After an introduction like that, I was dead," Lahr admits.

The ploy of referring to other comedians as "low comic" actually originated with Bert Wheeler when he and Fay played the Palace. Fay had been held over nearly ten weeks; he was a phenomenal success. Fay asked Wheeler to do a "bit" with him. Wheeler agreed, but wanted to know what skit they would do.

"We're just going to go out there and ask the audience to stay after the show and see the afterpiece, which we will do."

"Why does it take two people to go out there and do that? Let's rehearse something."

Fay's reply was typical. "Don't you know I'm probably the busiest and most popular comedian in this town and I haven't got time to rehearse."

Wheeler remembers the moment vividly. "I knew what I was in for. I get out on the stage with him and he starts on me. And I'm telling you he must have popped nine or ten gags off my head and the people are falling out of their seats laughing at this man. He expected me to answer him, but if I had answered him, he would have killed me double. He was just laying for me there. For once in my life I got smart. I let Fay run out of material, like a fighter out of steam. He got so mad because I wouldn't answer him he said, 'Aren't you going to do something for the folks?'

" 'Yes' I said, 'When you get through getting those titters . . .'

"Fay says, 'Titters?'

"I say, 'Fay, you have your method of getting laughs, and I have mine. What you consider a big laugh would be a snicker to me.'

" 'Well, go ahead,' Fay said, looking at me; I had been leaning against the backdrop while Fay performed. 'The hall is yours.'

"I said, 'Now would you like to see me get a laugh like you've never gotten in your whole life?' Fay nodded; and then I smacked him in the puss.

"Fay just stood there while the audience howled. When the laughter died down, he turned to the audience and in his dead-pan delivery said, 'That's what you get for mixing with low comedians.' "

When Fay used the term to describe Lahr, it rankled him. Despite the fact that Lahr respected Fay's ability and would in time become good friends with him, he got his revenge when the show came to Broadway by getting most of the good reviews. *Billboard* heralded the revue as "extravagant as anything Ziegfeld could offer." Lahr and Mercedes were singled out for their slick comedy skit.

> But what your correspondent wanted to see was more of Bert Lahr. The grotesque we seem to remember from a dim past of burlesque and small-time vaudeville. Lahr is terrifically funny, but he didn't have enough to do.
>
> *New York* Post

Lahr's caricatures were vivid in their wild brashness; his gestures were daring to a Broadway audience, whose taste leaned toward a more controlled, acceptable form of laughter. Lahr appeared in a few skits besides the cop act, and took part in a quartet by Billy Rose called "The Four Horsemen—Don Quixote, Paul Revere, Ben Hur, and Jesse James." He, of course, was the man outside the law, Jesse James. All of Lahr's old gags were there, but the difference was a new polish and sophistication for the $5.50 crowd.

The Broadway audience responded well to the anarchy he created on the plush stage of the Shubert Theater. Lahr was shocking and funny. One critic reflects the insularity of the Broadway comic stage and those who wrote about it at the time Lahr entered it:

> And then there is Bert Lahr. His name should be writ in gold on the programme. He is an extremely amusing comedian, new to me. I suppose he comes from where I never go—from vaudeville. Everything that is good in these affairs, I'm told, has been annexed from vaudeville. However, Mr. Lahr is excellent no matter whence he comes, and he is the real comedian of the 'Revels.' "

Harry Delmar's Revels not only introduced Bert Lahr to Broadway, it was also the showcase for one of the great musical standards of this century, "I Can't Give You Anything But Love, Baby." As Lahr recalls it, "Delmar wanted a 'jewel number' where the showgirls would come down in bizarre costumes. He wanted to do it in a different way. So Lew Brown (of DeSylva, Brown, and Henderson) came up with a song title, 'I Can't Give You Anything But Love, Baby.' I went with Delmar over to a music publishers, a place called Kalmer and Puck. Delmar gave Jimmy McHugh and Dorothy Fields the idea. 'Two young kids in front of a jewelry store. One says to the other, "I can't give you anything but love, baby." ' They took the title and wrote a song. The number didn't do much in the show at all. It wasn't done by important people; and the public didn't consider *Harry Delmar's Revels* a hit show. They put it into *Blackbirds of 1928* and it became one of the biggest hits of the country."

Despite approving reviews, Delmar's spectacular did not do well at the box office. Lahr was faced with an important decision. "I realized that this was my first show on Broadway, and in order to be seen, I'd have to stay there. The show was a flop. It would have closed. We needed money. Frank Fay put in some cash; and I invested five thousand dollars—which was all of my vaudeville savings. In the end, I was the only person who benefited by the exposure. Since we had put money into the show, we were also part owners. As performers we had taken a cut in salary. We weren't able to pay the writers. Billy Rose, who wrote some songs for the show, sued us for his money. Being part owner, I resented it. He sued me for forty dollars. I said to myself, 'How could he do this to people in this position.' So I went to the Pacific Bank on Forty-ninth Street and Seventh Avenue. I said, 'Give me forty dollars worth of pennies.' I was irate, incensed. Now, that's four thousand copper pennies. I carried them on my back down to the Loew's State Building where Rose's manager worked and threw it on his desk. I said, 'Here, you give it to the son-of-a-bitch.' He said to me, 'You better take it back, Bert. It's not legal tender.' So I had to lug the pennies back five blocks, four thousand copper pennies!"

His name sizzled in lights above the Shubert marquee for only sixteen weeks. Frank Fay was the headliner, but Lahr had been promoted to second place on the billing. He had seen his name on marquees before, but this was grander and larger than he had ever imagined. Thrilled, he kept a picture of that first Broadway marquee in his scrapbook.

NOTES ON A COWARDLY LION

"We opened the show with a trial scene," recalls Delmar. "Lahr was the judge. I used to know what kind of a house we had just by watching his face when he stuck his head over the bench." Usually, Lahr's face was not too jovial, but whatever his hopes for a full house, there were other things that pleased him about being on Broadway. The new celebrity he had achieved was reflected ironically in the National Shirt Shop Window on Broadway. The buffoon had suddenly become dapper. A picture of him with arms crossed, staring maturely into the camera in a well-tailored three-piece suit, filled the window. A placard read:

"LAHR"
A New Color Combination Neckwear
as Worn by Broadway's Best Dressed Comedian

He had a picture taken of the window display. It represented the way he imagined himself—opulent, genteel, and smooth.

If people began publicizing him in an image he had always desired, he also was delighted to find his name in the critical vocabulary. A clipping describing another comedian in 1928 reflects his new fame:

> Billy Bann, of the Bert Lahr school of funny men, is frequently funny. . . .

Five years after *Harry Delmar's Revels,* doctors explained the process Mercedes was exhibiting off stage as "blocking."

> She smiled when answering these questions. When certain other questions were asked, she "blocked" very decidedly, did not reply, paid no attention to the next two or three questions and then answered the first unanswered question pointedly. Q. What are your plans? Would you like to go back to the show business? (late answer) : There is room for me in the act when I get ready.

Lahr never understood her evasions of his questions and her silence, made more annoying to him by her elaborate facial responses, as if she were enjoying a private joke with herself. Mercedes had never been more stunning or effective in the act than she was during their only Broadway exposure. Lahr watched her move from the wings, waiting anxiously for the wink to come when he would proclaim himself her Uncle Succotash. She was still lively and crisp in her delivery. The only difference between her present performance and the ones in vaudeville was that her lovely mantilla and fine Spanish comb had been replaced by a scarf, which hid her short, unkempt hair from the audience. When Lahr watched her on stage, he thought of the inexplicable impulses that seized Mercedes and made her alien not only to him but also to herself.

"There is room for me in the act when I get ready." Mercedes always believed that the stage would accept her again. Her evasions about the theater, her performance, and her husband appeared in the mental barrier, the blocking, she put up to her emotions. Lahr could not keep the questions from his face, but he refused to speak them to her directly. How long could Mercedes remain on the stage? He feared for the worst.

Once during the *Revels,* he came into the dressing room before the show to find Mercedes drinking with a friend. She was drunk. Lahr could hardly control his rage. He ordered the other woman out of the room and glowered at Mercedes.

"What do you think you're doing? We've got to go on in fifteen minutes."

"Where's my brush, Bert?"

"Did you hear me, Babe? Let me look at you." He looked at her eyes and picked up the bottle to see how much Scotch she had taken.

"What are you trying to do to us, Babe? . . . What are you trying to do? I'm just starting to earn decent money and you start acting up. If it's anything I can help . . . You're acting crazy . . . unprofessional. Do you have anything to say?"

She paused; and Lahr waited for her response. Finally, she said, "If I can't find that brush I'll never be ready."

"Mercedes, will you talk to me? Talk, goddamit, talk."

"The brush."

"You're drunk," he said and struck her.

The image is still vivid in his mind. "I slapped her. It was the only time I ever raised a hand to her. She had to go on stage." Mercedes just stared at him. She laughed, and got ready to go on.

Lahr tried to be patient. He attempted to calm her, but she would cringe from his touch as if his flesh carried destruction. What was wrong with him? The question plagued him. He felt barren and sexless. She showed little interest in him when he spoke of the act. Mercedes had always ironed his clothes and kept their small accumulation of possessions neat and well organized. He respected her for this, and took it for granted. He never thanked her or acknowledged her actions, but it was tacitly understood, he thought, that this was part of the team effort. Now, nothing seemed to be in its place; the hotel room mirrored the confusion in her mind. He would ask for his shirts, and she could not find them nor remember where she had sent them to be laundered. He expected her to look nice for him, but, instead, he could see that the pride she had shown in her beautiful features was being forgotten. Before, she had spent hours doing her lips and combing her hair, now she dressed hastily and paid little attention to her appearance. He would scold her. "Darling, please dress nicely today. Why don't we go out and buy some new clothes? I'll come with you. Don't you want to look nice again?" She would not reply. He would buy her clothes, only to see them become wrinkled and uncared for.

For a man so conscious of the outside world and the sentiments of others, the humiliation was deep. People knew—how could they not see the difference? On stage, Lahr was free. He could run, jump, improvise with abandon. He was set apart from society. But now with money and acclaim within reach, his private world seemed strangely inflexible. Off the stage, he imagined people were judging him; worse than that, looking into Mercedes wide, dark eyes, he feared *she* was thinking things about him she would not share. He felt constricted, his freedom overwhelmed by an inarticulate guilt.

One day he answered the door to his hotel suite and found a policeman standing next to his wife.

"Bert Lahr?"

"Yes."

"Is this your wife?"

"Of course. What's happened, Babe?"

"She couldn't remember her name, sir. She was walking on the grass with her dog. And when I questioned her, she got all confused, cursed at me. I had to write a summons, sir."

Lahr tried to put the incident out of his mind and interest Mercedes in his next show. The *Revels* gamble had paid off. He had been signed by Vinton Freedley and Alexander Aarons, two of Broadway's most successful musical comedy producers, to a five-year contract. He remembers bringing home the announcement and pasting it in his clipping book.

Aarons and Freedley have engaged DeSylva, Brown, and Henderson to write their next musical comedy production. It will be entitled

Hold Everything. Bert Lahr is figured to have a prominent part in the piece, and Russ Brown will be engaged . . .

May 12, 1928

"We were finally there. Big dough, a Broadway contract. I came back one afternoon a few weeks after the police incident and Mercedes had locked herself in the bathroom. I knocked on the door, 'Mercedes, what are you doing in there? Open the door!' I waited. There was no answer. I pushed at the door, finally I smashed it open. She was squatting by the lavatory. She held a handful of dollar bills. I couldn't speak—that was money from our "boodle bag." She held the money tight in her hands. She was shoving the bills one by one down the toilet . . ."

All the actors knew what was happening. Nobody talked about it, and even now Delmar and Foy do not want to mention it. "It was so long ago, John. It's water under the bridge." Delmar glances at the reviews of the *Revels* laid out in front of him. He points to a name. He winks.

My father doesn't hide it. "I started playing around. Mercedes didn't want me, she didn't show any emotion toward me. Sometimes I'd stay out to two, three in the morning. When I'd get back, she didn't mind." He would leave her and return, silently convinced that Mercedes did not care, certain she did not realize the situation of her self-absorption. "A change came over me—I was looking for something, reaching out for something." He repeats it. "Reaching, reaching."

The excitement of going into rehearsal for his first Broadway musical comedy filled Lahr with a sense of urgency and anticipation. His professional concerns glossed the sadness of Mercedes's condition. Then, in September, she told him that he was going to be a father. Doctors Lahr consulted thought a child would take Mercedes's mind off the death of her mother and bring her back to reality. Lahr never told them of their Lake Hopatcong "marriage." In his own mind, they were married. But his fantasies prevented him from realizing that Mercedes had not made the same assumption; and that to be Catholic, unmarried, and pregnant could seriously add to the traumas that already threatened Mercedes's spirit and mind.

The doctors would uncover her curious responses:

> She has refused to give me the date of her birth, but when told all about her early life when a baby, she admitted it. She attended

school until 15 years of age, and then took up her profession as a singer and dancer. She took a position in a miniature revue, called "Mimic World" and after that trouped in various shows. She met her husband in one of these shows and married him (blocked on year of marriage) . . .

Lahr did not tell her of his discussions with the doctors. She had never wanted a child before, and now the sudden thought that one was growing inside pained her, creating complexities she could not express.

And Lahr remembers lying in bed with her thinking of *Hold Everything* and of the new child who would be born almost as a symbol of their twelve years of struggle. He tried to touch her, to kiss away her fears. He moved toward her and held her in his arms. As he embraced her, laughter rose from her throat. "She laughed at me, John. Laughed when I was making love to her."

BROADWAY
BEGINNINGS

Once when I was doing Flying High, *I played a benefit at the Metro-politan Opera House. Russ Brown said to me, "Do you realize that you're stepping on the same boards that Tetrazzini and Caruso trod?" I said, "Yeah, but it's a bad house for mugging."*

Lahr in conversation

When DeSylva, Brown, and Henderson talked to me about being in Hold Everything, *I asked them, "Couldn't I be a German fighter?" Buddy laughed at me. He knew I had the makings of a funny man. When I went into the part, even in those days, I said to myself—"Well, it would be sort of silly, wouldn't it." I just fell into this character of a bellowing, punch-drunk fighter.*

Lahr in conversation

B ERT LAHR'S COMEDY WAS ALWAYS CONTEMPORARY. IN 1928, WHEN middle-class America was still on its spree and prosperity still seemed assured, his laughter caught the pulse of the time while reminding an audience of what they had left behind. His humor was lavish and generous, boisterous and unsophisticated. Yet Lahr's good spirits and his outlandishness were the twentieth-century equivalent of the frontier tall tale—a preposterous stage language anticipating a world of success and safety. In every sketch or song, Lahr's comedy triumphed over adversity—confirming the audience's intuitive faith in the benevolence of American life.

Lahr's initiation into musical comedy was a fortuitous combination of his exuberance and the writing skills of DeSylva, Brown, and Henderson, a musical-comedy team whose shows reveled in the delight and wonder of the American experience. *Good News* (1927) sang about happy college days; *Follow Thru* (1929) about country-club life; and *Hold Everything* (1928), the first show they wrote for Lahr, gloried in the national fascination with prize fighting at a time when Jack Dempsey and Gene Tunney were folk heroes. Their shows demanded speed and a joyous celebration of the present—two ingredients of Lahr's uncomplicated buffoonery.

DeSylva, Brown, and Henderson were living out the prophecy of their own song—

> Oh Boy! I'm lucky,
> I'll say I'm lucky,
> This is my lucky day.

They shared, like Lahr and other Broadway journeymen, a boisterous faith in America's profusion. They appreciated Lahr's humor, his talent, and his "meteoric" rise to stardom. He was as new as Charles Lindbergh, as solid as a Model "T."

Just as Billy K. Wells had put Lahr into the healthiest burlesque environment, Lahr's talent, offering the howling variety of low comedy, had attracted the triumvirate at the peak of their success. Lahr could not have made his Broadway musical-comedy debut in more professional hands.

DeSylva, Brown, and Henderson called themselves "The Big Three." Their routine for writing *Hold Everything* followed a familiar pattern. In July, they checked into the Ritz Hotel in Atlantic City. They stayed in adjoining suites for a week to twelve days, venturing outside only for afternoon walks and late meals. Twice before from their Atlantic City hideaway the men had poured out songs that charted the romantic exuberance of the twenties, and remained a part of the American musical tradition for generations. In their first "book show," *Good News,* the team wrote "Good News," "The Best Things in Life Are Free," "Lucky in Love," "Varsity Drag." The previous year, for *George White's Scandals* (1926), they had contributed such songs as "The Birth of the Blues," "Lucky Day," and "Black Bottom."

Buddy DeSylva was the organizer of the group. He left the University of Southern California after his first year in 1916 and came to New York in 1919 because, as he told his friend and collaborator Jack McGowan, "By the time I graduated, I knew I'd be a rich man." He combined the discipline of a writer with a sense of phrase and romance that made his songs as scintillating as the decade in which they were written. He was especially effective in bridling the wild imagination of Lew Brown. DeSylva had been responsible for many famous lyrics before he teamed with Brown and Henderson. DeSylva had created such standards as "If You Knew Suzy" (with Joseph Myer), "Somebody Loves Me" (with George Gershwin), "Look for the Silver Lining" (with Jerome Kern), "California Here I Come" (with Al Jolson and Joseph Myer).

While Lahr, in an anxious limbo between vaudeville and Broadway, waited nervously to see the script, the team had to sandwich writing *Hold Everything* between a grueling schedule of commitments for films, stage shows, and their own publishing company.

There were no axioms to producing a musical score, but there was a definite pattern to which the team adhered. Ray Henderson, the only member of the trio still living, can recall the routine vividly. "We'd start laying out a show musically in New York. We might have a couple of titles, a couple of lines; we might even have a couple of tunes. And when we thought we had enough, we *always* went to Atlantic City to the Ritz. It got to be a habit. DeSylva and Brown would go into the bedroom and knock out a lyric, and then they'd bring it into the living room to me, and we'd set it. We'd work on a song that we might have started in New York or conceived in Atlantic City. We'd stick at it. We'd stay in the suite all day. If we got enough done, we might go out for a little fresh air, and then come back and work some more. That was the same routine, day in and day out. And to show you how meticulous DeSylva was—you see these pages of foolscap. We'd finally get the verse knocked out, and Buddy would write the song neatly on a piece of foolscap and fold it in half. He put it on the right side of the table near the piano. He got the biggest kick out of that. He'd go over and pick it up and feel it and say, 'Well, we're coming along.' "

While the score they completed in Atlantic City was not their best, it adhered to the musical recipe of the day. It was light, romantic, and tuneful. The book of *Hold Everything,* written by DeSylva and Jack McGowan, was about prize fighting—a theme that, even by 1928, had been exploited beyond its merit (there had been four shows with prize-fighting scenes that year). One critic observed about *Hold Everything:*

> Of course there is a gymnasium scene, a dressing room episode with
> the sweetheart busting in, and the battle itself. The story is unim-
> portant. This is a piece in which the clown is king.

In *Hold Everything,* the punch-drunk sparring mate (Lahr) of a championship contender fights the champion and, through a series of ridiculous twists of fate, wins. There is a love interest, and even an evil threat to the comic world in the crooked promoter, who is a spring-board for the situations. The producer, Vinton Freedley, had hired Lahr to play the pug and Victor Moore the wistful, droll manager of the champion. The love interest and drama were subordinated to the extravagance of the comedy.

"When I went to see *Harry Delmar's Revels,* I thought, 'There's a wonderful comedian and something new. He would make a beautiful contrast in his brazen manner to the little sweet trainer played by Victor Moore.' " That is Vinton Freedley's assessment nearly forty years after the show.

However, there was nothing funny about the show's initial reception. Freedley's million-dollar instinct—which led to the Gershwins' *Lady Be Good* four years earlier and would later mount such famous musicals as *Girl Crazy, Anything Goes,* and *Red Hot, and Blue*—was being severely tested. Originally budgeted at $65,000, the price of his venture had risen way above the norm of $125,000 by the time Freedley had absorbed the losses on the road.

"We opened in Newark. We lost ten thousand dollars and played to nothing. Went to Philadelphia and played to less business. I was very discouraged about the play. In the meantime, my then-partner, Alex Aarons (we had just built the Alvin Theater, which is named for him—Al, and me—Vin), had an extravagant production with Gertrude Lawrence and Clifton Webb called *Treasure Girl.* He looked down on my little flop as just one of those things I'd close up on the road. We changed our leading man to Jack Whiting and also hired a girl called Betty Compton whom Mayor Jimmy Walker saw in the show and later married. In Philadelphia, Brown and DeSylva came to me one night at the Sylvania Hotel with a couple of new numbers for the show. One was 'Too Good to be True' and the other was 'You're the Cream in My Coffee.' Those two songs plus the change in cast made the difference. We went to Boston and practically sold out. And then we came to the Broadhurst Theater and ran nearly two years."

The comedy Lahr and Moore provided gave *Hold Everything* the necessary originality for a long run that the book, limpid and often sentimental for all its ingenious turns, lacked. Even "You're the Cream in My Coffee" left some reviewers rankled rather than humming:

"Hold Everything" has several tinkling tunes to help it along, but the best of them is burdened with the most inane lyrics yet heard on our long suffering stage. Here is what the authors ask us to hum on our way home:

> You're the cream in my coffee,
> You're the salt in my stew,
> You will always be
> My necessity,
> I'd be lost without you.

Part of the reason for the show's mediocre reception out of town had been Lahr's inability to take complete command of his part. He had always been a "slow study"; and Henderson recalls that DeSylva was very worried about Lahr when they reached Boston. Lahr was nervous, worrying constantly about his part. He sat staring out into space, twirling the middle button of his coat. DeSylva would come over to Henderson and confide, "He's on the button again."

Whatever their apprehensions, Lahr had confidence in the Big Three. "I remember that DeSylva told the director, 'Let that kid alone.' I worked a special way. Nobody could direct W. C. Fields in a show. They'd just edit him. When you take a gal like Fannie Brice or Bea Lillie—you couldn't say do it *this* way or do it *that* way. They were distinctive talents."

The opening-night audience was treated to a brand of comedy new to the Broadway stage. Broadway had seen pratfalls and low comedians before, but Lahr's wildness and his dumb perseverance on stage were matched with vulnerability and pathos. The hilarity he could generate came from his ability as an actor to use his role rather than to go outside it. He was, in the true sense of the word "comedian," a comic actor. Occasionally, when he pressed for laughs, he went outside his part. But the instinct for acting was conspicuous. (This was not always the case with America's funny-men. The brilliant and individual comedy of the Marx Brothers and Bobby Clark went outside the characters of the play or its actions. They played themselves rather than their roles. Their humor lay in their unrestrained spontaneity, which mocked the conventions of the play. Willie Howard was a polished version of the dialect comedian. Even Ed Wynn brought self-consciousness to his stance as the "Perfect Fool.") With Lahr, the comedy was different. He had dropped his German dialect; and, while all his burlesque movements and bits of business were employed on stage, Broadway had never seen a comic so human yet so outrageous.

Lahr remembers peeping through the small hole in the asbestos curtain and seeing an impressive array of first-nighters. "Otto Kahn, who was a patron of the arts, was a backer of the show. He brought his friends. It was a high-class audience. A first-night crowd like I had never seen before in my life. I never played to anything like that in *Harry Delmar's Revels*. There were tiaras and diamonds. I was scared. But then when I came on stage, and I noticed after a few minutes Mayor Jimmy Walker almost falling out of his box laughing, that gave me confidence."

His entrance as Gink Shiner was made not with a cop stick or the ridiculous shuffle of the vaudeville days, but on a bicycle. He wore a beret and checkered pants. He rode it as if it were a bucking bronco. He went out of control on the machine, skidding across the stage in front of his trainer. He crashed into a tree and came back holding the battered bicycle frame. Gazing wide-eyed at the audience, he observed, "That's a hell of a place to plant a tree." This was the line that introduced him to musical comedy, and it brought howls of suprised laughter.

The carnival spirit of the play was embodied in the title song, "Don't Hold Everything." The action goes on around Gink as he struggles ridiculously to comprehend it. The comic world of *Hold Everything* was a safe and uncomplicated one, where people could sing—

> All moody folks,
> Sad, broody folks
> Should read old Doc Freud.
> For instance, his preaching is, his teaching is
> "Friends, don't be annoyed,
> Under no conditions
> Hold your worries in:
> You'll get inhibitions
> That are tough as sin."
> So free yourself,
> Just be yourself . . .

Gink tries to evade an infatuated woman and to summon enough courage and ability to get into the ring with Kid Fracas. Lahr's parody of the fighter's self-deception and his misguided confidence was similar to his treatment of the cop in "What's the Idea." His statement is not only in words, but also in gestures.

In the last act, Lahr, sporting boxing trunks and knee pads, is in his dressing room waiting to fight.

Gink, dubbed "The Waterfront Terror" for the bout, talks with his manager, Nosey (Victor Moore). Nosey has been watching Gink shadowbox, plainly disgusted.

Nosey: What you doin' now?
Gink: (matter-of-factly) Practicing ducking!
Nosey: What do you wear those pads for?
Gink: Cause every time I fight, my knees get scraped.
Nosey: Look out, you'll foul yourself.
Gink: (excitedly) Leave me alone. I'm winning.

Nosey: Come here! (Gink stops.) Sit down there 'til I give you the last rites.

Gink: (sits forlornly) Nosey—something seems to tell me this fight is gonna be the turning point of my career (becomes depressed).

Nosey: What are you feeling bad about?

Gink: (shamefully) Well, I bet on Kid Fracas against myself.

Nosey: (relieved) Don't give it a thought.

Gink: (breaking down and heaving his chest in despair) But I'm afraid I'm gonna win!

Gink is threatened by Kid Fracas's manager, who comes to look over the opponent minutes before the fight. Gink blusters at the manager, flexing his muscles in a tableau of hope over experience. After the manager leaves, Gink is aching for victory. His trainer tries to warm him up, throwing a soft jab to the belly. Gink sprawls on the floor, yelling "Foul! Foul!"

Gink marches off stage for his fight. When Gink enters after winning the bout, he struts like a peacock. His excitement is all arms and legs. "Did you see me?" Gink asks. "DID YOU see ME?" He prances around jabbing in the air, feinting courageously with his shoulders. "Didn't I flatten him pretty?" In the end, Gink not only gets the money, but the girl as well.

"I knew when the show was over," Lahr begins, shaking his head with a pained certitude, squinting in recollection of that moment. "I *knew* I was a big hit." He sat in the dressing room relaxing over a bottle of beer. He didn't want to go to the cast party. He felt private and exhausted.

Mercedes was not at opening night. Lahr thought of her, and decided to go home.

"I walked up Eighth Avenue. It was foggy. I saw a man throwing newspapers down from the tailgate of a truck. I went over and bought a copy of the *American* and opened it to the theater review." The review is preserved in his scrapbook on a special piece of paper. He read just the headline and the first paragraph:

New Comedy King
   Crowned In Music
      Play In Bert Lahr

A new comedy king was crowned at the Broadhurst Theater last night. In fact, he was crowned several times with beer bottles, brooms, blackjacks, and other miscellaneous tools of the slapstick trade. But he emerged from the fracas with the laurel wreath of triumph resting jauntily on his grease-painted brow, and up and down Broadway and for many a day to come you will hear talk of Bert Lahr.

"New Comedy King." Lahr's reaction to the review puzzles him to this day. "I continued up Eighth Avenue. The feeling I had was so strange. I felt—it's over. I did my job, and this is the way it was supposed to be. No elation. My whole life. All the hunger and the ambition and the fears and the hopes came to fruition. And then, when it happened, it was as if, well, it was coming to me. It was just a feeling . . . a feeling of . . ."

He returned to the Forrest Hotel and hurried upstairs to see Mercedes. "I said, 'Well, I think I was a big hit.' She looked at me and didn't say anything. No reaction at all. It was as if . . . as if she didn't know me."

The play did not draw unanimous raves, but the attitude of most critics was reflected in *Billboard's* notice:

> *Hold Everything* undoubtedly . . . will go down in theatrical history as the medium that carried Bert Lahr to Broadway acclaim. . . .

While some critics found Lahr's fun-making self-conscious and sometimes off the mark, they could not deny the freshness and boisterous energy he brought to the stage.

> . . . This man is funny. He can make old, tired stuff seem new and original. Believe me or believe me not, Mr. Lahr can obtain laughter by merely distorting his features. *Isn't that the oldest kind of clowning?* It is. Yet Mr. Lahr, I solemnly assure you, is able to cross his eyes and twist his mouth and *make people laugh.* You would not have thought that was possible? I myself would not have thought it was possible had it not happened . . .
>
> His resourcefulness is astonishing. He seems never to be at a loss for a way of making fun. If he cannot think of a facial expression, he uses a ludicrous utterance or some floppy posture, or, funniest of all, falls silent. The man, I repeat, is funny. His sparring business in the dressing room scene was so ludicrous that the entire audience was dissolved into laughter. This man is funny . . . there is more genuinely comic stuff in this piece than in all the other musical plays I have seen in New York put together.
>
> St. John Ervine, *Morning Telegram*

"Jes—us, why didn't I keep a diary or something of those days? I wish I'd written down all the things that happened to me during *Hold Everything*. I was in Seventh Heaven." He stops for a minute, forgetting Mercedes, remembering only the "hunger." "Rave reviews, a hit Broadway show, plenty of work. Seventh Heaven."

When he thinks back to *Hold Everything*, he envisions Victor Moore standing flat-footed and chubby like a partridge. Moore, with his quavering voice, was a fine comedian, with a soft, poignant delivery. Lahr had seen him in vaudeville in "Back to the Woods," an act he did with his wife. He was an important comic star when Lahr first met him.

"Young fellow," Moore said in their first encounter, "You've got the part in the piece. There's nothing I can do about it. Now, I'll help you all I can in these comedy scenes. But don't you do anything not to help me." Their rapport was instantaneous, and Lahr would always respect his professionalism and kindness.

In the reducing scene, in which Gink sweats off eleven pounds, Lahr spent most of his twenty minutes on stage in a ludicrous box that looked like a combination steam bath and laundromat. From inside the cabinet, only Lahr's head remained visible to the audience. When Moore applied the heat intended to hone him into championship shape, Lahr's face seemed to skitter out of control. Finally, the machine got too hot, and he disappeared into the box. When it exploded, the audience saw him with his face blackened, lying stunned in center stage. That was the end of the second act.

He devised many schemes to get a reaction out of the quiet comedian. "I used to break wind on stage to get Victor annoyed. You can't print that—some people will think it's disgusting. I did it purposely. I used to drink a lot of milk. One night during the reducing scene, Moore smeared Limberger cheese all over the top of the cabinet. It was in summer and very hot. We didn't have air conditioning. It was pretty uncomfortable. That was a hell of a way to get even with me. I didn't say anything. So I said to myself, 'What can I do to this guy?' I waited a few nights and then wrote him a letter:

Dear Mr. Moore,

There are twenty-five members of the Moose Club of Patterson out front, who are devoted fans. Would you kindly mention a few names. I'm sure the boys would get a great kick out of it.

John Angelo	—	loves his beer
Sam Carroll	—	likes the girls
George Simansky	—	always good for laughs

If you could make up jokes about them, I'm sure they'd not

only enjoy the show, but it will be something we'll talk about for many weeks to come.

Thanking you very much in advance,
Joe Spivack

"So I went into his dressing room. And he's sitting there with a script in front of him figuring out where he can place the names. That night on stage, he'd come out with a line like, 'I wonder if John Angelo is sober.' And there wasn't a sound. He kept throwing out these lines all through the first act, and there was no response."

Lahr laughs elfishly at the sight of Moore looking out at the audience, expecting laughter, and not being able to locate the Moose Club. To a comedian there is nothing more fiendish than silence. He recalls Moore's words as he walked off stage after the first act: "I'm a son-of-a-bitch, if I'm going to mention another name." Lahr never told him about the prank.

With *Hold Everything* a hit, Bert Lahr's name was now being mentioned by the public in the same theatrical breath as the Marx Brothers, Bobby Clark, and Ed Wynn. His familiar and humble circle of theatrical acquaintances was suddenly studded with friendships from the show-biz empyrean. Will Rogers befriended him, and Lahr remembers being so impressed that he asked if his ad libbing were really true. Rogers produced a slip of paper. "Bert," he drawled, "here's my show tonight." Mayor Walker, who had laughed so hard at him on opening night, came to see Betty Compton, and, during the courtship, he got to know Lahr. Even Noel Coward, then at the height of his long and brilliant theatrical career, came backstage after seeing Lahr's performance.

Hobnobbing with Broadway celebrities was not the only important gauge of Lahr's stardom. Other things marked his success—a bank account, his picture on the walls of the famous night spots, a fur coat for Mercedes. The mink coat was a special victory, a dream fulfilled from the vaudeville days. It was their first lavish indulgence, a luxury that had always been a symbol of the golden leisure which had now arrived. Having contemplated success for so many years, when his turn came, Lahr moved into the role with ease and enthusiasm.

How could he be so buoyant when Mercedes loomed in the shadow of every achievement? The answer is complicated. He gloried in his successes—the famous names, the reviews, the golfing. He took happiness also in the thought of the baby, and the possible good effect the birth would have on his wife. He cared about her and was concerned enough to ask friends to watch her while he was at the theater. At the same time, his ambitions kept him at odds with himself. They made Mercedes seem healthier than she was, the situation more hopeful than it ever could be.

During these two years of *Hold Everything,* Haley and his wife, Flo, lived in the suite next to Lahr's at the Forrest Hotel. They watched Mercedes retreat into herself; they knew Lahr's bewildered anxiety and the immensity of his aspirations. "His whole life was show business," Haley says. "His *whole* life. Now, in a way, it's just to get money. He hasn't told me this, but when I saw him after *The Beauty Part,* I could see it. There's a difference when you've got mileage on you, and you've been all down the road. You know you're not going to go any place. There's not going to be a bigger Bert Lahr than Bert Lahr was. You're not going to get bigger—just older." But in 1930, Lahr's stardom was just beginning. Haley was there to observe the ambiguity with which he faced Mercedes and life itself. "In the early days, those were the times when he was fired with ambition. Fired with ambition—and fear."

During her pregnancy, Mercedes was involved in an incident that confused and hurt Lahr. He claims that Mercedes fell asleep smoking, and that the fire which gutted their room was accidental. But Flo Haley, who smelled the fumes first, remembers the situation differently. "She set fire to the room. She was in there and the smoke was in there. It was like she didn't know it was on fire. We took her out in the hall. She wasn't crying. I said, 'You've got to get out, there's a fire . . .'" But Lahr cannot face the fact that, when they found her, she was sitting on the sofa in her fur coat. She had set the coat on fire.

"Bert used to ask me and the other girls to keep our eyes on Mercedes," Mrs. Haley explains. "In the beginning, before the baby was born, I don't think he realized what was happening. He was working too hard, rehearsing . . . She could fool you. She was like a little girl sitting in a chair. We'd play a card game called Fan-Tan and it would be her turn. I'd say to her, 'Honey, it's your turn.' I'd try not to notice what she'd do. I'd ask her something, and she wouldn't answer me. Then I'd talk to one of the other girls, and she'd reply to my question. We knew something was wrong. I told Bert about it. I only remember her as an immobile—face."

Lahr finally married Mercedes in August 1929, in Hoboken, New Jersey.

"Q. You have a little baby? Do you want to see the baby? (Late answer): The doctor told me that I should not have had the baby."

Lahr took his wife to the hospital when she went into labor. Jack Whiting had given him a bottle of rye in case he was nervous. He was so agonized by his sympathy for Mercedes's pain that he began drinking. "I got plastered. And then I passed out." When he awoke, Herbert Lahr, a large and healthy child, was at Mercedes's side. Lahr staggered out of the hospital exhilarated. He and Whiting went to a local bar frequented by the press and theater people. Overwhelmed with emotion, he recalls explaining the happenings of the afternoon to the newspaper pundit "Bugs" Baer. "If I had known the pain women suffer in childbirth," he said to Baer, "I'd have been a better son to my mother." Baer could not abide such easy sentimentality: "C'mon Bert, think of what a porcupine has to go through."

When Mercedes returned to the hotel, Lahr hired a nurse to care for the baby and also to watch his wife. Whatever his hopes for Mercedes and the child, it was apparent that his wife was not returning to reality. Like the doctors he consulted, Lahr was quick to rationalize her actions as postnatal depression. There was no other explanation for the curious indifference Mercedes showed toward her child. Even when Lahr saw that her motherly instinct was totally nonexistent, he did not realize that this had been foreshadowed in her previous behavior—in her laughter, in her forebodings about childbirth, and even in her intense love of her mother.

A few months after Herbert was born, Lahr was getting ready to go on stage when the nurse telephoned. "Mr. Lahr, your wife just tried to put the baby out the window." Lahr was stunned; he told her to stay with Mercedes until he finished his work.

Flo Haley and her card-playing entourage had been with Mercedes when it had happened. "Mercedes was very nervous putting on the baby's clothes. I could see it," she says. "The average person looking at her would not know anything was wrong until they spent some time with her. She walked over to the window. It was quite a wide window. She held the infant up as if she wanted to show him what was outside. But the window was wide open—it was summertime. That frightened me. I said, 'Let me show you another way,' so when I took the baby from her she followed me. He was awfully little. She didn't know. She thought she was going into another room, but she was going towards the window." Mrs. Haley told the nurse about the incident when she arrived a few minutes later. An actor's wife herself, Mrs. Haley had refrained from calling Lahr because she did not want to interfere with his performance.

The incident made its impression on her. "Then I saw that she was really sick," she says. "He was awfully worried about her. He sent for her sister. The doctors kept saying 'This can't go on. You've got to put her someplace.' He did not want to put her away in the beginning. He didn't want to separate her from the baby, either."

Whatever his emotions were when he left the hotel each night to perform, they are distilled now into a simple declarative sentence. "Sad. It was so sad." Still, his performances got cleverer and better as the season progressed. "Lahr got laughs that we never expected," maintains McGowan. Lahr's improvisation and growing confidence became something of a contest between the two men. "I'd buy aisle seats in the second row," says McGowan, whom Lahr dubbed the "Great Infuriator," "and every time Bert would get a laugh I'd point to myself. It frustrated him so. That mug of his would work overtime. I had him crazy doing this because I'd take the credit for the laughs he was getting. He couldn't take his eyes off of me. Every time he'd get a laugh, he'd look at me, and I'd point to myself and say, 'Me, me.' He got even. He'd screw up the lines so that he got a bigger laugh on what he ad-libbed. Then he'd point to himself."

The fun of performing transcended the personal problems. Off stage the question of marriage, his own sense of sexual identity, was not a laughing matter; yet each night the bumbling Gink would sing a duet with "Toots," the girl he evades with a passionate fear of matrimony and a total ignorance of womankind. The joke centered around his clownish ineptness. Gink's song was ironic:

> Sometimes I think that you hate me and
> Sometimes I wish that you would.
> I may be rough,
> But I know my stuff,
> You must admit that I'm good.

The stock market crash of 1929 and the depression that followed never touched my father. He never speaks of the bread lines or the poverty because the momentum of his career eliminated the fact of poverty if not the fear of it. He had his theatrical ambitions and his wife to occupy his mind. While people were setting up Hoovervilles in Central Park, Lahr could command five thousand dollars for a week's work in vaudeville when he was not in a Broadway show. The disparity never astounded him. No matter what the state of the nation, his salary did not seem illogical or curious. Perhaps a laugh-maker was never more valuable than during the bleak depression years. But since Lahr had no money in the stock market, he took only a cursory interest in its decline. People were still packing the theater.

Hold Everything was purchased by Warner Brothers late in 1929, in a year when only a few of the shows rated as smash hits were bought by the industry. Warner Brothers wanted to use Lahr in the film, but Vinton Freedley, hoping to attract large audiences on the road, held him to his contract. If the studio could not get Lahr, it did the next best thing—copied him. Warner Brothers hired Joe E. Brown, a comedian whose capacious mouth and lined face resemble Lahr's. When he went to see the *Hold Everything* film version of 1930, Lahr was shocked to find his comic business borrowed for the screen. *Variety* chronicled what happened:

> "Hold Everything" is probably the best comedy picture Warners has turned out since talking came in . . .
> The basic point of the picture is Brown. On the strength of this effort he of the wide grin grabbed himself a long and sweet starring contract with Warners. Which should make it an *event* for Bert Lahr. The latter has now made two people—himself and Brown.

Lahr was obsessed with the injustice. The week after the review of the movie version of *Hold Everything* Lahr answered it with a letter to the editor of *Variety*. His disgust at the incident can only be measured in proportion to his hatred of writing letters. He must have labored a full seven days over the one that appeared on March 28 under the headline:

BERT LAHR LABELS JOE BROWN "LIFTER"

> I have read the criticism of the picture "Hold Everything" in this week's *Variety*.
> I am greatly surprised and amazed to find that Joe E. Brown so boldly lifted my original business, mannerisms, methods, and phrases which I have been identified with for years and which I interpolated in the part of Gink Shiner of "Hold Everything."

It seems an outrage that a comedian can gain profit and recognition by deliberately lifting and copying another comedian's style of work. This is hurting my reputation, livelihood, and future in talking pictures.

Surely there must be some redress for an artist who has worked these many years as hard as I have to establish and attain the reputation and recognition I have as an original comedian gained by my creative and original style of work.

I am writing this in self-protection to let the *profession,* the exhibitors and executives of the picture world understand that I am the originator of all business methods, mannerisms, and unique phrases used by Joe E. Brown in the talking picture version of "Hold Everything."

Bert Lahr

The letter brought charges and countercharges by another comedian, who claimed that Lahr had imitated *his* style. Lahr wanted to sue for defamation of character; his lawyers advised him not to add weight to such absurd accusations by replying. Inaction may have been wise, but it did not assuage Lahr's temper. He stewed over the situation for months, his annoyance swelling with the success of the picture. In later years, he set a legal precedent for actors by winning a federal appellate decision (Lahr *v.* Adell Chemicals, 1962) protecting performers' mannerisms and speech against duplication for commercial purposes without their consent. In this case, his voice had been imitated in a cartoon for a detergent commercial in which a duck spoke with his intonations.

Lahr's annoyance was not without its humorous side. Joe E. Brown had taken more than Bert Lahr's mannerisms to the West Coast. His friend, Bert Wheeler, had been another victim. "Wheeler used to do a story; he was given permission by an old vaudevillian. He did it all over New York; he was recognized with the story called 'Mousie.' When Brown went to California before he did *Hold Everything,* he was telling the story all over and got known for it out there. So when he copied me in *Hold Everything,* I sent Wheeler a wire: "MOVE OVER, BERT, HE GOT ME TOO.' "

His friends never failed to infuriate him at the mention of Joe E. Brown. When Lahr was playing Baltimore on a personal-appearance tour in 1933, Victor Moore and Bill Gaxton were appearing in the same town with *Of Thee I Sing,* in which they both starred with Lois Moran.

When Lahr read the reviews of his opening night, he could not believe the print in front of him:

Bert Lahr, a comedian who is obviously making a living impersonating Joe E. Brown. . . . It seems appalling that one comedian should be allowed to take material from another and make his livelihood . . ."

As my father explains it, "I went over to their theater and talked to Gaxton and Moore. I was furious. I said, 'How do you like this son-of-a-bitch doing this to me.' And they were steaming me up, saying 'It's awful when you see this guy why don't you punch him in the nose.' And I said, 'Why I'm going down there and . . .' " His face shrivels up like a prune and his nostrils gape at me in mock defiance. "Finally Lois Moran came to me and said, 'Bert, this is a frame-up. This reporter is a friend of mine and we were out one night with the boys—Gaxton and Moore—and they framed you. He never even saw the show.' "

Lahr said nothing for a week. *Of Thee I Sing* was moving to Cleveland, and the night before the big move Lahr waited up until four in the morning for his moment of triumph.

"Gaxton went to sleep very early in order to make the jump. I got the operator at the Lord Baltimore Hotel, and I said, 'This is a matter of life and death. You *must* put me through to Mister Gaxton.' 'Why?' she says. 'Oh, I can't tell you, it's just so . . .' Finally she put me through, so I said 'Billy, Billy, is that you?'

" 'Yes,' he says.

" 'Billy, how's Madelaine, Billy?'

" 'Who's this?' Gaxton asked.

" 'Howard.' " Lahr imitates the tremulous voice he used.

"Billy, can you come down to the lobby for a few minutes. If you could bring Madelaine I'd appreciate it too," he continued.

" 'Who *is* this,' Gaxton demanded.

" 'Howard!'

" 'Howard who?'

" 'How would you like to go fuck yourself!'

"As I hung up, I heard him say, 'You dirty son-of-a . . .' " His eyes tear as he chuckles at his revenge. "Now I know it wrecked his sleep because about a month later I'm walking along Fifth Avenue and I meet his wife, Madelaine. She says to me, 'Remember what the boys did to you in Baltimore?' 'Yes,' I said, 'But do you remember what I did to Billy . . . remember him getting a call around four in the morning . . . ?' 'Did you do that?' she said. 'He blamed it on one of the chorus boys and punched him in the eye.' "

Although Brown's version of *Hold Everything* was well-received, it did not hurt the show's business on the road. Lahr brought his son and a nurse on the tour, allowing Mercedes and her sister to vacation in Europe as the doctors had suggested. Their trip cost ten thousand dollars—an indication of Lahr's urgency for a cure and the guilt he felt toward his wife. He was responsible and oppressed, sad yet seeking alleviation in others. On the road, he was in as much emotional turmoil as ever.

The trip to Europe proved a disaster. Anna returned a few months earlier than expected because Mercedes had not only remained indifferent to the beauty of the European summer, but, in her silent anxiety, had also taken to drink. "When we went to Rome, a reporter got us passes to have an audience with the Pope—and she didn't even want to go. She stayed in the hotel drinking wine. She wasn't exactly drunk, but she wasn't exactly sober either." Mercedes had some memories from the trip—she recalled the churches with their towering spires, the gondolas of Venice, and the endless horizon of glistening blue ocean. But after her return to the States, she seemed more agitated than before. Her speech and memory had deteriorated. She had difficulty readjusting to her son, and, if there had been any motherly instinct in her before she left for the Continent, it had vanished completely on her return. When Lahr met her at the pier in the spring of 1930, two things had changed in his life. He had a contract for a new show, and a lease on a Murray Hill apartment for another woman.

Rachel M. was a curious manifestation of the muddle in Lahr's mind. *"I don't know why, John, you see I was reaching for something, reaching . . ."* He wanted affection and beauty—neither of which Mercedes, in her illness, could offer. The girl he chose was an unlikely symbol of his own personal inadequacies. Typically unable to judge people, he did not realize when he began dating her that she was notorious. Rachel was a beautiful, Southern girl who had managed to make her way in New York by catering to out-of-town businessmen. "She was a nymphomaniac and a lesbian," says my father confidentially, like Dick Tracy on the scent. Although friends hinted at her reputation, he found himself drawn back to her. "We'd argue. I'd walk out on her, and then, ten minutes later, I'd be back at the door." He had nowhere else to go.

Whatever his private problems were, his stage career was bright. Although his relations with Aarons and Freedley were strained because they would not let him out of his contract to do the movie, the producing team was already planning to star him in a show called *Girl Crazy* with a new young singer called Ethel Merman. Lahr's talent, however, had attracted the attention of George White, who wanted to get him on Broadway in one of his own money-making vehicles. There was a hassle over contracts and legal action taken, but Lahr ended up in the company of White, a garrulous peacock who prided himself on getting what he wanted.

(When my father reminisces about this time with the few friends who are left from those ancient campaigns, he speaks wistfully about a Broadway whose entertainment centered around the comedian. "They're just not writing for me any more," he says, talking to his old friend and lawyer Abe Berman, who sits like a kindly panda bear nodding in agreement. "Remember the old days, I'd be playing in one show, and they'd be writing another for me. DeSylva would say, 'Let's write a show for Bert!' And somebody would say, 'How about a musical on flying?' And then, they'd do it." It was almost that easy—but not quite.)

White began litigation to free Lahr from his contract with Aarons and Freedley before he had a play in which to star him. He did not tell DeSylva or McGowan of his plans to use Lahr for a show when he commissioned them. According to McGowan, "All he told DeSylva was 'I want to do a show on aviation.'" McGowan, ironically, had just completed the *Girl Crazy* book for Aarons and Freedley. He had written the comedy part for Lahr and even typed his name on the list of *dramatis personae*. He never suspected he would be creating another show that would prevent Lahr from being part of one of the best remembered comedies in the first half of the century.

When The Big Three and McGowan took their ritual trip to Atlantic City, they drew a blank. They could not come up with either a story or songs. "We stayed there ten days," explains McGowan, "Then we came back and told George, 'Call it off—all we've got is a title, *Flying High.*'" White was astounded. As McGowan recalls it, he exclaimed, "For the love of God, I've got forty thousand dollars invested in contracts already for this." It was then that White intimated that

Lahr might be a possibility for the new show. When DeSylva balked at the idea of continuing and urged White to get someone else to dream up a script, White would not hear of it. He finally prevailed. Brown and Henderson returned to Atlantic City to create the songs. McGowan and DeSylva went to McGowan's farm in Connecticut to write a story.

The story for *Flying High*, a cross-country airmail race with Lahr as the pilot, evolved from a sketch McGowan had written for the Lambs Club and then forgotten. His satire lampooned the craze for flying and an actual situation where a Broadway starlet had attempted to fly the Atlantic with a male friend. The plane crashed off the coast of England. McGowan gave the idea to DeSylva one evening after their first few days of writing were unproductive. .The next morning at breakfast DeSylva exclaimed, "We've got it." The idea which evolved from that little scene was not the sex angle that McGowan had originally used in his burlesque of the incident. DeSylva had conceived a comedy situation where a man gets into the air and breaks the flying record because he cannot get down. With McGowan writing the first draft in one room, and DeSylva embellishing the construction and adding bits of business in another, the team was able to put together a script in three weeks.

Lahr had his contract soon after the play was completed. It was the highest sum he had ever been paid—$1,750 a week. "I remember coming in and showing Mercedes the contract. It was what we had been working for. The highest salary we'd received. She just laughed at me." Her reaction overwhelmed him. He began to spend more time with Rachel and was seen frequently in nightclubs with her. "She had him in full dress suit every Saturday night—a full dress suit!" says Nicky Blair, a friend. "We used to go to the Mayfair together. She was drunk half the time. She had him drinking, and, you know, he could never drink. She kept him going around . . . He never knew what to do in the woman department."

When my father thinks about the woman from Savannah, his voice lowers to a whisper, and he talks with a surprising objectivity about his lapse of judgment. "I knew in my heart what she was doing to me and what she was like, but I wouldn't let myself believe it. You know how you do when you're stuck on someone. It was all sex."

Rachel dragged him everywhere, and kept him from Mercedes and the child. "I was looking for something . . ." is all he can say to explain her allure. She even followed him to Boston during tryouts of *Flying High*.

One night in Boston, Rachel and Lahr got drunk after the show and ended up calling all over the country announcing to groggy voices who answered the phone, "This is Western Union. There will be a carton of eggs delivered to your door tomorrow morning . . ." When the person asked where they were from, Lahr would bellow, "From the chicken's ass, you bastard," and hang up.

They decided to call George White, who was in conference with The Big Three and McGowan about the book of the show that had stalled badly in Boston.

"This is the hotel clerk," Lahr said, disguising his voice in hollow, official tones. "You'll have to stop that noise, or we'll have to ask you to leave."

McGowan phoned downstairs to ask the operator where the call had come from. When she told him Mr. Lahr's suite, McGowan retaliated immediately. An Irishman of wide vocal range, he could produce a delightful falsetto voice. He called the hotel manager and in his most feminine tone, whined, "Please come up to room 409. This man is going to kill me . . . Please . . . Please. Hurry!"

The clerk, responding to the cry, got a house detective and policeman and rushed to the room. They rapped on the door, but Lahr, assuming it was a joke, did not answer. Finally, they broke the door down. Rachel ran into the bathroom. When the policemen pushed their way into the room, they demanded to see the woman who had just called them.

"What's going on?"

"Where's the woman you've been beating?"

"I haven't touched any woman!"

At this point Ray Henderson and Lew Brown came down the hall to see the outcome of the prank. The policeman stopped them. Lahr pointed to his friends. "These fellows will vouch for me." The policeman looked at the writers, who shook their heads. "We've never seen this guy before."

The manager made Lahr leave his room at once. They promised to send his theater trunk any place he desired, but they gave him and the woman who still refused to come out of the bathroom fifteen minutes to get out of the hotel.

With baggage in hand, Lahr left the hotel. It was five in the morning. He tried four other hotels, but each time he entered a hotel lobby the night clerk would not give him a room. McGowan had phoned all the neighborhood hotels explaining that Lahr had been evicted from the Ritz and had caused a tremendous disturbance with Rachel. No one would take him.

As a result, Lahr and Rachel sat in the park outside the Ritz Hotel until nine in the morning, when Lahr called the owner of the hotel and explained the prank. The owner checked the story, and finally let him back into the hotel on the condition that Rachel move to another floor.

There were more humiliations in store for Lahr when he got to New Haven. Rachel's sexual activities and her histrionics were not a well-kept secret. One night after Lahr had finished making love to her, he heard a volley of applause outside the door. A voice that sounded distinctly like George White's kept yelling, "Bravo, encore, encore!!" He put on his bathrobe and dashed to the door in a rage. When he opened it, he realized White had invited the cast to hear him make love. They had brought their pillows and sat outside listening to the performance.

As if the women in his private life were not enough of a burden, Lahr also courted trouble with one of his leading ladies, the popular Kate Smith. Miss Smith's large voice matched her figure, and her aggressiveness and jovial sense of humor combined to make her an effective subject for caricature.

In an interview with *The New York Times* (August 22, 1965) Miss Smith reflected on that period of her life:

> It was 1930 and I awoke the unhappiest girl in the world. I was 21 and in my third Broadway show. I should have been on top of the world but I wasn't. My claim to fame was as the helpless stooge of all the ad-lib remarks of the comedians.

If there was one comedian she despised and to whom this seems pertinent, it was Lahr. Kate Smith was a young actress and her lack of experience grated against Lahr's professionalism. Looking back to his relationship with her, he is penitent about his actions. "I was feeling my oats then. Laughs are very sensitive and having been in burlesque I knew what to do and what I was contending with. Kate and I didn't work well together, and she inadvertently hurt many laughs. She could have fed me my lines much better. When I tried to show her what to do one day out of town, she was furious with me. Lahr's vindictiveness must have been intense. "I didn't do anything to her, just called her 'Etna' under my breath when we were on stage." McGowan, who watched the feud from the stalls, concludes, "She was mad, but she didn't feel it the way he did."

One of the reasons for Lahr's anxiety was that the show was going badly on the road. White's friends had suggested he close it in Boston, but instead of chalking it up to experience, White doubled his bet and sent for Joseph Urban, the famous designer, to create a completely new set and costumes for the show. White himself took over the direction, and, being an old dancer, also took charge of the choreography. He not only suffered with the show, he also staged it, helped rewrite it, and kept the cast and production staff in their places. His iron will and staggering egotism managed to shape *Flying High* into a delightful evening. It was so eagerly awaited in New York that the show was the first to command a $6.60 seat on Broadway.

One sketch in the show caused McGowan and DeSylva quite a lot of annoyance. DeSylva had suggested a medical examination scene, and McGowan protested the gag on the grounds of bad taste. White liked it, and the joke remained in the show. McGowan, however, bet his collaborator five dollars that the bits of business DeSylva had conceived would not get laughs. This was his usual custom, and on opening night a lot of cash changed hands.

In *Flying High* Rusty Krause (Bert Lahr) is the exuberant and incompetent mechanic who gets up in the air and wins the race because he cannot get down. (Krause's trepidation is minuscule in comparison to Lahr's own fear of heights and planes.) The scene that McGowan was betting on took place at the end of the first act of *Flying High*, when Rusty is lured into the doctor's office by the wise-cracking, freelance photographer, "Sport," who sees the possibility of a good story and a better laugh in Rusty's plight. Rusty does not want to go, but with a love-lorn Amazon chasing him, he sees no alternative. "Lindbergh wouldn't take his cat," he shouts to Pansy who wants to come with him in the previous scene. She chases him off the stage for an explanation. In the next scene, Rusty finds himself in the doctor's office, trading quips with him. "Nationality?" asks the doctor summarily. "Scotch by absorption," Rusty replies. The doctor tries to push Rusty into a spinning machine or, as he describes it, a "tail-spin test."

> *Doctor:* Now I'm going to whirl you around several times. I'm going to have an object in my hand, and when I stop I want you to tell me what it is. You understand?
> *Rusty:* I don't want to be an aviator. I want to be a miner.
> *Doctor:* Now, if you feel sick, let me know.
> *Rusty:* Don't worry. You'll know it.
> (The doctor pushes his head down and whirls the drum several

times. A low moan comes from inside the cylinder. When the drum stops, Rusty's head emerges, wobbling from side to side. His eyes are hopelessly crossed. The doctor holds up a pencil in front of him.)

Doctor: What's that!

Rusty: It's a picket fence.

Doctor: (disgusted) Oh, my god—now we have to do it all over again.

Rusty: Let me out of here.

(The doctor pushes his head back into the drum and gives it a whirl. He goes to his desk and gets a banana. Meanwhile Sport comes in and sees the drum going and gives it a couple of extra whirls and exits. The doctor returns to the drum. Rusty is moaning fiercely. When it stops, his head lops out of it and hangs over the rim. The doctor holds up the banana in front of him.)

Doctor: WHAT'S THAT?

(Rusty looks nauseated. His hair is disheveled. He tries to move his head, but it lies limp on the side of the drum.)

Rusty: (shading his eyes) Take it away. Take it away.

Doctor: You're absolutely impossible. Come on, get out of there.

(Rusty staggers out of the contraption. He takes two steps and drops to his knees. And then gets up slowly. He staggers around the stage.)

Rusty: Gimme a lemon and seltzer! Gimme a lemon and seltzer!

(The doctor goes to his desk and gets a graduated glass for a urine sample.)

Rusty: Oh, there you are, bartender.

Doctor: (handing him the glass) You know what to do with that. (Rusty takes the glass, still staggering from the machine. The doctor turns to his desk and sits with his back to the patient. Rusty looks at the doctor, and then at the glass. The doctor expects him to urinate; Rusty doesn't understand. His eyes widen in befuddlement. Suddenly, a glimmer of comprehension flashes across his face. He reaches confidently into his back pocket with a quiet, knowing laugh. He takes out the flask and measures three fingers of the liquor in the glass. He staggers over to the doctor and hands it to him.)

Rusty: Here you are boy, that's all I can spare.

(Blackout)

McGowan lost his bet. He handed his five dollars to his mother-in-law who sat between him and DeSylva on opening night. "When she laughed, I knew it had to be funny." The scene he thought would be offensive to the audience became the biggest single laugh in the history of the American stage. Ray Henderson, who watched from the wings, saw people actually stuffing handkerchiefs in their mouths to keep from laughing. The next number could not continue and had to wait on stage until the laughter was low enough for the music to be heard. De Sylva clocked the laughter at sixty-two seconds. Robert Littell of the New York *World Telegram* wrote:

> George White's new musical is chiefly remarkable for three items, Bert Lahr, a fat girl named Kate Smith, and a very physical medical joke . . . Bert Lahr as a would-be aviator being examined by the doctor makes the farthest north yet reached on the stage by jokes about the human body. It was outrageous, but also, I must admit, very funny. When Bert Lahr presented the Doctor with a tall glass vessel into which he had poured some whiskey from his pocket flask, the house, especially the galleries, roared and screamed as I have seldom heard them scream and roar.

Lahr's comic moment played on the buffoon's innocence in the face of experience. The fact that he could pull off a joke which trod so thin a line between the heights of humor and bad taste illustrates his comic sensitivity as early as 1930. He articulated his knowledge of an audience many decades after he had capitalized on it:

> There are tricks in this business. If you play beneath an audience, if your character is a lowly character, do you see, the audience, although they like you, doesn't take you too seriously. "Oh, he's a schmo," they'll say, but they let you get away with it, you know what I mean. I have done things on stage that I don't think any other actor has ever done, and the audience never resented it . . . In "Flying High" I had this skit. . . . Now if a wise guy were to do that, a fellow with the wrong personality or that the audience did not respect, they could resent it very much, and it could be shocking. It all reverts back to how the audience feels about you out there, if they accept you as a guy that bumbles into something—that's in the writing and in the playing. *It's a matter of maintaining an air of innocence. You can do almost anything on stage, if you do it as if you haven't the slightest idea that there's anything wrong with what you're doing.* Some comedians can do that particular thing, but a lot of comedians make it vulgar and dirty, and the audience won't accept it.
>
> *Actors Talk About Acting*

Flying High proved that Lahr was not a one-show success. Yet his wild ambitions and his blindness to his own private actions are embodied with some irony in a song Rusty Krause sings after he has broken the world's flying record. Lahr never saw the irony. The song, "Mrs. Krause's Blue-Eyed Baby Boy," is sung with six girls who throng around him.

> Who'll be known from coast to coast?
> Who will be the nation's boast?
> Mrs. Krause's blue-eyed baby boy.
> Who'll be rich before he's through?
> Own his rolls—and coffee too?
> Mrs. Krause's blue-eyed pride and joy.
> And when the girls cry,
> "Some guy. Just think what he did."
> I'll say, "Hey, hey,
> Oh boy, some fun, eh, kid?"
> Who will rise and conquer men,
> Then become the bum again?
> Mrs. Krause's blue-eyed baby boy.

Through his triumphs in the show, Lahr has buried his failures. On April 27, 1930, Mercedes was committed to a sanitarium in Connecticut. He says that he was out of the house when they took her away. "It was just too sad." But the reports from the sanitarium indicate that he and Anna drove Mercedes to the hospital:

> Mrs. Lahrheim was brought to the sanitarium by her husband and sister. On admission she was silent but apparently did not wish to remain because she made an attempt to run away as soon as she arrived. She was assigned to a room, and night and day attendants were appointed. She showed no marked emotional reaction when left by her relatives and seemed apathetic and indifferent.

Lahr had always protected himself with one maxim: "I'll throw it out of my mind." On stage, as he sung about the success of Rusty Krause, he was able to forget his failures as Bert Lahr. His coarseness and his betrayal of his family he understood, but felt compelled to continue. There is no justification for his attitude; he has an ethical naïveté that is paralleled in his stage roles. The baby and the nurse stayed in his apartment; but he usually spent the night with Rachel. "Sometimes I'd come home and go into the child's room. I'd look at him, but I couldn't pick him up. I felt dirty."

Lahr's allegiance to Mercedes in the early months of her confinement was genuine. He called her and tried to visit her. Sometimes when he arrived she did not recognize him or talked with a marked deterioration. At other times, she was completely lucid.

He had not wanted to commit her, but nothing he had tried brought Mercedes out of her condition. "She was a good woman, and even though I fell out of love with her when she became ill, I had a great respect for her." There was no alternative but to commit her; even her child was alien to her.

If Mercedes's goodness haunted him, Rachel made him appalled at his weakness. "When I was with her, I'd say to myself, 'How can I unload this girl?'" But whatever his doubts, his flesh gave enough reasons for remaining. "I could have become a drunkard," he maintains when he thinks of what could have happened to him if he had stayed with Rachel. There was an alcoholic haze over their experience. "She was something new in my life. All I thought of before was work and Mercedes."

Rachel and he fought continually. Sometimes their grievances took on surrealistic proportions. Once when Lahr was out of town, Rachel called him and said she was going to commit suicide. There was a gun shot, and the voice on the other end of the phone stopped. Lahr called a friend in New York and asked him to go to Rachel's apartment and see if she was all right. He cautioned the friend about the possible suicide. When the man got to the apartment, he found Rachel passed out on the floor, with a blank-gun lying on the bed.

It is hard to think that my father, a man whose life reflected such singularity of purpose, ever allowed external situations to confuse him. But Mercedes and Rachel and the new child left him numb with uncertainty. "I was all mixed up. Success, disaster—I had everything."

Near the end of the New York run of *Flying High,* in 1931, he returned to Rachel's apartment after a visit to Mercedes. He was late.

When he entered the room, Rachel turned to him sardonically.

"Where were you?"

"I was at the sanitarium."

"With that *bitch* again?"

That word broke the spell. *"Bitch.* How could she call Mercedes a bitch?" In a matter of ten seconds, two years of humiliation were suddenly resolved. "The whole thing with Rachel left me just like that." He snaps his fingers. "Just like that."

SCANDALS AND FOLLIES

I F THE NATION FLOUNDERED IN ECONOMIC CHAOS IN THE EARLY
thirties, Bert Lahr's career was not so precarious. His talent was in
the hands of Florenz Ziegfeld and George White, two producers who
had placed their indelible stamp on musical comedy and whose names
were still golden theatrical currency. The difference between the two
men can be seen in Lahr's reaction to them. He still refers to Ziegfeld
as "Mr. Ziegfeld," while White he casually calls "Georgie." Lahr remembers Ziegfeld as part of theatrical history—a Broadway demigod
who had carved out of lavishness a kind of entertainment to which
every comedian aspired. White, on the other hand, was the renegade—
a dancer who had quit the *Ziegfeld Follies of 1919,* stealing its equivalent of fire—Ann Pennington—to start his own brand of musical revue.
When Ziegfeld wired him to return to the *Follies* after his debut,
offering two thousand dollars a week, White wired back that he would
pay Ziegfeld and Billie Burke three thousand dollars to go into his next
Scandals. With that, their feud was on.

Lahr was impressed by the overwhelming success of the *Scandals.*
White's personal flamboyance and street fighter's arrogance shocked
Lahr into admiration. White was a showman; he had made Lahr a
believer with his overhaul of *Flying High* in Boston. Above all, Lahr
respected White's ability to please an audience and manipulate it to
fullest advantage. "He knew something that Earl Carroll and Ziegfeld
never did. He knew something of comedy sketches. He knew how to
routine a show, where to put a sketch. If you played a jumbo comedy
scene, he'd follow it with a fast number. If you got into a dramatic
sketch, he'd put a love scene in front of it."

When Ziegfeld died on July 22, 1932, White became the un-
challenged king of Broadway. During the remainder of the thirties,
White reigned—a tattered royalty whose appeal would taper off
drastically by the end of the decade. He carved a flossy kind of
immortality for himself, not quite what he wanted, but a memorial
nonetheless. One of his crucial ingredients was the comedian who had
starred in Ziegfeld's last show—Bert Lahr.

Lahr has not forgotten the real beginnings of his association with
White. Deep friendships were as rare for him as they were for the
cantankerous producer, who had only a small coterie of acquaintances.

(Lahr seems amazed at the range of people who took a liking to him— Al Capone, who called Lahr "Ugly," Harold Ross, Samuel Gompers, Will Rogers. As a funny-man and a loner, Lahr posed no threat and had no ambitions outside his craft. He accepted everyone at face value and made no judgments. He moved freely without being part of any particular world.) Occasionally, and much to his astonishment, he made contact with people who remained an enigma to the public. White was one of them. The moment their friendship took root is still vivid in his mind.

"When I did the *Music Hall Varieties* (1933) for George, we opened in Philadelphia in a house that had tremendous capacity, maybe four or five thousand seats. I guess it was an opera house. He'd brought a show in there a year before with Rudy Vallee, who at that time was the biggest thing in the country. He did tremendous business. White thought he could do it again. Well, I looked at that audience out front and there was nobody out there. I was friendly with White and money came easily, then. I could do vaudeville in between seasons and make five thousand dollars. Radio was just beginning too. I said, 'Look, George, you don't have to pay me till you do some business with this show.' He looked at me—he almost had tears in his eyes. 'Ham,' he said, 'no actor's ever done this for me. As long as I live, you'll always have a job.' "

White produced thirteen *Scandals*. He owned each one outright. "A born gambler" is all that Abe Berman can say about his client of over thirty years. "He was Hungarian and gambling was in his blood." White gambled with talent more successfully than he did with horses. He knew the value of songs. George Gershwin, his earliest find, wrote more than forty-five songs for the *Scandals,* including "I'll Build a Stairway to Paradise" and "Somebody Loves Me." White hired him for fifty dollars a week for his 1920 *Scandals* and fired him five years later when Gershwin asked for a raise from his $125 salary. Undaunted, White brought Lew Brown and Buddy DeSylva together. The importance of his gambling instinct is sometimes overlooked even by historians who understand the value of the *Scandals'* music. Robert Baral makes it seem much easier than it was in his discussion of the *Scandals* in his book *Revue:*

> The Scandals probably would have wilted early, if George Gershwin
> and the DeSylva, Brown & Henderson trio hadn't come through
> the door—*but they did,* and these tunesmiths ripped Broadway
> apart with their blockbuster scores.

With Ziegfeld and the Shuberts also competing for revue laurels, White tried to stay one step ahead. He went to Paris yearly, returning with the finest novelty acts. He also had his costumes made there, but not stitched, in order to save U.S. duty. He hustled after American entertainers even harder than he did after the continental acts. If Lahr joined the *Scandals* late in their evolution, he was still in good company—Paul Whiteman, Eugene and Willie Howard, Ethel Merman, Lou Holtz, Harry Richman, Rudy Vallee, W. C. Fields, and Ed Wynn. None of these performers remained close to White except Lahr.

Lahr could overlook White's domineering attitude by keeping in mind the results of his theatrical tyranny. He had observed his friend in more scraps than any other person. "George was a cocky little fellow. He wouldn't take anything from anybody."

To outsiders, everything about the bantamweight producer was odious. Although photographs of him during the 1930's show him as he saw himself—handsome, affluent, chic—the façade hides a labyrinth of confusions. White's indifference to his many enemies and his outspokeness were always a source of amazement to Lahr, who once observed a delicious fistfight between Rudy Vallee and White where star and showman stood toe to toe. Through all the bluff, White managed to get off a feathery jab. Lahr was also present when an exasperated chorus girl, Jessica Pepper, crowned him with the *Scandals'* sheet music.

Despite all the vagaries of working with White, Lahr remained loyal to him. Their contract was a handshake. However, in *George White's Scandals* (1936), Lahr found that White's jealousy and cross purposes could overlook friendship. Lahr and Cliff Edwards headlined the revue along with Vallee and Willie Howard. Edwards and Lahr were good friends; but Edwards, enjoying great success as one of the most popular recording stars of the day, ran into trouble with White when he started dating one of the chorus girls. He was marked for revenge. "When White saw a guy with a pretty girl, he would say, 'Look at that bum with a pretty girl—why can't I have her.' He'd go after every girl in the show, but nobody else was allowed to date them."

When he discovered Edwards's transgression, White called the girl into his office and told her never to date the singer again while she was in the show. The girl, of course, had to tell Edwards when he asked for a date that night. Lahr, who shared a room with him on the road, was present when Edwards received the news.

"Edwards called White on the phone and said to him, 'I'm coming

down there, White. Who the hell do you think you are . . . I'm coming down there and punch you in the nose.' " Lahr laughs at the
thought. "Now you couldn't do that to White, who was a lightweight
you know, but had a lot of guts. So White says, 'You're coming down
here? I'm coming up there.' Edwards began putting on kid gloves.
'This is stupid,' I said, and called White on the phone. 'Look George,
I'm coming down.' White could hardly control himself on the phone
and kept muttering, 'Stay where you are, stay where you are. I'm
coming up there. I'm coming up.' "

Lahr went to White's suite and reminded him that there would be a
lawsuit, that the newspapers would get the story, and it would hurt the
show. White finally calmed down. When Lahr returned to talk to
Edwards, the singer was asleep. "If that was me, I would have been out
of town . . ."

It was not easy to forget White's anger. "He would blush when he
was angry and was at a loss for words." If White couldn't find the words,
he often found ways of expressing his disdain. "He was like an elephant,
he never forgot." He once got back at Vallee when Hollywood did a
movie version of the *Scandals* and the crooner had a scene when he was
momentarily suspended in the air. White kept him off the ground for
nearly an hour during the rehearsal. After the altercation over the
chorus girl, White tried to force Edwards to dress on the top floor of
the theater. When Lahr interceded and allowed Edwards to use his
dressing room instead of making the tiring trek up five flights, White
conceived yet another scheme. "He was unpredictable. The fireman at
our theater came into our dressing room one night cursing like crazy.
'That son-of-a-bitch White just told me if I ever caught you or Edwards
smoking to arrest you.' Now if he pinched me, he wouldn't have a
show, but George didn't care."

Lahr was flattered by White's nickname for him, "Ham." But
after the Edwards incident, Lahr admits trying a new mode of address.
"One day I called him 'God,' but I only did it once."

Occasionally, the dividends of friendship were unfortunate. White
asked Lahr to visit him at his rented penthouse at the Ritz Hotel in
Atlantic City. On one visit Lahr met a lovely redhead. A few weeks
later in New York, the girl came up to him at a nightclub and introduced herself. They left together; and a few days later Lahr contracted
what he euphemistically refers to as a "social disease." White consoled
him, saying, "Why didn't you come to me about it—she gave it to
me, too."

Their other social activities were healthier, but often as coarse. Lahr, who in the early thirties rented a Connecticut home for his son and nurse, invited White for weekends. The group that convened were not performers, but a wealthier crowd that lived on the periphery of entertainment—restaurateurs, agents, theater owners. They were loud and funny and kind. When White made his appearance, he brought a satchel filled with cans of Campbell's soup. It was embarrassing to Lahr, who could tolerate almost all of White's eccentricities. The outspoken producer answered his queries about the soup with a philosophy reflecting his attitudes toward theatrical productions. "Ham, how much do you pay your cook here?" Lahr told him. "Right, well, Campbell's pays their chef fifty thousand dollars to make soup, so why argue with success?"

When Lahr goes back to those times, he can see White dressed for golf, baggy and outrageous in his knickers. He stood only five feet five, but made enough noise on a golf course for ten large men. Golf had become Lahr's major relaxation. He played a sound game with a handicap of one. But when he went around the course with White and an equally eccentric agent, Harry Bestry, his game was understandably off. White took pleasure in baiting Bestry, whose hearing defect often made it hard for him to know where the static was coming from.

White did outrageous things on the golf course, such as cutting holes in his pockets to drop golf balls farther down the fairway than he had driven them, stamping his opponent's ball into the turf so it could not be found, substituting weighted golf balls on the putting green. His pranks reflected his hatred of losing and his fiendish delight in annoying his more serious golfing partners. During such outings, Bestry, who had to do business with White, directed his rancor at Lahr. Once, turning to him as he was teeing up, Bestry screamed, "I'm gonna hit you across the head with this three-wood if you don't quit heckling me." When Bestry turned back to his ball, White was urinating on it.

White's vulgarity, the brashness with which he met all conflicts, kept Lahr close to him. White was unpredictable in real life much the same way that Lahr was on stage. White's outlandishness, the mayhem his little body could create was exciting and irreverent in Lahr's eyes. They were both off the streets of New York; they had both risen to the top of their fields. Lahr appreciated White's gut energy and stubborn perfectionism. Lahr always pictured the young producer with his shirt sleeves rolled up, working with the dancers, grooming his property into a brassy, low-down reflection of himself. White never made a gesture that didn't spark excitement or hatred. Ziegfeld had been different. His humorless nasal twang was always a disappointment; it never excited Lahr like White's bravado. Ziegfeld was cut from a more cosmopolitan mold. He was tasteful and cautious where White was garish and rambunctious. When Lahr worked with Ziegfeld, Broadway's most famous producer was sixty-three and ill. His orders, especially in the last months, often came via a special telephone hook-up from his hotel room to the theater or in those famous ten-page telegrams. He worked with a quieter intensity. Lahr watched him in the painstaking process of dressing his chorus line, sometimes changing a pair of shoes on one chorine because another girl's feet showed off the color better. He too was a perfectionist, but he kept a distance from his performers. He was a formidable entrepreneur whose aloofness made Lahr nervous and unsure.

"Ziegfeld usually didn't like comedians. I think I was one of the few comics he liked." Ziegfeld admired Lahr the first time he saw him perform, at his debut on the Palace stage. In 1932, in the face of a depression and in an urgent attempt to maintain a name and a formula of entertainment begun in 1907, Ziegfeld picked Lahr to star in his last extravaganza, *Hot-Cha!*

Ziegfeld contacted Lahr on the Hollywood set for *Flying High,* where he was making his first motion picture. "I was flattered at the call. I didn't think much of the films then, I was going well on Broadway, so I came East." Ziegfeld offered him the added inducement of $2,250 a week plus a bonus of $250, the biggest salary Lahr had ever earned. To Ziegfeld, who was bidding high to maintain his reputation as a producer, the amount was insignificant. In a frenzied effort to keep the public's taste from changing, Ziegfeld attempted to glut it. Besides Lahr, he hired an astounding array of performers, including Buddy Rogers, Lynn Overman, Eleanor Powell, the DeMarcos, and the sensuous Lupe Velez, who was as popular in pictures as Lahr was on the stage.

Where White controlled his productions by his instincts alone, Ziegfeld, worn down and puzzled by the mediocrity of the script created by Lew Brown, Ray Henderson, and Mark Hellinger, could only turn to Lahr. Lahr cherishes the small moments of intimacy with Ziegfeld. "Did I ever tell you when Ziegfeld called me?" That call, perhaps as pathetic a gesture as Ziegfeld could make in his last years, is still memorable to Lahr. They met at Childs for coffee. "I'm not pleased with the show, Bert. I'm not pleased at all. What do you think we can do to fix it up?" Lahr suggested bringing in new writers to doctor the script, but Brown, Henderson, and Hellinger vetoed the proposal. Ziegfeld was hamstrung.

Ziegfeld's indecisiveness and insecurity made Lahr skeptical. "We opened in Washington, D.C. I wasn't too happy with the show; neither was Mr. Ziegfeld. It wasn't up to the standards of the other things I'd done." Nevertheless, Ziegfeld, like his revues, tried to whistle past the depression. He told the Washington *Times* (February 6, 1932):

> I look upon the Depression primarily as a lack of confidence. One of the songs in *Hot-Cha!* deals with it. "There's just as many flowers, just as many trees." It's all in the people's minds to a great extent. But people have less money and they spend it more carefully . . . There is still a market for a good product and maybe this Brown and Henderson song and Bert Lahr's comedy will help rid the public of fear. That will be worth doing.

In Pittsburgh, Ziegfeld came backstage to Lahr's dressing room after the opening night. "He never said, 'Good show, Bert,' or 'I think we have something.' " He smiled wanly at Lahr and looked around the room. For a moment he focused on Lahr's costume—the epitome of the Ziegfeld opulence—a sequined matador's costume with gold brocade and imported cloth. He fingered the material. ("There was nobody who could dress a show the way Ziegfeld did," Lahr says.) And then, he turned to the valet, saying, "Get a black bag for this outfit so the brocade doesn't tarnish." The show was not first rate and Ziegfeld knew it. In Pittsburgh, he was stricken with influenza, and by the time *Hot-Cha!* reached New York, he had developed pneumonia. Necessity forced him to take a hotel room close to his investment. The night the show opened he was nearly in a coma. George White never attended *Hot-Cha!* or inquired about Ziegfeld's health; by July there would no longer be an impediment to White's claim to the pinnacle of Broadway fame.

Lahr found the comedy scenes in *Hot-Cha!* mediocre. When he tried to improvise, Ziegfeld clamped down on his ad libs, disappointed in the sketches but suspicious of any free-wheeling departures from them. He wanted the leering zany who had pleased so freshly in *Hold Everything* and *Flying High*. Lahr went beyond his trademark responses in his scenes with Lupe Velez. "Working with Lupe was quite an experience. She couldn't laugh. She cackled—like a duck. I'd say

things under my breath to her on the stage and she'd start to cackle."
He imitates a duck and recollects the svelte body of Miss Velez, which
helped launch her film career playing opposite such sultry lovers as
Douglas Fairbanks, Sr. "Lupe never washed. When she'd go to the Mayfair or somewhere she'd just put on a dress. Nothing under it—nothing.
So when I'd be clowning with her on the stage and I'd notice her dirty
hands, I'd say, 'You've got your gloves on again.' It would break her
up." Ziegfeld, who watched his performers like a petulant mother-in-
law, got word of Lahr's joking. One day Lahr called him to inquire
about his health. He and Ziegfeld had a friendly chat. That night Lahr
received a long telegram from the producer, reminding him of his investment and scolding him for taking liberties with the script.

Ziegfeld's name insured a full fifteen-week run on Broadway despite
mixed reviews, but that telegram was indicative of his own misgivings.
"I think he liked me because in Pittsburgh he said, 'Wait for me, Bert,
and we'll drive to the station together . . .' He knew at the finish, that
he'd lost his touch." Even Lahr was not without trepidation. Soon after
Hot-Cha! closed, Lahr asked Jack Pearl to take a ride in his new
Packard. Pearl was commenting on how wonderful it was that both
of them had worked for Ziegfeld. Lahr interrupted him.

"How many weeks did you get out of the *Follies*, Jack?"

"Forty-one."

"I only got fifteen. Do you think Lew Brown tried to mess me up?"

"Don't be silly!"

"Jack—let me ask you this—do you think I've got a future in this
business?"

Pearl began to laugh. "You want me to tell you."

"No," Lahr said. "I don't want to hear."

His next vehicle was *George White's Music Hall Varieties* (1933).
There was nothing "artistic" about Lahr's reason for doing the show.
He had been riding high on Broadway, and despite his most recent tepid success, Broadway liked his brand of low comedy. He was
prepared to serve them the same style as long as audiences responded.
"I had nothing to do at the time. I thought it would be good for my
career to be working with Harry Richman, who was a big star then,
and Lili Damita, who was Errol Flynn's first wife. The show had
George White's name, and it was just to make money." Lahr's conservatism opted for the safe course; left to himself and without external

pressures, his comedy would probably have remained the same through the thirties, and he would have been forgotten by the end of the next decade.

George White, who stuck so closely to his own formulas for entertainment, encouraged his friend to experiment with a more satiric style to add another dimension to his performance. Too shrewd a businessman to demand that Lahr abandon his low-comic business entirely, he would, in the *Music Hall Varieties,* combine that with something untested in Lahr's repertoire—a satire on the popular English matinee idol, Clifton Webb, whose sophisticated and genteel dance routines seemed an unlikely target for Lahr.

Lahr balked at first. "I didn't want to do it because I'd never done anything like it before." But Lahr respected White's instincts. When he was nervous and uncertain about his sketches, White always pacified him with an axiom: "Never worry about a comic on the road; the dancer or singer will always be your hit out of town." White's dictum was well-founded. Lahr always needed practice to smooth his timing and flesh out his impersonations.

The Webb take-off, "Chanson by Clifton Duckfeet," was a stretch for Lahr. He was forced to be elegant instead of bumbling, controlled instead of excessive. In the sketch, Lahr appeared, as Webb did, from behind the curtain at center stage. He was dressed dramatically in tuxedo pants, a white bolero jacket and top hat. A gold watch chain stretched elegantly across his waist. He spoke delicately and lisped in an attempt at the clipped English monotone. When the spotlight discovered him, Lahr was standing, *à la* Webb, with his legs tight together and his hand jammed nonchalantly in his left pocket. He took out a cigarette, and after fingering it, threw it away as he began to sing. His song recounted springtime in Paris and a chance meeting with a Parisienne:

> 'Til midnight we chatted—romantic the scene!
> Adventure? Well, rather—my spirits ran high.
> The French are so friendly—if you know what I mean—

After the first stanza of patter, Lahr went into a delicate soft-shoe, swiveling his hips and emitting delighted gasps at his steps.

> A bottle and a bird . . .

White, in a box to the left of the stage, interrupted the song by giving Lahr the raspberry. Lahr countered, "Duck to you," and continued his tale—

> We were alone, the hour grew late,
> We sipped and sighed and sighed and sipped,
> A rendezvous, a tête à tête,
> For me pajamas—Alice blue,
> For her—negligée—and fetching too.
> I began to feel that "je ne sais quoi,"
> The night was like a symphony,
> And just as I began to unbend
> She said, "How about fifty dollars?"
> And I said, "RIGHT NOW LADY THAT WOULD BE A GOD-SEND!"
>
> And though it may seem absurd,
> It goes to show what can happen—
> from a BOTTLE AND A BIRD!

Lahr strikes Webb's confident pose, but the sound of a Bronx cheer fills the air. He does a disdainful double-take and makes a hasty exit through the center curtain.

In burlesque Lahr's ability to mimic people had been limited to a special socioeconomic class. Since that time, his mobility and range of interests had widened considerably. The *Music Hall Varieties* turned Lahr to other areas of comedy. "White saw that I had the capacity for satire. He thought I could do it, and he made me do other things."

The final, if less revolutionary, concession Lahr made to White's comic instincts was a dog act. "I had liver in my pocket, just like the trainer," my father says, winking. The skit began when he came out in a tuxedo to sing "Trees" by Joyce Kilmer. The liver was around his ankles. As he sang, the dogs rushed out on stage and sniffed around his legs. He continued to sing, kicking at them angrily. At the end of the song, the curtain behind him went up, exposing a fire hydrant. "There was even more liver around the hydrant." The dogs immediately left his legs and turned their attention to the stump. At another point in the evening, Lahr, assuming his burlesque Dutch dialect, to parody the dog trainer's comic introduction, returned to a style and excess as lowdown as any of his burlesque moments. He told the audience: ". . . Also you have to treat them with kindness and liver! And from there is where come the saying, 'Bring 'em back a-liver!' Always I carry in the pocket the best liver what gives. [He shows a piece of liver.] See the liver? Special liver for dogs only [eats the liver] . . ."

Although the *Music Hall Varieties* pushed Lahr briefly into fresh comic terrain, its general formula did not stray too boldly from that of White's previous *Scandals*. Not even an enthusiastic comedy buff like Brooks Atkinson of *The New York Times* could be coaxed to give it precedence over conflicting openings. The *Times* notice underscores the general static quality of the show. While the unsigned reviewer fails to see the significant new area in Lahr's comedy, his response illustrates the still waters that White and many of the famous entertainers were approaching:

> Mr. Lahr does not depart from his fantastic contortions of face or his impossible gutteral mouthings. . . .
> The material which goes to make up (George White's) *Varieties* has been tried and played so many times before that the performers don't need much rehearsal to go through with it.

But Lahr's first stab at satire was noticed immediately by most Broadway writers, and in *Life Begins at 8:40,* the following year, satirical content embellished his comedy. He was at ease with the more sophisticated material. When White contracted him for *George White's Scandals* (1936), it was precisely this urbanity which White had first nurtured that his shows could not, now, create on stage. In the interim between George White revues, Lahr found that he could say more with his pinky than a pratfall. He still took pratfalls, but the nonsense of his burlesque and vaudeville comedy was becoming more refined. He leveled his voice and face at targets foreign to his experience, like the British aristocracy.

The formula of White's *Scandals* allowed for a modicum of satire but not at the expense of spectacle. Satire was a special impulse that required a pace and subtlety the revues could not easily sustain. For White, everything had to be fast, funny, and please with good spirits rather than sophistication, even though the spectacle as Broadway entertainment was rapidly losing its public appeal. Movies could do it better; even radio's fantasy world was more successful than the revue's carnival spirits. White could not see the pressure of the other media on his work. In his urgency he stuck to his formula, while Lahr outgrew it. "If he could have realized that times change and treatments change, I think that White would be just as big today as he was years ago. But he wanted to do the old scenes; he would not change. He had a one-track mind."

Lahr found himself disputing his friend's comic judgment. "When we did the '36 *Scandals* (it was the next to the last one George did), it just wasn't as big as the others. I thought of a comedy scene. I went to the authors. But we wouldn't let White know what we were doing because he would meddle in it now and ruin it." The scene Lahr contrived was called "The Englishman and the Baby." This was an extension of the dry underplaying begun in the *Music Hall Varieties* and matured in *Life Begins at 8:40*. White would have wanted broader burlesque, would have forced his own ideas into the writing. The sketch was finally played; White accepted it, grudgingly, into the show. "It was his own egotism, his own lack of perspective that finally finished White. Things were shifting and he never noticed." Despite the attraction of Eugene and Willie Howard, Rudy Vallee, and Lahr, the revue managed only a modest run of 110 performances.

The sketch Lahr helped to write shows an attempt to remold his comic ground. The laughter is in the idea of Bert Lahr trying to assume the civilized airs of the English landed gentry. His instinct for parody assured him of a surprisingly realistic Oxford accent, but with a slight sibilance, he could take that reality and explode it. "It was an exaggerated Englishman. Everything very clip't, very adenoidal." He flares his nostrils to emphasize the round, hollow tones. His eyes, instead of crossing, become fastidious beads, the fleshy furrows of his forehead rise two inches higher in a formal bow to his nose.

The sketch played on the stereotypes of the English upper-class indifference, adding an American robustness to the image of civilized control. Set in the plush surroundings of a London club, Lord Marleybone (Lahr) and his acquaintance, Lord Tottingham, have a jowly talk about women with an aplomb that glosses their cool amorality.

Tottingham: And what was the matter early this morning? Did you get out of the wrong side of the bed?
Marleybone: Quite the contrary, you old scullery mop. I got out of the right side of the wrong bed.

The men get progressively drunker, gossiping and talking about old affairs.

Tottingham: I was just glancing through the *Times* here—I see where the Duke of Marmalade had to give up his yacht.
Marleybone: I'm not surprised. He told me last time I saw him it would have to be either his yacht or his mistress. He couldn't stand the expense of hauling her up on shore every year and scraping her bottom.

At the finale, Lord Marleybone's wife calls to inform him that she is pregnant. Tottingham, she explains, is the father. Marleybone puts down the receiver, orders a Scotch, and casually dispatches Tottingham. "I'm awfully sorry, and I know you won't mind, but I've got to shoot you."

Once the show found its rhythm, Lahr discovered that he was able to serve the impulses of both raucous and refined laughter. The pressure of refinement had its effect on Lahr's comic instinct. The sketch Lahr suggested to White for the '36 Scandals germinated in an understatement he had discovered painfully in Life Begins at 8:40, in a skit burlesquing those stereotyped English values: family, formality, stoic acceptance (see Appendix 4). In the scene, a much surer stab at class humor than Lahr's imitation, Lahr played the son, Richard, and Brian Donlevy was the father. Lahr enjoyed wrapping his tongue around English sounds—a luxury provided by the spareness of the language. He would learn from the experience; and then set out to find his own form.

Richard:	What is it?
Pater:	Gambling debt.
Richard:	Gambling debt?
Pater:	Can't pay it, broke?
Richard:	Borrow?
Pater:	Can't borrow, no credit.
Richard:	One thing to do.
Pater:	Right. Honor of family.
Richard:	Other way out?
Pater:	Not sporting.
Richard:	Right, stout fellow.
Pater:	Got a bite here.
Richard:	Poison?
Pater:	Right.
	(Butler enters with glass on tray.)
Richard:	Here you are.
Pater:	Thanks. (Pater raises a glass.) Give you the Duchess.
Richard:	How jolly.
	(Pater drinks.)
Richard:	Does it hurt?
Pater:	Rawther.
Richard:	Well, chin up.
Pater:	Chin up.
Richard:	Stiff upper lip.

Pater: Stiff upper lip.
Richard: Honor of family.
Pater: (prone) Honor of family. Cheerio, my boy. (Head drops.)
Richard: Cheerio, Pater. (Glances at watch.) Must dress.

The transition to new comic terrain in *Life Begins at 8:40* was eased for Lahr by the buoyant, tasteful overseeing of John Murray Anderson, an energetic Broadway director. Lahr speaks of Anderson with words he rarely uses for directors. "He had tremendous taste." Anderson's kindness and confidence helped Lahr control his material. The director had nicknames for everyone in the show. Harburg was "Zipper" (as opposed to his usual "Yipper"), Ira Gershwin was "Rock of Gibraltar," Arlen was "Old Man River," and his wife, Anya, was "Schmanda Fair." "I used to call him 'Punch,' " recalls Lahr, "because he had a chin like the Punch and Judy shows." Anderson referred to his clown as "Euripides."

The combination of the fine performers and inventive score had created great excitement on Broadway, and one of the wittiest sketches, "C'est La Vie," had originated on a Lahr impulse. "I said to Yip, I'd love to do something with an Inverness cape. It gave him the idea for his song and sketch on the bridge. Being known as a low comedian to do something that was directly opposite made it funny. It's the same thing I gave Jimmy Durante for his nightclub act. I said, 'Jimmy, why don't you come out in your act with a toupee under your hat. Just take your hat off, and say, "You can't fool your friends." ' He's kept it in ever since." In the Harburg sketch, Lahr and Ray Bolger are found staring gloomily into the Seine from one of the picturesque Paris bridges. As they chat, both realize they have been jilted by the same girl. They decide to end it all and leap into the Seine. Suddenly, there is a screech of brakes and their goddess (Luella Gear) enters.

Luella: Pierre. Jacques. What is it that you do. But non. You must not do it.
Both men: You do not love me. You do not love him.
Luella: You do not understand. I tell you I do not love you because I love you each so much and if I tell one, I hurt the other. But wait. I have a solution. Tonight before I get your terrible note I am in zeee cinema. I see la talkie "Design for Living."
Bolger: Ah, yes, it is by Noel Coward, non?
Luella: But yes.

Lahr: It is where the woman and the two men love each other and
the other each?

Luella: (smiling warmly) But yes. And they live happily together
after, for evermore. And I think to myself—Pierre, Jacques,
me, why not we so?
(Pleased with the idea, they all embrace. The men lift
Luella Gear onto the wall of the bridge and harmonize—
Lahr and Bolger begin a soft-shoe and sing—)

> Life is gay, we agree*
> When a heart it is big enough for three.
> Night and day, ma cherie,
> Me for you, and you and you for me.
> We're living in the smart upper sets,
> Let other lovers sing their duets.
> Duets are made by the bourgeoisie—oh,
> But only God can make a trio.

(With that, they dance again as Luella Gear laughs at their
romantic antics. As they glide past her, they push her off
the bridge.)
(*Blackout*)

Brooks Atkinson's reaction to Lahr's comedy in *Life Begins at 8:40*
is a sound barometer of the public's understanding of his development.
Atkinson, whose subtlest criticism focuses on comedy and clowns, was
reporting the beginning of a change he would analyze more critically
in *The Show Is On* (1936). In 1934, new dimensions in Lahr's comic
personality were emerging.

When he [Lahr] turned up in "Hold Everything" and a crimson
edition of the "Scandals" several years ago, he roared, and pranced
and mugged like a demented elephant. He is a low comedian. Most
of the material in "Life Begins at 8:40" is too subtle in *manner*
to release his native exuberance. Having more than one stop to his
instrument of comedy, he does remarkably well with what he has.

The uniqueness of *Life Begins at 8:40* as a revue and the new content added to Lahr's comic façade were in large part due to the songs
and sketches of E. Y. Harburg and Harold Arlen. At a time when Lahr
was groping for a laughter to match the times, Arlen and Harburg appeared—with an appreciation of his comedy and a genius of their own.

* © 1969 by New World Music Corp. All rights reserved.

Arlen and Harburg provided Lahr with some of his finest comic strategies. In his voice, they saw a wonderful opportunity to satirize the romantic and operatic stage clichés. Since they appreciated Lahr's theatrical acrobatics and his wit, Lahr's grimaces and grunts neatly punctuated their comedy songs. In *Life Begins at 8:40*, the lyrics by Ira Gershwin and Harburg managed to give verbal terms to the buffoon's self-deception and even capture the fundamental business of Lahr's leering good spirits. "I could say so many things through Bert's voice that I couldn't with my own," says Harburg, who saw Lahr in a completely different light from the songwriting company who had precipitated his stardom. "When DeSylva, Brown, and Henderson were writing for him, they saw Bert as the low-down comic, the average 'gnong-gnong' guy. He was the patsy; and implicit in that was the attitude of a semi-idiotic guy who always gets things wrong. I understood Lahr in a different way. In his comedy and personality I saw the little man; the pathos of a human being who is stuck with his society, who is put upon and exploited by it. His laughter is the laughter of a poor humanity, a sorry little guy who happens to be born looking like a comic and therefore everyone reacts to him not as if he were a human being, but simply a joker. All his reactions are those of a man society doesn't accept, but laughs at."

For Harold Arlen, the show was an important one, and Lahr helped him make a point to the Broadway world. The man whose rich and original music has produced "I've Got the World on a String," "Stormy Weather," "Let's Fall in Love," "Come Rain or Come Shine," and "It's Only a Paper Moon" wanted to write comedy with the inventiveness he had already exhibited with the blues. "This show [*Life Begins at 8:40*] really meant something," Arlen says. "I wanted to set sail into Broadway. I wanted people in the profession to know that I could write things they didn't expect of me."

They lavished attention on Lahr's comedy, finding just the right song for his stage personality. They came up with a take-off on a Metropolitan Opera baritone, singing a beautifully inarticulate song, entitled "Things." It was to be sung straight with no emotion and certainly no delicate phrasing. When Arlen thinks of the song, he cannot help smiling at the idea of Lahr standing regally in front of a Steinway, his hand resting pompously on it. "Anything he sings becomes absolutely asinine."

When Lahr sang in burlesque and even in the early Broadway productions, his wild, truculent movements were more important than his mangling of the lyrics. The humor in his rendition of "Peggy O'Neill," for instance, was its unabashed inarticulateness. With the Arlen–Harburg songs, the situation was reversed. The laughter came from his attempt at being coherent. In *Life Begins at 8:40,* Lahr was able to take advantage of the inconclusive lyrics and stiff operatic pose, joining the low comic bits of business with his monotone vibrato. The song was high parody. As Arlen recalls, "He fussed and fumed and was frustrated, and extemporized to get gimmicks into 'Things'—for instance, his toupee falling a certain way. It was an endless game for him, until he finally got as many laughs as possible out of it."

Lahr came on stage in a tuxedo and sporting a brown hairpiece that brought his hairline, like a dorsal fin, to an abrupt point on his forehead. A piano player sat beside him, elegantly poised for the recital. Lahr turned graciously to the small audience on the stage and began:

> Ladies and Gentlemen, the first number of my second group was written in a little garret on the left bank of Giaconda Canal and is entitled "Things," simply "Things."

Before he begins, Lahr's pinky shoots up to his tooth. He vibrates his finger like a tuning fork in the side of his mouth. He signals the piano player and smiles widely at the audience. His lips curl under, exposing an expanse of salmon-colored gums. His teeth are straight and clenched tight as if he were holding on to some terrible truth.

> When I was but a little lad*
> I used to think of things
> The only joy I ever had
> I had because of things.
> But now that I'm to manhood grown,
> Fond memory always brings
> The utter, utter, utter
> Loveliness of things.

His voice quavers with profound feeling at the word "things." His hand is outstretched in emphatic declamation. "Things . . ." Suddenly, the wig falls down over his eyes. He pushes it back quickly in exasperation. The readjustment is unsuccessful. The toupee sits like a sparrow's nest on his head. He continues nervously:

> Let others sing of Mandalay
> Let others sing of trees,
> Let others sing of mother,

And the busy, busy beeeeezzz . . .
But I'm happier far than a million kings are
When my soul sings of things.
Things, sweet happiness of things.
Things that ease the rocky way,
Things that look at God all day,
Things, sweet misery of things.
From birth bed to the grave,
Aren't we all to them a slave
What makes all the ocean wave
Things (ah, ah), things (ah, ah, ah) . . .

The piano player, carried away by Lahr's own emotional improvisations, embarks on an elaborate solo. Lahr scowls at the pianist as if to say, "I'm the artist."

When the frost is on the punkin',
And the sun in the west is sinkin',
Can't you hear those paddles chunkin' . . .

His wig rebels again, falling completely over his face. His hands grope in front of his nose trying to locate the hair that has covered his eyes. He finally gets hold of it and tries to smooth it in place. He tries the last line again. The pianist forgets again and goes into a strenuous solo. Lahr picks his teeth delicately and waits for the conclusion.

Lickity split and to beddy for things
Fit as a fiddle and ready for things . . .

When he says "ready," he winks at a woman in the front row of the stage audience.

You can have your smoke pipe rings,
Your Saratoga Springs,
But give me . . .

The trombonist in the pit hits a long note, so that he cannot finish the line. He turns and glares down at him. "Why don't you use a bellows!" After the statement, he forgets his lyric and looks helplessly at the accompanist, "Where the hell . . ." The piano player goes back to "smoke pipe rings." Lahr counters angrily, "I *did* that!"

You can have your smoke pipe rings,
And your Saratoga Springs,
But give me . . .

This time the violinist plays off key. Lahr yells down to the orchestra, "You must have a bad gut!"

Give me . . .

The saxophone drones on again. Lahr, finally determined to finish the song despite the outrages of the orchestra, throws his hands up in despair, "Oh, go home!" And in a crescendo of baritone lyricism, he finishes emphatically,

Give me *things!!*

The woman on stage at whom he has winked and directed his suave innuendoes rises at the sound of the last tremulous note and hits him in the face with a pie. (Blackout)

"I always wanted to do 'Things' so that when the baritone came out on stage his fly was open. The accompanist keeps pointing to it, and when he turns around to zip himself, his shirttail is out. But I never got to do that." When John Charles Thomas, one of America's most famous baritones and a friend of Lahr's, came to the show, the parody took him by surprise. "I remember he laughed so hard that he got up out of his seat and left the theater. As he stood up, I could see him laughing. He yelled up to me, 'You son-of-a-bitch' and left."

"I thought up the pie-in-the-face," says Lahr, as if that touch were some cultural refinement. The pie was a good indication that Lahr's burlesque instincts were not eroded by his new image; but by underplaying them, the elements of surprise and shock were even greater. Both Arlen and Harburg conceived their songs for Lahr with a mental picture of his face, in the same way that Herbert Berghof would keep photos of Lahr pasted in his script of *Waiting for Godot* many years later. They knew instinctively the possibilities for his voice; but, more important, they understood the philosophy behind Lahr's clowning. Arlen, a modest man, maintains that "no one could write for him better than E. Y. and myself." Many outstanding writers created material with Lahr in mind—S. J. Perelman, Abe Burrows, George S. Kaufman, William Saroyan—but none came as close to his buffoonery as Harburg and Arlen did. And although the Arlen–Harburg collaboration would not go beyond 1939, their special material for Broadway and *The Wizard of Oz* remained Lahr's trademark.

Even in satire, Lahr's humor found its way back to basic, physical situations. When the Arlen–Harburg lyrics were aiming their verbal dexterity at a serious idea, they used Lahr's foolery to give the songs the comic resonance that their intellectual sleights of hand lacked. In *Life Begins at 8:40*, this combination was most effectively used in "Quartet Erotica," in which four famous writers bemoan their decline in popularity. Originally subtitled "Rabelais, Balzac, de Maupassant, Boccaccio," the alignment was switched so that Lahr, as Balzac, was at the low comic end of the list. Donlevy was the stylish de Maupassant, Ray Bolger the gay Boccaccio, and James MacColl played Rabelais. When Lahr mugged at the audience and announced his *nom de plume* the emphasis was always on the first syllable. "I was really saying 'Balls,' so I'd say BALLSac." His eyes gleam at the idea of saying "balls" to any audience. The song is an interesting contrast to the hokey, curiously passé material Lahr used the following year in *George White's Scandals* (1936).

> We once won all the glories*
> For writing dirty stories;
> Sophisticated people thought our bawdiness immense.
> We stopped all the traffic
> With stories pornographic—
> But we can see the handwriting on the fence.
> > *Refrain*
> Rabelais, de Maupassant, Boccaccio, and Balzac—
> Once we were quite the lads:
> We thought that our erotica
> Was very, very hotica—
> But now we're only four unsullied Galahads.
> Rabelais, de Maupassant, Boccaccio, and Balzac
> Babes in the wood are we.
> The dirt we used to dish up
> Sad to say
> Wouldn't shock a bishop
> Of today;
> A volume like "Ulysses"
> Makes us look like four big sissies—
> Rabelais, de Maupassant, Boccaccio, and Balzac—
> Lost all our TNT.
> We're not what we used to be.

In the early thirties, the performing moments were more vivid than the private ones. Lahr's son, Herbert, was already showing the scars of growing up without a mother and with a father who could not handle him. Lahr tried. He was responsible in financial matters, but Herbert's face brought back his guilt. There was a Greenwich summer house for Herbert, a good school, fine clothes. But when he confronted his son, the boy seemed unruly and unpredictable. His son would imitate him not only in his voice but also in his gestures. When Lahr brought him to the theater, Herbert invariably would get himself involved in ludicrous escapades. He entered the girls' dressing room in *Life Begins at 8:40,* shut the door behind him, and then, knocking on the closed door, asked, "Are you proper?" Some of them were not.

Lahr could give nothing from his heart to his young son. In the same way, no one really shared Lahr's successes in those restless years, although two women tried. The marital pattern that seemed to be part of Lahr's material on stage was much easier over the footlights than away from them.

Mercedes tried to follow her husband's activities. Sitting stonelike in her room, she kept stacks of the *Daily News* by her bedside. In the spring of 1932, she was allowed to leave the sanitarium for a day to see *Hot-Cha!*

. . . She went to see her husband's show at the Ziegfeld Theater. After coming home she made little comment except to say "Buddy Rogers is a hot number."

Lahr meant to see her, but the memory of her lithe figure swollen now to nearly 170 pounds and the sudden stupor of her eyes kept him away. The doctors' reports verify the problem:

Mrs. Lahrheim has anticipated a visit from her husband for the past one week. He had just returned from Hollywood [*Flying High*] and had been telephoning her, but for some reason or other has not *ventured to call on her.* . . .

. . . She very often meets relatives, including her baby, indifferently and this disconcerts them. The more they prod her, the more stubborn she appears. She looks blankly into space, as if in a trance. When permitted, she wears old clothes and accumulates things. . . .

. . . Husband says he calls her frequently on the phone but cannot see her because it is too upsetting. He wants her to be allowed to go to the movies or have any clothes or comforts within reason. . . .

. . . The patient was visited by her husband today, and was much relieved when she was told that she was comfortable, happy, and *more free from worry than he.*

. . . She is inclined to answer most questions with a nod or interpretive facial expression. She says, "It is hard to get hold of Bert these days, he is so busy; he said he wanted me to stay here for a couple of weeks more."

"When she was in the hospital, I did the best I . . ." Lahr stops, weighed down by an anxiety he can never verbalize. "I was reaching for something. She was confused. She was sick—mentally sick. There was nothing you could do about it. Later on, you'd censure yourself, but. . ." Even talking of himself in the second person cannot put Mercedes at a safe distance.

What made it doubly difficult for Lahr to respond to Mercedes was the companionship that had developed between himself and the quiet, moon-faced blonde whom everyone called "Mil." Lahr met her soon after Mercedes had been committed. He saw her first in *George White's Scandals* (1931). At that time, he had asked to meet her. Although nothing was arranged, White did not forget Lahr's request.

Four months later, Lahr formally met Mildred Schroeder at a cocktail party given by White at his penthouse apartment at the Warwick in 1931. The chorus girls usually came alone, because White wanted them to be a decoration to his party, although he loathed the thought of them having any permanent attachment to his friends.

White liked Mildred. She was straightforward and simple. She combined a good-natured innocence with a well-scrubbed exterior. Once, they met accidentally in a bank where she was depositing her week's wages. White affected to be so impressed by this level-headedness that he matched the sum. Only twenty-six years old, Mildred was gullible, sincere, and parochial. She had been educated in a convent in Cincinnati and came to New York on a wave of confidence inspired by a long skein of first prizes in beauty contests. Sometimes when she felt insecure around the supersophisticates at parties like White's she would take a small clipping from her pocketbook and read it to herself:

> Miss Schroeder has, in less than two years in Greater Cincinnati beauty shows, won eight firsts and three seconds, a record which is said to be unequalled in this section. . . .

In her first Broadway show, *Fine and Dandy,* the brashness of the actresses shocked her. Dave Chasen, who gave up a successful career as a comedian to open a restaurant that made him world famous, remembers befriending her after finding her crying on the backstage steps. "Those girls could really push you around. I just wasn't used to those aggressive types. I wasn't brought up that way."

When Lahr met her at White's party, he was immediately attracted to her. She was not like the others there. She was nervous, twisting a lace handkerchief and smiling too easily at what he said. She was one of the most beautiful girls in the room, but one of the least polished. Her sincerity and shyness made her seem surprisingly old-fashioned.

Her features were stunning—a full, languid mouth, sharp, laughing eyes, and a body that was supple and energetic. Her voice was at once sweet and vibrant. Secretly, she only vaguely wanted the career that could so easily have been hers. A product of a broken, emotionally impoverished family, she longed for the kind of red-brick security that no actor could give. In fact, entertainers or anyone on the periphery of show business were not the people to whose company she aspired. Lahr was the first actor she had ever considered dating after two years on Broadway. "I never believed in marrying an actor. I thought that one should marry a businessman. I found Bert so different from my picture of an actor. He was a shy person, and that, I think, attracted me. I think he gave me his number, and I think I called him."

On their first date the contrast between Mildred and the other woman Lahr had been seeing was apparent to him. Mildred wore a long white pleated Grecian dress, with a small pillbox hat. It was her lucky outfit. They went to the Mayfair Club. As she sat talking with Lahr, Rachel M., whom Lahr had not seen since walking out on her six months before, approached their table. She was drunk.

"Got another bitch, Bert? Another easy trick like me?"

She spat on his dinner jacket. Mildred rushed from the table. Lahr followed her out in the street and tried to explain. They finished the evening at another nightclub. "From then on, he was never away from me." Lahr had found a companion.

Mildred, who believed in holding "good thoughts," who liked long walks and dancing, enjoyed looking nice and being a fine hostess, was a change for Lahr. She was a girl whose gaiety could be tapped at any moment, whose physical resources of energy were as deep as her will power. She was affectionate without being vulgar and warm without being scheming. She gave Lahr what no other woman had ever offered him—her complete devotion.

From the beginning, there was no question of competition. To Mildred, the bumbling clown was a "gentleman," a kind, soft, strange person who was in trouble. She did not stop to analyze him or understand his complexities. But faced with an emotional rapport she could not deny, Mildred accepted Lahr—his genius and his obsession. She liked the idea of being able to contribute something besides her good looks. She was a kind of straightman—a stable center around which he could radiate. "He hasn't ever been funny with me. I don't think he's ever said any great things to me, either."

Mildred was always there, after each performance, after the endless thirty-six-hole golf days, after the sad trips to see Mercedes. It was more than love that compelled her to stay with him. He was kind to her, but not thoughtful; gentle, but not spontaneous; loving, but strangely set apart.

Neither of them can remember any soft, romantic moments and only a rare present. What is recalled is the onus of worry that hung over Lahr and the kindness with which Mildred dealt with his continual "problems." Inconspicuously, she handled his fan mail, paid bills he left unopened on his desk, and listened quietly while he explained new laugh lines or pondered what the next season would bring. She persuaded him to visit Mercedes more often and urged him to take more of an interest in his son. When she first met Herbert, he threw a bottle at her. But, as with everything else, she persisted. She was the mother, the organizer, the mirror for all ideas. In a short time, Lahr began to have a confidence in her that he had never felt with a woman before. He respected her taste in clothes and liked the way she dressed. Occasionally, she would help him pick out a suit or a tie—a gesture of real affection to a man so conscious of appearances. His friends responded better to Mildred than they did, sometimes, to him. She was thoughtful and kind, never boisterous in public, always good-spirited. She asked few questions, satisfied to be a part of an undeniable and difficult genius.

Ziegfeld had asked her to join the Ziegfeld chorus line for *Hot-Cha!*, but an attack of appendicitis kept her from signing with the producer and complications left her bedridden for several months. Lahr, who always regarded hospitals the way most Americans regard black cats, visited her daily. "He was very kind to me when I was sick. He came to see me every day, and he'd bring flowers or something." That surprising attention was a debt of the heart that Mildred wanted to repay. She longed for the softness and understanding her own home life had lacked. In this comedian she saw a hint of it.

Mildred was healthy enough to make the trip to Washington, where

Hot-Cha!'s opening was front-page news. Her exuberance about being with Lahr was hard for her to conceal. She had never dated any other actor, so the public approval of Lahr's ability and his fantastic success filled her with apple-pie wonder. In a wire to her mother, the excitement of the experience is reflected in her overstatement. The trip to Washington sounds more like the final chapter in the Lewis and Clark journals:

FEBRUARY 16, 1932

MOTHER DARLING AT LAST I GAZED ON THE CAPITOL STOP WASHINGTON IS A BEAUTIFUL PLACE STOP CAME ON HERE FOR BERT'S OPENING IT WAS THE BIGGEST HIT EVER KNOWN IN ZIEGFELD'S LAST TEN SHOWS STOP I HAD A LOVELY BIRTHDAY WILL WRITE SOON.

Sometimes, Mildred's openness had its childish moments. Lahr's genuine affection for the eccentricities of Lupe Velez vexed her. Her unabashed sensuality made Mildred jealous. Once, after she and Lahr had passed hastily through a revolving door to greet Miss Velez, Mildred fell into a "faint." Lahr was by her side immediately and never realized that Lupe had been upstaged.

They had an easy relationship, but there were small fits of possessiveness from Bert that showed her that she was strictly his property. Once in Bimini, while dining on Harry Richman's yacht, a burly, bearded man made conspicuous overtures. "They were overtures—not exactly a pass, but an overture." Lahr was annoyed enough to speak up to the man who, somewhat embarrassed, introduced himself as Ernest Hemingway. In 1934, Sam Goldwyn, casting his film version of the *Ziegfeld Follies,* asked Mildred and her showgirl friend, Lucille Ball, to come to Hollywood to be in the picture. To her surprise, Lahr begged her to stay in the East. She remained willingly. "I think I could have made it in movies, so many of the girls who were with me like Lucy and Alice Faye did well out there." But at a moment crucial to her career, she stayed with Lahr.

Her allegiance had its rewards. She worked with Lahr on radio and did a few one-reelers with him that even now can be seen on old-time movie cavalcades. When he did vaudeville in the off season, she played the "other woman" (Marie) in his cop act, and was even in the chorus of *Life Begins at 8:40.* Between the work and a continual round of café society at Billy La Hiff's, the Stork Club, the Mayfair—memories filter down to long, gay evenings of talk and drinking—these were happy and, for her, anxious times.

Mildred, the girl who made Lahr wait before going out to dinner while Bing Crosby sang "A Penthouse for Two" on the radio, wanted a family and the kind of soft romance that Crosby's crooning implied. She asked Lahr about marriage. In her curious, unreflective way, she never expected that a divorce or annulment of his marriage was anything that could not be handled in a few days with the lawyers. "I was tired of being Bert Lahr's girl, I didn't want to have that label on me. I'd been brought up better than that."

Lahr tried to explain to her that it was legal to file for an annulment only after Mercedes had been in a mental institution for five years. This was true, but Mildred seems to have disregarded it and seen Lahr's explanation as a decoy. "I thought he was scared of getting married again." Her statement may have some validity, although Lahr denies it now. In any case, the problem was conveniently out of his hands, at least until the end of 1936.

Just before Lahr went into rehearsals for *George White's Scandals* (1936), Mildred came to him with an ultimatum. "I told him that unless he did something to make it possible for us to get married within a certain time—I think six weeks—I was going to date other men. I was pretty, I'd given him four good years, and I expected his intentions to be honorable."

"I thought she was kidding" is all that Lahr can recall about his reaction. Mildred's legal adviser had informed her that he would never be able to get a divorce or annulment on the grounds of insanity in New York State. This was true to the extent that there was no precedent up to that time. The six weeks came; nothing was resolved. "He *said* he was trying" is all that Mildred will say. She felt that where there was a will there was also a way.

In late January, while Lahr was in Pittsburgh with the *Scandals* and Mildred was in a show on Broadway, she had one of her friends arrange a date for her. Within days Mildred found herself deliriously in love with love. After six weeks of courtship, she and the man were discussing marriage.

Mildred saw Lahr often. He was upset, but not disconsolate, about the situation. Once she found him standing in front of the Barbizon-Plaza, where she was staying, waiting to catch a glimpse of the man.

Lahr did not need any more complications, especially not from the woman who had salvaged some of his peace of mind and happiness. He had showed his love with signs she could not read, involving her in his act, giving her a small diamond ring, the very same kind (perhaps more expensive) that he had saved for so long to buy Mercedes.

On March 28, a wire came to his hotel. There was nothing for the imagination to misinterpret:

IT SEEMS THAT OUR FATE IS NOT IN OUR HANDS WAS MARRIED TODAY SATURDAY TO MR JOSEPH ROBINSON ATTORNEY WE ARE ABOUT TO SET SAIL ON OUR HONEYMOON SOON WILL BE AT SEA AND BERT I LOVE YOU AND HAVE A GREAT ADMIRATION FOR YOU AS ONE MIGHT HAVE FOR A FATHER NOT A HUSBAND SO ON THE SPUR OF THE MOMENT DECIDED TO GET MARRIED THOUGHT IT BEST FOR ALL CONCERNED BERT DARLING TAKE IT LIKE A MAN I KNOW YOU WILL I AM TAKING YOU AT YOUR WORD I TRUST WE SHALL ALWAYS BE FRIENDS KINDEST REGARDS AND VERY BEST WISHES SINCERELY

MILDRED

He reached for the phone. He wanted to call his lawyer, Abe Berman. But then he put it back on the stand. He was crying too hard to talk.

BUFFOONERIES

If love . . . is a function of man's sadness, friendship is a function of his cowardice; and if neither can be realised because of the impenetrability of all that is not "cosa mentale," at least the failure to possess may have the nobility of that which is tragic, whereas the attempt to communicate where no communication is possible is merely a simian vulgarity, or horribly comic, like the madness that holds a conversation with the furniture.

Samuel Beckett, Proust

"ALL I CAN TELL YOU IS THAT IT WASN'T PLEASANT. I CAN'T REMEMBER much about the telegram except that it said something about 'take it like a man.' Let's just forget about that period of my life, O.K.?" Lahr wants to rearrange his life as if he were plotting a sketch, but the pieces do not fall together comfortably. His previous refusals to permit his biography to be written center on these humiliations of the heart.

"Sure I was hurt. It was a terrible thing, but I never missed a performance. It wasn't the end of the world." He has forgotten his frenzy. His acquaintances were not as easily fooled.

Because his sweetheart of many years ran away to Miami and married another guy, friends of one of the most famous comedians are watching him day and night. . . . sort of a spy system to see that he doesn't commit suicide. . . . before the gal skipped away she pleaded with the comedian to divorce his wife who had been seriously ill for a long time . . . and marry her. . . . He informed the gal that it was impossible to get a divorce in New York State. That it would ruin him, anyway under existing conditions. The actor was with a party of friends in a Broadway club when the news came in of Paul McCullough killing himself. . . . All said it was a pity, a tragedy. . . . All but the comedian, who sitting like a ghost, knowing his sweetheart was getting married (*but no one else knew*) spoke up and said, "Why shouldn't a man kill himself when he has nothing to live for? . . . I think McCullough was right!" McCullough too had lost a girl of whom he was exceedingly fond. When the story broke about the Miami marriage, the club gang remembered the comedian, as they knew his sweetheart well, and what she meant to him and how he worshipped her. . . . So now the gang never lets the broken-hearted man alone. . . . They are afraid of him following McCullough's example.

Bill Farnsworth, *Journal American,* 1936

"I was terribly upset, it was trouble on top of trouble. Naturally, if it happened now and I was older, I could cope with things. But I was inexperienced with women. I guess I acted irrationally. But men kill for love. It's with you all the time." Lahr was, in fact, forty, and had lived with two women for half of those years. Off stage, life caught him by surprise; it refused to be dismissed with the robust gaiety that scored so well on stage. "You don't sleep. You wake up in the morning and the walls close in on you. You walk and walk . . . I suffered. I anticipated marrying Mildred, but she didn't believe me."

A letter to A. L. Berman dated January 5, 1936, from the clinical director of the sanitarium, indicates that Lahr inquired about a divorce at least two months before Mildred's marriage. Lahr knew about the letter. It would have helped his cause with Mildred, but he hadn't shown it to her. Muddled by Mercedes's plight and a life that had suddenly become intolerably complicated, he remained silent.

The letter makes it clear that Lahr could never expect a recovery.

Her [Mercedes's] reaction, which I append will show you what Mrs. Lahr's thoughts are about her future. . . .

"I'll see that the child [her son] is taken care of properly. *I intend to live with Bert Lahr.* That is the only thing to do. He'll have to stand for it. I am going back to show business. I can't be without money. You know that. If I can't get it, nobody else will. Maybe I'll go in a play. I have a couple of thousand dollars worth of paraphernalia. Sure I have. My boy isn't being brought up properly. I don't like his appearance."

. . . For your information, I would like to explain to you that Mrs. Lahr has a defective memory for important events and dates in her life; she is unable to give even a brief account of her early childhood, career on the stage and her married life. Because of her inability to cooperate and to maintain a conversation, she could not possibly appear at a social or public gathering without causing comment and embarrassment. She is unfit to care for her son, and she must be forced to bathe herself properly and to take walks.

On April 7, Mildred returned from her honeymoon nervous and distraught over the rumors she had heard about Lahr's reaction to the marriage. She was confused by the ambiguity of her emotions and the silence at her return. Lahr knew of her arrival, but he would not phone her; he had made a decision and a difficult adjustment. "She was married. It was all over. I tried to make the best of it." But Mildred could not erase the previous four years. "I called him up. They said he was pretty sick, carrying a big torch for me. After all, we'd gone with each other for so many years. I was so confused. I didn't know whether I was right or wrong marrying Robby. I discovered I loved them both." A woman who longed for the affection denied her in childhood, Mildred could not give up her sentimental memories of Lahr or bear the thought of his pain. His voice on the phone was still wounded and sadly humorous. She knew he was drinking, walking aimlessly until sunrise. She knew he was taking friends by Mildred's new apartment, passing back and forth across the street and pointing to the window.

At their first meeting, a pavane of silence and tears, Mildred had no answer for his simple question of "Why?" She needed his friendship as much as the love that filtered through his anger. "I said, 'Why didn't you tell me?' She said, 'I didn't want to hurt you.' She hurt me more. I told her, 'If you'd been frank and come out with it, I wouldn't have felt so badly as this.' I was broken up. I couldn't work well."

In the months that followed Lahr and Mildred spoke on the phone and met occasionally in frustrated urgency. Mildred raised the possibility of divorcing Robinson. Lahr was stunned and humiliated. He loved Mildred, but after this torment he wondered whether he could ever care again. "I kept thinking 'Why should this happen to me at the height of my career?' I was full of self-pity." He could see no possibility for divorce if there were no grounds for it. Willingly at first to try and get over Mildred's sudden marriage, Lahr was ushered back into the drama of indecision. If Mildred wanted a divorce, he loved her enough to pay the costs, but his own conservatism winced at the ugliness of the whole proceedings. Frantic and lonely, he followed any advice that promised the possibility of resolution. His concern led him to one of his cabaret acquaintances—a detective named R. C. Schindler —who knew that marriages were not always made in heaven or dissolved by death, and who set out to find some evidence that would compromise Robinson. "You don't think when you're in that state of mind. I didn't know what I was doing. I just knew I was hurt and wanted to resolve this thing once and for all."

Whatever evil Lahr read into Robinson's character could not be validated in his private history. According to Robinson's subsequent appellant's brief, a friend of Lahr's approached him about the possibility of a "collusive divorce." Robinson flatly rejected the suggestion. Lahr cannot remember the incident; as with much of his life with Mercedes, he has blocked these painful months from his memory. Loving Mildred yet fearing involvement, committed to recovering his emotional equilibrium as well as his loved one, Lahr continued to call Mildred, lavishing husbandly attention on her. Mildred found New York suddenly bleak; it was not merely less ebullient than it had been with Lahr, it was actually hostile. His friends stopped calling or looked nervously away when she met them on the street. She felt alone, and worse, to a woman who longed for the safety of embrace, the object of deep antagonism. Her predicament was compounded by passion; Lahr's hurt was transformed into a frenzied desire to regain the only woman who had been able to order his life.

On July 10, 1936—four months after his marriage, Robinson made legal headlines as the attorney who won a $35,000 love-theft settlement for a cuckolded Florida socialite. Speaking after the trial, Robinson told the press:

> This verdict indicates to me that society still places a premium on the sacredness of the marriage union and the sanctity of the home and that here in Florida the rights of residents of other states are respected and persons who violate those rights are punished.
>
> It is against the laws of God and man for a third person to interfere with the marriage status and I hope this verdict will serve as a deterrent to other persons who fail to respect the holy state of matrimony.

Nearly a month after the legal victory, Robinson enclosed this press clipping with a warning in a letter to Lahr. Either Lahr would desist or Robinson would bring suit against him.

Mildred's indecisiveness and the sudden threat of legal action petrified Lahr. His immediate reaction was to bolt from the scene. With the *Scandals* already closed (it ran only 110 performances), there was only a blank space of time in front of him, time to think of his loss and a hazardous future. Everything in New York held a memory of Mildred, and the press was making good copy out of his jilting. He decided to set sail for London with White and movie director Gregory Ratoff. If he was going into isolation, he wanted good company.

They sailed on the *Paris,* a nine-day voyage that Lahr hoped would clear his head and soothe his sullen disposition. White took charge of his rehabilitation the minute the trio were on board. He demanded forty dollars from each of them, and immediately sent it down to the cook with a note of greeting. The steward got fifty dollars before the boat was out of New York harbor. Until the docking in Southampton, Lahr lived in luxury beyond even his most fantastic daydreams. For a man who was taking the sea air as heart balm, his memories are more vivid about his stomach. "I never ate so well in my life. A five-pound can of caviar on the table every day. You never saw such food. When we ordered desserts they would come in a swan—iced. We'd phone down ahead of time to order meals —*boeuf bourguignon*, steaks, *pâté de foie gras, coq au vin*—it was the best food I ever ate."

"I must have walked half way to London on that ship, but I had to force myself to have fun."

Gregory Ratoff was a small, portly man whose size and thick Russian accent made him a kindly focus of Lahr's pranks. Ratoff was going to England to make up with his first wife. He was nervous and excited about the trip. He carried a diamond necklace for her in his valise. It was a reconciliation present, which he inspected each day. Lahr, who should have been sympathetic to fine sentiments, was merciless about the present. He and White baited Ratoff about its price and kept claiming they'd seen a woman wearing a similar setting on the ship. Ratoff would grow gradually angrier, until, like a disturbed peahen, his head would incline toward his chest and his neck would swell in rancor. He would bluster, "Dees is as fine as can be gotten, yes?" And on that exclamation he would stuff it back into his bag and leave the room. But Lahr would not let the joke end on such an uncomplicated note.

"I played another gag on him." He says: "I went up to the radio operator's room and with a little persuasion I sent him wires." The first one read:

DEAR MR RATOFF

    ARE YOU INTERESTED IN PLAYING IN AND DIRECTING "MAYTIME" IN ENGLAND?

                                CHARLES COCHRAN

Ratoff, who had done the play in America and recognized the name of the well-known producer, was pleased. He cabled England at once.

"At dinner, after I sent the first wire, he kept saying, 'I've got to go on a ship to get a job. This is wonderful. I make money while I'm over there. I can pay for the trip.'"

The following day Lahr sent another wire:

DEAR MR RATOFF

    PLEASE DISREGARD PREVIOUS WIRE STOP WILL CONTACT YOU AGAIN
TOMORROW STOP NEW PLANS

                         CHARLES COCHRAN

Lahr giggles at the thought of seeing Ratoff worried. "He keeps saying to me, 'I don't like this, Bert. I wonder what it is. You don't think they've got somebody else, do you?'" Ratoff could hardly contain his excitement. Lahr was not quick to placate him. It was nice to watch someone else worry.

The next day he sent his final cable:

DEAR MR RATOFF

    FORGET THE WHOLE GODDAMN THING!

          CHARLES COCHRAN

Lahr never admitted the joke to Ratoff. While he walked the decks and thought about the misery of his own life, he didn't mind rankling his friends.

The trip to Europe was Lahr's first. He had read about Boswell's Grand Tour and imagined a similar kind of madcap elegance for himself. His own adventure could not have been more clownish. The day after he arrived, he received word that Mildred had finally left Robinson.

Confused while Lahr was in New York, beset by acquaintances who urged his cause, Mildred could not decide what to do. "The whole damn bunch haunt me so much," she confided to Robinson, "I'm almost out of my mind." While Lahr strolled in Hyde Park, Mildred was writing a note and placing it on the living-room table.

Dear Robby:

    I have received the copy of Arnold Bennett and thanks so much.

    Today I am checking out of the hotel and going away for a time. I really think it's the best and please do not be bitter toward me.

    Robby you have everything I admire in a man but I could not find happiness with you. I took $50 and paid the bill which I am enclosing marked "paid."

    Goodbye and may God bless you and give you happiness.

                   Sincerely,

                   Mildred

When Lahr heard the news, he visited one of Mildred's showgirl friends in London and asked her to go to America to keep Mildred company and protect his interests. Restless and disconsolate, he moved to Paris, where he saw the Eiffel Tower by accident and had a French model fall in love with him at the Ritz bar. She called him, sent him notes, but Lahr was not interested. His entire Grand Tour lasted five days. On the sixth, he was at Le Havre, still as empty and confused as when he had left, ready to set sail for home and an apprehensive future.

By the time Lahr arrived, Mildred had already moved to the American Woman's Club. Lahr inherited a situation he only half controlled. Mildred was not committed to him, and both of them recognized the capriciousness of their situation. There was absolutely no guarantee that she could get a divorce from Robinson or that Lahr could ever marry her. Nonetheless, she took the step for a man she could hardly understand and who could barely articulate his own emotions. "There was no romance with Bert—he never said things. You just knew he liked you."

Lahr himself was amazed by Mildred's decision. "I still don't know why she came back to me. He was younger, more handsome." In many ways Joseph Robinson would have made a much better husband than Bert Lahr. He was romantic and considerate. He remembered the little things that flattered her—the flowers, the birthdays, the surprise telephone calls. He liked picnics and long walks.

But Mildred now wanted a divorce. Lahr could only stick by her and prepare himself for what would be a long and, as he feared, dirty fight. On November 20, 1936, the long-threatened suit became national front-page news. Lahr was unmasked as a love-thief, an idea that seemed to amuse city editors.

BERT LAHR REHEARSES YELPS FOR $500,000 HEART BALM SUIT

Ooooo-wah!
Can't you hear it? It's Bert Lahr's cry of distress, and he was brushing up on it today because—
Someone is preparing to slap him with a half-million dollar heart balm suit charging him with stealing the affections of beautiful Mildred Schroeder, blonde showgirl.
And that someone—irony where is thy sting—is Joseph S. Robinson, the attorney who led the fight in the State Legislature to outlaw love-balm suits . . .

New York *Post*

To someone so concerned about his career as Lahr, these headlines brought fantasies of total disaster. The press, which had always loved his humor, was now exploiting his troubles. Lahr wisely let Abe Berman speak for him five days later when he made a rebuttal.

COMEDIAN LAHR READY TO DENY THEFT OF LOVE

Indirectly but vigorously, Bert Lahr, the comedian named as love thief, replied yesterday to the charges of Joseph F. Robinson, attorney, whose wife, Mildred Schroeder, deserted him.

The answer was made through A. L. Berman, counsel for the comedian in affidavits declaring the Brooklyn Supreme Court had no jurisdiction in the case.

Mr. Berman asked Justice Conway to vacate the order under which Mr. Robinson was authorized to examine the records of Mr. Berman, the Schindler Detective Agency, and telephone and telegraph companies before trial of an alienation of affections suit.

"My client would make categorical denial of the charges were there any charges to deny. But it is impossible for Lahr to make any defense in the present state of litigation, because there is nothing to defend here.

"Mr. Robinson declares that he has enough data to warrant a suit. If that is so, this order is unnecessary."

Mr. Berman declared that Mr. Robinson, a resident and voter of Manhattan courts, had sustained the new anti-alienation law and Brooklyn courts had rejected it. The statute is now on appeal.

Mr. Robinson charged that the comedian, whose real name was revealed as Irving Lahrheim, lured Mrs. Schroeder-Robinson from him on their honeymoon and is now maintaining her in a Beverly Hills cottage. Justice Conway reserved decision.

New York *American*, November 25, 1936

While Lahr at no time tried to inveigle Mildred away from her husband while they were on their honeymoon, as the New York *American* said that Robinson charged, the fact remains that he was supporting her while she got a separation.

Robinson maintained to the press that Lahr, with the help of a detective agency, had tried to uncover information that might lead to a fraudulent divorce. That he was foolish and the agency bumbling Lahr cannot deny. A letter from the detective remains.

Dear Bert,

The enclosed appeared in yesterday's paper. Of course, it is a matter of considerable embarrassment to me as the rat implies that we tried to frame him, and it certainly doesn't help me with the type of clients for whom we do business. However, there is nothing you can do about a situation of this sort.

But Lahr, angered by the publicity and gross mishandling of what had begun as a whim, refused to honor the detective's bill.

Having tried and failed to obtain a Florida divorce, Mildred decided to move to California as a stepping stone to residence in Reno. Robinson tried to bring an injunction against a Nevada divorce, restraining her from obtaining legal decree out of the state of New York. As the tension and court appeals mounted, the legal questions blurred. Lahr was cast as the Diomedes to true love. In a full-page story in the *American Weekly* ("Persevering Mr. Robinson vs. Wicked Reno"), a caption describes Robinson as he muscles his right arm in fierce debate in the picture above.

Mr. Joseph Robinson, who, whether he wants his wife back or not, is determined Funny Mr. Lahr shall not have her.

The adjudication was harrowing; and although Lahr stuck by Mildred, he shrank from each news story. While he never believed what drama critics said about his work, he began to question his own dignity when reporters classified his private life. "They called me a love thief—it was humiliating. Nothing like that had ever happened to me before."

Lahr was trapped between his career and his suddenly public private life. His nerves were frayed; he lived in constant disgust about the recent past and fear of the future. Lee Shubert, who had signed him for *The Show Is On* late in 1936, called Lahr into his office to talk about women. Mr. Shubert, small, sallow, with an aquiline nose, was a businessman who rarely dealt with the dilemmas of his performers' personal lives. But Shubert was worried that Lahr might suddenly skip town to join Mildred in California or go on a drinking spree. He wanted to try to stabilize his comedian. He had never met Mildred; but he knew from reading the papers the circumstances that perplexed Lahr.

"Shubert was a hard businessman. It was the first time he ever talked to me like this. He sat me down—I can remember it so vividly, and he said, 'Young fellow, I was once madly in love with a woman. She was known in show business as the most beautiful woman of the stage. Justine Johnston. I found she was untrue to me. I found there was another man. I took it very hard. The nights became months. I kept walking, nobody could talk to me, everybody was concerned. I walked the docks. I couldn't eat, I couldn't sleep. Finally, after many months, one morning I woke up and it was gone. The whole weight, that sadness, had left me like a bad dream. In later years, when I looked back at it—it seems so silly, so laughable. It was puppy love. Don't do anything rash, Bert. Try to forget this thing, Bert. You won't, I know—but try. Because one day, you'll wake up and it will be gone. Like the snap of a finger.' "

Lahr remembered Shubert's words. The confession surprised him. "Here was the head of a theatrical empire, this calculating, brilliant businessman, and he was under the same stress as I was. He had felt the same pangs." But Lahr could not be so easily consoled. The experience compounded his suspicion of the world, and even of Mildred. His view of himself fluctuated with his mood; at times he felt flippantly above society and at others, nervously under the scrutiny of the public eye. Before going into rehearsals with *The Show Is On,* he visited Mildred. Even with her, he was, in his imagination, some kind of social leper. A distressed letter from Mildred to A. L. Berman indicates his obsession.

Dear Abe,
   . . . I have been staying in every night because B. L. is ashamed to be out with me since the publicity. Truly, I sometimes feel that I am a criminal the way he acts. Do you think, Abe, that I have committed a great act? I know I made a mistake but did feel, at the time, I was doing the right thing, even if it turned out miserably. If only B. L. had some of your understanding qualities. I hope you believe me, Abe, that I have made every effort to do the right thing by B. L. since the day he left for London. But as the years pass by, he throws it up to me and seems unforgivable to the point of making me a bundle of nerves. Waking up and asking me what I did with what man and so on . . .

Mildred always tried to comfort him; but with every attempt at intimacy he moved away. Lahr could manipulate people on stage with the audience's approval; off stage, he was vulnerable and suspicious.

Bea Lillie co-starred with Lahr in *The Show Is On.* Despite the genuine pleasure of working with the comedienne and trying out fresh material, Lahr brought to his rehearsals the weight of his personal problems. Annulment proceedings had begun with Mercedes; the Reno divorce seemed stalled by a temporary injunction; and his son,

Herbert, was beginning his Christmas vacation. Lahr brooded; the show suffered. To those who did not know him well, his anxiety and inability to concentrate were the galling affectations of a star. His unwillingness to explain his nervousness made him an object of anger and mystery—at least to his director.

An article for *The New York Times* ("So You'd Like To Direct the Sketches"), quotes Edward C. Lilley in his justifiable irritation at Lahr:

> Neither does the attitude of Bert Lahr during rehearsals fill a director with delight. Mr. Lahr, as everyone knows who has traveled long in his company, is just about the worryingest rehearser in the business. As Mr. Lilley puts it, "He's a button waster . . ." Nothing ever strikes Mr. Lahr as funny. He never laughs during rehearsals; he fidgets through his lines with nervous haste and comes off twisting a button and saying, "Yeah, but I don't think it'll do."
>
> Another demoralizing habit which the sad-faced Mr. Lahr indulges according to Mr. Lilley is that of "Lawyer calling." In the middle of a sketch rehearsal, he will ask somebody for the time and then rush off with an explanation that he has to phone his lawyer, A. L. Berman. Just why, nobody seems to know. Or he'll bellow like a hopeless bull for "Louis" and then wait in anxious suspense until his agent Louis Shurr comes to his assistance. . . .

At a time when all his friendships seem to be caving in around him, he found in the inimitable Bea Lillie a woman who inspired trust.

"Working with Bea was one of my great experiences in the theater. We never had a cross word. I never saw her make one bad move. She was entirely professional." E. Y. Harburg, brought in to doctor the show, recalls Lahr's energy, not his peckishness. "Bert rehearsed like a darling child. He'd want to get every last bit of laughter out of the rehearsals. He never held back; Bea did. Bea got onto all his tricks; but she didn't come out with hers until the opening night in Philadelphia. She pulled about six or seven on him which floored Bert and broke him up on stage. He was worried about her. She represented elegance; he represented the low-down."

The two seemed an unlikely combination. Bea Lillie, elfish and delicate, spoke with a fluttering urbanity. Her satire, like herself, inspired gentle, dry laughter. She was a lady; and the sense of refinement that filled her comic pose brought hilarious surprise on stage. She was not beneath using a Seltzer bottle, or wearing a pair of roller skates with an evening gown; but when she used them, the laughter came from the disbelief with which she viewed her own comic personality. In comparison, Lahr was wild, inarticulate, and loud. He was not used to underplaying. His energy contrasted with Bea Lillie's feyness.

Bea Lillie had always been a comedienne of manners; Lahr was evolving in the same direction. They both enjoyed deflating the pretentious. They delighted in playing off their comic personalities in sketches that took them into unfamiliar ground. Lahr learned a lot from watching Bea. Her gasps of laughter, like a child careening down a hill, her quips, her pillbox hats became familiar landmarks.

The admiration was mutual. "I liked everything he did," says Bea Lillie. "And he liked everything I did. We thought the same about things. It took me a long while to know him personally—because he always looked so worried."

Lahr's affection for the comedienne had a paternal tinge. He remembers the evening they headlined a special New Year's bill at the Majestic Theater in Brooklyn, doing some of their vaudeville material. Each of them brought a sketch to do together. *"That,"* she says, winking, "was *quelque chose.*" Lahr is more explicit. "We had been warned that the second house on New Year's Eve might be a little rough. A lot of people in the gallery were drunk and giving the performers, as Bea would say, the *'rahsb'ry,'*—you know, the Bronx cheer. Well, I went on first, and they gave it to me. I went down front and said something which was in good taste like, 'Bad stomach?' When I came off, Bea was in the wings. She said to me, 'Oh Bert, I'm frightened.'

"I had a few moments to think, and when we both made our next entrance I said, 'You don't mind what I say if they do that to you?' She said, 'No,' and we went on.

"The minute we began somebody gave the Bronx cheer. And I looked up and yelled, 'I'd hate to be the guy who does your laundry.' The audience howled."

"I didn't get it for a minute," Miss Lillie confesses. But when she did, it hit her with overwhelming delight. "She yelled out that 'eeeeeeh' laugh of hers and broke up on stage. It was such a big laugh that from then on they let us alone."

Bea could have the same effect on him. Lahr visited her in England at her Henley estate. The first supper was served by a very distinguished butler ("and two maids in the kitchen, thank you very much") who entered with the soup.

"Old retainer?" Lahr asked.

"I've never seen him before," said Bea indifferently.

The next thing she remembers was seeing Lahr's face on the side of the table, crumpled with laughter.

"Sometimes she'd interpolate things on stage for me. There were types of humor that didn't impress her. If a story had something about getting hurt in it, falling off a chair or something like that, she'd say, 'That's sad, how tragic.' She never thought that kind of business was very funny."

In one scene of *The Show Is On* their good spirits got the best of them. "We did a scene where Bea was the ticket-taker at the Guild ('the Geeeeld—it was veddy graaand'). In those days Cain's Warehouse was the place where all the shows that flopped would take their scenery. Anyway, in this scene, Bea was the ticket-taker and I played the advanceman for Cain's Warehouse. I came with a tape measure to take measurements of the scenery. On opening night, when the performers and the theater crowd came, the situation was a riot. At one point the audience laughed for five minutes. Bea said, 'Do you move a show quickly?' And I replied, 'We moved a show so fast the other night the actors had to take their bows from a crate.' The second night, the scene was just fair, and by the end of the week, when the regular customers came in, they didn't get it at all. So Bea and I started kidding around on the stage. She'd say to me under her breath, things like 'Get off! Get off!' or 'Drop your pants, maybe you'll get a laugh.' I'd whisper, 'You're not funny tonight, Lil,' " Whether the audience laughed or not, they had so much fun with it that the producer finally had to take the scene out because it was disrupting the momentum of the show.

Lahr's big number in *The Show Is On* was "Song of the Woodsman," which became one of the treasures of American comedy lyrics and his trademark for many years. It was a parody of the famous bass, Chaliapin, and of the operatic sentimentalizing of the outdoors, which had been epitomized in Nelson Eddy's "Rose Marie."

The song was written especially for Lahr by Harold Arlen and E. Y. Harburg. Lahr had given them the general idea of what he wanted, hoping they could come up with a song that would beef up the material he had in the show.

"I always wrote Bert's material easily," explains Harburg. "No lyricist is worth his salt if he can't get inside the personality he is to write for. Bert always had artistic hopes and feelings; but the life he was given squelched that. His comedy was always conscious of a lack of privilege. He wants to be the artist; he wants to have the vignette of the enlightened guy. He knows he can never attain it; and so he laughs it off. The audience laughs with him, while he's slipping on an intellectual banana peel. Look at the first few lines of 'Woodsman.'

> The day's at the dawn,
> And dawn's on the morn,
> The morn's on the corn
> The corn's on the cob . . .

I was parodying part of Browning's 'Pippa Passes'—

> The year's at the spring
> And day's at the morn
> The hillside's dew-pearled;
> The lark's on the wing;
> The snails's on the thorn;
> God's in his heaven—
> All's right with the world!

Bert is precisely at the opposite of that lip-smacking romantic instinct. He was exploding the pompous baritone. I couldn't write those words for anyone else. 'Choppin' and 'Chaliapin' for instance, is Bert Lahr language. To get a lyric to sound funny you need amusing sounds. To imagine Chaliapin chopping a tree is witty. The more fascinating the sound collection, the more interesting the song."

"We made a record of 'Woodchopper' after we had written it, and sent it to Bert," says Arlen. "I got to the point where I could do him."

When Lahr received the record, his delight and enthusiasm for the song was immediate. Bea Lillie was with him. "I remember when a record of the 'Woodsman' came from California; I was so happy for him because it was a wonderful number, but I didn't have a good stopper myself. When he put it on, I guess my face dropped. Anyway, he sensed it, and after we'd played it a few times, he said to me, 'Never mind, Bea, I'm going to get the boys to write you one too.' I never got over that."

When the curtain came up, it uncovered an unlikely woodsman. Lahr was posed preposterously next to a scrawny tree with an ax in his hand. He wore a checkered hunter's shirt and a toupee matted on his head. He began raising both hands delicately toward his chest and then unleashing an outrageous sound.

After the first stanza, he stops to let the logic of the lilting words sink into his own befuddled brain.

All's right with the world
All's rah-rah-rah-rah-rah-rah-right, with the world.

O, a Woodsman's life is the life for me
With an all wool shirt, 'neath an all wood tree
For the world is mine, where 'ere I stand
With a song in my soul
And an a-a-a-a-a-a-a-a-ax in my hand.

The orchestra plays a throbbing melody. Lahr strikes an operatic pose.

For I chop and I chop and I chop
Till the sun comes up
And with every stroke the welcomes ring
When my truest friend, my ax I swing
What care I if the stocks should drop
Long as I can chop, chop, chop, chop.
Songs were made by fools like me
But only a baritone, a vari-bari-baritone
Can sing while the tall trees flop
So let me chop, chop, chop, chop, chop, chop.

He backs away from the tree and shoulders his papier-mâché ax, swinging boldly at the tree.

Heave-Swing! Heave-Swing!

As he swings, a barrage of wood pelts him from the wings.

Heave-Swing! Heave-Swing!

Another bombardment. This time, as he covers his head to protect himself, his wig tips over his eyes. He tries to stick it in place. It is a hopeless struggle. He stuffs it on sideways and continues singing even louder to cover up the embarrassment.

There's no stoppin' me or Chaliapin
When we're choppin' a tree
When we're cho—opin a tree.

He pauses, fussing with his wig. Then, with eyes aflutter, he begins softly—

What do we chop, when we chop a tree?
A thousand things that you daily see.
A baby's crib, the poet's chair,
The soap box down at Union Square.

A pipe for Dad, a bat for brother,
An extra broom for dear old mother.
Pickets for the fence,
Buckets for the well,
Poles for American Tel & Tel.
Cribbage boards for the Far West Indies,
Toothpicks for the boys in Lindy's.
Croquet balls for you and me,
That's what we chop when we chop a tree.

His voice rises an octave in passionate declamation—

Whadda we chop when we chop God's wood?

And then, reverently—

Guns to protect our womanhood,
The better mousetrap, the movie mag,
The mast to hoist our country's flag.
Handles for the Fuller brush,
Plungers for the obstinate flush,
Comfort seats, all shapes and classes
For little lads, and little—lasses.
Modernistic beds built just for three
That's what we chop when we chop a tree.
Heave—Swing! Heave—Swing!

As he finishes his swing, he tenses up to receive the onslaught from the wings. Nothing comes. Again—

Heave—Swing, Heave—Swing.

He covers his head, and when nothing happens, he looks in disgust at the stagehands and continues—

For I chop and I chop and I chop

At the crescendo of his song, with his arms dramatically outstretched, he is bombarded again. He cowers, but struggles on—

Till the sun comes up,
There's no stoppin' me or Chaliapin
When we're choppin' a—tree.
(*Blackout*)

"They threw everything at me. Everybody backstage wanted to get into the act."

"I couldn't wait to get in the wings for that number," confides Bea. "I'd throw boards, brooms, anything I could get my hands on at him. I couldn't wait to see it."

With the "Woodsman," Lahr moved closer to a more controlled comic image. The sketch was economical, simple, and relied not so much on his fund of energy as on the attitude of mind he was parodying. Bea Lillie caught the difference in his comedy, which brought their work closer together. "I've never seen anybody as dignified as Bert Lahr when he plays Lord This or an Englishman. He is *so* grand in everything he does, if you know what I mean—even in his comedy. He has great dignity in chopping that tree. He took all that wood in the face with great dignity. There was no slapstick—and if there was—it was dignified. That's me, that's me—whatever happens I rise above it."

Lahr did another sketch called "Income Tax," which was very successful. What is interesting about the scene is how so many of the laugh situations parallel his own life. If he was not the obnoxious radio star, Bert Clarkson, trying to fast-talk the tax inspector, he was Bert Lahr who had been called down to the Office of Internal Revenue the previous year to explain a deduction of four hundred dollars for nose putty. When the inspector protested that four hundred dollars was out of the question, Lahr nonchalantly answered, "Well, I put rhinestones in it!" Unlike the character in the sketch, he did not have a nubile Indian traveling with him, but Mildred was waiting in California, and he was contributing to payment of her expenses.

The Show Is On played 237 performances. Lahr was greeted with good reviews, which, much to his surprise, did not capitalize on the publicity of his private life. While there was something bold and courageous about facing an audience and the critics under the circumstances, it was safer than private recriminations. "The audience either laughed or they didn't; they loved you or you flopped. There was no in-between. Off the stage, there were so many complications and alternatives. So many ways to read the same facts. Nothing was quite as clear and immediate."

While Lahr could not chart the changes in his emotional life, the shifts in his comedy were easier to read. Brooks Atkinson described the evolution in Lahr's humor over the previous four years to which *The Show Is On* gave new, important focus.

When Bert Lahr was fresh from burlesque houses, bellowing his 'ung-ung-ung and throwing his arms out of joint, he was funny enough for *comfortable theater going.* But he has gone through a considerable metamorphosis since those days. Now he dresses at times in ornate evening clothes or splendid livery and stands around the stage like a brilliant fashion plate . . .

Although satire is usually not the low comedian's stock-in-trade, Lahr has become a satirist with a comic strength that virtually annihilates the subject of his material . . . [with] his coarsely demure presentation of E. Y. Harburg's and Harold Arlen's "Song of the Woodsman," the braggart baritones of the musical stage had better take warning. For it is the author's belief that baritone balladry is fraudulent stuff, that the masculinity is mendacious, and it is Lahr's belief that a bum song is a buffoon's triumph. This one is his. For the two B. L.'s (Bert Lahr and Bea Lillie) the carnival stage has individual ways of arriving at the same ludicrous conclusions.

The New York Times, January 10, 1937

The Show Is On solidified Lahr's comic reputation and brought him together with Bea Lillie. As a team they shared many gay moments on stage. They also suffered through their private torments. Bea was a confidante. She witnessed more than she will relate. She was present when Lahr received the letter from Mercedes asking to come to *The Show Is On.* The letter, scrawled in a delicate, halting hand, was addressed to the Winter Garden Theater. Her doctors had intercepted it and sent it to Abe Berman, knowing that his counsel would bring quicker results than Lahr's own intuitions.

Dear Mr. Berman:
I would sincerely urge that Bert answer this letter. It would satisfy Mrs. Lahr. She is always speaking to us about being cut off from outside contacts.
December 29, 1936

Dear Husband,
Please have your travel agent arrange for a transportation for me for the big city and also to see which day will be best for me to see your show. I feel very hurt you didn't let me know you were in town and that I had to wait to see you. Hoping you will see it my way and grant me this favor and with thanks. I will close sending my best love,
I remain devotedly yours, Merc. Babe.

Lahr talked to Bea about it, and while she never offered suggestions, her quiet maturity consoled him. But he found no answers and sought no solace. He would have to see Mercedes. What could he say? "It was through by then. It was gone, what love I had for her. I felt pity. God knows I took care of her—sent her to Europe, the best doctors there and in America—but, by then it was through."

On March 16, 1937, Lahr received a letter from the clinical director that clarified Mercedes's position:

> Mrs. Lahr has improved very much since coming to the sanitarium, especially since she has received the insulin therapy. My reason for writing to you is to get your reaction to having her leave here on trial for one week or so, during which time she would live with her sister, Anna. She has promised me that she would cooperate with this sister and not do anything which might incur your displeasure or embarrass you in any way. . . .

The next week Mercedes and Anna visited Lahr backstage.

Standing in the white light of the dressing room, she must have looked even bigger than she was. She weighed 160 pounds. She wore a black dress, new for the occasion. Her lipstick was smudged. She didn't seem to notice the strands of hair that hung loosely about her head.

Her eyes would focus on objects in the room, and Lahr tried every conversational gambit to keep her animated. In each glance, he felt the guilt of the past. She gazed at the dresser. Had he put Mildred's picture away? Yes. And then, for a long time, while he asked her about New York and how she felt, Mercedes seemed preoccupied with the dressing-room wall. He recalled the last page of the report in 1935 that he had scanned for hopeful signs of progress.

> One evening she was found sitting huddled up in a cold room with all the windows open and announced that she was cold because the walls were so bare.

He could never read the reports after that.

Lahr talked nervously to her. He could not look at her directly, afraid that her glassy stare would somehow rivet on him, and that he would cry. She would not answer all the questions he asked. Her silence upset him.

When she did speak, her words were uttered with restraint. She talked to him about show business. When she spoke of coming back to the stage, her responses were quicker. She told him what she would express again to psychiatrists a year later when they came to visit her at the Martinique Hotel, where she stayed with her sister. "She said she thought she could take part in a musical revue, that she could dance and perform just the same as she had in the old days. We suggested to her that her physical condition had changed very much since the time when she was actively on stage, that her weight had increased, that she had become flabby, but that didn't bother her." As she talked, Lahr remembered that she sometimes danced at sanitarium parties and that, when she hurried up the stairs to her room, her new weight shook the staircase. Between the memories that flooded his imagination and his forced conversation, Lahr found himself silent. "I never talked about an annulment; I never talked about love. She wouldn't have understood. Most of the time she wouldn't answer my questions."

Lahr recalls the meeting as the "saddest moment of my life." Standing there, trying to be kind, but hopelessly incompetent with words and unsure of his emotions, he only wanted Mercedes and her sister to leave. When she was away from him, he could always hope that she would recover. Face to face with her, all the money, the dreams, the anxiety over her seemed hopeless. She had changed so much. As Anna was getting ready to take Mercedes back to the hotel, Mercedes broke the silence. Turning to her husband, she said, "Let's go home, Bert."

"You go with Anna," he said, "I'll be along later."

He never saw her again.

OTHER EDENS

"Despite a few temporary excursions into radio and motion pictures, they have never forsworn their allegiance to the stage."
Brooks Atkinson on Lahr and Bea Lillie,
The New York Times, *1937*

"How do you—an old Broadway Boy—like acting in the movies?" Mr. Lahr shrugged: "I like anything so long as I'm making money."
Lahr to Bosley Crowther, The New York Times, *1939*

WHEN MAURICE CHEVALIER ACCEPTED A RADIO CONTRACT IN 1931 for five thousand dollars a week, star radio was born. The next year Bert Lahr was on the air coast to coast. There are pictures of those days, Lahr standing handsome and nonchalant in front of an NBC microphone. He is smiling, and he holds a script at his side. His tie is undone. His hat (he wears it despite the fact that his coat is off) is cocked at a self-assured angle. In the picture, he is the image of control.

As one of the bright new stars of Broadway, Lahr was an obvious attraction for the new medium. Many stage comedians made the transition to radio. Some, like Eddie Cantor or Jack Benny, did it easily; others like the raconteur Lou Holtz were mysteriously ineffective. Lahr had all the accouterments for a radio success: a big name, an unusual delivery, and a sense of verbal idiocy, all of which made the idea of a "Bert Lahr Show" viable.

He rarely talks about radio, which for more than a decade fed him at fees as high as $2,500 a performance but which often left him dissatisfied. Between 1932, when he featured in his own show for Lucky Strike, and 1938, he appeared regularly with the most successful radio personalities of the day: Fred Allen, Bing Crosby, Rudy Vallee. By his own estimate, he was a guest on the Vallee show more than thirty times. His own verdict of his radio talent is harsh. "I wasn't on too long. I wasn't too good." Whether he liked the medium or not, Lahr was effective enough to be in demand; and he never gave up radio. "I stayed with radio as long as it was fruitful. When television came in, then radio went out. The money wasn't there anymore."

When he began his radio career, the medium was primitive. It had not separated its technique from that of the stage, a fact symbolically illustrated by the audience at all studio sessions. Since tape was not extensively used by the industry until after World War II, it was not unusual for a show being broadcast to the West Coast to be performed twice on the same night. Different audiences were provided for each performance.

The difficulty in making the transition to radio rested in a failure to understand its uniqueness. Unlike the stage, it was graphic but not visual, private more than public. When Lahr made his radio debut on June 20, 1932, critics pondered whether his ribald humor could adjust to the larger, less sophisticated fireside audiences.

> If Bert Lahr can project his own particular style into the air without having to use dirt—then he'll outshine any radio comic so far developed.
>
> New York *Sun*

But Lahr's maiden voyage into personality radio was disastrous, floundering not simply because of the material but because of the naïveté of radio personnel to their own medium. Lahr was headlining at the time in *Hot-Cha!,* and the radio director was intent on capturing Lahr's Broadway performance for the listening audience. "The director kept telling me, 'I want you the way you work in *Hot-Cha!.*' I worked the same as I did on the stage. He kept saying, 'Come on, come on, like the stage, just like the stage.' It was awful. I had a thirteen-week deal, and after four weeks they paid me off for all thirteen. The first experience was so painful that I think it gave me a mental block."

Although Lahr was a darling of the press, the radio critics were not as easily overwhelmed as the Broadway first-nighters.

> At first blush, Mr. Bert Lahr . . . gave me the impression that he hadn't quite grasped the radio technique. Possibly the same thought occurred to Mr. Lahr after the initial performance a week ago for he came to the microphone this weekend with more confidence and a greatly improved delivery.
>
> New York *Journal*

The same thought *had* occurred to Lahr. At first, there was too much to worry about: the live radio audience, speaking with the right intonation, limiting his gestures, not biting his cues or hurrying his delivery. Years later, listening to replays of his performances, he would shake his head, mumbling, "I was reading too fast. I could have humored it more." To Lahr this meant a way of reacting, the manner in which he embellished his performance with glances, pauses, ludicrous sounds. But on the air, his boldness and security vanished.

Some performers, like Cantor, were fearless. Cantor even got into costume for his radio shows. His "I don't give a damn" attitude helped his comic delivery. Lahr's shyness came through all the bellowing. "Bert was always afraid it wasn't going to go," says Carroll Carroll, one of the men who wrote his radio comedy. "His own timidity about his ability had an influence on him."

While the writers sharpened the jokes, they could not resolve the fundamental problem. Lahr was a comedian whose laughter relied heavily on gesture. In front of a microphone with one hand on a script, he was as effective as a hobbled horse. "In those days, I was a fellow who was always moving. When I got in front of that microphone and had to hold a paper in my hand, I had fear. If I did it today, things would be different. But standing there, trying to read, I'd fluff something, and then I'd fight it."

The importance of the body and movement as a buffoon's tool is never more apparent than when he is without it. "I was always ahead of my script. I couldn't read it because I wanted to move all the time. The same holds true of Bobby Clark, who was one of my favorite comedians. After years of working with a fellow named McCullough who stood in one spot through the whole act, Bobby couldn't keep still. He was a wonderful guy, but he just couldn't stay within a scene. He was always playing Bobby Clark. We did a scene together at the Lambs Club, it was one of the biggest laughs I ever got there. The situation was this: I was supposed to be in my bedroom at the Lambs. I was just ready to go on, and I was listening to the other acts getting tremendous laughs. It was a knife in my heart. (I played the part of a self-centered, nervous comedian who worries about the next act.) I didn't know what Bobby was going to do because we'd rehearsed without make-up. When he came on, he had everything—goggles, the coronet, the cane. So I said, 'He has to work up an entrance to come into the bedroom.' In this scene he had to sit down with me, but I couldn't get him to do it. I ran downstage and grabbed him by the arm and said, '*Bobby, stop underplaying!*' It was a big laugh. I was like Bobby when they put me in front of a microphone. I couldn't keep still."

Lahr's mobile face, his impulse to pierce through a morass of words with a single gesture, made it difficult for the radio writers to forge an effective comedy image of him.

Carroll Carroll, who spent many long hours trying to solve the problem of Lahr's radio personality, recognized the dilemma. "As a writer you were constantly trying to write something funny. At the same time you knew where Lahr was going to make a funny face. He could not resist doing that. Sometimes you might come up with a straight line which the studio audience would laugh like hell at because Lahr was mugging. It was a problem when the studio audience was breaking up and Bert simply said, 'How are you?' It confused the listener."

Like most of the best radio writers of the time—Herman Wouk, Parke Levy—Carroll's life was spent in long frenetic writing sessions. He was sympathetic to Lahr's comedy (he wrote the last television sketch Lahr ever commissioned) and knew radio's limitations. "What Lahr really thinks is funny are the things he does, the faces he makes, the articulations which have a relation to other people. He's an actor. His reactions to people are frequently more funny than anything he does or says. Of course ninety per cent of this was lost on radio."

Nor was Lahr used to working with a team of writers. He liked to ponder his humor, plot his gestures, practice until he had found just the right word for every situation. But a Sunday show each week left no time for perfection. The writers met with Lahr at the Warwick Hotel. He strolled nervously around the room in his kimono, twisting a piece of cellophane in his hand and muttering, "I think I've got something."

"Working with him was not easy," says Carroll. "We suffered a great deal because he suffered so much. We used to sit for hours looking at each other. I remember we were trying to get a name for an Indian tribe—Seminole would have done. I suggested Potowatami. I thought it was a funny name, with an explosive sound. For some reason Bert didn't like it. I don't know how long we argued the point, whether it should have been Mohawk or Onondaga, but you'd continually find yourself coming to a Mexican stand-off with him."

Lahr's initial impulse in radio was to return to the burlesque raucousness which, in 1932–3, he had not yet abandoned on stage. He did not understand that the microphone would not accommodate his wild energy. "When we had these sessions," recalls Carroll, "it was apparent that Bert was trying to translate the humor of burlesque into radio. It was too physical and, in many cases, too salty."

Lahr's self-consciousness missed the moments of genuine fun that were broadcast. "Bert isn't much of a reader, although when he read a line wrong it was usually funnier than when he read it right. He tried very hard to be a good reader, and as a result, it came out at times a little childlike. It sounded as if he was actually reading instead of that free spontaneous play he did so well on stage."

Because the radio audience could not see his uncomprehending squint, Lahr had to convey his physical responses with language. There was no way to signal the audience that something funny was coming, as he did on stage with a gesture. The best he could substitute was an affected "huh, huh" before every laugh line. Sometimes, in back of these radio situations, a cackle, small—almost elfish—could be heard. The sound was Lahr actually enjoying himself, instead of the dumb show with which he usually delivered his lines.

Carroll and the other writers found Lahr helpful when it came to mangling the language. "He was a great contributor of the ludicrous. When you got to a point where you needed something utterly absurd, it would generally come from Bert. Once, we did something about psychoanalysis, and he came up with 'Don't probe into my subnoxious.' He was good at picking out the words that he could say, while looking funny as he said them. He's a mugger. He'd do a lot of it on radio to build a joke. The live audience was firmly pledged to him."

Lahr's ability to invent language that created not only amusing sounds but also a vivid mental picture is illustrated in one of his ad-lib remarks on the Chase & Sanborn Coffee Hour. The writers created a character called Balzac, who was continually pestering Lahr. Balzac was a scamp who rarely talked, but played havoc with Lahr's good nature. Lahr always managed to get even. In one sequence, Lahr described a confrontation this way:

> I woke up this mornin', the birds were tweetin' in the trees, the sun was shinin', the bees was buzzin' and I had to run into poison ivy.

Carroll watched Lahr pace the Warwick carpets trying out the word "Balzac" in a variety of tones. "He was fascinated with the word. He could do funny things with his lips; his mouth would quiver like a bloater fish, and his face shrivel into an unexpected angle."

Lahr's reading on the air could be very funny. "He did a lot of fumbling around," says Carroll, "but that was part of what was amusing." Lahr's tongue could never quite wrap itself around the words. A good comic ploy, it was also true to life. When he made a mistake on radio listeners were surprised to hear him exclaiming, "Lumpy printing" or "Now I'm reading my thumb." When things went wrong on radio, a performer still had to say something. Lahr's ad libs, like his language, were always graphic. One can see a man reading his thumb.

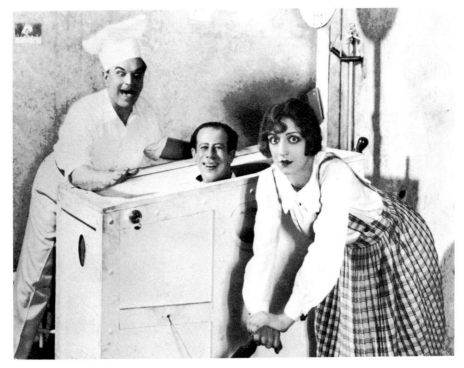

With Victor Moore and another cast member in *Hold Everything* (1928)

Boxing in *Hold Everything*

The Spin Test in *Flying High* (1930)

Overleaf
In *Life Begins at 8:40*
(1935)

As an English peer in
George White's Scandals (1936)

In *Flying High*

With Lupe Velez in *Hot-Cha!* (1932)

In dressing room (1935)

With Mildred (1933)

A radio sketch with Ed Wynn (c. 1933)

A portrait of Mildred (1929)

Singing "Song of
the Woodsman"
(1937)

With Bea Lillie in *The Show Is On* (1937)

With Claudette Colbert in *Zaza* (1938)

With Ethel Merman in *Du Barry Was a Lady* (1939)

Portrait as King Louis XV

With Mildred on wedding day,
February 11, 1940

Privately, Lahr considered his use of words to be a technical device he had developed for the stage. He was the most inarticulate man ever to consider himself adroit with words. But the combination of confidence and misuse made his passion for language valuable to his comedy. "I read a lot. In burlesque even, I read. Words. Words. I used to say, 'You're a despot,' and I'd get laughs. I knew what a despot was. I put it in a situation where it was ludicrous. I could have said 'You're a villain.' I used this a lot in radio. I sounded stupid on the air, and my use of big words was surprising to listeners and funny. When I did Louis XV in *Du Barry* I felt I knew how he behaved." He raises his head regally. "I read about Napoleon. Very dainty, and the hands." Lahr's fingers, usually lying like potatoes in his lap, flutter with frantic delicacy. He reaches out as if taking a mint. "Language. I'm a New Yorker. I've got a New York accent and give the impression of being terribly erudite. I don't say that I'm a scholar. I do a lot of crossword puzzles. I digest a lot of it. I'm not crass and coarse."

The Chase & Sanborn Coffee Hour was a moderate radio success for Lahr. Certainly Carroll and the other writers did not consider it, as Lahr did, a total failure: "I don't agree entirely that it wasn't a good show. As writers we were limited to a fixed format which broke down to two or three individual scenes, so that we weren't in any position to do an extended situation or anything with a real beginning, middle, and an end—the kind of thing Bert was used to doing on stage. We thought we had to set up a premise, get a few laughs, and get off in about six or seven minutes. And then do another seven-minute spot later. The main reason Bert wasn't as good as he could have been was simply that he was conscious of what people will laugh at when they are looking at him rather than *listening* to him."

One of his best radio broadcasts, on October 11, 1939, was with Fred Allen, the master of radio satire, whose cracker-barrel twang and wry wit made him one of the nation's foremost radio personalities. Lahr felt confident in his company and, privately, looked upon Allen with special amazement. Allen's carefully planned routine and the simplicity with which he controlled his life were a source of wonder to Lahr. He admired Allen's efficiency—a man who kept lists for everything from eating at a different restaurant every night to giving money to the many unemployed actors he'd befriended. "I never cared about the money when I worked with Fred. *I knew I'd be protected.* I mean the material would be there. Allen used to write it."

On stage, Lahr had learned how to defend himself from the audience and other actors. There was no recourse on radio, no way to recoup an error or ingratiate the faceless thousands waiting to be entertained. "Allen was wonderful to work with because he was so unselfish, he acted as a straightman to the comedian. He was most generous with other people."

Lahr's radio style had matured. The Fred Allen broadcast was much more refined than his earlier ones. Lahr still read too fast, and his voice was still too loud for the microphone. He spluttered, howled, slurred his words; but the microphone could never let him run his vocal range. Lahr was now able to assume an aristocratic hauteur, missing in the old Chase & Sanborn shows. His facility with words had increased to the point where he could tickle the fancy with more difficult tongue-twisters than his burlesque "despot." Allen tries it with "poltroonery." The effect was hilarious. For radio, Lahr's physical image had to be replaced by a voice and material that conjured up the simpleton, the bluff egotist who didn't realize the consequences of what he was saying. Allen was able to get the most mileage out of Lahr on radio by steering the humor very close to his personal frustrations: laughter, Hollywood, love life, the stage. He saw instinctively what Lahr could never see—how much his comic character resembled the private one. Lahr was never funnier, as his friends understood so well, than when he was bemoaning his fate.

Lahr: . . . People think if one comedian is funny, two comedians should be twice as funny.

Allen: Oh, that's silly. Now, here we are. You're a comedian, and I'm a comedian. We're together. Are we twice as funny?

Lahr: (struggling with the words which are sounded out of his nose) To the contrary, to corn a phrase.

Allen: (laughing at Lahr's miscue) 'To corn a phrase." Well, let's stop the whole thing. Say, how come you left Hollywood, Bert, you must have had a reason?

Lahr: Yes, Fred, Hollywood went too far . . . It was up to me.

Allen: (laughing at surprise arrogance) What did you do?

Lahr: It was my turn to go too far. (laugh) So I got on a train and came East.

Allen: Oh, you mean out there, you were getting in a rut, artistically?

Lahr: Yeah, I was tired of being a great lover.

Allen: You wanted to get away from it all?

Lahr: Well, most of it. (laugh) There was a little blonde at Metro who might have intrigued me, but, huh, the silly little minx let me get awaaaaaay.

Allen: You must have taken it hard.
Lahr: I was momentarily frustrated. I denounced the human race. I
sought solace in the animal kingdom.

The response to the show pleased Allen. Lahr enjoyed appearing
with him, despite the fact that the money—as he kidded in the script—
was considerably less than he could command. Two weeks after the
performance Lahr received a note from Allen.

Dear Bert—
Thank you for the wonderful job. Please accept this token.

"That money was over and above my regular salary. I had never
heard of anyone doing that before." The gesture symbolized a kindness
and generosity that radio, in general, never showed Bert Lahr.

The abyss between public approval and artistic accomplishment
plagued Lahr in films as well as on radio. To the world, he was a success; privately, the specter of failure haunted him.

Lahr's career in movies was arranged by his agent, Louis Shurr, who
had induced him to go to the Coast to do Buddy DeSylva's *Merry-Go-
Round of 1938* and make a more lucrative career in films.

Louis is five foot three, and pale. Although styles have changed, he
looks much the same as he did in the early thirties, when he was show
business' most successful agent. He prefers conservative, custom-made
suits and elevator shoes. Everyone has always called him "Doc" since
George White first dubbed him that. And no one in the vicinity of the
Brown Derby, where he lunches daily at table four facing the entrance,
would ever deny that Doc Shurr has managed some of The Big Ones.

Marilyn Miller, Clifton Webb, Jack Pearl, and Lahr were "his" in
that golden age of revues, which spanned the twenties and thirties. The
stable of talent has dwindled since, but almost all the famous stars have
passed through his well-carpeted office. To the Brown Derby set who
don't remember those halcyon days, he is associated more easily with
Kim Novak, whom he discovered. They will tell you that he got himself
photographed in *Life* pursuing Miss Novak on foot while she peddled
through the Brentwood streets on a bicycle. They may also add that
she doesn't work for him any longer. But there are others who still
remain—names which have managed to bridge decades: Bob Hope,
Betty Grable, and Lahr.

Shurr is a curious man. He lingers almost sensually on facts and figures. He is not as smooth as the silk-suited young agents he employs, but he is very conscious of appearances. When Lahr thinks of him, the image is of a man checking his cuffs and collar to see if they are clean.

On the table beside his desk is an assortment of well-framed and carefully dusted photographs. Lahr is among them, an old picture from the late thirties. This is how Louis would like to remember him—a smooth, wealthy, "hot property." Bob Hope is at the front with his arm around Louis.

"Your father and I have been together a long time," Shurr says. "A very long time."

He stops to consider their relationship and nodding sagely says, "If there was one thing I learned about him, he was a worrier. That's it mainly—a real worrier." He swivels in his chair. "Oh, we've had our quarrels," Shurr adds, "but he's a great artist."

The phone rings. He turns away and reaches for a list that is taped to a small table insert he can pull out from beneath his desk.

"Yeh? How many weeks? . . . But they don't have to be that young for a Western . . . Yeh. Let me see. I can give you Andy Devine . . . No. Gabby Hayes? No. What about Bert Lahr? . . . Hey, I've got somebody here. I know I can work something out for you."

Shurr turns back, smiling. "Like I was saying, your father is one of America's finest performers . . ."

There was a time, even after the scripts had stopped coming as frequently and Louis was no longer there at the train station to greet him on his trips West, when Lahr defended him vehemently to his family. "Don't tell me about my business." But privately, he has always understood the problem of his management. When a script comes from California, Lahr eagerly opens it. He looks at the front page. An Elvis Presley picture. He goes back to his crossword puzzle. Later he exclaims, "Jesus, what does Louis think he's doing?"

The bond between Shurr and Lahr is memory, not understanding. Perhaps there was a point in Lahr's career when he should have sought subtler, younger guidance. But at seventy-two, it seems more important to keep things in order.

"As far as I'm concerned, if a call comes in for me, I guess he'll work on it, but he won't waste much time." Even when Lahr was new to Hollywood, he was suspicious of the way he was being handled. "Louis was never a mentor, if you know what I mean. He was just an agent. If they'd call him, he'd sell me. At the inception of my movie career, I don't think I was managed properly. He got me jobs, but he didn't care what kind of script it was. He'd give you a rubdown, and make you think things were rosier than they were."

Lahr bumbled into associations. For the stage he could tell a good script and know how to improve a mediocre one. In other media, without his own knowledge to fall back on and with virtually no intimate friends to give him advice, he floundered. "When I went out to Hollywood, I was just a comedian, a caricature. Even now people think of me as I was in those days. But my main source of fame, if I've achieved any real recognition, was on Broadway. In radio I had many opportunities, but I never . . . Let's just say I was a Broadway specialist."

As a comic actor, Lahr's instrument of entertainment was equal to, if not greater than, the funny-men of the screen. His face was as distinctive as Keaton's; his energy drew on real emotions and could match the more artificial mayhem of Harpo Marx. In 1938 he could also claim a comic style that raised a point of view, less self-conscious but as special as Chaplin's. On top of these assets, he possessed one of the definitively funny stage voices, and like all of the excellent fun-makers, his personality on stage or screen created an instant affection.

When he set off for Hollywood in 1938 he was conscious of the risk he was taking, but his instinct for survival pushed him to develop a performing flexibility. "I realized that good scripts didn't turn up every year on Broadway. I couldn't afford to sit around waiting for a year. If I wanted to stay alive I'd have to go into other areas of entertainment. Today, I think I've learned enough to make myself qualified for any medium."

There were many reasons for Lahr's departure to the Coast. The primary one was, of course, money. But closely allied was his desire to be with Mildred. "A lot of my friends were going out to California and doing pretty well. I thought it would be good for me . . ." Typically, he had no faith in the success he had attained. At the height of his Broadway career, he intended the move to California to be permanent. Critics have praised his loyalty to the stage; Lahr himself has claimed indifference. "I never go to see plays; I don't like them. I can always outguess them." As he embarked for California, he was hounded by what seemed to him an undisputed failure in radio. In forsaking the stage again, he must have wondered whether the gilded world of Hollywood and its new technology would betray him in the same way radio had.

Lahr looked on California like Pinocchio at the fair. His image of it was a child's vision of leisure and simple fun. He told a reporter soon after arriving in the new Xanadu—

> Forget the glory. I've had plenty of it rising from the bottom of show business. Now I ask myself, "What do I get out of life."
>
> I like to see prizefights. Most of them are as good around Hollywood as in New York. So are the football games. There is nothing wrong with the golf courses either.

Even in 1939, while he was joking about Hollywood to Fred Allen, Lahr was making plans to build a house there. He would make sorties to New York to do a show or a guest appearance. But it was in the parched, craggy Hollywood Hills that he settled. He was forty-three, and while he might be able to tell the world there was glory in rising from the bottom of burlesque, he bore the scars of a struggle that had been long and, in his mind, far from glamorous.

Coldwater Canyon, which he had picked out as the site for his home, was then rolling, sparsely populated territory. The comedian of many disguises, the chameleon of laughter, found himself adapting almost immediately to the new terrain. "Space. You had room to move around. Air. You could breathe fresh, clean air. It was—it was—very green." When he thought of California, he imagined the lovely dog-leg at the Hillcrest Country Club, a long, crooked tongue of emerald turf with palm trees rimming the side. California, as he would paint it for Eastern friends, was the clink of glasses, the laughter of old acquaintances enjoying the leisure of their success, names that later made him smile with happy memories: Jimmy Cagney, Frank McHugh, Spencer Tracy, Pat O'Brien, Eddie Foy, Jr., Ralph Bellamy. All of them were refugees from the legitimate stage. They had found their way to California, and Lahr, surrounded by Nature and old companions, felt he had never had it so good.

Broadway was Lahr's bailiwick, but his exuberance in the early months of his arrival in California indicated a confidence in the new life.

> —Bert Lahr entertaining some of the boys at Dave Chasen's with a broken down rendition of "My Heart Belongs to Daddy."
> —Bert Lahr, so busy telling stories on the Metro set that he's never ready until they yell, "Camera."

The buffoon who laughed at his inarticulateness on the stage was gaily passing out his "bon mots":

On Hollywood:

Hollywood is the only community in the world where the entire population is suffering from rumortism . . .
If you want to be a success in Hollywood. Be sure to go to New York.

On Woman:

She's not so bright, but she's got an enormous scandal power when she's lit.

On Screen Technique:

He'll wind up behind the eight-ball unless he stops stealing scenes from himself . . .

Lahr had performed in two-reelers made in 1928 at the Warner lot in Brooklyn for Brian Foy. "It was pretty bad. Foy just said, 'Go ahead in there.' I had very little script. It took three days." Later, Lahr had been transported to California to do the screen version of *Flying High* (1931), a year after Joe E. Brown had impersonated him in *Hold Everything.* He gave virtually his stage performance on screen; but to the disappointment of the moguls and himself, it failed to come across as richly as it did on stage. He did not care about films at that time. His memory of his first screen exposure is not of the material but of two of the industry's pioneers: Irving Thalberg and Louis B. Mayer. He recalls the humility of Thalberg, who in 1931 summoned him to his office, from which he presided over the creative end of the Metro-Goldwyn-Mayer productions. "Bert," he said "I want you to help me cut this picture. You know where the laughs are." Lahr was flattered. (Lahr met Thalberg with his wife Norma Shearer two years later in the Astor Ballroom. Thalberg approached him. "Perhaps you don't remember me. I'm Irving Thalberg." Lahr, who had not spoken to him for fear of being presumptuous, was touched by the attitude of a film magnate to a performer. "I thought he'd forgotten who I was.") It was not the way most movie moguls, like L. B. Mayer, who handled the business end of Metro, behaved.

At M-G-M, Mayer was a man of astounding power and callousness. His genius for showmanship had manipulated his films to a success and quality still unparalleled in the movie industry. Mayer himself was the single highest paid man in America for nine years in the thirties and forties, earning as much as $1,300,000 in 1932, but he was notoriously stingy with his performers. His struggles for power within the industry and his ruthless exploitation of talent created many enemies. (This was never so clearly indicated as in the reaction to his death. Explaining why so many people had come to the funeral in 1956, Samuel Goldwyn, who knew the bitter in-fighting, quipped, "The reason so many people turned up for his funeral is that they wanted to make sure he was dead." Lahr, a victim of Mayer's philosophy of entertainment, said, "If you want a full house, you give the public what it wants.")

Lahr's contract for *Flying High* called for a substantial sum for the eight weeks of filming. For any extra time on the set, Lahr was to be paid at a special rate. When it became evident that the film would take longer than two months and that Metro would have to pay a conspicuously large salary to Lahr, he received a summons from L. B. Mayer. When Lahr arrived, Mayer, a toad of a man, small and bilious, was seated at his desk. His assistant, Ed Mannix, stood by the door. Lahr's initial nervousness was assuaged by Mannix, a large, friendly man who had once been a bouncer at Palisades Amusement Park.

Mayer began his talk with Lahr quietly, dispensing his words with a fatherly consideration.

"America is a wonderful place, Bert, isn't it? I mean where else could a man build a great company like Metro which has brought the best talent together to make movies? Where else could a guy like me who came from Russia be able to control all this? It takes diligence, and thrift, and the hand of God."

Lahr nodded, surprised and confused by the typical Mayer introduction, calling on Metro, the homeland, and Divine Will, in that order.

"We want you to stay out here, Bert. But we can't afford to pay you *pro rata*."

Lahr was astounded. His contract with George White had been a handshake. No one had ever balked at paying his salary.

"Mr. Mayer, Florenz Ziegfeld called me a few weeks ago to do a show for him in the fall. I've got to go East to firm the deal."

"We can't pay you that money, Bert," said Mayer, chomping on his cigar.

"But it's in my contract. I want to go back to New York. I've got business there. We agreed to this a long time ago."

Mayer got up from his desk and leaned on the glass top with fingers jammed against it like a tripod. "We can't pay you *pro rata*. You'll only be here a few more weeks."

"I can't give in to that."

Mayer went to the water cooler and took some pills from his vest pocket. "He tried to cajole me. He kept walking around me, talking. Sometimes I couldn't see him."

When Lahr persisted, Mayer lost his reserve. He shoved Mannix, screaming, "Why did you bring this man in here? Get him out of my sight! Get him out!"

Mayer turned to Lahr. "Actors are a dime a dozen out here. We won't do any close-ups of you. We'll do it our way or not at all. We won't finish the picture. Go back East if you want." Mayer stormed out of the office.

Lahr's first impulse was to pack for New York. "But I discussed it with friends who thought I was making the wrong move. They said, 'This man is very powerful. It's not going to do you any good if you come back here.' "

A few days later, Lahr called the front office and said he would stay for the cutting and close-up shots. M-G-M offered to pay him one thousand dollars a week "expenses." In three weeks he was shuttling across the country to receive a much warmer welcome from Florenz Ziegfeld.

The Mayer incident left Lahr with an abiding distrust of movie management, even seven years later, when he returned among the palm trees, an exile eager to cash in on Hollywood's fabulous prewar boom. Nearly everything the movie industry marketed turned to gold, and Lahr began living as if he would be part of that gilt-edged currency. He purchased a cream-colored Cadillac convertible, ordered his casual custom-tailored suits from Eddie Schmidt, Hollywood's tailor for the "stars," and waited for the scripts to arrive. He had high hopes, and a Guild card that read: "Support." When the offers arrived, they were not what he expected. The anticipation was mingled with suspicion. John O'Hara, a frequent drinking partner who as a writer suffered the same frustrations that Lahr faced under the lights, remembers that he and Lahr "shared among other things a distaste for the men who were producing motion pictures."

From the beginning, Lahr's anxiety about Hollywood scripts reflected the battle between his standards of comic excellence and his desire to make California his home. The buffoon's anarchy on stage capitalized on immediacy, extending into the twentieth century an impulse that could trace its heritage to the amphitheaters of Greece and the streets of Italy. Now, not only his body but also his comic personality would be subjected to the electronic distortions of a new medium.

In 1938 the quantity of work disguised the quality of Lahr's experience in front of the camera. Like so many others, he suffocated in roles that neither used his talent nor cared for it. *Merry-Go-Round of 1938* was only a modest success, despite the insertion of Lahr's popular Woodchopper song and the ego balm of being the highest salaried comedian on a term deal in Hollywood. Universal Pictures, however, dropped his contract; and Darryl Zanuck gave him a six-month contract at Twentieth Century-Fox. The next two films, *Love and Hisses* and *Josette,* were no better. Lahr's word is "failure," but the problem lay as much with the system as with the management. Neither Lahr nor his agent fought it. Believing in affluence and aspiring to gargantuan leisure, they could only bemoan the dearth of material and acquiesce.

If Lahr was perplexed by the inability of studios to find decent scripts for him, his friend Jimmy Cagney had pointed out the economic score. Cagney, soldier-straight and surprisingly aloof from the Hollywood idiom, had served on the Screen Actor's Guild. Lahr was a visiting member of the "Irish Mafia" (as they jokingly called themselves), and heard the facts and figures of Hollywood discussed at nearly every weekly meeting of the clan. According to a Screen Actor's Guild survey, despite the large movie output, approximately only four hundred performers were employed. The average amount of time worked came to three and a half weeks a year.

Lahr did not count himself lucky. He had been one of Broadway's highest paid comics in the thirties. In Hollywood, he had to hustle to make a comparable living. This inevitably meant playing inferior parts, sometimes, humiliatingly, to a twelve-year-old star like Shirley Temple, which he did in *Just Around the Corner.*

In the show Lahr was paired with Joan Davis to supply comedy relief. A few weeks before the release of the picture, a movie executive told him, "They previewed your picture. You're a big hit."

"I was very happy about it. I never had a part up to then where I could stand out. I was working on the Fox lot, and the job was the first of any consequence I'd had."

Since Lahr seldom went to see himself in pictures (and today rarely watches his taped television performances), he sent Mildred to see the show. When she returned from the picture, she announced that he was hardly in it. He called the director, who could only explain: "You and Joan were too strong. Mrs. Temple saw to it that you were cut down."

As a comedian Lahr was banished to either playing a friend or a guest. "In other words, the comic was incidental to the picture's value. If you're not part of the story and you're put in as comic relief on the periphery of the script, you're the first thing that is cut."

Lahr's problems in adjusting to the Hollywood scene reflected a shift in public taste. Sound had changed the focus of movies. By 1938, comedy no longer dominated films. Romance sold best. As James Cagney said to Lahr, "This is a boy-girl business." There were exceptions like W. C. Fields and the Marx Brothers, but significantly, their humor was distinctly more verbal and subdued than Lahr's. Films did not want the eccentricities of comedy to overshadow the romance.

"The answer was this," explains Lahr. "The Buster Keatons, the Harold Lloyds, the Charlie Chaplins—that kind of humor went out. For years great Broadway comics like Ed Wynn, Bobby Clark, Jack Pearl never were a success in pictures. The studios never went after them unless they were *legitimate*."

Lahr had to teach himself film technique because none of the directors wanted to tamper with his highly successful approach to laughter. "The directors, I think, held me in awe. Whatever I did, they thought was right. But I've done a lot of things in pictures which, when I saw them afterwards, I almost vomited."

The comic mechanism Lahr had spent a lifetime adjusting seemed to be off kilter in front of a camera. "Different movements which got laughs on stage came out overplayed, 'funny-funny' on the screen. They were very obvious. I shuddered at them." The camera itself distorted and, in some ways, destroyed the basic responses of buffoonery. Lahr was aware of the difficulty. "The camera made every reaction twice as large. Instead of underplaying, I was way over. I was a caricature. In moving pictures, I learned that the audience subconsciously expects everything to be *real*. On stage, if you had a rock, it didn't look real, it signified a rock. But on screen it had to be a rock or a real pie or a real dog or a real emotion. Everything had to be real, if it wasn't, the audience wouldn't believe your story."

The camera worked against him in another way. Lahr's responses were isolated from the larger dramatic environment. He was still funny on screen, but the camera's limitations—the close-up and various angle shots—depleted the energy of his performance and the richness of response. The comic event became more literal, deprived of its improvisational spontaneity and surprise. Mervyn LeRoy's dictum about filming illustrates the problem: "Where the camera sits, everybody sits." Lahr's humor relied upon his response to the stage world. He was larger than life and yet related to all of it. The stage's frame contributed a sense of formal control to clowning's anarchic energy. The tension fed comedy. On screen the comic was cut off in the picture frame sometimes at the head, at other times below the knees. By isolating part of the body or by separating the comedian from the total environment of his humor, the resonance and theatrical momentum of Lahr's laughter was severely hampered.

Lahr's first breakthrough in pictures was a dramatic role in George Cukor's *Zaza* (1938), a story producers felt might do for Claudette Colbert what it had done for so many others. Originally a stage play produced by David Belasco, it made Mrs. Leslie Carter the belle of Broadway. When the first film version came out of Paramount in 1915, it launched the career of Pauline Frederick. The remake of the film in 1923 bolstered the career of Gloria Swanson.

Cukor cast Lahr as Cascart, an admirer and vaudeville partner of the scintillating Zaza. The backstage melodrama chronicles Zaza's shattered romance with a married man and her rise to stardom with the faithful Cascart as her manager. The choice of a low-comic surprised the movie colony, but Cukor, who needed a vaudeville warmth in his film, understood the considerable acting talent that went into being a funny-man. Although Lahr was apprehensive undertaking a legitimate role, his disgust at the comic parts he was getting and the need for work made the decision easy.

Cukor, a director whose insight and flair for light comedy was especially strong when directing women like Greta Garbo, Katharine Hepburn, and Audrey Hepburn, was able to explain to Lahr what his previous directors could not. The part was a challenge to Lahr. "Cukor edited me. He would take me aside and say, 'Simple, Bert, simple. Cut it down to half. Give me half of that. You've got a microphone above you. You don't have to kick it out to an audience of a thousand people. Let the camera do the work. You don't have to reach out to an audience and hand it to them.' He was the first man to try and adapt me to films."

On camera, Lahr's acting resources were often amusing to the cast, and indicative of an approach to performing not learned on a movie lot. Erskine Johnson, a Hollywood reporter on the *Zaza* set, captured the freshness of comic response:

Director George Cukor is rehearsing Claudette Colbert and Bert Lahr in a scene from *Zaza*. Miss Colbert is lying in bed, heartbroken over the necessity of giving up Herbert Marshall, who has been found to have a wife and child. Lahr's opening line is—

"Oh, come now, you'll cry your eyes out over a dozen worse fellows yet."

"And then," prompts Cukor, "when you see she is unimpressed, you try some other way to cheer her up. Use that funny laugh you used on the stage."

Lahr goes through the routine of ludicrous laughs, six in all. The sixth is the one Cukor had in mind. The scene is taken, Miss Colbert responding to the laugh, pleading—

"Don't tease me. Just—just." She doesn't complete the sentence. Instead, she bursts into hysterical laughter.

"Cut," says Cukor. "What's the trouble?"

"That wasn't the right laugh," Miss Colbert sputters between giggles. "It was a brand new one."

"Yeah, yeah, it was," Lahr confesses. "I've got a dozen of 'em. I couldn't remember which one we decided on. Anyway, they're liable to come out differently every time."

Lahr took great pride in *Zaza*. He collected enough material on that picture to fill two complete scrapbooks. His enthusiasm was real because of the economic leverage it gave him in Hollywood. One theme is included repeatedly in his *Zaza* memorabilia.

Bert Lahr, in this his first straight dramatic part, impresses with a sincerity and skill in modulation for important assignments outside his customary comic parts. He plays the patron and theatrical partner of Zaza and shows, perhaps, unsuspected ability in the emotional register.

Thirty years later, the film seems surprisingly sentimental even for a Cukor product. Its best moment is the vaudeville routine of Zaza and Cascart. Arms akimbo, Lahr thrashes his elbows, rolls his eyes, rubs up against his partner with the grace of a Persian cat. The gestures, the excitement of seeing the performers before an audience are more accurately portrayed than the usual backstage melodrama. Lahr's song and dance are not as fiery as the real burlesque fandangos, but the performance is still vital. In his serious moments, Lahr is dutifully controlled. With his face robbed of distortion, it becomes surprisingly smooth and shallow on the screen. "Unfortunately the Hays office cut the picture to shreds, but I got the notices. If it had been a hit, I would have been made as a dramatic actor."

Zaza was moderately successful at the box office; and, despite a performance that was severely cut before distribution, Lahr's press agent was pleased to slip a surprising announcement to the trade late in 1938:

No More Stage
For Bert

Plans of Broadway producers to star Bert Lahr in a show will not materialize since the comedian is scheduled for another heavy season in the cinema capital.

While Lahr did not have any immediate plans after *Zaza*, the optimism created by the picture overwhelmed him. He began building his dream home. The opulent standards set by Mary Pickford, Harold Lloyd, and Douglas Fairbanks, Jr., were not the ones to which theatrical expatriates aspired. Although their homes were well-appointed and attractive, they were comparatively modest palaces. "To be living in a fixed place was something new to any performer." It was the first time in his life that Lahr owned the roof over his head.

The wonder and excitement Lahr felt is evident in his plan for his home. The house would have a den, a bar, a swimming pool, and even a driveway complete with an electric gate. But more significantly, the comedian from the streets of Yorkville would surround himself with a jungle of flowers and fruit trees. His trees created a dense orchard of eucalyptus, grapefruit, avocado, orange, lemon, lime, almond, and fig. ("Figs that big," he says, holding his fingers as if asking for a double whisky.) Clusters of exotic flowers blanketed the lawn: gardenias, camellias, birds of paradise, orly andrews, Gabriel's horn, and even bougainvillaea over the garage.

The profusion is what he remembers. He walked among his trees, feeling the softness of the fruit, worrying like a nervous aunt about the health of his orchard. When the fruit ripened, he helped gather it himself, and then gave it away to anyone who asked—and to some who did not.

Friends of Bert Lahr claim he shipped avocados from his orchard to "21" with instructions to serve them to friends without charge.

The story was true. He could not begin to use all the fruit his orchards yielded. But, fascinated with the bounty of nature, Lahr even planted a truck garden. When he felt a fit of insecurity, he grabbed a spade and tended to the vegetables he had planted. In his first "crop" he discovered that the cantaloupe and cucumbers, planted next to one another, had cross-pollinated, creating a weird, inedible fruit he named a "cucolope."

Gardening was no substitute for work, and Lahr was in his usual state of despondency when Louis Shurr sent him a script from the Metro lot early in 1939, a fairy tale that neither of them had heard of. It was called *The Wizard of Oz*.

Lahr and Shurr were attending a wedding the next day. At the church Lahr found himself sitting in front of his agent. When the bride came down the aisle, Shurr, a hard-boiled sentimentalist leaned forward and whispered, "Doesn't she look beautiful?"

Lahr replied immediately, "Yes, I read the *Oz* script. It's wonderful."

The Wizard of Oz was a unique property, ideally geared to the world of film and the panoply of talent on the Metro lot. The idea of a fantasy had come separately to the producer of the film and his assistant. Producer Mervyn LeRoy had dreamed of filming the L. Frank Baum classic for years. Arthur Freed, who had been writing lyrics for Metro musicals, saw it as a means of launching his own producing career. "Louis [Mayer] wanted me to produce. There were two properties I was interested in buying—*The Wizard of Oz* and the Rodgers and Hart musical *Babes in Arms,* which I later made with Mickey Rooney and Judy Garland. I had been writing for Judy, and I was interested in her." Freed finally got Garland for the picture after the studio had lobbied hard for Shirley Temple.

The picture was an immense technical accomplishment, expanding the potential of film-making by going against the rubrics of Hollywood's formula realism. No make-up man had ever faced the problem of turning a Jack Haley into a Tin Woodsman, a Ray Bolger into a Scarecrow, or a Bert Lahr into a Cowardly Lion; no special-effects engineer had shown life from the inside of a cyclone. "A bigger job than merely creating something unreal descended upon us all," LeRoy wrote in *The New York Times*. "The task of putting realism into the fantastic." *The Wizard of Oz* (a complete departure from the cartoon fantasy of Walt Disney), was a collaboration that invented a new world and strange events that nonetheless had to convince an audience of their actuality.

The price of invention was high. Both LeRoy and Freed had to battle Metro executives to do the film. The opposition came from Nick Schenck, Mayer's business partner, who thought the fantasy a waste of money. The picture would cost Metro an astounding $3,700,000 to make. LeRoy recalls, "Schenck wanted to stop the picture. He thought I was ruining the company, spending too much money. I remember I told him, 'Mr. Schenck, I wish I had three and a half million, I'd buy it from you. It's going to be worth more than that.'" But L. B. Mayer, a man who spoke out loudly, if not too clearly, for wholesome fun, put his weight behind the production, and his insight started Metro on one of the most imaginative and popular pictures in its history. What seemed a gigantic financial risk in 1939 became a national favorite which, with television, would earn $800,000 for a single replay.

Freed commissioned Harold Arlen and E. Y. Harburg to do the music. As a writer for musicals himself, he knew the value of Arlen's music and Harburg's lyrics. "Harburg had a great sense of fantasy in his lyrics." Freed was right, and his proof was the beautiful realistic flights of imagination that Harburg concocted in "Follow the Yellow Brick Road," and "Ding Dong the Witch Is Dead." *The Wizard of Oz* would become the most memorable of the Arlen–Harburg film collaborations.

Harburg promoted Lahr for the part of the lion. As a lyricist who could imitate his sound, he began ad-libbing lines from the script to the producers. "'Put up your dukes! Put up your paws!' Can you imagine Bert doing that?" LeRoy and Freed liked the idea. "They accepted Bert because they thought he was funny," says Harburg. "I didn't. I never do that. I accepted Bert and wanted him for the part of the Cowardly Lion because the role was one of the things that *The Wizard of Oz* stands for, the search for some basic human necessity. At the heart of this seeking after courage is fear. Call it anxiety now; call it neurosis. We're in a world we don't understand. When the Cowardly Lion admits that he lacks courage, everybody's heart is out to him. He must be somebody who embodies all this pathos, sweetness, and yet puts on this comic bravura. Bert had that quality to such a wonderful degree. It was in his face; it was in his talk; it was in himself. To me that kind of comedy is on a higher plane approaching a more humanitarian, universal statement about Man. It is not a temporary gag. A lyricist is lucky to have a Bert Lahr in his lifetime, who incorporates humor and humanity in his performance."

To both producers, Lahr was a natural. They associated a lion, like the Metro image, with a proud roar. But Harburg had worked on two shows with Lahr, and he knew how much more lay behind the caterwauling. In an inscription of a book of his short poems, Harburg wrote:

To Bert—
   Still King of the Forest.
   With "ruff" and "luff."

     Yipper

The Cowardly Lion embodied the very best parts of a buffoon's instincts: gut responses, frenetic gestures, a touching and elusive sense of the world. The roar he made created affection, not fear; yet it kept the audience and the people around him at a distance from a more disturbing private self.

Although Hollywood has been known to film successful pictures many times, milking the public's fascination with one particular vehicle, it is generally agreed that no one could undertake a re-make of *The Wizard of Oz*. Not only would cost be prohibitive, but no finer cast (Ray Bolger, Jack Haley, Judy Garland, and Lahr) could be assembled for the major parts. Nor could a sufficient number of midgets be rounded up to play the inhabitants of Oz.

According to LeRoy, 350 midgets were difficult to amass even when vaudeville entrepreneurs managed midget acts. The responsibility for bringing all the midgets to Culver City fell on the casting director Bill Grady, an old Broadway agent who had handled W. C. Fields. Although Singer's Midgets are listed in the picture credits for *The Wizard of Oz*, Grady maintains that Singer had nothing to do with acquiring the little people, although many of them had worked for the impresario. Grady explains it this way:

"Of course the only guy I could get them from was Leo Singer of Singer's Midgets. Leo could only give me a hundred and fifty. I went to a midget monologist called Major Doyle. I told the Major my problem, and he said he could get them all for me. I said I had one hundred and fifty from Singer." Doyle despised Singer not only because he would give him no work, but because the five-foot-five manager was known to exploit his clientele. He answered Grady in a Boston Irish brogue, as rich as it was stubborn.

" 'I'll not give you one if you do business with that son-of-a-bitch.' 'What am I gonna do?' I said. 'I'll get you the three hundred and fifty.' 'I'm almost committed to Leo Singer.' 'If you do business with Singer, you'll not get any from me.' So I called up Leo and explained the situation. I said that I could get all the midgets from Major Doyle but if I did business with him, I couldn't get any from the Major. Leo raised hell, but I explained that there was nothing else I could do. When I went down and told the Major that I'd called off Singer, he danced a jig right on the street in front of Dinty Moore's.

"The Major gets these midgets for me. They come from all over the world. Now I've got a date. I'm going to bring them out West in buses. The meeting place was the Times Square Hotel on Forty-Third Street. I had these buses pull up there. We were going to bring about one hundred and seventy midgets out of New York, the rest I was going to pick up out West.

"The first three buses are loaded. They are to go through the Holland Tunnel and on through to Chicago. The first bus starts *up Broadway*. They are supposed to go down Eighth Avenue. I grabbed a cab and followed the bus. Major Doyle is sitting in the front seat of the first bus. I yelled out, 'Hey, Major, where we going?'

" 'Come with me,' he yelled.

"So I followed him. Leo Singer lived at Sixty-eighth Street and Central Park West on the fifth floor. Major Doyle took the three buses and arrived at Central Park West. They waited at the curb in front of Singer's house.

"The Major got up and went to the doorman. 'Phone upstairs and tell Leo Singer to look out the window.'

"It took about ten minutes. Then Singer looked from his fifth floor window. And there were all the midgets in those buses in front of his house with their bare behinds sticking out the window."

"Major Doyle's Revenge," as it became known in movie circles, was not the last the movie executives heard from the midgets. Once they got to Culver City, there was a problem of controlling them. The polyglot group of little people came from a wide range of professions. Many of the "Munchkins" were midgets who, in fact, made their living by panhandling, pimping, and whoring. Assistants were ordered to watch the crew of midgets, who brandished knives and often conceived passions for other, larger Metro personnel.

"I remember one day," smiles Lahr, "when we were supposed to shoot a scene with the witch's monkeys. The head of the group was a little man who called himself 'The Count.' He was never sober. When the call came, everybody was looking for the Count. We could not start without him. And then, a little ways off stage, we heard what sounded like a whine coming from the men's room. Somebody investigated. They found the Count. He got plastered during lunch, and fell in the latrine and couldn't get himself out."

The midgets were also a problem from the production angle. Victor Fleming, the director who stayed longest on the film, had a production philosophy that probably accounted for his tenure. (Dick Thorpe and George Cukor tried to direct the picture and gave up. King Vidor finished the last black and white segment of *Oz* when Fleming left to direct *Gone With the Wind.*) Fleming's dictum was simple: "Don't get excited—*obstacles make a better picture.*" There were many outrageous problems: a flying witch, bolts of fire, simulated tornadoes. How do you get a rusted Tin Woodsman off his mound of earth on to the road for a dance? How will the Cowardly Lion wag the tail of his one hundred-pound lion suit? How do you teach 350 Munchkins to sing "We Welcome You to Munchkin Land," when only a third of them speak English?

The idea of having the midgets sing their song seemed natural enough. Fleming gave them the song, but the first day they performed on camera his problem was apparent. Jack Haley says, "Some of 'dem sang mit de Cherman agzent. They couldn't speak English and when they sang together it was the damndest conglomeration of noise you ever heard." Fleming solved it by having the Munchkins mouth the words while the voices were dubbed.

Although Lahr had wanted to do the picture immediately and Twentieth Century had let his contract run out, Metro wanted his services for only three weeks at $2,500 per week. Lahr balked. "I said I wanted a five-week guarantee. When they wouldn't give it to me I said 'The hell with this, I'll go back East and do a show.' I wasn't getting the right parts. Nobody knew what to do with my comedy." It took Metro a month to accept Lahr's terms. Its prediction was significantly unrealistic. Lahr worked five weeks on one number, "The Jitterbug," which never got into the picture. The studio exhibited little understanding of the complexity of the undertaking or of the future of their venture into realistic fantasy. Lahr spent twenty-six weeks as the Cowardly Lion.

Staring out of their offices, the executives of Metro were treated to a panorama of grotesques that even Nathanael West could not equal. These were not fusiliers, bandits, or cowboys going to work on Stage 36, but people with green skin, a man walking in what looked like a tin box, his face tinted silver, a lion sauntering erect carrying his tail to avoid tripping, hundreds of midgets with red fright wigs and pointed beards scurrying to the lot. The window watchers were always being surprised; the people never stayed the same. Sometimes the man with the silver face looked rusty; the midgets with their rosy cheeks on Monday would be transformed into cloud gray on Tuesday.

For the actors, the metamorphosis began promptly at seven each morning. The principals had a make-up man apiece; and twenty make-up men processed the Munchkins at the rate of nine an hour.

The Wizard of Oz was the first large-scale make-up job in Hollywood. Metro had to have special make-ups created for the Wicked Witch, and for the Tin Man, whose silver skin and blemished, rusty quality had never been attempted before. Metro also had to invent tricks of its own. The primary one evolved in *The Wizard of Oz* was the use of sponge rubber. The Tin Woodsman's helmet was made of rubber, his bald head simulated by a plastic cap that the studio had just developed. Lahr's lion snout was also composed of sponge rubber; so too were the Wicked Witch's hooked chin and the Scarecrow's sandbag head, which was made to look like a burlap sack. The rubber was applied to the face and then colored to match it.

The make-up, which was applied fresh and with new rubber fixings each day, took two hours to put on. Jack Dawn, the head of the Metro make-up department, worked on the Cowardly Lion. He remembers that Lahr was never too enthusiastic about getting into character. "He would wait reluctantly for the exact time to start putting on the make-up. He'd just hesitate and keep looking at the clock." Although Lahr was surrounded by two old cronies in Bolger and Haley, *Oz* was grueling. "You couldn't have fun," says Haley, "it was awful. I had a radio show at the time. I had to drag myself to work." Even the Munchkins were unenthusiastic, not prepared for the incessant waiting and painstaking preparation. The make-up men also had a problem with the midgets. "There was a great deal to learn about working with them," Dawn says. "They were adults, not children, and sometimes we forgot. They did not want us to touch them or lift them up into the make-up chairs. They clambered into the seats by themselves."

The costumes for Lahr and Haley were particularly burdensome. Haley, encased in his Tin Man's garb, was nearly immobile off the camera. The studio designed a leaning board so he could lie down. Lahr's situation was even more preposterous. Already burdened with a heavy wig, he bolstered the cumbersome lion's suit with shoulderpads. The make-up, which was so funny on the screen, was no laughing matter off it. The sponge rubber that covered his upper lip prevented the snarling Lion from eating a regular lunch. Lahr took his meals through a straw since the make-up was too elaborate to strip down. The other principals ate in their dressing rooms. "They wouldn't allow us to eat in the commissary," Haley recalls. "If we put on our dressing gowns—as we were supposed to—it would have caused too much of a commotion."

In 1939, before the color process was perfected, it took more light to illuminate a set. The heat from the arc lights made the costumes unbearable and the hours long. "Each day Judy [Garland] had to go to school. Her tutor—an old woman—would come on the set and someone would yell 'School Time!' We used to long for that sound—it meant we had an hour's rest." Too keyed up and uncomfortable to sleep, Lahr ambled next door to Haley's dressing room to enjoy a cigarette and a chat. Usually he found his friend asleep on his special board.

Off camera, adversity was something often overcome with good talk. Among friends like Bolger, Haley, and Lahr, a continual patter of stories and pranks persisted. If the work was difficult, the actors felt that the picture and their parts were excellent. Their high spirits relieved the boredom of retakes. When Haley or Bolger were preparing to perform, Lahr bellowed the triumvirate's private anthem, "Smith's premium ham!"—a radio commercial of the day. "Vic Fleming had never experienced guys like us," Lahr says. "Some legitimate directors can't imagine anybody thinking about something else and when he yells 'Shoot,' just going in and playing. We'd kid around up to the last minute and go on. You could see he got mad and red-faced. Some actors try and get into the mood. They'll put themselves into the character. I never did that. I'm not that—let's say—dedicated."

When the trio told dirty stories, they tried to keep them from the inquisitive ears of Judy Garland, who was then fifteen. "Little Judy would sneak around. We'd joke with her and yell 'Get outta here . . .' " Their affection for Judy was genuine. At the conclusion of the picture Bolger gave her a fine edition of "The Raven" by Edgar Allan Poe, who was her favorite poet. In later years, as the picture became a Hollywood legend, stories about how the three comedians tried to nudge her off the Yellow Brick Road would circulate. But the Tin Man, Cowardly Lion, and Scarecrow never acted maliciously toward the talented young star. As Haley points out, "How could that be? When we go off to see the Wizard we're locked arm in arm, and every shot is a long shot. How can you push someone out of the picture with a long shot?"

Sometimes their jibes came very close to the bone. Bolger, who had worked with Lahr in *Life Begins at 8:40,* was often the good-natured brunt of their pranks. He was not as outgoing as the other two, but his generosity of spirit extended to his particular brand of blarney. His tall tales made him a perfect foil for Lahr's clowning. Lahr's overtures always began with, "Hey, do you wanna have some *fun?*" When Haley agreed, Lahr made his proposal.

"Lahr said to me, 'Say that you'd like to be somebody or do something. If you dwell on it, Bolger will tell you he's done that.' I agreed to go along with it. Everyday we had lunch together I'd say, 'You know Ray, Bert and I worked together many years ago in a show called *Folly Town.* He was in terrific shape. He used to work out boxing with other guys, and he had a belly on him like a washboard. He used to box with this guy practically every day.'

"Then you wait. And here's the line. You know this line is coming; you could lay book on it. Bolger says, 'I was a boxer once.' You were? 'Yeah, I wasn't very good, but I had a few fights.' And then he'd tell you an incident about one of his 'bouts.' "

Bolger's harmless tales were the source of amusement during many of their off-camera moments. But Bolger had his own revenge. Once, after a heavy rainstorm, he had a friend call Lahr to warn him that soil from his newly acquired land in Coldwater Canyon had been swept down the road in the torrent, and it was necessary to send a truck to collect it. Lahr panicked, and made a few frantic phone calls before he realized that he'd been duped.

On camera, Victor Fleming won the respect of all the performers. Lahr was flattered when Fleming would take him aside and ask his opinion for improving a scene. But Haley saw this tactic in another, more realistic perspective. "Fleming had a wonderful understanding of people. He knew that the make-up was wearing on us. After a couple of hours it was depressing to have it on. In order for us not to lose interest in the picture, to try and keep our animation, he would call all three of us together and say, 'Fellahs, you've got to help me on this scene.' Well, I knew this guy was a big director, and he didn't need actors to help him. He'd say, 'You guys are Broadway stars, what do you think we should do here?' The scene might be waking up in the poppy field and we'd give our suggestions on how to play it . . . But I always thought he was just trying to keep our interest."

But Fleming's inquiries produced results. In the scene where Dorothy and her companions fall asleep in the poppy field and wake to find it snowing, Lahr inserted a key line—"Unusual weather we're havin', ain't it?"

"Fleming couldn't see it," he recalls. "I said, 'Vic, I'm sure it's a laugh. He trusted me. In that situation, I was right. It was a big laugh."

Many of the pieces of business that earned Lahr awards for his portrayal of the Cowardly Lion were the fortuitous consolidation of his Broadway experience. Lines ad-libbed in the picture stand out as interesting grafts from his stage performances. Assuming much the same boxing pose as Gink Shiner in *Hold Everything,* the Lion roars, "Put 'em up, put 'em *uuuup."* The slurred words, the not-quite-articulate diction are all part of the stage comic's machinery. When Oz awards him a medal, Lahr reacts like the cop to Nellie Bean. "Read what the medal says, 'Courage.' Ain't it de truth. Ain't it de *troooooth."*

With the Arlen–Harburg score, Lahr's inability to keep up with the erudite, polished lyrics is part of the humor he'd mastered so well in *The Show Is On.* While a stage hand controlled his tail with a fishing rod from a catwalk above the set to keep him from tripping on it, Lahr even managed to sneak in a hint of his English accent when he proclaimed—

Yes—it's sad, believe me, missy
When you're born to be a sissy
Without the vim and verve.
But I would show my prowess,
Be a lion, not a mouesse
If I only had the nerve.

Lahr's mugging of the Harburg puns forced *The New York Times* film critic, Frank Nugent, to exclaim, "Mr. Lahr's Lion is fion."

Awaiting his audience with the "Terrible Oz," the Lion pondered being "King of the Forest" in an elaborate excursion into nonsense verse. The song became Lahr's most famous comic gambit. (See Appendix 5.) Lahr delivered "King of the Forest" as if it were open season on lions as well as baritones. All the trills, dainty exclamations, and hoots are heightened in lion's costume; and Lahr's performance is more vibrant and complex than in his other films. His special comic spirit and excesses of gesture were easily incorporated into this "realistic fantasy." The role that came closest to his imaginative life and stage energy became the public's finest memory of him on screen.

At the conclusion of the picture, Mervyn LeRoy recalls, the crew applauded the Cowardly Lion. Secretly, Lahr was confident in his performance; but he could not forget a remark that Frank Morgan, who played Oz, made to him during the filming. "Bert," said Morgan, "you're going to be a great hit in this picture. But it's not going to do you a damn bit of good—you're playing an animal."

"If I'd made a hit as a *human being*," Lahr muses, "then perhaps I'd be sailing in films now."

With the picture completed, Lahr bided his time at home, nervously awaiting the studio's verdict and eager for work. "One day, I'm sitting on my lawn, and 'Square-Deal' Grady pulls up at a light and yells, "Hi ya, Gnong-Gnong.' This surprised me. Grady and I had been friends in New York, but since he'd become an executive, many of the actors, including me, felt he'd upstaged us. Out there you know by the attitude of the executives what your fate is. When he yelled at me, I was surprised. It was the first time he'd given me a tumble since we'd been in Hollywood. I said to myself, they must have previewed the picture, and I'm a hit. So I called Louis, and he called the front office. He called back. 'Bert, they've shown the picture. You're a real hit.'"

Hollywood was humming with the news of his performance. To Lahr it was sweet revenge on the Twentieth Century-Fox producers who had welcomed him to the lot only to mysteriously stop talking to him.

Louis Shurr suggested that Lahr do a Broadway show. Buddy DeSylva and Herbert Fields had an interesting property called *Du Barry Was a Lady*. "Lahr wanted no part of it," Shurr recalls. "Bert said, 'Metro's going to keep me for life after what I've done for this picture. I'm going to stay out here for a long time." Shurr wanted Lahr to protect himself with a Broadway show. Lahr, never one for taking a risk with his career, felt his performance was protection enough.

He was astonished when Shurr brought him the gossip from Metro a few weeks after the preview. "I had just checked with Mervyn LeRoy. He said that Metro was going to stop making musicals at the moment for financial reasons. They're dropping your contract as well as Haley's and Bolger's." Lahr couldn't believe it.

A month later, *The Wizard of Oz* opened in Hollywood. Lahr was so optimistic that he attended the premiere at Grauman's Chinese Theater with Shurr, Mildred, and Buddy DeSylva. "He was the smash of the picture," recalls Shurr. Walking out of the theater Lahr confided to him. "I'm not going to do a show. I want to stay out here and make pictures!" Shurr, a man who understood the facts of Hollywood, could only defer to his client. "I told him I'd try to talk to the executives and see what I could do." In the meantime Lahr went to New York, impatient at waiting for so crucial a decision from the studio and to wind up the painful technicalities of his annulment from Mercedes.

Lahr was in New York when *The Wizard of Oz* opened there at the Capitol Theater. His picture was in the window of Lindy's, directly across the street from the theater; the maître d'hôtel at "21" and the Stork Club recognized him as if he'd been away only a week. By 8:15 on the day of the opening, ten thousand people had lined up to see the film. By the evening, *The New York Times* was telling the city— *"The Lahr roar is one of the laughingest sounds since the talkies came in . . ."*

Lahr reported his pleasure to Mildred in a letter: "Believe me it was a tonic for my inferiority complex which is so readily developed in Hollywood."

But the two weeks in New York also disturbed him. These should have been happy times, he kept telling himself. His movie was a success. His private life was straightening out—Abe Berman had explained how the Domestic Relations Law, Section 7, subdivision 5, would enable him to finally be free to marry Mildred early in the New Year. Everything seemed so straightforward; yet his future in a town that now knew him as one of its finest exports seemed as uncertain as it had been when he was much younger.

People were swarming to the theater; *Variety* was blaring the *Oz* grosses all over its Picture Section—and yet Metro was thinking of letting him go. He was loved by a woman, and yet after so many years of waiting, he was uncertain about marriage. In his self-absorption, Lahr never suspected that his relationship with Mildred had been in jeopardy. But the painful and complicated legal proceedings had frazzled Mildred's patience and made her apprehensive of any future with him. Lahr never knew she had written Berman about her marital prospects as late as December 1938.

> Abe, how is BL's case straightening out? Do you feel that it is working out or is it proving a wasted six and a half years? I get so afraid when I think of going out on my own. But know that if I must do it, I cannot afford to wait much longer. I get older each year, and each year that youthful spirit I was endowed with weakens, and grows dimmer. I am certain by the time you come out here, you will know definitely.

Berman could not tell her anything when he visited California, but she never left Lahr. He would never know, even with the success of the legal struggle, how close he came to losing her.

The annulment placed another financial burden on him that made a Metro contract imperative. He had spent nearly a quarter of a million dollars to cure Mercedes; and now he had to establish a fund of over $150,000 to take care of her. She would live in Arizona with her sister and son.

The bond of so many performances and private aspirations was reduced to a few pieces of legal foolscap. He would be able to return to California and tell Mildred that the papers for the annulment would be filed in the Westchester County Clerk's office.

In the last page of the fifty-page documentation, one of the examining physicians and a practicing psychiatrist for thirty-seven years, replied to cross-examination with a sad decisiveness.

Q: Doctor, in your practice have you ever seen another patient suffering the same ailment as you have described this person (Mercedes Lahrheim) suffering from?

A: I have seen post-encephalitic psychoses and I have seen lots of simple dementia praecoxes. I have never seen them both tied up together in this most interesting and unusual type.

Q: Have you ever seen any patient that had it, that was eventually cured?

A: No.

Q: Do you know of any in the medical books?

A: No.

Lahr could return to California with his life intact. If he thought of it one way, everything was good—he would marry Mildred; they had the house; he would continue in films. But, in truth, he saw himself stalled like the Cowardly Lion. He was heading back to California and away from the stage. He was going "home" to a career that was still in the hands of movie executives who threatened to drop his contract. He was making money; yet his financial responsibilities were suddenly graver. The business of comedy was now more pressing than ever. He had to work. But for whom?

His emotional circumstances scared him: there was a woman who was now a mask, living in a silence he feared he had helped create, and there was her exact opposite, the buoyant, beautiful Mildred. She was still not legally committed to him. Would she change like Mercedes? Would a woman so stable, so patient, and so generous grow apart from him the way Mercedes had done?

When he returned to California, Louis Shurr confirmed what he knew before Lahr left—Metro was dropping his option. Lahr seemed resigned, but totally distraught. He talked with Buddy DeSylva, and a contract to do *Du Barry* was drawn up.

He signed for the show in Shurr's Hollywood office. Putting Louis's pen back in its jade holder, he glanced up at his agent. "Well, after all, how many lion parts are there?"

He would return temporarily to Broadway, where comedy and the name of Bert Lahr were still King.

"...BUT WHAT DO I DO NEXT YEAR?"

A S FAR AS MRS. HELEN SCHROEDER WAS CONCERNED, THE TELEGRAM postmarked February 11, 1940, should have been written years earlier.

> DON'T LAUGH JUST MARRIED
> MILDRED AND BERT

But nobody was laughing. The relationship had undergone too much—even after Mildred had been granted a divorce on October 4, 1937. On January 4, 1938, the temporary injunction that had made it impossible for her to return to New York was finally reversed by the State Court. Up to that time, Mildred had been guilty of contempt of court and failing to obey injunction orders. Now, Mildred was exultant and secure. The gaiety of the telegram reflects her ebullience. But it was not funny to her mother, and certainly not to her new husband. It was he who chose to be married on a Sunday, in the quiet town of Elkton, Maryland, three days after an interlocutory judgment of the annulment of his first marriage had been filed with the Westchester County Clerk's Office. Lahr picked Elkton with the care he usually reserved for selecting a fairway wood. His desire for anonymity is an indication of how heavily his guilt about Mercedes and the legal battle with Robinson weighed on him. "We had to get married as quickly as possible. That *whole* thing would have come back at us."

Standing in front of the Episcopal minister, the only one available when they reached the town at midday, was not what Lahr had imagined. He was uncomfortable; a spastic colon had developed during the annulment proceedings and, aggravated by his usual worries about a new play, was acting up. But the comedian who never got the girl on stage was finally taking the leap again.

True to his distrust of sentiment and his inability to sustain a romantic moment, Lahr suggested the mezzanine of the local hotel for the wedding. Amid smoke, musty sofas, and the clink of dishes, he and Mildred were married. As the proceedings were about to begin, the receptionist's radio bleated its own special irony. "The theme song from this radio program echoed up to the mezzanine. It was 'Here Comes the Bride.' Everyone smiled, but then we heard the announcer give the name of the show, 'I Want a Divorce.'"

Through the ceremony, Lahr noticed that the minister kept looking up at him and reading the ceremony very dramatically. After it was over, the Reverend asked the nervous groom, "Haven't I seen your face before?"

"Perhaps you saw me in *The Wizard of Oz.*" With Bible still in hand, the Reverend glowered and threw up his fists, "Put 'em up! Put 'em uuuuuuuppp!"

Afterward Lahr and his new wife had dinner in Wilmington and then returned to New York. He recalls only its uneventfulness. Too many thoughts about his emotional past and his theatrical future separated him from the day.

"I was fearful about the success of *Du Barry*. I don't know why. That was a time in my career when I was a little mixed up. As the show went on, I got more confidence."

Eighteenth-century France provided the musical-comedy idea that eased his always-troubled comic instincts. In *Du Barry,* he played Louis XV. When a subject bowed before him, Lahr, with a democratic good nature at the base of his comedy, dismissed him saying, "Skip the dip." The phrase is Lahr's invention, but the eighteenth century was a world that amazed him and that he found both ribald and touching. He knew Boswell and Johnson, and for the show he had made a study of Louis XV.

In *Du Barry*, a washroom attendant (Lahr) wins a sweepstake ticket, and then, through a misplaced "Mickey Finn," finds himself transported into that daydream of largesse, the elegant court of Louis XV. It was the first sustained parody of the upper classes Lahr had ever attempted, yet it came close to his frolicsome burlesque. The Hollywood country gentleman had come to court.

The musical had a golden ring to it, which few of his previous entertainments, despite their excellence, had. Cole Porter, the Alexander Pope of American musical comedy, created lyrics whose complexity captured the veneer and exuberance of a world as confident in its coherence as the heroic couplet. The producer, Buddy DeSylva, was as eminent in show business as he was successful. Lahr's co-star, with whom he shared eight per cent of the gross, was Ethel Merman. Her meteoric rise to Broadway lights was built around a voice and personality both unique to musical comedy.

There was little tinkering with *Du Barry* on the road. One song, Miss Merman's "Give Him the Ooh-la-la," was added in Boston, where the supersophisticated show attracted an unlikely crowd of children and parents who expected clean, wholesome fun from the Cowardly Lion.

The only complication in the book was getting the washroom attendant into the court of Louis XV. In Boston, DeSylva realized the transition was weak, and, trusting his old friend's sense of theater, he consulted Lahr. DeSylva called at any hour of the night and his opening sentence was always the same: "We're under it, Bert. Can I come and see you?" Lahr dressed and went down to the front door of his hotel where DeSylva met him in a taxi. They would drive around the city until they came up with a solution.

In this case, their answer came after only a few minutes of touring. As a lovesick washroom attendant, Lahr plays a scene with his protegé, Charley, in which he teaches the bathroom tyro how to brush a coat, to fill a wash basin daintily, and finally to snatch a tip with the voraciousness of a hammerhead shark. The laughs were strong ("We could have stayed on with it forever"), but just how Lahr and Charley, his rival for the love of May (Ethel Merman) would get their Mickey Finns mixed, move into the dream sequence, and get off with a laugh was a real problem.

"All I had to suggest was that the washroom attendant yell, 'Get an ambulance.' Let the situation play it, and then go into the fantasy of the French court. The minute I said it, DeSylva laughed like hell. 'That's it. Let's go home.'"

Lahr was beginning to understand that humor did not always come from pressing an audience or a situation. In the car Lahr pantomimed how he would say, "Get an ambulance." His hands clutched at his stomach, his eyes went wide, and his body shook as if it were attached to a reducing machine.

When Lahr first heard the *Du Barry* score, he was not convinced of its excellence. The fault was in Cole Porter's piano playing. "Cole was a horrible piano player. Oompah, oompah. He played with a slow, wooden tempo. If you didn't know who it was, you'd have thought he was a learner. The same with Jerome Kern. I once heard him play at Billy Rose's house. It was embarrassing. You couldn't believe that the melodies which are part of Americana came from the same fingers."

If the first full orchestra rehearsal proved that Lahr's fears about the music were groundless, Porter's bitchy, urbane lyrics raised another problem. His songs were riotous; but they contained bawdy overtones. Although Lahr appeared wild and spontaneous on stage, a sense of decorum modified his antics. The clown always had to please; and Lahr was always conscious of creating "sympathy" on stage. He balked at some of Porter's words; DeSylva agreed. "If we use all of these lyrics," he told Lahr, "they'll walk out."

No matter how antiseptic the comedy song, both Lahr and Merman had voices and movements that brought any restrained lyric abruptly back to earth—Lahr with his mouthings and leers, Merman with that brassy coarseness she epitomized later in *Annie Get Your Gun*. In the dream sequence of *Du Barry*, Louis is trying to woo La Comptesse Du Barry (Merman). As Louis, Lahr had somewhat better luck in attracting his love than he did as the washroom attendant. "But in the Morning, No" is a sophisticated song of seduction set to a minuet. To see Lahr in high-buckled shoes, a lorgnette, and periwig ridiculed the fustian eighteenth century. The play of wit between Louis XV and Madame Du Barry puts the elegance of that time back in its proper physical perspective—close to the stomach.

DeSylva chose only four verses; the others, heretofore unpublished, were not sung. The song received encore after encore. "When Cole got dirty," Lahr says, "it was dirt, without subtlety. Nothing I sang in burlesque was as risqué as his lyrics. It would never have been allowed on the burlesque stage." Lahr's love of biological laughter had become tempered by a sense of propriety that came with theatrical success. But when he reads Porter's words to himself, he cannot stifle a laugh at nearly every line.

The song, with at least ten refrains, reached the epitome of stage ribaldry in this stanza, matched only by Porter's private performances in his early days at the Palazzo Rezzonico in Venice:

He: Are you good at figures, dear?
Kindly tell me if so.
She: Yes, I'm good at figures, dear,
But in the morning no.
He: D'you do Double Entry, dear?
Kindly tell me if so.
She: I do Double Entry, dear,
But in the morning no . . .
When my pet Pekinese
Starts to mind her Q's and P's
That's the time
When I'm
In low . . .
He: Do you like Mi-ami, dear?
Kindly tell me if so.

She: Yes, I like your ami, dear,
But in the morning, no, no—no, no,
No, no, no, no, no.

The Porter score was inventive and wry; and if Lahr worried about how the audience would react to an occasional line, the general effect was one of immense pleasure. The show produced no immediate "hits," but through the years three songs emerged as "standards": "Friendship," "Do I Love You, Do I?" and "Well, Did You Evah!" which became famous when rewritten for the movie *High Society.*

Porter had written comedy songs before—but never for a comedian whose gestures and personality allowed him to pull out all the stops. Much of the comic material in his earlier shows had been provided by the male performers themselves. This was true, to a large extent, of Danny Kaye (*Let's Face it,* 1941) and Jimmy Durante (*The New Yorkers,* 1930; *Red, Hot, and Blue,* 1936). Although Porter had concocted comedy songs for Victor Moore in *Anything Goes* (1934), they hardly had the verve or wit he displayed for Lahr.

Lahr's own comic imagination—his instinct for the liberties he could take, his ear for funny sounds and words he could mangle—helped Porter sharpen the thrust of his laughter. Lahr's comedy was graphic and precise; Porter's lyrics, whatever his devilish intentions, were often wordily sedate. In collaboration, Porter's songs could play off not only Lahr's blundering stage coarseness, but also the impact of his physical presence. In "It Ain't Etiquette" Lahr was to expound on manners as a bathroom attendant with a taste for "class." Where Porter inclined toward the general statement, Lahr pushed him for more specific song ideas that carried greater possibilities for movement and response.

A Porter stanza begins—

> When invited to hear from an Op'ra box
> Rigoletto's divine quartet,
> Don't bother your neighbors by throwing rocks
> IT AIN'T ETIQUETTE.

The lines seemed improbable to Lahr, whose comedy thrived on the outrageously real. He suggested building up to something about a Bronx cheer. These lines, scribbled in the *Du Barry* prompt book, were the more effective alternatives.

> If invited one night to the Met to hear
> Rigoletto's divine quartet,

> Don't shower the cast with a loud Bronx cheer,
> IT AIN'T ETIQUETTE.

Porter appreciated Lahr's uniqueness. The song's final stanza, written before he had worked with Lahr, began:

> If a very proud mother asks what you think
> Of her babe in the bassinette,
> Don't tell her it looks like the missing link . . .

Instead of being cute, Porter was as blunt as Lahr's body. His revision acknowledges Lahr and gives the joke resonance:

> If a very proud mother asks you to see
> Her babe in the bassinette
> Don't tell her it looks exactly like me
> IT AIN'T ETIQUETTE.

The element of fey surprise in Porter's lyrics was matched by Lahr's delivery, which, no matter how fastidious, mocked refinement. Off stage, Lahr balked instinctively at some of the Porter *double entendres*. But his image of himself as censor for the audience was laughably hypocritical.

His affection for Betty Grable illustrates this. Miss Grable, whose famous figure was as stunning as her face was sweet, had a fine time jesting with Lahr. "She was a lovely kid. When she opened in *Du Barry*, she was new to New York. She had a lot of vivaciousness. Then she got the cover of *Life*, and from then on she sailed." The one fact that sticks in his mind is not her considerable beauty, but the delightful lamb-and-mutton image she could create in the same moment. To Lahr, a man who lived with artifice, this deception was hilarious. He laughs when he thinks about it. "Betty could say the filthiest things and they sounded . . . well, you never took offense." This paralleled Lahr's own feelings about getting away with anything on stage as long as one did it with a sense of innocence. Both Lahr and Grable used to delight in mocking Broadway decorum while performing. "Under our breath, we used to say things that if the audience heard, they'd back up the wagon."

Lahr was not as comfortable with Ethel Merman, whose talent he admired, but whose strength made him nervous. Lahr's humor depended on the reactions of others to him. He had difficulty with Miss Merman. "She's an individual with a special way of working. There was nothing vicious in what she did, she is a great performer. But she's tough. *She never looks at you on stage.* She's got her tricks." Lahr had his tricks too, and an inevitable, if friendly, friction developed. It fed their stage roles.

As a musical-comedy team, Merman and Lahr generated an energy and noise as unique as they were appealing. Miss Merman's brash truculence made her a perfect foil for the dim-witted, kind soul Lahr portrayed. On stage they moved within their own field, as forces that attracted and repelled each other. Both Lahr and Miss Merman created spectacles of excitement, gorgeous but strangely unapproachable. Lahr's body told his own intimate tale, always finally a lesson in loneliness and private failure. Miss Merman, firmly planted on the stage, challenged the stage life with a voice that dwarfed any frequency around her and that set her apart from the play. On stage, their personalities were radiant assets to each other; off it, they did not always mesh as well.

In *Du Barry,* their final number was "Friendship," a song that had its own irony. Lahr never saw how close the good-natured stand-off that May sings to her unsuccessful suitor, Louis, mirrored the situation between Merman and himself. The fantastic success of the song was, in part, due to their own sporting criticism of each other. The wink at the audience was also a private jab in the ribs.

Louis: If you're ever down a well, ring a bell.
May: Bong! If you ever catch on fire, send a wire.
Louis: If you ever lose your teeth and you're out to dine, borrow mine . . .

The song allowed Merman to marshal her finest clarion tones, and it gave Lahr a chance to embellish the words with burlesque dancing turns. During the chorus, he would pivot on an elbow with the pride of a ballet dancer or undertake a potbellied *pas de deux.* In Boston, the audience refused to let them stop. They hollered for more of Porter's barbs. Lahr had to yell, "That's all there is. Come to Philadelphia."

They took two encores, and the nonsense lyrics of the final line were reiterated through the encore. As Porter wrote them, they were—

Chuck, chuck, chuck,
Quack, quack, quack,
Tweet, tweet, tweet,
Push, push, push,

> Give, give, give,
> Good evening friends . . .

But Lahr, experimenting, plumbed for funnier sounds. In his prompt book, he had penciled in his own clownish additions—

> Zip, zip, zip,
> Chuck, chuck, chuck,
> Za, zu, zaz,
> Razmataz,
> Go, go, go,
> Give, give, give,
> Good evening friends . . .

His instincts directed him to the vaudeville routine he and Merman were incorporating into the body of musical comedy. He refers to the song as a "two-act," and his lines underscore both its "show-biz" flavor and the low-comic prancing.

After the opening night performance, Louis Shurr burst into Lahr's dressing room. "I stopped a couple of critics on the way out, Bert. You'll be here forever."

"Yeah," Lahr replied. "But what do I do next year?"

The press was very favorable to both Miss Merman and Lahr, if not enthralled with the story. Brooks Atkinson devoted a Sunday *New York Times* piece to "American Comic: In Praise of Bert Lahr—Leading Zany, Showman, and Comic." It was royal kudos.

> . . . Bert Lahr is the most versatile comedian in the business. . . . During the years, Bert has quieted down. He still does something foolish with his right arm, but in moderation. And the brassy bellow, like a terrorized fire gong, has practically gone out of existence. What we have now is a nimble and roguish comedian who is still low enough to be good company and who can change pace according to the mood of the scene—laying it on thick when the occasion needs buffoonery, but simpering through the impish high society scenes.
>
> Since the supermen should be beyond criticism, it must be confessed regretfully that music hall comedians as a lot do not have such range. Victor Moore's teetering walk and quavering voice, Jimmy Durante's steamy ferocity, Ed Wynn's lisp and giggle are, respectively, their stock in trade—excellent in kind but not *continuously* inventive. If you are a producer or author, you dutifully concoct a show around their characteristics; and since repetition

rubs the ecstasy from an act, an appearance once in two seasons is probably enough . . . As an actor, [Bert Lahr] can follow the convolutions of a plot with considerable ease. If he wears the loud costume of a washroom attendant in the first act, he also wears the intricate costume of King Louis in the dream sequence, not in the hang-dogged absurdity of a low comedian, but with an actor's assurance . . .

What Bert Lahr has accomplished this last decade rests on a solid footing. . . . It is the burlesque background which gives depth and richness to his comedy. Toward the end of "Du Barry" he reverts to type with uproarious exuberance. He is singing Cole Porter's travesty on sentimental balladry in "Friendship" and he decorates the choruses with all sorts of old-time clowning—mugging, quick steps, and finally a series of non-sensical capers at random. It has the liveliness of burlesque revelry—taking falls for a laugh . . . *always with the grimace of satire.*

Burlesque as it operates today does not train comedians. Perhaps we shall never again have comedians who can run and jump like Bobby Clark and Bert Lahr.

September 1940

In spite of this high praise, Lahr had little faith in himself as a legitimate performer. The low comic still pressed for laughs. As the show wore on into the 1940 season, Lahr took liberties with the script. His excesses were always to preserve the fun at the core of the musical. "I'd get away from the script. I'd clown. I'd kid. It was really the laughter in *Du Barry* which made it. The love interest was a disagreeable one, in the show each character wanted a divorce and couldn't get it, and already the story line wasn't too tasteful. Even with that situation, the audience could imagine a clandestine romance. When you come to think of it, the production, songs, Ethel, and myself put the show over, not the story."

Lahr's deviations from the script did not please DeSylva. But the producer, already involved in another show, had little time to monitor Lahr's performance. "The author and stage manager would tell him the things I was doing." Lahr refers to the informers as "spies," and, although the term may be laughable, the results were not. Lahr received a long, acerbic letter from DeSylva, in nearly the same spirit and length as the telegram Ziegfeld had sent him eight years before.

The letter was not DeSylva's intention alone, although Lahr always assumed it was. Many people associated with the DeSylva enterprise, including A. L. Berman, had a hand in it. The letter was written on

DeSylva's letterhead and signed in his absence. Because DeSylva rarely put pen to paper, Lahr did not notice any discrepancy in the signatures. But, whoever the original author, the letter overwhelmed its recipient. Lahr was chagrined at its charges and annoyed at the implication of unprofessionalism.

Dated April 26, 1940, the letter made clear that the customers as well as the executives of the theater had complained about Lahr's performance. DeSylva accused him of clowning and playing parts of the show lackadaisically.

He had spoken to Lahr privately about this before, but now he was angry. Emphasizing his reputation for keeping his word, DeSylva went straight to the point: either Lahr shaped up immediately or DeSylva would close the show at the peak of its profitable run—$29,000 a week.

To be sure, the implications were clear; DeSylva spelled them out. Indicative of DeSylva's understanding of his star, he anticipated Lahr's dollars-and-cents reaction to such a threat. If DeSylva closed the show when it was so popular, the blame would fall on Lahr; if, however, DeSylva let the show dwindle on its current haphazard course and then closed it, the blame would be laid on him. DeSylva stressed that he would not let this happen.

DeSylva ended his indictment by adding an appreciation of Lahr's talent and pointing out how lucky Lahr was to get *Du Barry Was a Lady* at such a crucial time in his career.

Lahr offered to hand in his notice, but DeSylva would not accept it. "DeSylva was a great admirer of mine. I never had words with him, but the letter created sort of a rift. We saw each other during the show, but it wasn't the same. I was very hurt by his accusations. I thought he was perfectly right in what he said, but there was no vicious intent in my ad-libbing. I did it just to keep the show in good spirits."

The friendship was patched up in California, two years later, when the trust Lahr felt had been betrayed was symbolically restored by an oil painting DeSylva did of his comedian in *Du Barry*.

1941–2 was a time of excitement and nostalgia for Lahr. It did not begin that way. When he returned to California in the spring of 1941, he was haggard and feeling old after a year with *Du Barry*. In the quiet of his garden, he had time to ponder his forty-six years, his expanding midriff, and an immense disappointment. Red Skelton, a younger comic, had been given his role in the movie version of *Du Barry,* a disastrous choice for the film and a perplexing one for Lahr.

Moreover, Lahr's continual brooding about his career was mixed with more ominous thoughts. The talk of the movie capital was of war. Lahr had not been touched by the First World War, and now, suddenly, his friends were leaving their jobs to go into the service.

Then, a few weeks after his return, Mildred told him he was to be a father. Amid a sense of death came the hope of life; and in the face of disaster (real or imagined) grew a strange peace.

Bert Lahr did not begin his life as a new father—my father—on the strongest footing. My mother was scheduled for a Caesarian operation at 8:30 a.m. on July 12 and had been taken to the hospital two days in advance. The night before the operation, the expectant father, nervous and always squeamish, had dinner at Chasen's with his good friends Julia and (later Senator) George Murphy. He drank too much and awoke on July 12 at 10:30, his head aching from the previous night's drunk and already two hours late for the birth of his second son.

Lahr rushed to the hospital. When he arrived, Mildred was recovering from the anesthetic. One look at his unshaven face, and she knew what had happened. She was not pleased. Lahr was ushered out to see his son. He remembers the conversation with the nurse who led him to the New Arrivals room.

"What are you going to name him?" the nurse asked casually as they walked.

"I think we'll wait until he's eighteen—maybe we'll have to call him Lillian."

Lahr's feeling about his second son was much the same as Jacob had shown for him. "You looked like a prune—the ugliest kid I've ever seen. Even uglier than me." But the most unnerving part of the birth was not the sudden appearance of another mouth to feed or his throbbing head.

An old lady with a Bavarian accent approached him and smiled. "Oh! the grandpapa's very happy."

In March 1942 Lahr was chosen to take part in the Hollywood Victory Caravan, a three-week whistle-stop junket, involving Hollywood's biggest names, to raise money for the war effort. The Caravan was symbolic of the curious foothold the professional actor had carved out in American life, a denizen of a dream world respected and relived in every town in the nation. At a time when the movie industry was handing him only B-scripts, Lahr was thrilled to be included, because a Screen Actor's Guild poll of the sixty most popular entertainers had not listed him. The organizers of the tour realized that seasoned performers would give an audience more pleasure than the insipid starlets the public demanded on their polls.

The array of talent was astounding. The Caravan amassed the largest number of entertainers ever to tour the country. The performers who began the tour included Bing Crosby, Laurel and Hardy, Groucho Marx, Cary Grant, Bob Hope, Jimmy Cagney, Pat O'Brien, Frank McHugh, Jerry Colonna, Desi Arnaz, Charles Boyer, Merle Oberon, Claudette Colbert, Joan Blondell, Joan Bennett, Faye McKenzie. For Lahr, it meant seeing and meeting many performers. As stars, most of them, like Lahr, operated in their own orbits and rarely mingled with a wide range of people. The keynote of the trip was fellowship—an emotion strangely alien to most of Lahr's relationships. He could speak with disdain of one of the famous actresses on the trip. "She had the 'star' feeling—very aloof." No one was more aloof, ordinarily, than Lahr; but surrounded with other performers, he had an unaccustomed opportunity for camaraderie that he rarely sought himself.

Each actor had a compartment on the train, with chaperones dutifully separating the men's section from the women's. The train was equipped with a barber shop, a dining room, and an observation car where the performers, along with the band, passed the early morning hours. When the Caravan came into a town, the actors made their way to a hotel in the town, and rested during the morning. A parade through the streets in the afternoon was a usual part of the ceremony; and the show in the evening—a three-hour extravaganza—ended with the stars and starlets going out into the audience to ask for donations. "The show was so big," recalls Frank McHugh, "that someone like Marlene Dietrich could join us for a few days as she did in Washington and you wouldn't know she was there." At the end of the day, the performers returned to the train. Dinner was served at midnight, and "good times" really began with the early-hour libations. "We hardly got any sleep," Lahr recalls. "We had a doctor on the train who gave us sleeping pills to calm us down at night, and Benzedrine to wake us up in the morning."

The trip held many highlights for Lahr. Perhaps the most vivid was his entrance into the White House with Groucho Marx.

Although Lahr had held the scepter of royalty in *Du Barry*, had mocked every form of authority in his early burlesque days, and would later impersonate Queen Victoria, he felt there was something both hilarious and marvelous about being invited to a White House garden party.

Lahr might have made it through the day unscathed, if he had not chosen Marx as his companion. Groucho, dressed in a seersucker suit and white-rimmed glasses, looked more like an Ivy League professor than the court jester he became on the Caravan. Lahr was a perfect foil for Marx. Groucho's quick, acerbic wit would defer to no one; too insecure and timid for this kind of humor, Lahr was a fine audience for his cigar-smoking friend.

The tenor of the day was proclaimed when Marx, McHugh, and Lahr stepped into a car driven by a well-dressed member of the American Women's Voluntary Service.

"Where would you gentlemen like to go?" the lady asked in upper-class tones.

"Is there a cathouse in the area?"

"We were a bit uncomfortable," recalls Lahr, laughing. "But Groucho would overpower you. Maybe three or four of those jokes wouldn't hit, and then one clobbered you. He was always gagging. Groucho was never at a loss for words. He had tremendous confidence. If you weren't sure of yourself, he'd skewer you."

Lahr was on his best behavior at the White House, and wishing he were not. Standing behind Groucho in the receiving line, both comedians had time to watch the attaché ask each member of the troupe his name and then announce it to Mrs. Roosevelt, who in turn would say, "It's a pleasure to have you here, Mr. ———." When it came Groucho's turn, the attaché announced his name to Mrs. Roosevelt, who proceeded in her formal greeting. "I'm very happy to welcome you here, Mr. Marx." "Are we late for dinner?" Groucho said.

The joke nearly reduced Lahr to tears of laughter; he cannot remember shaking hands with Mrs. Roosevelt, although he recalls biting his lip to maintain decorum in the receiving line.

The chandeliers and the shaded colonnades impressed Lahr with their splendor, but also with the irony of their lavishness. The White House was conservative enough, but to Lahr as well as Marx, there was a touch of Hollywood about the place—a world fitting itself to its own image. The spectacle was amusing, and the actors mingling with attachés and military leaders longed to deflate the self-conscious importance which filled the House. Lahr kept his tongue; Groucho did not.

"I remember a general coming up to Groucho and me and asking where Mrs. Roosevelt was. You wouldn't have believed him—medals all over him. 'She's upstairs filing her teeth,' Groucho said. The general walked away."

At the garden party the Marine Band was part of the scheduled entertainment, and their music was a source of great amusement, especially to Lahr. "These Marine bands are always the same—and the one which played for us was composed of old men. They must have been in the band for half a century. They were God-awful." Lahr cringes and cups his hands over his ears. "FDR wasn't there that day, and when the band began to play, Groucho turned to Mrs. Roosevelt and said, 'No wonder the old man didn't come.' "

On the White House lawn, the performers had their picture taken with Mrs. Roosevelt. The photo is a curious one—all of these actors, so used to being photographed in public, are clustered together with the nonchalant anxiety of a high school class. Even Lahr, who professed to being indifferent about coming to the White House, is struggling to make himself visible from behind a starlet's wide-brimmed hat. "I was in the last row. Everybody was in front of me. Nobody knew who the hell I was."

The problem of positioning was even more conspicuous in the parades. Lahr was a Broadway star, a face whose most popular image had been distorted beyond all recognition by a lion's mane. While McHugh recalls "parade time" as a general "bedlam" and a scramble for any car a performer could find, Lahr was always placed carefully between the cars conveying Cary Grant and Pat O'Brien. "You've never seen so many people. They'd be lined up—perhaps five feet from the cars. We'd round a corner and there would be a tremendous cheering. You'd hear 'Hurray!' Then my car would pass, and suddenly, there would be a hush. Everybody was saying, 'Who's this bum?' And then five or ten seconds later, you'd hear 'Hurray.' That was Pat O'Brien.' "

Actors, like Lahr, who appreciated audiences but not crowds and whose success set them apart from the "people," found this hysterical adulation exciting and strange. At a time of national crisis, they had been elevated to the empyrean of folk heroes. The actors began to understand the mythical power of the film on the public's imagination.

The impact of the motion-picture idol was stamped into Lahr's understanding during an afternoon parade through Chicago. A man suddenly leapt out of the crowd and ran toward the car carrying Charles Boyer. "You've ruined my marriage," he shouted. "My wife's crazy about you." The man's obvious seriousness perplexed Lahr. "Boyer had never even seen this man." If the triumphant procession of film stars made some seem larger than life, others, like Lahr and Marx, suffered because they were not recognizable. Marx's distinctive mustache was not his own; and he never wore his prop off stage. Without his mustache, the public had difficulty identifying the scholarly looking comedian. Lahr remembers the ruckus when Marx tried to ascend a railroad platform where the troupe was being photographed. A policeman stopped him at the gate.

"Where do you think you're going?"

"I'm Groucho Marx."

"Sure. And I'm Jimmy Durante," said the policeman as he began muscling Marx toward the exit. Marx wore his mustache in public from then on.

The stage performances were delightful. Lahr did his "Income Tax" scene with Cary Grant as his straightman and also the "Song of the Woodsman"; Bob Hope and Bing Crosby got together on stage for a little snide *patois;* Pat O'Brien and Frank McHugh did a World War I song and dance routine; and Laurel and Hardy went through one of their innumerable comedy skits. But the memories of the performances have faded. Lahr never saw a complete show; neither did McHugh or Cagney. The laughter was in the dressing room; and after each performer's stint the stars returned to the make-shift quarters to gossip and trade stories. For Lahr, these were memorable, quiet insights into show business and its personalities.

No matter how early a performer got to the theater to make up and to calm himself for a performance, Babe Hardy and Stan Laurel were always ahead of him. When Lahr arrived at the dressing room, Laurel and Hardy had already assumed their seats in the corner of the long dressing table. Their make-up would be set out neatly in front of them, with a clean towel folded carefully over it. Between them each day was an unopened bottle of whisky.

Laurel and Hardy waited quietly as the actors came in. Gradually everyone moved down toward their corner, sharing a drink and theater talk. Boyer was the only performer, besides Laurel and Hardy, to bring make-up. Lahr used to pilfer it at each performance. When Boyer was on the stage the other actors helped themselves. Once, when Boyer was making himself up, he looked at his can of grease paint, now greatly diminished, and said, "They're not making it like they used to." Nobody told him the truth.

In St. Paul, Lahr discovered that the toupee he wore in his "Woodsman" sketch had been stolen. He was distraught. "I depended mostly on that toupee for the laughs in the scene. When I chopped the wood, the toupee would slip and I'd get some fun out of it being in the wrong position. When I lost the toupee in St. Paul, I couldn't do the act. I remember bemoaning the fact to Groucho. Here I was, in the middle of the country, with no place to get another hairpiece and the train was leaving that night for a two-day junket to Texas."

"Go out and buy yourself a pair of toe slippers," Groucho said, "and change your act."

The toupee was mysteriously found en route to Texas.

On stage, there were many touching moments. The personal magnetism of the performers and the audience's response could be best calibrated from the wings. McHugh remembers "Wonderful show business things happening. I used to watch certain bits of the show while I was waiting to go on. When the orchestra played Laurel and Hardy's sign music, you've never heard such an ovation. There was another one. Bob Hope and Bing Crosby did one of their routines. They weren't with us the whole trip—they had other commitments and would leave and rejoin the train. But when they were on stage, they were tremendous. After a while, Hope made his exit and Bing leaned over the footlights and asked the orchestra, 'I wonder if you could give me a couple of bars of something there.' He never asked for the song he was going to sing. The orchestra struck up 'Blues in the Night.' As soon as the music began, there was a deafening roar of applause." Lahr was fascinated by the activities of the Caravan. Olivia de Havilland, whom Lahr sometimes escorted to the theater in a cab, was always unpredictable. Once she stopped the cab to go to the local library. "She was daffy. She'd disappear during the afternoon, and then, somehow, don't ask me how, she'd show up for the show—she once asked me to let her play comedy in my act." And there was the beautiful Joan Bennett, whose dependence on her glasses made her hilarious when she had to appear in public without them, trying not to squint and wrinkle her face.

Merle Oberon joined the circle of Cagney, McHugh, Lahr, and O'Brien early in the tour. They became good friends by the end of it. To the stunning and civilized Miss Oberon, Lahr once quipped, "You know the reason we like you, Merle—you're hairy-assed!" She didn't wince. From the company she was keeping that was accolade enough.

Oberon was the constant companion of the foursome. She ate dinner with them and listened quietly while they reminisced about a theater world she had never known. In Chicago, "the boys," as she called them, escorted her to the lavish Pump Room in the Ambassador Hotel. McHugh remembers it vividly, "She was beautiful—just beautiful. When we'd go into the Pump Room this gorgeous creature would enter followed by Lahr, Cagney, and myself. Everybody looked at her and then at us, and you could see them saying to themselves, 'What is going on?' " Miss Oberon handled herself like a princess. "Everybody called at our table," says Lahr with a wink. "Just to see her; but she never asked anyone to sit down." Once a man stopped her in the lobby of the hotel and asked querulously, "What are you doing with those three men all the time?" Miss Oberon is reported to have replied quietly, "Oh, I love baggy pants comedians."

Lahr remembers watching one of the screen's most famous lovers waiting at a table for two and arranging a flower for one of the starlets of the show. She never came, but sent a friend in to have dinner with him. "We all saw it; but we didn't say anything. I thought it was kind of dramatic and sad—here's this great lover doing all these niceties, and then being stood up by the girl."

But, more often than not, the spirit was festive. Lahr can remember Cagney standing on a chair by the transom of one of the compartments hushing the group to keep quiet. From inside came the familiar whisper of a famous matinee idol. "Oh, my darling . . ." and then a high-pitched young voice, "No, I like to sleep alone!"

When Claudette Colbert was joined on tour by her husband, a doctor in the Navy, the couple did not emerge from their compartment for two days. When they finally did, they found a note on their door in Groucho's hand—"Isn't this carrying naval relief too far?" Pat O'Brien was also a great source of amusement and mystery—more outgoing than the others, O'Brien never seemed to sleep. When Lahr finally returned to his room for sleep, O'Brien would be sitting in the club car; and when he stumbled out in the morning, O'Brien would be sitting, fresh and chipper, having his coffee and reading the paper. Not until the third week of the trip did they realize how he managed his miraculous transformation. Instead of returning to his room at night, he went to the train's barber shop and fell asleep in the barber chair. The Caravan's barber arrived at eight and gave him a shave and hot towel to spruce him up for the day's activities. Unlike the other performers, who stayed to themselves when they reached a town, O'Brien was continually in demand. "If you walked into his hotel room in any given town, you were likely to find the local police force or the local diocese being entertained. His social activities became one of the biggest Caravan jokes—prompting Bing Crosby to jibe, "You son-of-a-bitch, you play Sherman Billingsley all night, and Father Duffy all day!"

After midnight dinner, the performers went back to the observation car and put on a special show for themselves. Everybody performed. There was a piano and small band for accompaniment. There were no critics and no contests. Lahr felt an affection and safety in the company that he had rarely known around performers. He would later refer to the troupe as "a caravan of love."

Lahr always enjoyed harmonizing; it had been a long time since he had sung in Crotona Park. But now, Crosby and Frances Langford would be singing. Groucho, in his high-pitched tones, would go into one of the famous Gilbert and Sullivan patter songs which he knew *verbatim*. O'Brien, standing with his left wrist on his hip and his right hand extended toward his delighted audience would swing into "Ooooh, shake hands with your uncle Mike, me boy . . . !" Lahr, of course, improvised a loud burlesque of many of the popular romantic numbers, but when it came to harmonizing, his comedy voice was unwelcome. "We'd sing harmony; but every time I'd try to get into a group, they'd kick me out because I was always off key. They wouldn't let me in it."

When the train made its final stop in Glendale, California, there were many wistful moments. Lahr tried not to cry, and he managed better than most of the others. He recalls seeing the massive Babe Hardy, so outgoing and confident a funny-man, trying to look away from his friends to hide his tears. He looked large and rumpled from the journey. "Don't let's lose this. Keep in touch." The image of Hardy, standing on the platform saying goodbye to the many new friends he had made, lingers in Lahr's memory. "He looked, I don't know how to say it—he looked so isolated, so alone."

The trip was not allowed to end on a sentimental note; the following day, each member of the troupe received a telegram from Joan Blondell and Joan Bennett. It read, "ARE YOU GETTING MUCH?"

Lahr remembers the Caravan as a moment of confidence in a business that had conditioned him to continual private torments. Hollywood was never so generous and responsive as the communal spirit generated by the trainload of performers. In the two years that followed, he did only three pictures—all embarrassing grade-B productions: *Sing*

Your Worries Away, Ship Ahoy, and *Meet the People.* He remembers nothing from those pictures, forgotten as quickly as they were made. Instead, he recalls the few private moments of content—standing knee-deep in his pool teaching me to swim, waiting quietly in the garden to watch the sun teeter on a mountain ridge and finally sink beneath the canyon wall.

If there was a ray of hope in Lahr's Hollywood career, it lay in the hands of Jack McGowan, his good friend and the writer of his first two Broadway hits. McGowan had been equally as iconoclastic and success-ful in Hollywood, and the word about a new idea for a Broadway show he was writing for Lahr became Hollywood gossip. Lahr and McGowan worked up an idea for a musical comedy, the title of which was based on one of Lahr's famous catch phrases, "Oh, you kid." In the show, Lahr was to play a policeman in a story which focused on the infamous Boss Tweed. McGowan wrote the script; and, when M-G-M heard about it, they asked to have a look. The result of the cursory inspection was a fifty thousand-dollar check for McGowan, and the promise of the starring role for Bert Lahr. "They hadn't treated me well in Holly-wood. They never seemed to have the right parts for me. This was finally a picture geared to my comic personality."

Lahr's spirits were at their nadir when McGowan brought the news of the picture sale. Lahr had steadfastly refused to play politics for his jobs. "I wanted to give parties, like the other stars did, so that Bert could meet the right people—but he never would let me," says Mildred.

Mildred was expecting their second child in the first week of Sep-tember 1943, and Lahr's instincts as a provider were sensitive. There were no jobs, but the promised role gave him a reason to relax. He told himself that the McGowan script on which he had collaborated would change his luck in Hollywood and secure his popularity.

Mildred again went to the hospital two days before the birth. On the night she left, Lahr opened the Los Angeles *Times* to read that Wallace Beery was to star in *Oh You Kid.* (Later M-G-M announced that Red Skelton would do the picture, and finally it was dropped com-pletely.) Lahr's name was not mentioned. He was stunned. "It was a double-cross. They had told McGowan I would do the show in order to get the script from him. I was terribly depressed. Without telling Mildred, I put the house up for sale. I just didn't know what to do."

On September 2, my sister Jane was born. To Mildred, the birth of a daughter completed the family for which she had waited for a dec-ade. She had fashioned her own family community with a kindness and concern her early life lacked. Her home in Coldwater Canyon was the first solid base to her dream. When Lahr came to see her, Mildred smiled at him with tired eyes. As he spoke she began to cry.

"I've sold the house," he said.

Within six months, he was stepping onto the Super Chief bound for New York and a Billy Rose extravaganza. With him on the train were the remainders of his Hollywood idyll: a wife, two children, a maid, a valise of dolls, and a carton of avocados.

Lahr's occasional returns to Hollywood thereafter were far from triumphant; not only did his agent stop meeting him at the train, but he often found that Hollywood had lured him West under false pretenses. He remembers three fiascos above all.

In *Always Leave Them Laughing* (1950), starring Milton Berle, he signed a contract for five weeks, only to discover on arrival in Hollywood that he had almost been written out of the picture. "In the movie, I played an old comedian, married to a young girl. Berle portrayed a hustling young comic who stole my material, then my wife. When I got out there, I looked at the script and there was hardly a thing for me to do. I made one appearance as the cop in my old cop act, and that was only included as a plot point, to show the audience how I worked so that Berle could copy me."

The script was finally rewritten to give Lahr a song and a sentimental scene where the old comic shows the young one how to be a professional.

Off camera, the same struggle was taking place. "Berle was watching the picture very carefully—it was his picture." This attitude led to conflicts. The first was the day in which Lahr's "sentimental scene" in a hospital took place. "We shot all morning. I came in early to see what I was going to do. I look out by the camera, and there is Berle. He stayed there all morning watching my scene. I was so upset I blew my lines. The only way it got into the picture was that I convinced him there were no laughs in the scene. I don't think he knew the difference at that time. It's just as much value getting interest and sympathy as it is to get laughs."

In another scene, where Lahr and Berle did a song and dance routine together, Berle protested and almost brought the two performers to blows. "When we were doing this song and dance together, I had on a Sulka tie with a little design in it. Berle objected to the tie because he said I was trying to take attention away from him." Lahr capitulated, but the experience remained "one of the most unpleasant situations I've ever had in pictures."

When Lahr came to Hollywood to do a remake of *Rose Marie* (1954) with Ann Blythe, Howard Keel, and Marjorie Main, he found that he had again been "oversold." He had a fine part—a Mountie who never got his man—and the picture was being directed by his good friend Mervyn LeRoy. LeRoy called him to his office when he arrived in California.

"You're riding in this one, Bert."

"Riding?" replied Lahr, already upset. "I get dizzy sitting on a foot stool. I don't want to get on one of those things. I don't know how to steer 'em."

"Louis Shurr said you were up every morning in Central Park riding."

"To feed the pigeons. I don't go near animals."

"Well, Bert, you're riding in this one. Go out to the back lot and learn to ride a horse."

Lahr's first confrontation with the Wild West was painful. "To a cowboy, if you don't know how to ride a horse, you're a square. When I got to the back lot, the cowboy in charge kept me on a horse for fully two hours. Well, I have a fear of heights, you know. When I got off, I could hardly walk. I came home and my posterior was completely raw from saddle sores."

The next day Lahr hobbled into LeRoy's office.

"I can't get up on a horse. The only way I'll do it is if you get me foam rubber and put Malibu tights on me so I can sit on the horse without getting sore."

Lahr became the first member of the Canadian Mounted Police to have foam-rubber underwear. The results were astonishing. "When we did the picture, of course, they got a double for me because I had to ride very fast. But I did have to come in on a horse, and then go out on one. They'd cut to my stand-in, who would be speeding away. They tell me the biggest laugh in the previews was my exit on horseback. I came in all right, but going out, the camera stayed on me a little longer. I couldn't hold the saddle. With rubber underwear, I bounced about a foot off the saddle."

The part required even more athletic prowess. Lahr was chased by a woman of low-comic aplomb, Marjorie Main. Their song and dance number was an athletic jaunt that required Lahr to evade Miss Main's aggressive passes. Technical problems proved disastrous.

"In motion pictures, you've got to be on your mark to be photographed because of the lighting. There were certain places in this number where we had to hold and sing the lyrics. Marjorie was not adept at it, and, of course, song and dance is my business. When we were rehearsing I was always on my marks, but when the cameras rolled she'd always get me off it. There was a big oak mantlepiece, and I was supposed to fall back against it. They had to cut out a large chunk of the mantlepiece and insert rubber, painted to look like the wood. I kept getting off my mark every time. Finally, Mervyn said, 'Don't worry, Bert. I'll come around and get you in a close-up.' We started shooting again; I did the song, and then fell back against the mantlepiece. I missed the rubber and cracked my head against the oak. I finished the song with a gash in my head. When I looked out at the camera, I saw Georgie Stoll, the musical director, rolling on the floor with laughter. It wasn't funny."

While on location, Lahr wanted to take advantage of the fine fishing in the Rocky Mountains. Despite his fear of heights and loathing of horses, he set off with some friends and a guide to find fresh streams at higher altitudes. The cowardly mounted policeman in *Rose Marie* was never as full of trepidation as Lahr on a mountain trail. "The trail was five feet wide. I was petrified. I remember each turn. And on the way down it was harrowing. The horse looked around at me as if to say 'Who is this bum?' " Lahr cranes his neck to the side and points his nose arrogantly in the air, nostrils flaring. "When we got to level ground, the horse made a beeline for the corral."

There were some consolations. "You know I can make noises like a moose." Lahr makes a moose noise. "On the way up the mountain, we saw a deer. I gave my moose call. It started to move toward me. The guide offered me twenty-five dollars a day to call deer."

Lahr's last completed movie, *Ten Girls Ago* (1962), was an experience that confirmed his cynicism about films, and left him with a special sadness about the inevitable change in comic tastes. The film was never released. But Eddie Foy, Buster Keaton, and Lahr, who provided comic relief for the rock 'n roll love story, were a significant part of the American comic tradition.

The trio met at Grand Central Station. It was like a family reunion. Lahr had almost grown up with Foy; and while he had not known Keaton until 1931, he had seen his original family act, "The Three Keatons," at Hammerstein's Forty-second Street while waiting for work in his pre-burlesque days.

Lahr first met Keaton on the back lot of M-G-M, when the flamboyant figure was riding the crest of his popularity. Keaton's dressing room was called "Keaton's Kennels"; his personality paralleled the name of his quarters—carefree, playful, and exuberant. Lahr's company had been requested at a dressing-room banquet of venison steak. His price of admission was a barrel of beer. This first raucous evening cemented a relationship that was carried on intermittently through the years.

Keaton's fall from stardom was as famous as it was precipitous. Like all of them, he had tried commercials, TV, grade-B films; but he had not weathered the changes in entertainment fashion. His stoic face, once silent in survival, now looked like a gutted building. Yet what amazed Lahr was not Keaton's history, which was part of theatrical legend, but his tranquillity. He envied Keaton's contentment. "He never bemoaned the fact that he'd lost stature. I remember him telling me that he went to Berlin where they were running his pictures, and that he was still a big star. He seemed very satisfied. He had a lovely wife and a nice house in California. He talked a lot about gardening. Years ago, when he was married to the Talmadge girl, he was kind of a playboy, but by now he was a solid citizen. He used to drink a lot; but, with us, he'd only have an occasional beer. He talked about his pantomime— he was very theater wise. In the last years, he was making a pretty good living."

Keaton's body seemed brittle; in his youth, Lahr had watched, amazed, when Keaton, wrapped in a gunny sack, was thrown around the stage. The instincts were still there; but his body was no longer as agile. Keaton brought along his ukelele, and accompanied himself when he entertained his friends.

The three comedians, together after three decades of association, seemed to counterpoint one another. Foy was already baiting Lahr about an old stage humiliation. While the others stood immobile and tired, Foy was ready to spring into a buck and wing. With arms extended, he did a pantomime of a soft shoe. Keaton, unlike the others, was distinctly rumpled, tired, and uncommunicative except for an occasional carefully considered sentence.

Lahr did not make the movie out of pure artistic considerations.

"They came to me. I read the script. It wasn't good. They were giving me a three-week guarantee for a tremendous amount of money. When I read the script, I realized they couldn't get it done in twenty weeks. It was a real amateur situation. Everything was a montage shot when one scene fades into another. It takes a long time to set up a montage and light it. They had at least one hundred of them. So, right away, I knew. They needed somebody to play the other comic part—I suggested Foy."

What Lahr did not realize was that Foy, typically nonchalant, would accept without reading the script.

"Eddie read it on the train. He phoned me from Albuquerque. 'I don't want to do the picture!' "

On the train to Canada, the three comedians discussed ways they could improve the film. "You should do the hanger bit," Lahr told Keaton. "You know, the one where you get mixed up with the paper and glue and everything. You can invent something." They laughed about ad-libbing, with Foy reminding Lahr of the quick talking he had had to do when he followed the Hickey Brothers in Texas. "We had a hell of a time," says Lahr. When the customs inspector came through at the border, Lahr turned to Keaton: "Did you bring the cocaine?" Keaton's face held its deadpan. "The customs man looked around quick and realized who we were; I don't think he liked it too much."

The picture was as much of a fiasco as the three men had expected. Although the company hired an "ace" cameraman, Lee Garmes, who filmed *Gone With the Wind,* it had not found a director until the last minute. There were only to be two sets: a park and a delicatessen. The story involved a show that was going to be put on in the delicatessen. "One day during the first week," recalls Lahr, "the writer got in a fight with the scenic designer. The writer was yelling, 'It needs red paint in this scene.' The scenic man kept saying, 'The red will clash with the costumes.' That night the writer snuck onto the set and splattered the scenery with red paint."

Dion, the popular singer who struck out on his own after a series of successes with a group called "Dion and the Belmonts," also had a three-week guarantee; but unlike the other performers, he was signed to do a coast-to-coast tour after his picture contract ended. The miscalculation about the time it would take to direct and light the sets meant that by the time Dion's three weeks were up, the love interest's role was not complete. The answer: change the script. In the end, Lahr had to sing the title song—a love song to the young girl.

The three comedians tried to put order into a full-blown disaster. There were moments of nostalgia only they could understand. There was a tacit sense of expertise between them. A reporter on the Toronto *Telegraph* recorded an incident with a naïveté that must have read strangely to the three veterans:

> At one point, Dion, who seems to worship the old-timers, came over carrying a policeman's night stick. Lahr took it from him. Then he remembered a line from an old vaudeville (or possibly burlesque) routine.
>
> "Stop in the name of the station house, stop," he said with a mock snarl. Then he turned to Foy, "Remember that?"

The film took six weeks to make, during one of which Lahr was bedridden with pneumonia. "They kept calling me up and asking me when I would be out to the studio. Finally Mildred said to them, 'Do you think you could be funny with 104° temperature?'"

On the fifth week, the comedians' salaries were not delivered on time. Lahr called his New York agent, who tried to pressure the production company. They were always elusive. Finally, Lester Shurr called Mildred. "Go out there and tell Bert and Eddie not to shoot."

It was a ten-dollar cab ride to the studio, and when Mildred arrived Lahr and Foy were in the middle of a scene. "I saw a woman in the back waving. I yelled 'Cut,'" recalls Lahr. "I said to Eddie, 'Who's that?' I yelled, 'Whaddya want Mildred?' She says, 'Get off, get off.'"

Foy still laughs at the incident. "If you could have seen Mildred standing there as belligerent as a policeman, yelling for us to stop work, you would have laughed too."

Luckily for Lahr, the assistant director, sizing up the situation, called a lunch break; otherwise, the production company could have taken legal action against him. Lahr, Keaton, and Foy received their money that day, but they were never paid for the final week's work.

Despite the debacle, there were memorable moments. Lahr played a few scenes with a Bassett hound—one of his most pleasant memories. "The trainer evidently trained him with a whip. I'd come on the set with a pocket full of meat. When the dog could hear my voice, he'd start to whine. I wanted to buy him, but they wouldn't sell. He got to love me, you know. The dog just looked at me with loving eyes, and his tail would wag all the time. He really loved me."

BACK TO BROADWAY

There is no place in the adult musical plays for the extravagant clown-ing of Bert Lahr. . . . The shows in which Bobby Clark, Ed Wynn, Willie Howard and W. C. Fields used to appear could not compare artistically with Oklahoma! *(or* Annie Get Your Gun)*. In point of fact, the clowns generally appeared in revues which have become victims of technical obsolescence since America became swamped in television.*

By abandoning buffoons, the musical stage has lost one of its most legitimate assets. They belonged to the musical stage because they, too, were larger than life and inhabited a fantasy world. They were as legiti-mate as the music, dancing and decor.

Brooks Atkinson, Introduction to
The American Musical Theater *(1967)*

LAHR'S EXPERIENCES IN HOLLYWOOD AFTER *The Wizard of Oz* AND *DuBarry* crystallized his love of the stage and his faith in Broad-way. However, the Broadway to which he eagerly returned in 1944 was already changing. There had been fifty-three new musicals in 1927, when Lahr made his Broadway debut; three years later the number had dropped drastically to twenty-seven, and by the year of *Seven Lively Arts*, 1944, there were only eleven. Musical *comedy*, Lahr's métier, was in decline. Like Hollywood, Broadway was beginning to concentrate on romantic fantasy.

Until *Oklahoma!* (1943), most of the men creating musical comedy molded their sophisticated diversions from the contemporary urban experience. Even when musicals were set in faraway places, their spirit was that of Shubert Alley. But the year Lahr returned to Broadway, musical entertainment had given first notice that comedy was an un-wanted appendage for a theater of escape. *The Song of Norway* opened three months before *Seven Lively Arts*. The inundation of the exotic continued with *Bloomer Girl* (1944), a Civil War tale that took place in upstate New York. In time, even the most conservative Broadway producers would drop the term "comedy" from their descriptions of musicals. And with this careful distinction, the form—the most signifi-cant American contribution to the theater of the Western World—would gradually decline.

Comedy was the vehicle that gave the wooden fantasy of the plot the grit of reality. Lahr entered musical comedy when the form was drawing from experience: the spontaneously real comic gesture completing a faith in the present. Lahr's talents had first been matched, in musical comedy, by those of DeSylva, Brown, and Henderson, who were masters of the good-natured adulation of national heroes and cultural passions. His work later for Ziegfeld and White had been successful because the laughter he generated, as income tax collector or English aristocrat, mirrored America's immediate dreams and despair. He never admitted in song or gesture the sadness of the depression; yet within frothy musical paeans to the nation's benevolence, his laughter never lost sight of private torment.

Seven Lively Arts, whose avowed purpose was to resuscitate a splendor of the past, received more publicity than any show, musical or dramatic, on Broadway in 1944. No other show could boast a half-million-dollar advance in wartime; no show would have such an awesome array of talent. No show would be such a devastating disappointment to the theater world.

Produced by Billy Rose, the pint-sized impresario of spectacle, *Seven Lively Arts* was intended not only to reopen Rose's newly acquired Ziegfeld Theater, but, once and for all, to transcend the Great Ziegfeld. The production brought together the foremost performers and artists in the world. Rose coaxed Bea Lillie out of a self-imposed five-year retirement from the American stage and brought Lahr back from Hollywood. Cole Porter was commissioned to write the score, Igor Stravinsky to provide ballet music for prima ballerina Alicia Markova. William Schuman contributed a composition entitled "A Side Show for Orchestra," and Rose hired Benny Goodman and his famous Quartet for the downtown element. Moss Hart and George S. Kaufman wrote the sketches, with Ben Hecht helping out and contributing incidental monologues spoken by "Doc" Rockwell. Hassard Short directed. The production opened in Philadelphia with two acts, twenty-three scenes, and ten train-car loads of scenery.

From the beginning, *Seven Lively Arts* was a $1,350,000 theatrical anachronism. Rose was trying to serve up spectacle in an archaic formula. He proudly confided to Lucius Beebe for a New York *Herald-Tribune* interview that *Seven Lively Arts* did not contain an "ounce of significance, a suggestion of social, economic, or political implication or a trace of moral purpose. . . . It's the last word in complete escapism, a super Christmas tree, a grab-bag of fun, anything you want to call it."

Escape was possible in a faraway land; but to mount a show whose laughter and lavishness were an arrogant fist in the face of universal carnage was severely misjudging the public's taste. Rose had moved the show's New York opening to December seventh, a commemoration and denial of Pearl Harbor. A nation still at war would see an opulent extravaganza that attested not only to the stability of America's theatrical history, but also to a carefree attitude that the country would never regain.

Eventually, this affluence spelled the death of spectacle as a theatrical entertainment. Rose's tepid vision indicates how insensitive he was to the satire of both Lillie and Lahr, whose responses to the world (however unwittingly) exposed its foibles. By bridling them with a "sense of fun" stripped of any social insight, he was making both performers return to a good-natured type of humor and style of entertainment from which they had graduated. Without the vinegar of serious comic content, there was little hope of making their humor register.

Rushing to get *Seven Lively Arts* in shape before the historic December day, Rose planned only one out-of-town tryout. Dissatisfaction was brewing long before the show reached Philadelphia (Bea Lillie was already calling it *Seven* Deadly *Arts*) ; but the audience, at least, seemed pleased.

> . . . From 8:35 to 12:15 last night as many as could be squeezed into the Forest Theater saw the world Premier of the apotheosis of stage revues. True, it follows the general pattern of all these shows from W. C. Fields through Ziegfeld and George White, but for sheer beauty of scene and diversity and wealth of material *Seven Lively Arts* is tops. . . .
>
> *Variety*

Lahr had misgivings about his material. Rose had tried to con him in *Harry Delmar's Revels* and he felt that *Seven Lively Arts* was another fancy bill of goods. "I was unhappy with the show from the beginning. Billy Rose didn't get me the proper material. I could see my sketches were thin, and I kept asking if he would fix them up. He said he'd try, but he didn't do much. Fortunately for Bea, Moss Hart wrote her scenes."

Lahr's annoyance surfaced at the Philadelphia opening night when Rose came backstage to present him with a wreath of flowers. His excitement jarred with Lahr's obvious displeasure. Rose, once again, promised to do something. He handed Lahr the flowers, saying, "Your talent is as fine as this bouquet."

Lahr cut his speech short. "You know where you can put them!"
Anxiety over the material and Rose's obsession with bringing the
unpolished production to New York hung over the show. Porter and
Bea Lillie found Rose hard to work with—tight-fisted and lacking any
sense of excellence. When Miss Lillie claimed a sore throat and failed
to appear at a Broadway benefit preview, *Variety* reported that her
absence was a gesture of protest against Rose's mismanagement.

(Even Igor Stravinsky got the special Rose treatment. Contracted
by the producer to write a fifteen-minute ballet for five thousand dollars, Stravinsky's score had pleased Rose at rehearsal. When Rose heard
the music from the pit on opening night in Philadelphia, he fired off
a telegram to the composer:

YOUR MUSIC GREAT SUCCESS STOP COULD BE SENSATIONAL STOP IF
YOU WOULD AUTHORIZE ROBERT RUSSELL BENNETT RETOUCH OR-
CHESTRATION STOP BENNETT ORCHESTRATES EVEN COLE PORTER.

Stravinsky wired back:

SATISFIED WITH SUCCESS.

The ballet was not presented in its entirety until the winter of
1945, when it was performed by the New York Philharmonic.)

The possibility of an inglorious return to Broadway put Lahr on the
defensive and clouded his comic instincts. His self-consciousness
squelched valid comic ideas. "Moss Hart wrote one scene for me that
was good, but I didn't think it was right for my kind of comedy."
The sketch was about an English officer who gives a lecture on the evils
of women to his troops. As he talks, he becomes progressively more
excited, until he has to be cooled off with a bucket of water. "The
water was a little uncomfortable for me. I didn't like it. I didn't want
to get drenched every day. It wasn't worth it. Being unhappy in the
show anyway, I just couldn't do the sketch. It was dropped from the
show, but it was much better than I thought at the time."

Lahr also refused to sing a chorus of a Cole Porter song that rhymed
"cinema" with "enema." "When you said a word like that on stage,
you could feel the audience freeze up." Lahr's prudishness and his
nervousness about the audience did not do justice to the song, which
cast him as an old man singing out his venom. (This hilarious comic
idea would be employed later when S. J. Perelman and Lahr discovered
the red-baiting ice-cream tycoon, Nelson Smedley, in *The Beauty
Part*.) Lahr's testiness during the rehearsals is measured by the mild-

ness, not to mention the wit, of the Porter song he would not sing. Disgusted with the show, he misjudged not only material, like Hart's, which looked toward the past, but also ideas, like Porter's, which offered something new.

Porter's song "Dainty, Quainty Me" would have given Lahr's material the sophistication and variety it lacked. The song was certainly stronger than much of the comedy business he performed. His attitude at rehearsals and his gripes against government and society were strong enough to have made the comic statement hilarious.

I'm "Dainty, Quainty Me"
And from care completely free.
You may ask me how I can still feel gay
Why, by merely ignoring the world of today.
When e'er I feel like mis-behaving
I go out and buy a French engraving
So like the lark, I'm as happy as can be
Little old, "Dainty, Quainty Me."

The patter was a glib commentary on life in the early forties.

When people talk about those columnists, such as Walter
Winchell, Ed Sullivan, Westbrook Pegler, Hedda Hopper,
Dorothy Thompson, Dorothy Kilgallen, and that frightfully
vulgar girl they call "ELSA"
I take BROMO SELTZA.

When one mentions Martha Raye, Carmen Miranda, Lana Turner,
Anita Louise, Joan Davis, Betty Hutton, Gregory Ratoff,
Red Skelton, Monty Woolley, Don Ameche, Jack Oakie, Sir
Cedric Hardwicke and other stars of the CINEMA
I have to take an ENEMA.

The song was suited to the sophisticated intention of *Seven Lively Arts;* but Lahr's anxiety put him at odds with himself. He wanted fresh material—but not *that* fresh! Porter continued to polish the song with the hope of convincing Lahr to use it. Lahr's absolute veto scotched the idea. In later years, Lahr's decision still rankled Porter, who once confided to Mildred, "Your husband doesn't think I can write a comedy song."

Porter too sensed the show's mediocrity. Writing under not only the burden of such an unwieldly enterprise but also his own private problems, he could not find the comic or melodic flare that had distinguished his earlier scores. The only song to come out of *Seven Lively Arts* was

"Ev'rytime We Say Good-bye." Although Porter fitted Bea Lillie with a few fine comedy numbers, he did not provide the material Lahr had so confidently expected from the creator of *Du Barry*. One unpublished song shows Porter playing with the comic personalities of two of his favorite laugh-makers—Lillie and Lahr. In "Where Do We Go From Here," he tried to pit Lahr's obstreperous mug against the alabaster whimsy of Miss Lillie.

> *He:* I loves yuh, lady, 'cause you're so refeened,
> It musta been on champagne that you was weaned.
> I loves yuh 'cause you're crammed fulla blood that's blue.
> *She:* Strangely, sir, I loves yuh too,
> Your Grecian nose, I simply idolize,
> I adore the lack of distance between your eyes.

The lines are smooth, and although they pay attention to Lahr's body, they miss his speech patterns. They are not particular enough to develop the sense of variety that makes Porter's best lyrics unique. If Porter's inventiveness seemed momentarily stale, he could still parody the musical tradition he had done so much to revolutionize.

"Rose promised me material; but I never got it," Lahr says. "Finally I had to try and protect myself—I suggested to Cole a burlesque on the old Shubert drinking songs. He liked the idea, and 'Drink, Drink, Drink' became the only decent number I had in the show." Porter set Lahr in an admiral's costume, with a large he-man chorus providing harmony as his baritone voice mounted to heroic proportions and he got progressively drunker.

But the song was not enough to assuage Lahr's bitter disenchantment. If the audience howled at the final stanza, it was laughing at old wine—

> Drink to *The Student Prince* that show sublime,
> And please don't forget Jeanette, in *Apple Blossom Time*.
> Drink to Nelson Eddy, before you faint,
> And here's to J. J. Shubert, our patron saint.

The gaudy façade of the production perplexed Lahr. Opening-night tickets sold at twenty-four dollars a seat. The scene outside the theater and in it had been spectacular and grotesque. After the show, Lahr would read Lucius Beebe's approving account:

> . . . The gangways seethed with the names that made news hoisting

fire pails of champagne at the expense of the management. The limousine line stretched from the theater's blindingly lighted marquee all the way to Central Park. The speed guns of news cameramen were once more busy as ever they were at the openings of 1939, and neither grand opera nor any other social clambake save perhaps the horse show has in recent years brought out such an undulant red carpet of chinchilla and boiled shirts as populated the orchestra stalls when the first curtain went up.

Lahr went to Bea Lillie's dressing room to wish her luck. He found her at the make-up table, crying. "I didn't say anything. It was about then, I think, that her son was missing in action. And now, on Pearl Harbor Day, she was going on . . . I wouldn't have done any good. I knew how she felt."

For Lahr, there was a certain gluttony in the enterprise, which contrasted violently with his beloved co-star bent over her dressing table in tears. Lahr understood the sadness intuitively, yet he could not relate it to his own life. "It was the only time I ever saw Bea cry."

The war had not touched him as it had Bea. He had suffered nothing; he was at once safe in his profession and yet strangely threatened by an optimism as artificial as the sumptuous Ziegfeld Theater lounge that Dali had decorated for the occasion. His faith in Bea's unerring comic sensibilities and her quintessential professionalism was challenged by a wonder that politics had somehow intruded into the sacrosanct province of laughter. His humor had always been based on a buffoon's anarchy; it was indisputably apolitical. But Bea's tears hinted at a world that could no longer dismiss history.

The first-night audience enjoyed themselves, stopping the show several times for encores. The good spirits were self-conscious; the rapport between the performers and eager audience strained by the emotional vacuum backstage. Lahr was disturbed by the audience's apparent enthusiasm and the inability of the best of America's professionals to meet that demand with excellence.

The critics were kind to the performers despite the fact that the show was top-heavy, uneven, and, in some cases, like Stravinsky's *Scenes de Ballet,* extraneous. The lavishness Rose imagined would be part of the fun was only occasionally amusing. "Fragonard" placed Bea Lillie on a swing engulfed in a pink arcadia. Lahr in matching pink pantaloons and a periwig pushed her gently in a parody of eighteenth-century manners. Miss Lillie recalls, to her delight, the night the swing clipped Lahr on the chin and sent him sprawling. Rose's instincts for extravagance were foiled on another occasion when Benny Goodman refused to don Rose's elaborate costumes for the finale. He made his appearance in a modest set of tails. Perhaps the most trenchant observation on the show was made by *Saturday Review's* John Mason Brown. Commenting on Rose's Lucullan intentions he turned the other cheek to his hospitality. "Had Mr. Rose succeeded in making those seven arts lively, one might have forgiven him his gold plate, even in wartime. What we resented, so far as entertainment was concerned, was being overfed and underprivileged."

Seven Lively Arts was intended to be a bromide to the war's doldrums, to paint over anguish with a show of splendor that asked nothing of the future except that it be like the past. The decadence of the show was apparent even to Lahr. Its array of burlesque and vaudeville turns, its extravagance in homage to another era seemed curiously old-fashioned, a wistful recollection of a more innocent time. Behind the faltering material and lapses in taste that Lahr could see was a fear of something larger and more elusive. The war would change laughter. Although *Seven Lively Arts* had delighted first-nighters and eked out a respectable run of 183 performances, it was not merely a bad show. The people were not responding. It spoke to a different society; and no return to an earlier bravado could gloss the fact. Lahr was no prophet. Continually misled by his sense of historical fact, he nonetheless feared for his career in a postwar environment. The image of Bea crying stayed with him through the gayest moments of *Seven Lively Arts* and after it. "I don't know why. It made me sad. I just couldn't get it out of my mind."

As a father Bert Lahr emerged from the shadows of midnight kisses and occasional walks only slowly. Jane and I barely understood that there was someone else besides Mother and an endless succession of foreign nurses who were responsible for us. His behavior during *Seven Lively Arts* and the two years of relative inaction that followed certainly did not seem normal—even to children as young as we. He rarely played with us, and on a Sunday morning we could never gain access to his room much before noontime. We wanted to hear stories, and he would always begin one—the same one—which he never finished. It was about a street cat—or dog—who never had a home. He wandered around the city, and my father would describe what the animal saw.

We wanted him to embellish his stories with tales of birds and goldfish, which interested us at the time. He never did.

He was an upsetting man. His voice could be volcanic. It would sometimes crash through the world of comfort he had created for himself: suede shoes, tweed jackets, Of-Thee-I-Sing cologne, cigarettes in every cigarette box. Now, I know there was fear in his voice; but, unable to read it then, the sound was simply stamped on our imaginations as Authority. He surrounded us with toys, and answered every one of our material needs. He protected us. Jane and I never knew there had been a world war until we entered grade school.

My father was aloof. A game of catch in the park was two or three tosses. I did not know he worried; he simply cast no aura over the household. Even the birthday cards and Christmas presents from him were written in Mother's hand.

Once, soon after *Seven Lively Arts* closed, he went to a costume party. It was the first time I had seen him in disguise. He went as Whistler's Mother. He seemed like one of the sweet, puckered old ladies who took us to the park. I woke up when my parents came home from the party. Mother's voice was loud in the hall. I crept to the door and saw her giggling. She was laughing at my father, who had passed out in his dress. Years later, he would tell me that people came up to him at the party (he went complete with rocking chair) and pinched his cheek, saying, "What a cute old lady!" He would turn around, completely inebriated, and say something gross. Dead drunk, in his outrageous costume, the personality beneath scared me. He was different from the other more reliable grownups my friends had as fathers. I hated to see him drink. But I remember that often when I'd lie awake waiting for my parents to kiss me goodnight their kisses had a perfumed smell. It made me sad.

There were no Broadway parts that seemed to be right for my father in the year and a half after *Seven Lively Arts*. Having cast his lot for Broadway, Hollywood was not a place he visited often, although he would sometimes tell us about his home and his orchard. It was a restless time, and he had to resign himself to waiting for the right part. His anxieties about his comedy were never expressed to us, but we were aware of the tension. Muffled voices behind locked doors suddenly blurted out into harsh, sometimes teary sentences, and then, tantalizingly, fell back into whispers.

The mystery of my parents was my chief pastime. I would eavesdrop in the early hours of the morning—trying to listen or peek through a keyhole. Sometimes I regretted my snooping, because I found out more than I expected. I recall seeing my father throw a suitcase on the bed, waving his hands wildly at Mother. He walked out of the room, and then out of the house. What annoyed me was not that he'd left, but that he had not bothered to kiss me goodbye. He hadn't kissed Mother either. That was some consolation.

We often tried to ferret out the secret of Father's job, which he would never explain. When he took the family to see *Peter Pan* so many people at intermission wanted his autograph that there was a line all the way up the aisle. My father recalls walking with Jane on the street. People would gape at him. "Why are they staring at me, Daddy?" He never explained. He always evaded our questions. Sometimes he told us he was a pitcher for the Yankees (but when he broke Mother's antique vase with a pitch he called the "dipsy doodle" she didn't act as though he were a professional athlete). He said he was a big-game hunter, an aviator, a golf pro, and only after he came up with so many answers to the same question over a period of years did we realize that these responses were red herrings. Even when we were told that he was an actor, he was different from other fathers. In front of audiences he danced, he sang, he put on faces he never showed us at home.

Why did he hide himself from us? He had a vision of his profession as harsh, vulgar, and coarse—a world he did not want us to comprehend. But his secretiveness at that time, I think now, came much closer to the dilemma he was facing in his comedy. The scripts were not coming; the material was not there. Comedy situations written for him after *Seven Lively Arts* seemed old-hat. There was no way, at the moment, to present his kind of humor on stage. The spectacular failure of Rose's revue and the endless stream of bad musical comedies on his desk corroborated for him the mercurial situation of Broadway. If he was not on the stage, if he was unsure of the pertinence of his comedy, he could never be sure of himself.

In the summer of 1945, he tried out *Burlesque,* the Arthur Hopkins–George M. Watters chestnut, in a dingy theater at Brighton Beach, New Jersey. The choice seemed an odd one; the play, a great dramatic success in 1927, was undeniably dated. Burlesque was an art form that had been moribund for a decade when the play with its artless sentimentality eulogized this particular breed of American performer.

Despite its mustiness, Lahr tried the play out. "I wanted to see what *I* could do with this show."

What Lahr was testing was his dramatic ability. With his career seemingly stalled, his instinct for survival needled him into developing another facet of his talent—just in case. He was trying a script in which he might be able to incorporate much of his old comic material in a fresh format. Nobody, either on stage or in films, had chronicled burlesque as he knew it. His interest in the play was not just a yearning for the past.

The play was not good in New Jersey; Lahr's first dramatic performance was unsteady. Arthur Hopkins had traveled to New Jersey to see it, and Lahr conceded, "I don't think he was too impressed." However, in the summer of 1946, still without a promising theatrical property, Lahr tried out *Burlesque* in Greenwich, Connecticut, with additions he had made in the story. The show was a great success. "I was easy in it. I had the conception of the show."

The public's response to the Lahr version of *Burlesque* impressed an ex-vaudevillian—Jean Dalrymple—who had watched Lahr's cop act from the wings and knew both its pathos and comic potential. She decided to produce the play with Arthur Hopkins even though she had not seen the Greenwich production. "I remember that when I saw Bert's performance in *Du Barry*, it struck me as a wonderfully legitimate characterization. I felt he should do a straight play. When I heard he was doing his cop act in the burlesque show within the play, I thought to myself, 'That would be marvelous, it can't fail, it's foolproof.' Sight unseen, I decided to bring it to New York."

Getting *Burlesque* into the Belasco Theater, where it finally outran and outgrossed the original Hal Skelley–Barbara Stanwyck version, was not as easy as the audience reaction to the show indicated. To Hopkins, a man as averse to comic improvisation as he was to busy scenery, Lahr was wrong for the part. Hopkins kept protesting to Miss Dalrymple, "The play was written for a hoofer." Undaunted, Miss Dalrymple insisted that the play made continual references to the hero's humor and the melodrama could use some comic flair. "Mr. Hopkins wouldn't even go up to Greenwich to see Bert. Finally, one Friday he called me and said he was going up. I couldn't go with him. I was astonished."

The next day Hopkins called Miss Dalrymple and announced "You were right. You can do the show!"

When Miss Dalrymple met him the following Monday to begin laying plans, Hopkins insisted that he direct it. "I was very disappointed when he said he'd have to direct the show himself." Hopkins liked the show in Greenwich, but thought it was too hokey. "I said that I thought the hokiness was honest and precisely what made it a hit. In order to get it done at all, I finally agreed to let Hopkins direct. That was a great mistake. He tried to make Bert unfunny, too legitimate. Unfortunately, it seemed to me, Bert listened to him and played very straight. Hopkins used to call me a 'nervous Nellie' when I'd complain about the play being 'flat.' I said I didn't think it was funny at all; he replied, 'It's not supposed to be funny.' "

The cast had two types of performances: one, when Hopkins was in the theater, played the story; the other followed Lahr's more relaxed instincts. Lahr used to whisper to the actors, "Talk fast, talk fast," hurrying through the dramaturgy to the burlesque entertainment. Still, Hopkins's presence was an important source of confidence to Lahr. Hopkins respected Lahr's talent and let him direct the burlesque play "within the play" in the third act. Hopkins did not seem to care about the musical-comedy numbers, and Lahr remembers his surprise when the famous producer-writer put him in charge: "You do the musical numbers, Bert; I'll direct the piece." He was distinctly the mentor; and Lahr listened. "He would 'edit' me. He never told me much. He would say, very quietly, 'I wouldn't lay on that line too much' or 'play that down.' We had a most wonderful association. He had great taste. He was to me what a literary editor must be to a writer. He doesn't tell the writer what to write, but sometimes he points out what to embellish and clarify. When he died, I couldn't go to the funeral. I'm too emotional at funerals; it's embarrassing. I couldn't see him."

Hopkins provided an important creative catalyst to Lahr, who was eager to absorb all of his directional suggestions. Gail Garber, who played a character part in *Burlesque,* recalls coming back to Lahr's dressing room after the first rehearsal under Hopkins.

"What did he tell you?" Lahr inquired.

"He told me to keep my head up and my chin down. When I looked up, Bert was staring into the mirror and trying it."

Hopkins encouraged Lahr's dramatic capacities. "When a director can't tell me what to do, I can't learn from him. He stifles me. He's like a hand around my throat." Hopkins, however, provided the security and intelligence that let Lahr take risks he had never before attempted. Lahr was able to meld the dramatic with the comic moment on stage. He found himself with not only directorial control of one of the play's most important sequences, but also the responsibility for writing some of the material.

One of the few letters Lahr kept for his scrapbook is from Hopkins, dated seven days before the show opened on Christmas Eve 1946.

Dear Bert,

Working with you has been a real pleasure. I cannot emphasize too strongly that there is a wide and rewarding field for you in straight plays. Character comedians become rarer each year. You can be the answer to what hitherto would have been a serious casting problem.

Free yourself entirely, Bert, from the idea that you have to be continuously funny. Your straight passages can be just as rewarding. I think with Skid, you have only started. Use him to supplant in people's minds the limited category in which your previous success has placed you.

Remember good character stars have never failed to find a gratifying and rewarding place for themselves.

Above all, don't worry if they don't laugh. If there is a laugh there, you will get it. If not—you don't want it.

I hope the performance has steadied down again. It is unfortunate that we got sidetracked after the Sunday matinee. Anxiety can be the most harmful of meddlers.

Hopkins was speaking to Lahr's two most pressing desires—getting the laughs and prolonging his career. "Nothing should imply that Mr. Lahr has now taken off into middle air and improved himself culturally," wrote Brooks Atkinson after seeing *Burlesque.* "If you are a full-ranking merry-andrew . . . there are no higher glories. By comparison, acting Hamlet is only a monologue booking."

Lahr had no qualms about directing the burlesque scene because he knew what was honest about the form of entertainment and what the public had romanticized. The sensitivity and wit managed to surface through the melodramatic ice.

Lahr brought to the Hopkins play a fondness for the burlesque ambience and intimate knowledge of the friendliness and loyalty that characterized the burlesque performer. Directing the part that made the greatest impact on both audiences and critics, his impulse was always one of respect for not only the people he employed but also the institution he was re-creating.

Ironically, the song that opened the show was singled out by Eric

Bentley for embodying an attitude toward entertainment no longer possible in a postwar society. The song is nonetheless the recognition of a sad farewell, looking backward to a romantic excess that had dwindled to formula and boredom on Broadway by 1947.

Lahr's song—his only attempt at Tin Pan Alley—was squealed by a handful of young ladies who peered out over the footlights to sing—

> Hello, hello, hello,
> You in the very first row.
> We are the Gaiety Girls
> We hope you like our show . . .
> We hate to overtax you
> We're here just to relax you
> So, hello, hello, hello
> Let's get on with the show.
> Goodbye to cares,
> We'll show our wares,
> Hello, hello, hello.

Lahr's song was not merely a nostalgic interlude. It contained humor and its own self-criticism. Eric Bentley, writing in *In Search of Theater,* picked up the point:

> The intention behind the show—*Burlesque,* by Watters and Hopkins—is clear. For those who sell, it is a profitable commodity. For those who buy, it is a way of keeping awake after dinner . . . But the even surface of routine entertainment is broken by eruptions of sheer art. . . . Bert Lahr needs only show us a tithe of his extraordinary talent and we are transported to a realm that no entertainment-monger could possibly be interested in. Lahr's performance has about it that very embarrassing quality—beauty. His personality—like that of all first-rate comedians—expresses a criticism of life and thus calls into play a faculty more formidable than the aesthetic sense: the intellect. . . ."

Lahr was exploiting the moments of pathos and humor he always found absurd. The tall, buxom woman and the short man; the inarticulate, flustered policeman, the braggadocio tenor whose voice is funny to all but himself. This playful irony was the arena of burlesque laughter. Lahr entered it without any other intention than putting on a realistic version of a burlesque show that would allow him to do his cop act.

The precision with which Lahr approached the job was impressive. He hired many old burlesque artists: Gail Garber, Bobby Barry, Irene

Allery. Barry had been a burlesque headliner and had worked with Lahr on many vaudeville bills. When he hired Miss Garber as the formula "Beef Trust" girl, Hopkins objected. The chorus line needed a dancer who was continuously off-stride and absentminded. If Hopkins and Lahr differed in their choices, they also had different ways of getting results. As Gail Garber pointed out, "Hopkins would hire a good-looking girl and made her look dumb. Lahr wouldn't do that. He'd hire an ugly dope of a chorus girl and make her think she was beautiful."

Lahr played this private game often. He employed a bald-headed violinist for the reason that all burlesque orchestras in his memory had a bald-headed violinist. On opening night, the violinist wore a toupee. Lahr never had the courage to say anything to the man. In the burlesque show within the show, Lahr wanted a tenor voice to sing the hokey "Sheik of Araby." He wanted it done in the same ornate, melodramatic manner he'd seen on the burlesque wheel, complete with musty costumes and tarnished larynx. Lahr could not find the right man. "I wanted an Irish tenor, a fellow who sings so loud you think he's going to break a vein. A fellow came in one day and said to me, 'I'm an opera singer.' He was just what I wanted. He thought he was great, but he was horrible. In his dressing room, he'd be doing the scales and squirting his throat with an atomizer. I had him come out and close his arms very sternly and lean against the proscenium and sing. The audience used to laugh at him, but he never heard them. He thought he was wonderful. I remember Bea Lillie came to see the show. I knew she'd only laugh at certain fey things that had some satire in them. She'd seen my cop act many times; and I knew she wouldn't be surprised by that. We all watched her from the wings. When this tenor began to sing—'I'm the sheik of Araby! And your love belongs to me,' I heard Bea's special laugh—eeeeeeh. It was the only thing that caught her fancy in the show."

Burlesque was the first show where Lahr's comedy and his own taste were the complete focus of attention. The songs were of his choosing, recollected from his good-humored image of burlesque: "Get Out and Get Under," "Put Your Arms Around Me," "Tiger Rag." He even had Hopkins reintroduce "Ballin' the Jack," a number he had done in *Keep Smiling*. The accuracy of the burlesque show was matched by the intense concentration with which Lahr assumed responsibility for its success. He watched the production closely. Gail Garber recalls the night she opened in the show. "Bozo—that was Bobby Barry—was pulling me away from another chorus girl. I was supposed to say, 'Leggo me, you shrimp.' But I forgot. Suddenly, I was conscious of somebody calling me a shrimp from the wings. I turned around, and there was Bert with a prompt book in his hand, whispering 'Leggo me, you shrimp.' "

Lahr unexpectedly called Bobby Barry and Miss Garber aside after the performance. "Bobby, I don't want you moving on my lines or anyone else's in this show!" The old comedian took Lahr's criticism with a smile. He'd been caught red-handed. Miss Garber, who was singing "Something About a Soldier," was the victim of the upstaging. She was amazed that he had been doing anything. "Bert, how did you know he was moving?"

"I was watching your shadows from the wings."

"Something About a Soldier" was one of Lahr's favorite old burlesque routines. He had hired Barry specifically for it. Barry, who stood about five feet two, played a fife and did a trollish tap dance, while Miss Garber, decked out in a majorette's hat and wooden rifle, towered above him. Lahr's obsession for improving his own material carried over to the burlesque show he was directing. He was continually revising it and putting in new ideas. Sometimes, however, as a neophyte director, he forgot to relate these ideas to everyone concerned. So, when the idea of the impish Barry making his exit by jumping on Miss Garber's broad back came to him, he told Barry, but in his excitement forgot to warn Miss Garber. When Miss Garber pranced smartly off stage during the Broadway performance, Barry hit her from behind, latching onto her back like a monkey to a tree. She careened into the wings.

Lahr's only surprising innovation was adding a stripteaser. He used the striptease to update his cop act, and where in vaudeville Mercedes had done a Spanish dance, now Irene Allery came out and did a bump and grind. "We never had strippers in burlesque when I was part of it. The girl I hired was very cute. She had a little figure nobody resented. You'd look out and see old ladies smiling. She was very *petite*. I used to surprise her on stage. I'd try and break her up. Then her breasts would jump up and down, you know. I'd say, 'You laugh like a mixmaster.' The audience would laugh *with* us because I could break her up by just moving my nose. I wanted a stripper for a reason. She didn't do much of it, just a chorus. When she began to get violent, I'd come out in a cop suit, yelling 'Stop! In the name of the station house, stooooop!!' We'd do our act in one. Hopkins was delighted with it. If he hadn't liked it he wouldn't have kept it in; he never wanted anything cheap."

In choosing an artist whose body was not gargantuan and keeping the bawdy to a minimum, Lahr matched the affection with which burlesque people were described in the play and in his own mind. Hopkins once told him, "The success of Burlesque is this—very few backstage plays have ever been successful. But these people are nice, kind people. That's why it's a success."

As a director, Lahr was benevolent. The actors came to him to intercede with management when they wanted a few days off. And it was Lahr who, after the dressing rooms at the Belasco had been robbed, paid the chorus girls, who had lost a few hundred dollars, out of his own pocket. As the same time, he kept order backstage. His co-star in the original show, Jean Parker (later replaced by Faye McKenzie) was married to her manager, who was continually causing trouble. His thick-rimmed glasses and even denser Austrian accent earned him Lahr's nickname, "Dr. Cyclops." Finally, Lahr had to ban him ("I forbad him to enter" are his regal words) from backstage.

Jean Parker was a delight to work with, but sometimes galling. "She was beautiful—a fine comedienne and a fine little actress." At one performance, however, she went on with a cold. When Bonnie goes off with a rich cattleman and is confronted by Skid (Lahr) in his usual inebriated state, she is forced to sing "In the Gloaming." Skid, sarcastically, asks her to sing, but the Cattleman genuinely wants to hear the song. "Now she's got a cold, but she starts to sing and hits a clinker. She walks down to the audience and says, 'I gotta cold,' then steps back into the play and sings. Well, I'm fit to be tied. When the curtain came down I said, 'You dumb son-of-a-bitch, don't ever do that again.' "

Flouncing her brief burlesque skirt arrogantly up in back, she countered, "All right Pappy!"

In the next act, the cold prevented her from hearing the orchestra. At the climax of the show, when Skid faints on stage and is carried off, Bonnie comes on to sing "Peggy O'Neill." "The song was a dramatic moment, because Bonnie is playing a scene as well as singing. But she could not hear the music. She looked down into the orchestra and said, 'Where is everybody?' " Even Lahr had to laugh.

At one point, Bobby Barry had come to him and asked for a few days rest. Barry, then in his seventies, "a sweet snaggle-toothed old man," as one of the cast called him, was going to visit relatives in Pennsylvania. Lahr got him the days off. However, Lahr had not seen Barry on the day of his return, and went on stage expecting to confront his old burlesque cohort in much the same shape as he'd left him. "I'm on stage and Bozo (Bobby Barry) is supposed to knock on the door. There's a knock and I say, 'Come in Bozo.' Well, Barry came in and said, 'Hiya Skid.' I took one look at him and all I could see was this beautiful set of pearly teeth. Before, every time he smiled you'd see his upper gums, now he looked like Satchmo. I went—'aaaaaah.' I couldn't stop laughing. Then Bobby started laughing, and the entire cast laughed for five minutes on stage. Isn't that awful."

Lahr's performance created a pathos, a careful counterpoint between flashy burlesque activity and genuine sadness. The melodrama in the lines was made honest and poignant because Skid's emotional decline paralleled Lahr's own private life at one time. One of the play's most touching moments is the second-act curtain, when Skid is present at the marriage of his girl, Bonnie, to the Cattleman. Lahr found himself mouthing words which drew on his own resources of grief: "Why do people get sore and crab when they lose out in marriage? Why don't they join in the festivities? Come on, Jerry, play the weddin' march and play it fast."

No matter how flexible an actor *Burlesque* showed Lahr to be, there were some situations that even *his* talent could not gloss. Once, when Jane and I were watching the scurry of legs, we heard the orchestra strike up, and Dad's familiar voice. We opened a door by the set and watched him sing, "Here Comes the Bride." We particularly liked this part of the show because he skipped around the stage and acted both the bride and groom, as we often did in front of mirrors at home. The audience laughed throughout the number, disconcerting my father, who finally stopped and turned to look behind him. He stared straight at us. We were standing in the middle of the stage. Gail Garber lured us away, and the show tried to regain the lost momentum. On another occasion, I accidentally locked Faye McKenzie in her dressing room and put the key in my pocket, which kept the performance stalled for five minutes.

Burlesque left Lahr with not only a sense of accomplishment ("I felt I was on the right track again"), but also a camaraderie he had not felt in *Seven Lively Arts*. Many of the Broadway cast would tour with him around the country and again in summer stock. An affection for the show as well as the people in it, was inevitable.

Off stage, things could be as grotesque and slapstick as they were on it. He was accorded the honor of being best man at the wedding of his striptease artist, Irene Allery, to a Hungarian wrestling champion. Jean Dalrymple was maid of honor, and the entire wedding, in true burlesque tradition, took place on the stage of the Belasco Theater. As a publicity stunt, Miss Dalrymple had hoped to get the Mayor of New York to marry the couple; but when he could not appear at the celebration, an aged judge was called in.

"It was the funniest thing I ever experienced," Lahr says. "When we first made our entrance through the door behind the stage and stood in a row in front of an improvised altar, the band played 'Pomp and Circumstance' instead of the 'Wedding March.' I'm standing there next to this brute and looking at the judge, waiting for him to begin the ceremony. He was very old; he had glasses the size of bottles. He leans over to me and says, 'You're getting a lovely wife.' "

"I'm not getting married; he is!"

The wedding celebration was even more outrageous. The buffet dinner had been attended to by the stage manager, who, being Jewish, had provided Kosher meats. More unusual than the bill of fare was the guest list. Sitting on the groom's side were forty wrestlers, mixed with actors and other theater people. "You've never seen so many cauliflower ears. I saw the Swedish Angel take ten sandwiches in one hand. It was like a plague of locusts."

The cast recalls Lahr fondly—aloof, unpredictable, professional, and talented. On the road, he took complete charge of the show. Once, tired of the nonchalance with which the show girls were dressing in the hotel, he called them together. "I want this group to come down looking shipshape in the morning." The next day, Lahr's dumb blonde, who, according to another member of the cast, "thought she looked like Hedy Lamarr but was closer to Marjorie Main," came down to the hotel lobby in an evening dress and a picture hat.

The cast always listened to Lahr, sometimes out of reverence and sometimes out of fear. In Brooklyn, Lahr found that his policeman's coat was missing. He was furious. As a prank the stripteaser tipped him off that the tenor, Santo Scudi, had stolen it. Gail Garber recalls seeing Lahr storm into the wings while Scudi was giving his rendition of "The Sheik of Araby," yelling "Where's my coat, where's my coat?" Scudi, continuing his song, kept shaking his head and pleading ignorance. Lahr finally recovered the prop, but not before his wrath had threatened the entire cast. The stripper's tip-off was retribution on the tenor, who had acquired a ring that squirted water, with which he doused her as she exited.

Lahr's anger was not reserved for members of the cast. Once, a drunk in the front row took exception to Lahr's imitation of one. "Go home you drunken bum!" he yelled at Lahr's most dramatic scene, when Skid passes out on stage. "When we came out to take our bows," recalls Gail Garber, "Faye McKenzie and I had a death grip on him. He wanted to jump over the foots after the guy."

Many stories grew out of *Burlesque*. Members of the cast will tell you about the five-minute ovation Lahr received when the show played Hollywood and its star returned after a three-year absence. "I don't remember it," is Lahr's reply. "I went over all right, I guess." But Gail Garber is more precise. "When he walked out, he got a standing ovation; I've never heard a response like that before. He finally had to step out of character and acknowledge their kindness."

Lahr's hypochondria is another theme for the stories. Once one of the chorus girls in *Burlesque* fainted. She was brought into Lahr's dressing room while the doctor examined her. Lahr was doing his make-up for a Wednesday matinée. Miss Garber, a registered nurse as well as a performer, was aiding the doctor and present at the examination.

"Have you had dizzy spells before?" asked the doctor.

"No."

From his dressing table, Lahr puzzled. "Sometimes I get dizzy."

"Stomach cramps?"

"No."

"Say, Doc," Lahr said, "sometimes I have cramps."

"Does your mouth often go dry?"

"No."

"Mine goes dry all the time, Doc."

Exasperated, the doctor turned to Lahr, "If you don't mind, Mr. Lahr, I'm trying to find out if this woman is pregnant."

Lahr's fear of illness was intensified by the death of his father from cancer during the *Burlesque* run. The fact was kept from him until a Friday performance. According to the cast, he never showed any outward emotion. At home, however, things were strangely different. I remember asking about the candle he left burning on his desk. He never explained; and he never did it again. It was the only time he ever exhibited a religious awareness. Lahr's sadness over his father's death was immense, but whatever he felt he rarely expressed. Occasionally, he would recollect the times when we'd visited his father at an old age home, and how we'd played checkers.

On the road, Peggy Cass took Faye McKenzie's part. Miss Cass recalls seeing Lahr sitting glumly at a table one night. She asked him how he felt.

"Not so good," he said. "I think I've got the Big C."

After this Broadway success, Lahr once again played a waiting game. His potential as a legitimate performer had been impressed on audiences and critics, but not on producers. No one capitalized on his acting ability. If theatrical management was nervous about breaking commercial stereotypes, Lahr also contributed to the situation. In his three-year absence from Broadway, he toured in the Sid Caesar vehicle *Make Mine Manhattan,* appeared frequently on television, and made a few unmemorable appearances in films. He had defied Hopkins's good advice for axioms closer to his heart. "I'm a mercenary. Any dramatic parts I got after *Burlesque* just couldn't pay well. I had dependents, and a lot of obligations. Comedy was the only thing I could afford to do."

In 1951 *Two on the Aisle* brought Lahr back to Broadway. Just as Ziegfeld's last extravaganza had starred Lahr, *Two on the Aisle,* conceived and directed by Abe Burrows, was Broadway's last big-time revue, "a bright and authentic flashback to the nearly forgotten formula" as *Theater Arts Magazine* referred to it. (Later, smaller-scale revues like *New Faces of 1952* and *1956, La Plume de Ma Tante* in 1958, and *Beyond the Fringe* in 1961 found admiring audiences on Broadway by offering not only more acerbic satire, but also an economic format that counterbalanced spiraling Broadway costs.) *Two on the Aisle* was the last flamboyant breath for the star-studded cast and opulent extravaganza, a form that had nursed comedy and comedians on Broadway into an important force.

If the show was an anachronism, Lahr was happy to be with it. "I waited a long time for this show. Good sketches are tough to develop." The difference between *Two on the Aisle* and previous revue attempts was the quality of material. An impressive array of Broadway talent was concentrated on bringing the revue format up to date. Abe Burrows and Nat Hiken created the sketches; Jule Styne, Betty Comden, and Adolph Green wrote the music and lyrics. None of the songs have lived, but two of its comedy bits, "Schneider's Miracle" and "Sawsie Dusties," have become part of the American comic heritage. Beside fresh, contemporary situations, they allowed Lahr to sport costumes and disguises, key props of the buffoon's fun. The audience could see him decked out as Queen Victoria, a Wagnerian Siegfried, a baseball player, and a park attendant.

The sketches satirized modern targets with a more intellectual flavor than most of Lahr's previous material. Abe Burrows concocted the first American science-fiction routine for the show; a satire on television that betrayed the lie of sportscasters and, in the time of the Kefauver investigations, the embarrassing intimacy of the television camera's microscopic scrutiny of public events for private viewing. One sketch took Lahr into an urbane triptych in which a love scene is played in three different styles: burlesque, T. S. Eliot, and Cole Porter. While some critics moaned (John Chapman of the New York *Daily News* said, "When is Santa Claus going to bring Lahr some new material?") , the show was more literate than many of its predecessors in the Golden Age of the revue.

It was particularly exciting to be around my father at this time of his career. With more good material to run through each evening than he had had in a decade, he was at his comic peak. His security in the laughter (while never complete) was strong enough to warrant moving to a fourteen-room duplex on the West Side. He suddenly had become a collector and self-proclaimed expert on porcelains. Fleshy paintings on the scale of "The Rape of the Sabine Women" and still-life studies of "Nature Morte" kept cropping up on the downstairs walls. In October 1951 he brought home a copy of *Time* Magazine with his face, in baseball costume, on the cover.

He never decorated his dressing room. It was barren, except for an occasional press picture. Most of the attention was focused on the soft-drink cooler. But in *Two on the Aisle* a special gaiety pervaded even his somber surroundings. After each scene Lahr would come back soaking wet. The room had a washline for costumes. It was cluttered with a Superman outfit, Viking helmet complete with bull's horns, a New York Giants uniform, and a ridiculous set of royal robes for Lahr's impersonations of Queen Victoria. What was laughable was seeing Dad standing in his underpants and bare feet, wearing basketball kneepads and holding out his arms for his valet to slap the next change on him.

With so much to amuse us, we spent many matinées in the dressing room. The family would sit, eating, playing with the props, listening to the ball game on television. Even without an afternoon performance, he was often at the theater by four, checking the box office, waiting for the eight o'clock curtain. On the surface, everything seemed placid and secure. It wasn't.

Lahr did not take the show on the road—a final gesture of disgust with Dolores Gray, whom, regardless of talent, he could not abide. The difficulty began when the show opened in New Haven. Miss Gray, just returned from London, where she was a hit in *Annie Get Your Gun,* had a big voice and an ego to match. Burrows, following revue format, had slotted Lahr for the number three spot, the position allotted to the first star. (Its importance was read into contract law when, in another show, it was stipulated that Bea Lillie was not to appear before 8:50.) The second number went to the show's second star, with the opening number usually a boy–girl production. Miss Gray argued that she should be placed at number three. "That was unthinkable," says Abe Burrows, who finally settled the dispute. "I won it by threatening to quit the show."

The continual tension created by the threat of upstaging and other demands made Lahr nervous, and sometimes his concentration on the laughter went to ludicrous extremes. Burrows recalls that "periodically during the show Lahr's valet, an enormous six-foot-four ex-boxer, would appear at the dressing room of a younger actor and summon him to Bert's dressing room. Bert would talk to him and explain where he'd hurt a laugh. One day, Bert insisted an actor was moving on laugh lines. I watched the scene and I didn't see it. I said, 'Bert, the guy didn't move!' He replied, 'He was moving his facial muscles.' "

To a director like Burrows, who was just beginning a Broadway career, Bert Lahr was certainly a tough first-draw. "I walked into my first rehearsal scared. Bert said, 'Hello, *Abele'*—that means little Abe. He made me feel ten feet tall. I was a green director; and he made me feel good." But Burrows, squinting nervously over white-rimmed glasses, managed to instill confidence in Lahr while remaining critical of his performance.

"Lahr understood me and appreciated my work. I had a sketch that I'd written for myself—the baseball sketch. I turned it over to him and rewrote it for him. He knew I was on his side. However, there came a point when periodically I felt he was going after the audience too hard. He's America's greatest technical comedian, who over the years had to rely on his comic talents more than he did on his material to carry the scene. Obviously, I never asked him to throw a line away. He's not a drawing room comic in that sense. I also felt he was a real actor. If he would play just the material the laughs would come. We clashed at that point. I guess I was looking for underplay."

Whatever the tension, it was creative. Burrows, who would go on to become one of Broadway's most famous comedy directors and writers, learned a lot from working with Lahr. "I saw him do my scenes. I argued about it, but I appreciated it. He helped me enormously in my direction. I'm an actor's director. I'm a good one, I think, because I started with Lahr. I learned to use what the actor had, instead of superimposing my attitude immediately. I always try and see what the actors do first and work from that. The point is not to get so dazzled that you immediately toss out your concept."

Burrows marveled at the way Lahr maneuvered around the stage. "He's the freest man on stage I've ever seen. The little movements I had in mind for his sketches didn't fit at all, because Bert roams the stage in huge strides. I had to adjust to that. I seem to inherit those guys. Every so often I get a free-wheeling comedian like Robert Morse. I think it was my experience with Bert which made me so successful with Morse. I had Morse in two shows, *Say, Darling* and *How to Succeed in Business.* In both of them, remembering my experiences with Bert and realizing that a certain kind of talent shouldn't be changed or stifled, I provided direction that enabled him to flow. Instead of getting impatient because his movements changed the patterns I had in mind, I just went with them and used them."

Lahr's complete control of a stage fascinated Burrows, who often watched him from the wings. "If anybody moved on stage he was furious; yet, at the same time, the son-of-a-gun would turn around and help break the actors up in some scene. He used to blow on his upstage cheek. You couldn't see it from out front, but the actors would start to giggle. One day I threatened to fire anybody who broke up on stage; and he, being a good guy, stopped immediately."

Burrows was an admiring audience for Lahr's ad-libbing. "Bert has tremendous control. I used to stand in the wings some nights. He'd be in the middle of a scene that wasn't going too well. He'd see me standing there, and, still in character, stride toward the wings, and say, 'They're from the moose country tonight!' Without missing a beat, he'd go back into the scene."

Lahr's ability not only to make the stage his own territory, but also to turn the sketches into his special view of the world impressed Burrows. The Baseball Sketch (see Appendix 6), according to Burrows, "was a comic conceit of mine. When I wrote the sketch I was much more interested in the character of the announcer. Bert took it and made it his own, which was a marvelous transformation. He made it a scene about the ballplayer."

Lahr's love of baseball was not the only element that made his characterizations true. As a man constantly besieged by people who glowed over his talent only to ask him his name or mistake him for Joe E. Brown, he was suspicious of hail-fellow good spirits. Like Lefty Hogan, in Burrows's sketch, Lahr was continuously being discussed in romantic-heroic terms he never understood. His matter-of-factness about his business was an amusing contrast to the hifalutin questions people asked and the trite answers they expected in return. ("Everybody says I've got wonderful *timing*. Young actors have actually stood in the wings with a stop watch charting when a certain laugh would come. But you wanna know something, I don't know what the hell they're talking about.") Lahr was always skeptical of smooth, glib media men. As one of the first commercial television performers, he was continually thrown up against the egos of fast-talking reporters, and his interpretation of Lefty Hogan was drawn from his fund of experience and whimsy. Behind Lahr's lampoon was the firm belief that "television is small time."

The sketch skewered television's impulse to make myths out of men instead of confronting them. Lefty Hogan, squinting dumbly into the television light, is everything the announcer is not: inarticulate, ugly, bumbling, uncouth. He is human; the announcer tries to make him superhuman. Lefty pierces his heroic rhetoric with straightforward honesty.

> *Announcer:* And finally Lefty, you became a professional—you had to. You had to because of that deep love you possessed for this great sport! Because of that you wouldn't rest until you became part of this beloved game.
>
> *Lahr:* No, I wanted to make some dough.
>
> *Announcer:* Magnificent sportsman that you are . . . and what a great pitcher you were. Tell me, Lefty, after being so great, what made you decide to take off your armor and cease to do active battle on the field of honor with the other knights of baseball?
>
> *Lahr:* I never played night baseball . . . only daytime . . .

Burrows articulates what Lahr has always understood in his "flop sweat" and his button pulling: "I guess to somebody out of the business it might sound silly. 'What the devil is a laugh?' A laugh is a laugh. It's like radar. Radar operates by sending out a message and it bounces back . . . You send out an impulse; it hits an object and sort of echoes. By measuring the echo you know the distance, size of the object. A comic is like radar, he sends out a laugh—his personality—if nothing comes back, it's death. Literal death. Comedians always used the phrase, 'Boy, I died last night.' That's no accident. They are literally comparing it to death. On the other side, they use terms like "I killed them," "I fractured them," "I had them laying in the aisles," "I murdered them." This is really like a bullfight, but it's more than a contest, it's a life and death battle."

Lahr never spoke to Burrows about these feelings; but Burrows's ability to understand them in Lahr's work made their collaboration fruitful. After the show's successful opening, Lahr bought Burrows a suit, a vaudeville tradition that indicated his approval. *Two on the Aisle,* dedicated to laughter, opulence, and sheer enjoyment, was always serious for Lahr. The show, which ran 267 performances, was a comedian's *tour de force.* Burrows recalls sitting with Lahr before the curtain went up opening night.

"Do you think they'll laugh?" Lahr asked.

"I think so."

"They'll laugh. If they don't, I'll make them laugh."

WAITING FOR GODOT

THE PLAY THAT CAME FROM MICHAEL MYERBERG'S OFFICE IN AUTUMN
1955 was unusual on two counts. First of all, it caused my father
himself to pad to the door to take it from the messenger—a chore he
usually delegated to someone else. Second, it was not a script at all, but
an already-published paperback version of a play. On the cover was a
photograph of two hobos moving around a distinctly unrealistic tree.
The play was Waiting for Godot.

He did not return to his room, but sat down at the dining room
table and began reading. Since Two on the Aisle, he had been through
this process often. The messenger, the hasty reading, the pondering,
the call to Lester Shurr, his New York agent and Louis Shurr's brother.
No play seemed right. He had moved from his fourteen-room duplex
to a small five-room apartment on Fifth Avenue.

But that day his attention was riveted on the book. For the first
time in many months an excitement was visible.

"What's it about?" I said. He rarely remained quiet for such a long
time.

Without looking up he mumbled, "It's about two bums."

Bums. The word seemed incongruous in a room full of porcelains,
a room dominated by a huge portrait of him as Louis XV in Du Barry.
No one except my father looked at the china; everyone but he accepted
the secret of his favorite painting. The picture shows him standing
haughtily with scepter in hand and costumed in gold brocade, lace cuffs,
and a shoulder-length periwig. The fantasy pleased him. He did not
mind that the eyes beneath the wig were not proud or that the nose

was disconcertingly wider at the base than any French aristocrat's. He often studied the painting with a magnifying glass, forgetting, or perhaps awed by, the final joke—that it was not a painting at all, but a retouched photograph.

A play about hobos did not seem to fit into his carefully planned luxury. He had eliminated the harsh brutality of poverty from his life. Yet the play fascinated him as if some secret frequency had penetrated this sedate comfort. He got up and walked into the bedroom as he read. He shut the door behind him.

An hour later, the bedroom door swung open, and Lahr was sitting near the telephone stand, book in hand.

"Hello, Lester . . . it's the damndest thing . . . Yes, I read it . . . Yes, I don't know. It's not like anything that's been done . . . I've never done anything like it. Do you think I could do it? . . . What do you think about it? Do you think it's commercial? . . . Yes, but do you think I could play it? . . . Sure, it's funny . . . Yes, but it's funny . . . I know, Lester, I know it's supposed to be tragic, but there are lots of gags . . . I'm not sure, but the writer's no phony. How many weeks do you think I could get with it? . . . Yes . . . I'll call you back when I've read it again."

Lahr held the book out to Mildred. "See what you think." As she reached for it, he opened it and thumbed through the pages again. "There's something in here. Something . . . Read this, John. What does it mean?"

He read the following words, with his finger pressed closely to the lines he spoke:

> *Vladimir:* Was I sleeping, while the others suffered? Am I sleeping now? Tomorrow, when I wake, or think I do, what shall I say of today? That with Estragon my friend, at this place, until the fall of night, I waited for Godot? That Pozzo passed, with his carrier, and that he spoke to us? Probably. But in all that what truth will there be? . . . He'll know nothing. He'll tell me about the blows he received and I'll give him a carrot. . . . Astride of a grave and a difficult birth. Down in the hole, lingeringly, the grave-digger puts on the forceps. We have time to grow old. The air is full of our cries. . . . But habit is a great deadener. . . . At me too someone is looking, of me too someone is saying, He is sleeping, he knows nothing, let him sleep on . . . I can't go on! . . . What have I said?

"You're a student—what does it mean? I don't get it." He didn't wait for an answer. "All right. Two bums. They're hungry. They're scared. They wait for something that never comes . . . It's too intellectual for me. The words say something, they're plain enough, but somehow the ideas aren't."

He stopped and picked up the phone. He cradled it under his chin and talked as he dialed.

"What is this 'habit is a great deadener'? . . . Hello, Lester. Bert. How many weeks did you say . . .?"

Waiting for Godot intrigued my father. No intellectual discussion intensified his appreciation. The play which would have a revolutionary effect on ideas and form in contemporary drama, was discussed, instead, with others whose advice he had always heeded in musical-comedy matters—with Jack O'Brian, the columnist and ex-drama critic, and Vaughn Deering, a friend and professor of drama at Fordham University who occasionally helped him rehearse. Both of them counseled Lahr to do it. However, the final and most forceful voice of approval came from Mildred, who had long advocated that her husband extend his talents into other areas of theater.

He was tough to convince. Without academic training he felt unsure of the play's complexities and of his ability to stamp it with his own personality. Even while deliberating whether to perform the play, he seemed to delight in its mystery and theatricality. "When I first read it, I realized that this was not stark tragedy. Beneath it was tremendous humor, two men trying to amuse themselves on earth by playing jokes and little games. And that was my conception."

Millions of critical words have been lavished on *Waiting for Godot*; Lahr conceived of it as a vision of action that reduced itself to a few simple sentences of explanation. While friends, and later the press, reacted to a low comic entering the intellectual arena with amusement, Lahr understood the play not from a literary point of view but strictly from a theatrical one. Once, while still undecided, he came into my room and read these lines:

Estragon: In the meantime let us try and converse calmly, since we are incapable of keeping silent.
Vladimir: You're right, we're inexhaustible.
Estragon: It's so we won't think.
Vladimir: We have that excuse.

Estragon: It's so we won't hear.
Vladimir: We have our reasons.
Estragon: All the dead voices.
Vladimir: They make a noise like wings.
Estragon: Like leaves.
Vladimir: Like sand.
Estragon: Like leaves.
   Silence.

"He writes beautifully, doesn't he? His meter—he's a poet, isn't he? His rhythm is crisp; there's meter to it, same as in poetry. It's not cumbersome; it's in character. It flows."

That was all he ever said to indicate his appreciation of Beckett. If he had a reassuring sense of the play's poetry in private, he did not trust the weighty impact of its repetition so easily on stage. In the Miami tryout, he wanted to cut the lines he read to me so admiringly. Years later, talking to my Hunter College drama class, he recollected how sad and beautiful that dialogue was, adding, "And after the last repartee, there was a momentary silence in the audience and then laughter, as if they had held their breath and suddenly been allowed to relax."

As an actor, he understood the subtleties of the spoken word without ever having read poetry. He never read any other Beckett plays or novels. Lahr's simple words reflect an understanding of the pathos and meaning of the play that went beyond critical generalities. Lahr lived with silences; his understanding of language was commensurate with Beckett's precise, philosophical use of it. His appreciation of the playful potential of words went back to his burlesque days and his use of the malaprop; at the same time, Lahr was conscious of his own inability to make words convey his exact meaning. He didn't like to talk merely to pass time; he would rather remain silent—even with his family. Yet there were reasons why others talked—a motive that in his own shyness he understood. In a radio play, *Embers,* which Lahr would never read, Beckett gave an insight into the significance of his particular type of dramatic language. Talking about the sea, a man (Henry) remarks to his wife, Ada—

   . . Listen to it! . . . It's not so bad when you get out on it . . .
   Perhaps, I should have gone into the merchant navy.
Ada: It's only the surface, you know. Underneath all is as quiet as the
   grave. Not a sound. All day, all night, not a sound.

The languid rhythm of Beckett's speakers, the endless gabble of trivialities between Vladimir and Estragon, creates precisely the surface activity that Beckett's characters refer to in the sea. The insight is also embedded in the laughter of Lahr's comedy scenes, from the inane blathering of the cop to cover his own embarrassment to the TV announcer's verbocity that reinterprets the baseball player's simple sentences. Lahr talked about playing Beckett "instinctively," a term by which he hints that Beckett spoke to his own immediate and intense private experience.

If he understood the play's poetry in a curiously unacademic way, his faith in Beckett as a craftsman came only after struggling through the play's interior structure on stage. "You never laugh at a blind man on stage or people with their legs cut off. But Beckett wrote in Pozzo and made such a heavy out of him that, by the second act, when he comes back blind, we play games with him. He falls down, he cries for help. Vladimir and Estragon are on the stage. We taunt him. We ask him how much he'll give us. We slide. We poke—you understand? The audience screams. If Beckett didn't know what he was doing, as so many people at the time claimed, he wouldn't have put the show in that running order. When I read it, and saw how deliberately he had placed Pozzo in the script, which was against all theatrical convention, I wasn't sure it would work. When I played it, I realized how brilliantly he had constructed the play. I always thought it was an important play—I just didn't realize how important."

Lahr decided to do the play, with the idea that if it worked well Myerberg would bring it to Broadway. On the surface, Lahr was pleased; but from the beginning his uneasiness with intellectual ideas, his fear of failure, the strange format of the show, and a young director bred anxiety. Myerberg had contracted with Alan Schneider to direct the production after Garson Kanin, his first choice, backed out at the last minute. Schneider, with only two Broadway credits—*Anastasia* and *The Remarkable Mrs. Pennypacker*—had been recommended to Myerberg by Thornton Wilder, who had seen Schneider's revival of *The Skin of Our Teeth*, which Myerberg had originally produced in 1943. Beckett's play extended Wilder's early fascination with the philosophical and dramatic consequences of the flux of time. Beckett was hardheaded where Wilder was sentimental, poetic where Wilder was folksy.

Schneider recounted his first introduction to Beckett's work and also his meeting with Beckett in an article for the *Chelsea Review* (Autumn 1958). As the director who later became Beckett's chief interpreter in the United States as well as the director of Edward Albee's major plays, Schneider's reactions are important. Beckett's significance in America at the time was limited to a small coterie of intellectuals; only after *Waiting for Godot* did he become the important literary and dramatic voice in America that he already was in Europe.

Schneider met Beckett; Lahr did not. Schneider saw the play in other countries; Lahr did not. Schneider's experience with Beckett is important because, as director, his vision of the play and how to convey Beckett's meaning were different from what finally evolved in Lahr's interpretation.

In 1954, Schneider saw *Waiting for Godot* in both its Zurich and Paris versions. Captivated by the play's strength of thought, he set about tracking down the seclusive Beckett. As he chronicles his exasperating search—

"Finally a friendly play-agent informed me that the English language rights had been acquired by a British director, Peter Glenville, who was planning to present the play in London with Alec Guinness as Vladimir and Ralph Richardson as Estragon. Besides, added the agent, the play was nothing an American audience would take—unless it could have a couple of topflight comedians like Bob Hope or Jack Benny kidding it, preferably with Laurel and Hardy in the other two roles. An American production under those circumstances seemed hopeless, and Mr. Beckett was as far removed as Mr. Godot himself. I came home to New York and went on to other matters.

"The next spring [1955] I had occasion to remember once more. *Godot* received its English language premiere in London, not with Guinness and Richardson at all, but with a non-star cast at London's charming Arts Theater Club. Damned without exception by daily critics, it was hailed in superlatives by both Harold Hobson and Kenneth Tynan (the Atkinson and Kerr of London) in their Sunday pieces, and soon became the top conversation piece of the English season. At the same time, the English translation was published by Grove Press in New York.

"I read and re-read the published version. Somehow on its closely spaced printed pages, it seemed cold and abstract, even harsh, after the remarkable ambience I had sensed at the Babylone. When a leading Broadway producer asked me what I thought of its chances, I responded only half-heartedly. Intrigued as I had been, I could not at the moment imagine a commercial production in Broadway terms.

"One day in the fall of that same year I was visiting my old Alma

Mater, the University of Wisconsin, when to my utter amazement I received a long-distance phone call from producer Michael Myerberg asking if I would be interested in directing *Waiting for Godot* in New York. He had Bert Lahr and Tom Ewell signed for the two main roles . . . It was like Fate knocking at the door. After a desperate search in practically every bookshop in Chicago, I finally located a copy, stayed up all night on the train studying it with new eyes, and arrived back to New York to breathe a fervent 'yes' to Myerberg.

"Followed a series of conferences with Lahr and Ewell, both of whom confessed their complete bewilderment of the play; and with Myerberg, who insisted that no one could possibly be bewildered, least of all himself. He did think it might be a good idea, however, for me to see the English production, perhaps stopping off on the way to have a talk with Beckett himself. To say that I was pleased and excited would be a pale reflection of the reality. And my elation was tempered only by the fear that Beckett would continue to remain aloof—he had merely reluctantly consented to a brief meeting with 'the New York director.'

"At any rate, a week later, I found myself aboard the U.S.S. *Independence* bound for Paris and London—and by coincidence, the table companion and fellow conversationalist of Thornton Wilder, who was on his way to Rome and elsewhere. He greatly admired Beckett, considered *Godot* one of the two greatest modern plays (the other one, I believe, Cocteau's *Orpheus*), and openly contributed his ideas about an interpretation of the play which he had seen produced both in France and Germany. In fact, so detailed and regular were our daily meetings that a rumor circulated that Wilder was rewriting the script, something which later amused both authors considerably. What was true was that I was led to become increasingly familiar with the script, both in French and in translation and discovered what were the most important questions to ask Beckett in the limited time we were to have together. More specifically, I was now working in the frame of reference of an actual production situation—a three-week rehearsal period, a 'tryout' in a new theater in Miami, and, of course, Bert and Tommy. It wasn't Bob Hope and Jack Benny, but the Parisian agent of two summers before had been correct so far. Was she also going to prove correct in terms of the audience response?

"Beckett at that time had no phone—in fact, the only change I've noticed in him since his 'success' is the acquisition of one—so I sent him a message by pneumatique from the very plush hotel near the

Etoile where Myerberg had lodged me. Within an hour, he rang up saying he'd meet me in the lobby—at the same time reminding me that he had only an hour or so to spare. Armed with a large bottle of Lacrima Christi as a present from both Wilder and myself, I stationed myself in the rather overdone lobby and waited for the elusive Mr. Beckett to appear. Promptly and very businesslike he strode in, his tall athletic figure ensconced in a worn raincoat; bespectacled in old-fashioned steel rims; his face was as long and sensitive as a greyhound's. Greetings exchanged, the biggest question became where we might drink our Lacrima Christi; we decided to walk a bit and see if we could come up with a solution. Walk we did, as we have done so many times since, and talk as we walked—about a variety of matters, including, occasionally, his play. Eventually, we took a taxi to his skylight apartment in the sixth arrondissement and wound up finishing most of the bottle. In between I plied him with all my studiously arrived-at questions as well as all the ones that came to me at the moment; and he tried to answer as directly and honestly as he could. The first one was 'Who or what does Godot mean?' and the answer was immediately forthcoming: 'If I knew I would have said so in the play.' Sam was perfectly willing to answer any questions of specific meaning or reference, but would not —as always—go into matters of larger or symbolic meanings, preferring his work to speak for itself and letting the supposed 'meanings' fall where they may.

"As it turned out, he did have an appointment; so we separated but not before we had made a date for dinner the next evening. On schedule, we had a leisurely meal at one of his favorite restaurants in Montparnasse, then I persuaded him to come along with me to a performance of *Anastasia* at the Theatre Antoine . . . it turned out to be very artificial and old-fashioned and Sam's suffering was acute. Immediately after the last curtain we retired to Fouquet's, once the favorite café of his friend and companion James Joyce. . . . Shortly before dawn—since I had a plane to catch for London—we again separated. But not before Sam had asked me if it would be additionally helpful if he joined me in London at the performances of *Godot* there. He had not been to London in some years, had never liked it since his early days of poverty and struggle there, but he would be willing to come if I thought it helpful! I could hardly believe what I heard. Helpful!

"Two days later, Sam came into London incognito. . . . That night, and each night for the next five days, we went to see the production of *Godot*, which had been transferred by this time to the Criterion in Piccadilly Circus. The production was interesting, though scenically over-cluttered and missing many of the points which Sam had just cleared up for me. My fondest memories are of Sam's clutching my arm from time to time and in a clearly heard stage whisper saying, 'It's ahl wrahng! He's doing it ahul wrahng!' about a particular bit of stage business or the interpretation of a certain line. Every night after the performance, we would compare what we had seen to what he had intended, try to analyze why or how certain points were being lost, speak with the actors about their difficulties. Every night also, we would carefully watch the audience, a portion of which always left during the show. I always felt that Sam would have been disappointed if at least a few hadn't.

"Through all this, I discovered not only how clear and logical *Godot* was in its essences, but how much and how easy to know Sam was, how friendly beneath his basic shyness. I had met Sam, wanting primarily to latch on to anything which might help make *Godot* a success on Broadway. I left him, wanting nothing more than to please him. I came with respect; I left with a greater measure of devotion than I have ever felt for a writer whose work I was engaged in translating to the stage. . . ."

Myerberg's conception of *Waiting for Godot,* after seeing the London production, was more certain than Schneider's. Where Schneider had questioned its commercial nature, Myerberg was immediately impressed at the play's ability to hold an audience despite a production he considered, in general, to be mediocre. "Let's face it, *Waiting for Godot* is not everybody's cup of tea. It's a theatrical property; it might be called a great play. I call it a theater piece. I don't know what a play is myself. Everybody else seems to know, but I don't. I look for material that can be put on the stage and hold an audience for an evening. I don't know what a play is. . . ."

Schneider, in his article, registered little surprise at the suggestion of two stand-up comedians like Jack Benny or Bob Hope playing Vladimir and Estragon. Myerberg's first reaction was to envision Lahr in the role of Estragon. "Knowledge of performers is part of the producer's equipment. I have a kind of card index mind which riffles through them. I get one casting in my mind and that's the casting I go for. When I contracted for the play, I said 'I'll produce it only if I can get Bert Lahr to play in it. How I'll sell it to him, I don't know. If I don't get him, I won't produce it.' "

Myerberg's cunning led him to another important decision that had a bearing on the final performances. He would do *Waiting for Godot* on Broadway, not, as in London and Paris, in the experimental non-commercial theater clubs or off-Broadway houses. The choice, which astounded many, was not daring to a producer of Myerberg's frame of mind. *"Waiting for Godot* was a revolutionary play that had never been done here. Beckett had not really been introduced to the public. I regarded the problem of production this way: either you do it or you don't. I don't feel you can have the opportunity unless 1) you have the proper stage, 2) you attract the proper actors. I couldn't have gotten the final cast I got—E. G. Marshall, Kurt Kasznar, Alvin Epstein, and Lahr—for off-Broadway. It's just a question of professionalism. You couldn't have done the play off-Broadway on the scale it demanded. After it's established, then it can be done any place."

Myerberg's statement is an interesting backward glance; but the initial tryout of *Waiting for Godot* was handled in such a myopic fashion as to suggest that even Myerberg, for all his assurance, did not quite know what he had on his hands.

Myerberg himself admits that mistakes were made. He had mounted the play on a highly stylized set that not only made it difficult for the actors to move, but also detracted from the words and action. As Myerberg later told *The New York Times,* "I went too far in my effort to give the play a base for popular acceptance. I accented the wrong things in trying to illuminate corners of the text I felt were left in shadow in the London production. For instance, I cast the play too close to type. In casting Bert Lahr and Tom Ewell I created the wrong impression about the play. Both actors were too well known in specific types of performance. The audience thought they were going to see Lahr and Ewell cut loose in a lot of capers. They expected a farcical comedy, which *Waiting for Godot,* of course, is not."

Myerberg had sold out the two-week Miami engagement a month in advance by advertising Beckett's play in the finest tradition of P. T. Barnum. The people who rushed to the box office had Myerberg's advance notice humming in their minds.

> Bert Lahr, the star of *Burlesque,* and Tom Ewell, the star of *The Seven Year Itch* in the laugh sensation of two continents—Samuel Beckett's *Waiting for Godot.*

(By the time Myerberg brought his controversial property to New York he had learned how to sell it. He ran an ad in *The New York Times* asking for seventy thousand intellectuals to support the play and warning audiences who wanted casual entertainment to stay away. His statement to the *Times* about going too far in giving "the play a popular base" is a ludicrous understatement.)

No one was pleased about opening at the Cocoanut Grove Playhouse in Miami except Myerberg, who had covered expenses with a large guarantee. Schneider, unhappy with the set and with Miami, liked the idea of doing *Waiting for Godot* with Lahr and Ewell in principle, but confesses "I was terrified of doing the play with stars. I was scared that ego problems would get in the way of the play."

Lahr has his own recollections. "Playing *Waiting for Godot* in Miami," he says, "was like doing *Giselle* at Roseland." He was skeptical about opening there, but never completely pessimistic. He brought his fishing tackle and his family to Florida, expecting to enjoy a little of both during the run.

Schneider is haunted by the anxiety of the first production. "We were all babes in the wood. We were groping around there with our shoes off." Even Lahr, riddled with doubts and petrified of public rejection, clung vehemently to comic simplicity that made sense out of (what seemed to him) intellectual confusion. His childlike recalcitrance caused more uneasiness than he would ever realize. Schneider sensed the problem that would materialize in Miami as he wound up his meeting with Beckett in Europe. "Bert was terrified of it from the beginning. I kept getting telegrams from Myerberg urging me to change my ship reservations and fly home":

LAHR AND EWELL NERVOUS AND DISTURBED URGE YOU FLY BACK
FRIDAY.   MYERBERG

LAHR SLOW STUDY STILL FEEL YOU SHOULD RETURN BY AIR AT ONCE
                                                          MYERBERG

Finally, Lahr himself tried to use his own powers of persuasion:

WE FEEL VERY NERVOUS ABOUT SHORT REHEARSAL THINK IT URGENT
BEGIN REHEARSAL MARCH 5TH PLEASE MAKE EVERY EFFORT TO RETURN
TO MAKE IT POSSIBLE AS SO MUCH SCRIPT AND BUSINESS TO LEARN
APPRECIATE MUCHLY CABLE ARRIVAL   BERT LAHR

Lahr's relationship with Schneider is a study in misunderstanding, their association a wry commentary on Beckett's play. Like *Waiting for Godot,* it emphasized not only the limitations of language to convey experience but also the compulsive love-hate relationship of people engaged in a single enterprise. Vladimir and Estragon play a game to survive life. Lahr did not understand Schneider's language; and Schneider's inexperience and new conception of Beckett would not allow for the comic leeway that Lahr insisted would make the play "work." At the root of the problem was Schneider's understanding of the symbolic movement of the two main characters and Lahr's lack of it. Schneider's attitude, on one level, is accurate; but Lahr's intuition for play grated with Schneider's idea of its rhythm. "Estragon is rooted in the earth. Restless. Uncomfortable. Hungry. Rooted. Vladimir is the wanderer. He's curious. He's the Intellect. I would have to keep saying to Bert on stage 'Get back there. Stay on your mark.' Bert didn't like to do comedy standing still. I kept saying, 'Bert, you can't move around so much, remember Estragon's got sore feet.' "

In saying this, Schneider was not recognizing another symbolic movement, one closer to the rhythms of human relationships, which also clearly pervades Beckett's play. Beckett's stage directions indicate a flexibility and possibility for movement that Schneider did not see, but which Lahr suspected and could not verbalize.

(1) They look at each other, recoiling, advancing, their heads on one side, as before a work of art, trembling towards each other more and more, then suddenly embrace, clasping each other on the back. End of embrace. Estragon no longer supported, almost falls.

(2) They listen, huddled together. . . . They relax and separate.

(3) . . . Exit Estragon left, precipitately. . . . He looks up, misses Estragon. . . . He moves wildly about the stage. Enter Estragon left, panting. He hastens to Vladimir, falls into his arms.

(4) He draws Estragon after him. Estragon yields, then resists. They halt.

(5) They turn, move apart, turn again and face each other.

Vladimir and Estragon come together out of necessity, yet the closer they get the more impossible it is for them to unite. They grope toward one another, then move away with the frantic momentum of burlesque comedians. Beckett's stage directions chronicle their friendship—a pantomime of loneliness and cowardice that Lahr had distilled in his own comic world through the lion, the prizefighter, the cop. The tramps' movement is never able to resolve itself and end in a lasting embrace. They bounce back from their pratfalls unaware of their plight.

Comedy without movement was impossible for Lahr. He balked at Schneider's dicta, at being asked to harness his energy. Lahr was suspicious and ignorant of the allegorical reasons at the basis of Schneider's demands. When the director would go on stage with masking tape and place strips where he was to stand, Lahr was shocked. "I began to think to myself—this is all wrong. It's stark. This is the wrong approach to the play. It's dire; it's slow. There isn't any movement."

Schneider's reverence for Beckett may have accounted for his inflexible direction. His intentions and Lahr's were at a Mexican stand-off. Lahr felt stifled; Schneider felt hostile. Finally, Lahr confronted him: " 'This is a comedy scene. These are music hall bits.' I could see it. I could see it because that was my basic training—burlesque. He said, 'I don't know anything about humor.' "

At that moment, the fate of the play seemed sealed in Lahr's imagination. "He was convinced it was his play from the beginning," says Schneider. "My problem working with him was to make him realize that there couldn't be a 'top banana' (a word he kept using) in a show of this kind. The play was a game of give and take, a partnership. Lahr kept insisting, 'There's a feed, and there's a joke.' "

The experience was painful, but Lahr would learn from his mistakes as would Schneider, who would go on to become one of the most successful directors of contemporary theater. However, in Miami the production of *Godot* met with conflicts at every turn.

Schneider was saddled with Myerberg's stylized set—a mound that faced the audience like a parabola. It hindered the actor's movements, and made the stage environment uncomfortable. Schneider was also disturbed by the fact that Lahr and he were staying in the same hotel, a tactical mistake for anyone who could not cope with Lahr's compulsive worry. Lahr would knock on Schneider's door at six a.m., already groomed and fretting over the day's work. "He wanted to discuss the play," Schneider recalls. "He didn't want to talk about meaning. He would ask me: 'Am I right for it?' 'Is it going to work?' 'Are we going to be a success?' "

Lahr's predictable perfectionism was matched by a predictable hypochondria. He was extremely difficult, beset nearly every day with a new ailment. A doctor was finally hired to sit in on rehearsals. Schneider felt Lahr's continual interruptions for medical reasons were symptomatic of something else. "We had more doctors around that rehearsal hall than I've ever seen. It was always something about his throat, his voice, an ache here or there. It all had to do with the fact that ultimately he didn't want to be there."

Schneider's insistence that he refrain from using old mannerisms made Lahr particularly nervous. The pressure was upsetting to him, but ultimately more creative than he acknowledges. Lahr originally wanted to substitute "gnong, gnong, gnong," for Beckett's pointed and pathetic "Ah!" He argued, but Schneider prevailed. "If he had inserted his old catch phrase, the tone would have been something else. It would have reminded everyone of *The Wizard of Oz.*" Schneider, aware of the uniqueness of Beckett's play, did not want it filled with Lahr's famous musical-comedy mannerisms from the past. Lahr found new ones that matched his body's potential and the play's content.

Schneider's battles to preserve the text seemed incongruous to Lahr, who wanted to approach experimental theater on the only basis of experience he possessed—the musical-comedy stage. The ultimate arbiter of value was the audience. Anything that was not clear to the people out front or stymied their attention should be immediately disposed of. On that theory, Lahr's first instincts were to cut many of Pozzo's and Lucky's longer speeches. He was unable to relate the minor characters to the broader philosophical propositions of the play.

If Lahr's demands for textual changes were unreasonable, his instincts for the tragicomic had a potential that Schneider's own uncertainties kept him from exploring. While Schneider insisted that the play was a partnership, the melding of mind and body, privately he saw the mind dominating the belly ("The play is not about Estragon, but Vladimir"), a moot distinction that shades the comedy toward tragedy rather than vice versa.

Lahr's insight was from the gut. He knew that laughter would complement Beckett's poetry. Schneider leaned toward the poetry, but was afraid laughter would turn it into a romp. Lahr wanted to move away from the weight of philosophical statement as in Beckett's most beautiful passage, where the hobos try and distinguish the quality of sounds. The passage ends:

> *Vladimir:* They make a noise like feathers.
> *Estragon:* Like leaves.
> *Vladimir:* Like ashes.
> *Estragon:* Like leaves.
> *Long silence.*
> *Vladimir:* Say something!
> *Estragon:* I'm trying.
> *Long silence.*
> *Vladimir: (in anguish).* Say anything at all!
> *Estragon:* What do we do now?

The laughter highlights the poetry; by deflating the emotion, the sadness of the situation comes closer to the heart. Schneider appreciated the poetry of that particular passage, but felt that "if *that* dialogue gets laughs, it's over my dead body."

Lahr sensed laughter even at the height of the tramps' chaos. A messenger from Godot appears but cannot offer any information about his master or when he will arrive. The reaction of Vladimir and Estragon to the boy mirrors not only the blundering sadness of their interminable vigil, but also the laughable intensity of any zealot's commitment to values based on a faith not borne out by experience.

As Estragon shakes the Boy, trying to find out the truth, Vladimir intercedes—

> *Vladimir:* Will you let him alone! What's the matter with you? (*Estragon releases the Boy, moves away, covering his face with his hands. Vladimir and the Boy observe him. Estragon drops his hands. His face is convulsed.*) What's the matter with you?
> *Estragon:* I'm unhappy.
> *Vladimir:* Not really! Since when?
> *Estragon:* I'd forgotten.

The laughter in the situation is not ebullient burlesque laughter; but that of paradox which acknowledges a darker side of comedy, where pain treads the thin, ambiguous line between pleasure and sadness. Schneider disavowed the comic element here also. "When Estragon says 'I'm unhappy'—to me that's not a comic moment."

Lahr's disenchantment with Schneider made it difficult for the director and the rest of the cast. "He'd listen to me when he wanted to. I was a kid director." This lack of trust created conflicts over simple lines. Schneider recalls Lahr could not understand the line "boldly ignorant apes." "He wouldn't listen to the line. On stage he would throw it away."

At other times, Schneider tried to devise methods of communicating the intellectual intention of Beckett's play to Lahr's comic intuition. One of his most successful gambits was known to the cast as "the ping pong game." Schneider would say to Lahr, "Bert, the game is simply to bat the ball over the net." When Lahr would stumble on lines that involved this kind of playful repartee, Schneider would remind him, "Bert, that's a ping pong game." Once he understood the spirit of the tart return, he would leap into the lines with gusto. One of Lahr's fondest passages of the play is precisely one of Beckett's hilarious volleys:

Vladimir: Moron!
Estragon: Vermin!
Vladimir: Abortion!
Estragon: Morpion!
Vladimir: Sewer-rat!
Estragon: Curate!
Vladimir: Cretin!
Estragon: (with finality) . Critic!
Vladimir: Oh!
      He wilts, vanquished, and turns away.

Schneider recalls this moment of success with Lahr vividly. "He loved that. You're dealing with a child, in the best sense of the word."

No one knew what to expect. To Lahr, Schneider grew progressively more hostile and impatient as the older men had difficulty with their lines. To Schneider, Lahr became a *bête noire.* He found Lahr "elusive, evasive, constantly trying to get out of rehearsing the play." For Schneider, it was a conflict "to reach him either physically or mentally." He likens Lahr to his experience with Buster Keaton, whom he directed in Beckett's only movie, *Film.* "Lahr's reactions to Beckett were just like Buster's. He would do anything for you, but he didn't understand it. Buster always wanted to put in old bits. He'd say, 'Why don't you let me pick up a pencil the way I did in ——.' Bert wanted to interpolate old business, too. Keaton was quieter, less persistent."

Lahr's insecurity mounted with each rehearsal. He wanted to help the material; but the content of the play was not easily within his grasp. His only moment of reassurance come when Tennessee Williams, an investor in the production and also in Florida for the opening of *Sweet Bird of Youth,* which followed *Waiting for Godot* into the Cocoanut Grove, introduced himself after a grueling afternoon of rehearsals. "Bert, you're the only one that feels this play." The moment was important for Lahr—"It gave me confidence."

The family hardly saw him. Even when he moved from the hotel near the theater to the house where we were staying, his cloth rehearsing cap was always on his head and his mind was on his work. He would return late in the day and immediately hand Mildred the script to go over his lines. Since he could not always see the logical progression of ideas, memorizing was painful. Sometimes he would ask me to help him. He worked furiously, but was secretive about how the show was going. Lester Shurr came down for the New Year's Eve Party a few days before the opening. Through all the festivities, Lahr remained somber. He went to bed at the same hour we did. The part, which we never saw him perform in Florida, seemed to sap his energy in a way that no other had done. We were sent home a few days before the opening—a gesture that should have told us what to expect.

The day of the opening, Schneider called a line rehearsal for six p.m. The cast was testy and anxious. During the rehearsal Lahr fell asleep. "Part of it was nerves," explains Schneider. "Part of it was trying to get away from the play." Neither the director nor the rest of the cast was pleased with Lahr's siesta.

Walter Winchell, who was in Florida for the premiere, came into Lahr's dressing room before the show. "What's this about, Bert?"

Lahr found himself saying, "I really don't know. It's very strange. We'll see."

The opening night was as gala as Miami could make it. Among the audience moving past the huge fountain, down the thickly carpeted aisles, were Tennessee Williams, Joseph Cotten, Joan Fontaine, Gloria de Haven, Winchell, and Myerberg.

The next day the Miami *Herald's* headline recounted the devastating effect of the occasion—

MINK CLAD AUDIENCE DISAPPOINTED IN WAITING FOR GODOT

The audience, gilt-edged and giddy with expectation at the "'laugh-riot" the ads had promised, was completely dumbfounded by what it saw. As one local critic reported, "The audience was more in the mood for *Guys and Dolls*." It was openly hostile to the event.

Lahr found himself living through a comedian's nightmare. He met a complete stone wall. "I have never experienced anything like this in the American theater. I don't think anybody has. Two thirds of the audience left after the first act."

Lahr's horror at the audience's reception sent him into a frenzy of activity. "He tried to do a one-man show," recalls Schneider. "He was trying to salvage the evening. There was nothing malicious in his gestures, but he would ride in on Tommy's laughs. I had to restrain Mrs. Ewell from going on the stage. Bert just couldn't believe that Vladimir could get laughs. The two of them ended up killing each other on the stage."

Lahr could never comprehend Ewell's reaction to him. In his mind, Estragon demanded the movement he brought to the part. "Tom thought I was moving on him; he'd wrap his arms around me on stage and hold me.

"I didn't do anything to him. I wasn't trying to hurt him. We'd been in this thing together—in fact, he'd finally convinced me to do the play. It was only a two-week run, and anyway, he was bigger than I was."

The next day there was a line in front of the Cocoanut Grove Theater, not to buy tickets, but to demand refunds. Lahr himself began receiving protest mail. One day soon after the opening, he approached Schneider and held out a letter for him to read.

Dear Mr. Lahr,
    How can a man, who has charmed the youth of America as the lion in *The Wizard of Oz*, appear in a play which is communistic, atheistic and existential.

After Schneider glanced through the letter, Lahr asked, "What does existential mean?"

But Lahr's intuitions about the play changed gradually during the two-week run. He began to understand parts of the play that Schneider's careful words had not been able to convey.

Although he swore to Schneider that he would have nothing to do with another production, he could not deny that the play spoke to a vast, inarticulate region of his experience. Beckett's limbo would elicit similar responses from convicts in San Quentin who saw the San Francisco Actor's Workshop production in 1957. Middle-class audiences, however, found the experience unsettling and treated the production with an aggressive dislike. Walter Winchell wrote the first of a handful of notices that would characterize their typical arrogant obtuseness. While Lahr could not forget the caverns of emptiness the play dramatized, Winchell illustrated the antagonism of a class that refused to recognize it.

As one of the most influential of the old guard on the Broadway scene, his hostility, verging on hysteria, is pertinent. Some, like Walter Kerr, dismissed it ("an intellectual fruitbowl"), but Winchell wanted to destroy it as if it were subversive and those who took part in it insane.

Waiting for Godot will appear in Washington, Boston, and Philadelphia before it challenges New Yorkers at the Music Box. Lahr and Ewell are on stage throughout, trading double talk. The thing opens with Tom Ewell's trousers unzipped. . . . It ends

With Jack Haley as the Tin Woodsman (left) and
Ray Bolger as the Scarecrow (right)

M-G-M

Overleaf
As the Cowardly Lion in *The Wizard of Oz* (1939)

On the Hollywood Victory Caravan (1942)

With Oliver Hardy, Bing Crosby, and Jimmy Cagney
backstage on the Caravan junket

With Bea Lillie at *Seven Lively
Arts* rehearsal (1944)

Changing a scene at
Seven Lively Arts rehearsal

With Bea Lillie in *Seven Lively Arts*

With Jean Parker in *Burlesque* (1946)

As Queen Victoria in
Two on the Aisle (1951)

As Lefty Hogan, ballplayer,
in *Two on the Aisle*

With Dolores Gray in *Two on the Aisle*

As Estragon with E. G. Marshall as Vladimir in *Waiting for Godot* (1956)

With Kurt Kasznar as Pozzo and E. G. Marshall. *Waiting for Godot*

Overleaf
Portrait from *Waiting for Godot*

with Lahr's pants falling to his ankles. In between there is considerable chatter about madness, boredom, human suffering and cruelty. . . . There are several profane utterances . . . some of which have never before been heard on the stage before. . . . Even the vulgarians who people the premieres found the dirty words vulgar. . . . "Unnecessary" exclaimed a hard boiled Broadwayite. George E. Engle, a multi-millionaire who loves theater people, renovated the Cocoanut Grove Playhouse and will play Broadway shows old and new. Mr. Engle is also the proprietor of 440 producing oil wells.

"What on earth possessed Myerberg to put on such a show," he asked John Shubert the Broadway showman. "Don't underestimate him," he said. "Myerberg was laughed at by experts when he put on Wilder's *Skin of Our Teeth*. He made so much money with it that he bought the Mansfield Theater! . . . *Life* photographers "shot" the elite audiences as the stars were taking alleged bows . . . If published, these pictures cannot help the new show since half the spectators fled after the opening stanza. . . .

The debacle was completed when Myerberg canceled the out-of-town tryouts and folded the show. Much of the fault lay with Myerberg himself. He had billed the production falsely, mounted it outrageously, and brought it to a town with no sympathetic audience to sustain an experimental play. But Schneider had an even unhappier experience, for he was not asked to direct the New York production, as he had expected.

For Schneider, however, the real sadness was in not having done justice to the Beckett he understood. As he wrote in the *Chelsea Review,*

> The failure in Miami depressed me more than any experience I had had in the theater, though I had for a time anticipated the probability and done all in my power to avoid it. It is typical of Sam [Beckett] that his response to Miami was concerned only with my feelings of disappointment and never stressed or even mentioned his own. Nor did he utter one word of blame for any mistakes I might have made along the way. . . . We met several times. I told him the story of Miami as objectively as I could and he spoke to me of what he had heard concerning both productions. Somehow he made me feel that what I had at least tried to do in Miami was closer to what he wanted to do—though he never criticized the efforts of anyone else. . . ."

Schneider never saw the New York production.

The play's dismal reception in Miami never numbed Lahr's faith in its fundamental theatricality. There were dimensions of the play he felt his performance had not been able to tap because of the director, the set, his own fear of the material.

"Everybody has their own interpretation of *Godot*. At one point in the play, you thought the tramps were waiting for God. But then Beckett would go off on another tangent. Then you knew it wasn't God. At the finish, they were still waiting. It was Waiting. Hopelessness. It was waiting for the best of life; and it never came. I think he meant the two characters to represent both sides of man. Estragon, my part, was the animal: Sex, Hunger, Eating, Sleeping. The other, Vladimir, was Suspicion, Inquiry, always examining everything. Intellect. He had kind of an animal's love for the other. He cared for him almost like a baby."

Even Myerberg realized that "Lahr seemed to know the character better than anyone even from the beginning."

What did Lahr know? Questions of the Bible, of philosophy, and social organization that the play raised had never crossed his mind. His theatrical friends urged him to scrap the idea of playing *Godot*. Yet he found himself defending the play without being able to verbalize its special force. In 1964, when Beckett went to London to oversee another production of *Waiting for Godot,* he discussed approaches to the play that might have calmed those who scoffed at Lahr's persistence.

> This play is full of implications and every important statement can be taken three or four ways. But the actor has only to find the dominant one, because he does so, does not mean the other levels will be lost. . . .
> *Sunday Times,* December 20, 1964

Lahr found his approach to Beckett; the audience's violent reaction in Miami had solidified his idea. "When I saw them walking out, I knew, I knew." Many of Lahr's theatrical associates regarded his fascination with the play as childish. If he lacked the words to express his appreciation, his "instincts" would prove Beckett's statement correct, peeling layers of meaning and emotion from the play that neither actor nor author could have originally visualized.

A few weeks after returning to New York, Myerberg asked Lahr if he would do another production of the play. Despite Lahr's bad experience in Miami and his distrust of Myerberg, he agreed on the condition that he have final say about the director.

Two weeks later, Lahr found himself in Lester Shurr's Broadway office talking to a director whom he'd never met and whose acting-school productions of *Waiting for Godot* he'd never seen—Herbert Berghof.

Berghof did not look like a man with a flair for comedy. He was heavy-set; his bald head and thick Viennese accent reminded Lahr more of a philosophy professor than a director. Berghof had come to the interview with a mixture of confidence and trepidation. He had directed *Waiting for Godot* in his acting studio and played the part of Estragon himself. Since he knew the play and had heard about Schneider's approach to it, he felt that he could offer an alternative. "Myerberg had said to me 'It's all up to Mr. Lahr. If he accepts you, then it's fine.' I wanted to direct the play very much, but I was frightened of that meeting. I had seen Bert in all his great parts, and I was a fan of his. I was really frightened."

Lahr stood at the window watching a mammoth cardboard Yogi Berra blow Camel smoke rings onto Broadway. He listened and nodded while Berghof explained his feelings about the play. "Although I had never seen the Miami production, I had very definite ideas about Beckett. My complete conviction was that the play was affirmative. There was nothing fanciful or strange in it. There was no raised finger. To me it didn't have the false significance of an arty play. In Miami, it was directed for style and crucifixion and I don't know what. I felt the play was comparable to clowning—the sublime clowning of Grok or the Fratellinis. The meaningless notions of Beckett are meaningful. We *do* eat carrots and go into delicious ecstasy about them. That gesture has meaning; it's not just being silly. In comedy, what matters is that you truly see. Take a drawing by Saul Steinberg, who is a metaphysical clown among cartoonists; he's able to X-ray something—emotionally, psychologically—with two lines. His illustration is true; he has captured an absurd moment of a human being, but with precise understanding. The same happens with Beckett's laughter. The play in Miami was directed for significances, meanings. My understanding of Beckett was different, more affirmative. Only somebody who loves life strongly could see all the flaws and weaknesses in an attempt to find out what it was all about. The exploration of existence becomes a sublime clown's act. There was no negation in Beckett's play; but the kind of affirmation you get when you love someone and see all their faults. Life to Beckett seems to have all these absurd, unexplained aspects; and yet, he is on the search because he loves life." Berghof's conception of the play allowed for the comic leeway that Schneider's did not. Lahr immediately warmed to it, expressing his humiliation and bewilderment at the Miami production.

Lahr described the elaborate set design. Berghof replied, "I think that's phony."

"You're right. I wouldn't set foot on it again."

Berghof understood clowning and directing comedy and could see immediately how the set imposed its own limitations. "There were very complicated ramps, which made it impossible to operate like a clown because a clown basically needs an empty stage. First of all, the complicated set detracts from Bert's gestures; secondly, the whole attitude of the play with platforms seems fanciful and out of order."

Having found a sympathetic ear, Lahr confided, "I just couldn't walk or talk on it. What do you want as a set?"

"I don't want anything," Berghof said flatly. They discussed casting, and again Lahr was surprised at how many of Berghof's ideas paralleled his own. "I did feel it was wrong to cast Tom Ewell with Bert. Their type of comedy is too similar—naïve, simple, innocent. Bert has this same radiance or innocence. I thought the character should be played by somebody who had comedic elements but was a sharper player, more intellectual. I suggested E. G. Marshall. He had a kind of New England acuteness, a cerebral quality to contrast with Estragon's vulnerability."

Lahr, who had been cordial up to this point, became more involved. He moved away from the window and stopped pacing.

"I think it's music hall. But in Miami, I couldn't get a laugh for two hours."

"If it's not comic," replied Berghof, "it's nothing. It becomes completely dry if it is played with a raised finger and all kinds of symbolic overtones which do not communicate the meaninglessness to an audience."

Lahr struggled with Berghof's terms and began analyzing the play on the philosophical level Berghof had broached. He didn't get far. Berghof stopped him, echoing Beckett's sentiments written in 1964: "I don't like to talk intellectually about a play which has to be played simply in order to be an intellectual play. I would like to talk about how you go to sleep or how you eat the carrots. The words are there. If they have meaning, the meaning will come out."

Berghof's attitude intrigued Lahr. He seemed comfortable with ideas, and, at the same time, extremely theater-wise. He began to put Berghof to the test. "Now, for instance, how would you play the opening speeches? There's no laughs in them?"

Berghof proceeded to act out the situation. "Now I'm not as good an actor as Bert—certainly not as good a comedian—but I'm pretty good. At least I could make things clear. He liked that. I was showing him instead of talking. We went through the play. We had an absolute rapport. I don't like to talk either. I have been on the stage since I was sixteen; and I know what is a legitimate problem and what is a lot of talk. What matters is that something is true and human, that you get true sensations."

Berghof's demand for theatrical honesty paralleled Lahr's attitudes. They continued reading through the play. "Bert had a very clear and simple attitude toward the work. One of his words which I really adore is 'That's phony,' 'No, that's not real,' 'No, that's hokum.' These are the words I remember most about his reaction to production ideas. He wasn't satisfied with being funny; it had to be true and real too."

The interview had taken ninety minutes, but Berghof could not gauge whether Lahr's questions and enthusiasm were a vote of confidence. Lahr himself was still uncertain whether laughter could be coaxed up from the interpretation Berghof outlined. They came to the final image of the play, where Estragon, having failed to hang himself with his rope belt, speaks the final lines with his pants down. The technical problem of sustaining an audience rapport during this moment had plagued Lahr in Miami. It had never created the sense of sadness or the laughter that Lahr felt was on the printed page.

"Well, how are you going to make *that* work?"

"I worked on that for a long time in my studio," said Berghof. "I've got a very simple device."

"How are you going to get away with it and not be offensive?"

As Berghof recalls, "I said, 'That's very simple,' and then dropped my trousers."

Lahr did not laugh. He stared at Berghof; and then glanced at Lester's paneled office. Looking back at the director, he said "You're going to direct this play. You're my man. Anybody who drops his pants for a moment in the theater is my man as a director."

Berghof had been accumulating information on *Waiting for Godot* since its European debut in 1954. On the cluttered shelves of his study were boxes crammed with programs, pictures, and articles about the various productions. (Lahr would never see that den or realize that Berghof kept a picture of him, frozen in a wild grimace, on a bulletin board in front of his desk.) Berghof's extensive research on the play and his fluency with the characters as well as with the personalities of the actors playing them made rehearsals much smoother than the Miami production.

A cast was assembled quickly. In early April, two months after Miami, rehearsals began. "One of the rules I established with the cast was that I was not going to intellectualize the play, but work." Privately, Berghof interpreted the play on a very intellectual level, but he feared that any discussion of ideas would limit the human experience he was trying to evoke from his actors. "I studied Bosch and Brueghel in detail. I used certain attitudes in the paintings for the visualization of the images in the play. I'd never tell actors that. But in Brueghel and Bosch, you have actions pertinent to Beckett. They are doing something very strange and often very silly, but with great intensity and naturalness. I go to such things because you absolve yourself from theater gimmicks."

Berghof also did not tell Lahr that he kept pictures of all the actors pasted throughout his script. "I like to see what actors look like in others parts. If I'm supposed to help an actor to be good, I have to understand him: his face, his cheekbones, his arms. I like to understand everything, so that when I ask an actor to do something, I know his responses."

The other members of the new cast were better acquainted with Beckett and the problems of production than the Miami entourage. E. G. Marshall had seen the play twice in England; and Kurt Kasznar, who played Pozzo, flew to England to view the production before going into rehearsal. Berghof capitalized on the enthusiasm and expertise of his actors. A seriousness of purpose and a sense of direction pervaded the rehearsals. For Lahr, it was like discovering a new play. "With Herbert's direction the play began to open up. E. G. was brilliant; Kasznar was right. I began to function properly."

Berghof tried not to push Lahr into false significance, but let him discover his own emphasis. Lahr responded with confidence and immense energy. "Bert has a way of rehearsing," recalls Berghof, "that I wish other actors would learn. He came to rehearsal half an hour before it started, got into his working clothes. He was very anxious to get to work. He kept saying to me, 'Let's get on the floor.' And he worked— sometimes seven hours straight. We got an unbelievable amount accomplished. In two weeks we were practically ready."

Berghof worked hard at building Lahr's confidence. He had realized long before rehearsals that his main task would be assuaging Lahr's fear of another failure in the role. Alvin Epstein, whom Berghof had signed as Lucky, remembers that the director made him come down to his studio to go over his part two weeks before the production went into rehearsal. "Once we go into rehearsals," Berghof told him, "I can't spend any time with you."

Berghof's method of directing the play gave run-throughs a special flavor. "He would prod you and push you and giggle and laugh," recalls Epstein. "It was like making love to the actors, a constant dance back and forth. He'd get up and show you. Then he'd say, 'You do it better. You do it better, darling,' and then you did it, and he'd say, 'Oh, that's *wonderful!*' It was like that for four weeks."

In rehearsal, Berghof was often astounded by Lahr's ability to respond to a dramatic suggestion. "When you looked at him (sometimes I was only two feet away) he was absolutely true, unfailingly true. Every experience—the crying—everything. It was absolutely unheard of. He never knew how he knew; it came to him. His instincts to look for where he could get emotion were there. Gide once said, 'All the tedious research becomes worthwhile if you have one inspired moment.' Lahr was inspired. I believe acting is a game of make-believe, like children play. Bert plays that game; he goes into a rehearsal like a child going to the park. I found Bert's style came from content. I hate 'style.' Everything Bert did came from an experience and made a form. He didn't find a style first, but rather the experience made a form."

Lahr's face took on new dimensions in the play. He ate a carrot with hungry joy; he took off his shoe with a peace beyond satisfaction. He crawled; he whined. Berghof was amazed to see how he could convey insight without extraneous gesture. "Bert once told me that as a young actor he was called 'one-take Lahr.' He had only to look at an object once and he'd get a laugh. What is a double-take anyway? You look at an object; you see it, but you don't understand its meaning. You leave it and walk away from it. While you are walking away, it dawns on you what the object really is. You look back. Delayed recognition. Now Bert was able to look at something—a tree, a carrot, a shoe—see it, and it suddenly dawns all over his face. He doesn't need to go away from the object. That is fantastic. It shows an immense acting sensitivity."

Lahr's gestures found the rhythm and purpose of Beckett's prose. He was used to doing funny things with his arms and legs, turning the costume into part of his personality. Epstein, who had worked with

Marcel Marceau and studied with Etienne Decroux, was amazed. "So much had to do with the kind of clothes he was wearing, the shoes, the hats. The idea of his movement, the physical feel of it seemed to me the perfect Beckettian tragicomic gestures. It wasn't campy. In another context it might have seemed like a put-on. It wasn't. It was absolutely right within the framework of the play, sluggish and sloppy, but precise."

The recognition of excellence was not one-sided. Once the stage manager came to Epstein's door. "Mr. Lahr would like to see you."

Epstein was flustered. "I immediately thought, 'Oh my God, what have I done?' He never summoned me to his dressing room; we were on very good terms."

When Epstein came to see Lahr, he found him edgy but affable. "He hemmed and hawed and said, 'You're a very talented young man, Alvin. You've a great future.' I didn't know what he was driving at. But I knew I hadn't committed the irrevocable crime of stepping on a laugh. He was embarrassed. He finally blurted out, 'I hope you don't mind me saying this. I think you ought to change your name. I did. Lahr's not my name.' "

When Berghof told a New York newspaper, "Lahr's a primitive, God bless him," Lahr read the statement with interest. He checked the word in his dictionary, making sure it was not pejorative. He relaxed under Berghof's careful respect. Their association (Lahr refers to it as a "marriage") led him to many discoveries.

In rehearsals, Lahr made his own personal additions. "I never changed a word of the text; but I put in business like crawling and saying 'Aaah!' The reaction was in the text, but not the way I did it —with the pointed finger, as much as to say, 'I do understand, but I don't.' When the messenger boy came with news of Godot I'd shake him; E. G. would sometimes shake me, saying 'What are you doing?' I'd cover my face. When I took my hands down, my face would be this horrible mask of torture and frustration. I'd crawl off sobbing. A shock went through the audience. I could hear them gasping . . ."

Lahr's inventions and the fine work of the other actors gave the play an immense dramatic potential that even Lahr had not imagined. In his mind, it began to take a shape equivalent to the praise heaped on it from literary circles. Tennessee Williams had called it "one of the greatest plays of our time." Jean Anouilh had called the Paris debut of Waiting for Godot "as important as the premiere of Pirandello in 1923." The previews played to an enthusiastic audience. Lahr found himself exhilarated by the play, which, under Berghof's direction, he saw for the first time,as revolutionary. He was aware that many people looked upon its production in America as an event of crucial importance to the theater. William Saroyan had said, "It will make it easier for me and everyone else to write freely in the theater."

But the memory of Miami lingered. Lahr still feared that laughs would not come. He pestered Berghof with the same statement daily: "There are not going to be any laughs."

Ironically, on opening night, Berghof's big worry was that laughter would dominate the delicate balance of the play's mood.

Berghof called Lahr aside at the last run-through. "You know Bert . . . be careful not to do too much out there."

"Herbert, I'm not going to do anything opening night. Oh no. Not on opening night."

Berghof recalls that "as I walked away I thought to myself, 'What does he mean now? Is he going to do anything or not?' "

Berghof's answer came soon enough. At the end of the play, the entire audience at the Golden Theater stood up and applauded Lahr. "They bravoed, standing on their feet," Lahr remembers, "like if it was a symphony."

The production was a triumph, but Lahr's performance made it special. "It was a unique evening. Bert was so unfailing in his instincts on how to play to a first-night audience. He gave his best performance on opening night—it was his purest. He somehow felt that if he was really pure it would be acceptable. He's quite right because everybody is there waiting for the actor to send the laughs out; and he wasn't doing it. I'd never seen him as clear, as simple and to the point."

In the dressing room, Lahr was besieged by well-wishers. One woman came to the door and asked to speak with him. When he turned to greet her she began crying. "Oh Mr. Lahr . . . Mr. Lahr," she said, and ran from the room.

Lahr can recall only one other moment of an evening he considers his greatest theatrical triumph. Moss Hart, who had come backstage, turned to Mildred as he left: "Tell Bert to hang up his dancing shoes."

Berghof referred to the critical praise Lahr received as "unheard of" and compared the notices to those received by Kean, Barrymore, and Duse. Lahr simply remembered the respectful tone which most people took toward his work, and the strange excitement he felt. "I couldn't wait to get to the theater each night. It was an experience I'll never forget; it was the most satisfying moment on stage I've ever had."

Lahr's personality charted the wasteland of Beckett's play. As Richard Watts observed in the New York *Post*—

> Mr. Lahr, in addition to being enormously funny and touching in the role, somehow managed to seem a kind of liaison between the narrative and the audience, a sort of spiritual interpreter whose warmth and humanity extended across the footlights and caught up every spectator in a shared experience.

Once during a performance, he forgot his lines. Impelled by the play's movement and its sense of dreamlike repetition, he turned to the audience and confided, "I said that before." His instinct was right; the break with his own strict sense of professional propriety, shocking and insightful. The audience sensed Lahr's struggle as their own.

Panel discussions about the play were held on the stage after each performance. Lahr and the other actors took part in the talks, with literary personalities and critics spicing the discussion with contemporary analysis. Myerberg felt this theatrical innovation in a Broadway theater helped sell the play to the public. The debate fermented both inside the theater and beyond it.

Variety and Walter Winchell, the most anachronistic wings of Broadway criticism, continued their attacks on experiment and ideas on the Broadway stage, prompting *The Nation,* an intelligent journal usually above commenting on the humdrum of daily theater columns, to remark on their aggressiveness—"a savagery even for them."

While Myerberg was pleased at the controversy Winchell tried to create, Lahr was angered at his destructive remarks. "He did everything to castrate us." A typical broadside read:

> "Waiting for Godot" the dramatic whatzit which brilliantly discusses the philosophy of so-what is returning to Broadway. The history of frammis never had anything so rillerah. Undoubtedly the controversy will be revived, Samuel Beckett, the alleged author, was recently interviewed. The reporter, seeking an explanation of *Godot,* inquired, "When you have nothing to say, do you do what others do—go right on trying?"
>
> Beckett's gloomy reply: "There are others who threw themselves out of windows after years of struggle." (Happy pecans and merry almonds) . . .

The debate had interesting ramifications. If Winchell represented vindictive ignorance, another pugilist with literary credentials added his own kind of double-talk about the play. Writing without having seen the production, Norman Mailer tried to run the play up a Freudian flagpole.

> . . . But at the very least, the critics could have done a little rudimentary investigation into the meaning of the title of *Waiting for Godot* and the best they have been able to come up with so far is that Godot has something to do with God. My congratulations. But Godot also means " 'ot Dog or the dog who is hot, and it means God-O, God as the female principle, just as Daddy-O in Hip means the father who has failed, the man who has become an O, a vagina. Two obvious dialectical transpositions on *Waiting for Godot* are To Dog the Coming, and God Hot for Waiting, but anyone who has the Joycean habit of thought could add a hundred subsidiary themes. As for example on Go, Dough! (Go Life!)

Mailer, who had quit the *Village Voice* a week before seeing the play, returned for an unexpected encore to register his disapproval of the production, which he found chi-chi.

Lahr often took part in the theater debates, but his outlook was hardly as elaborate as Mailer's. He did not offer the press any easy answers or account for the motivations behind his performance. When Berghof was asked by reporters, "What do you think Mr. Lahr means when he says he doesn't understand the play?" the director's reply would surprise the reporters and even Lahr himself: "I think he understands it better than any critic I've ever read, better than anybody who has ever read about it, and I think he understands it better than Beckett."

The play lasted ten weeks on Broadway. Economic confusions between the cast and the producer forced an early closing of the show, which could have run throughout the summer and perhaps toured the country. Despite the short run, Beckett, at least, had been established in America as an important intellectual force.

The play had the shortest run, and was the most unconventional and the least financially rewarding of any of Lahr's major enterprises. Yet, those ten weeks live in his memory as a much longer time. When he thinks about the play, he will walk to his bookshelf and pick out Kenneth Tynan's *Curtains*. "Did you ever read what Tynan said about me?" he asks with an air of honest amazement. Then, placing the book in front of him, he glances over the words that have become the only chronicle of his energy. Memory cannot isolate the event, but the printed page makes his performance and his satisfaction stand still. With a magnifying glass he reads:

> Ten days ago *Waiting for Godot* reached New York, greeted by a baffled but mostly appreciative press and preceded by an advertising campaign in which the management appealed for 70,000 intellectuals to make its venture pay. At the performance I saw, a Sunday matinée, the eggheads were rolling in. And when the curtain fell, the house stood up to cheer a man who had never before appeared in a legitimate play, a mighty and blessed clown whose grateful bewilderment was reflected in the tears that speckled his cheeks, a burlesque comic of crumpled mien and baggy eyes, with a nose stuck like a gherkin into a face as ageless as the Commedia dell'Arte: Bert Lahr, no less, the cowardly lion of *The Wizard of Oz*, played the dumber of Samuel Beckett's two timeless hoboes, and by his playing bridged, for the first time that I can remember, the irrational abyss that yawns between the world of red noses and the world of blue stockings.
>
> Without him, the Broadway production of Mr. Beckett's play would be admirable; with him, it is transfigured. It is as if we, the audience, had elected him to represent our reactions, resentful and confused, to the lonely universe into which the author plunges us. "I'm going," says Mr. Lahr. "We can't go," snaps his partner. "Why not?" pleads Mr. Lahr. "We're waiting for Godot," comes the reply; Whereat Mr. Lahr raises one finger with an "Ah!" of comprehension which betokens its exact opposite, a totality of blankest ignorance. Mr. Lahr's beleaguered simpleton, a draughts-player lost in a universe of chess, is one of the noblest performances I have ever seen.

"Did I ever tell you," he says, closing the book, "that sometimes, when I crawled off the stage, I could hear the audience. They were gasping."

A DECADE OF MOMENTS

At this stage of life, I like to do important things. . . . No actually, I don't want to do anything. I want to fish. . . . I don't think there's such a thing as a good fisherman. There's just stupid fish. But fishing makes me tired, hungry, and sleepy. I throw off all my worries. I'm very fortunate but I still worry. . . . At this stage of life, what the hell do I gotta prove?

Lahr to Newsweek, *July 11, 1966*

Bert Lahr should be preserved like a fine old wine, or in one, it doesn't matter which. As the years go along his tang gets headier, his lifted pinky gets daintier, his moose call to the great beyond gets mellower and mellower, and furthermore, he is beginning to carbonate. . . ."

Walter Kerr on Foxy

Getting old is harrowing.

Lahr in conversation, *1967*

SURVEYING THE LAST DECADE, BERT LAHR CAN CLAIM A NUMBER OF successes, but not satisfaction. He has grown into something of a theatrical institution during the sixties; but the America that gave him fame now eludes his comprehension. The society is changing; and although Lahr cannot cope with the shift in values, he nonetheless has had to evolve with them. The youth of today, whom he excoriates like a Jewish mother for its protest and long hair, has adopted him. Walking on Third Avenue, young girls sport his face as the Cowardly Lion on buttons with the same laughing delight with which they wear mini-skirts. And Bert Lahr, potbellied and persnickety, has become Camp.

This public nostalgia disturbs him; it lacks the moral conviction to match the style. If it has affected the art world and high fashion, it has missed the theater. In the sixties, Lahr has tried the musical, the revue, satire, even the classics. He has succeeded; but no wide popular audience has been secured. "If they value me," he asks himself, "then where is the support?" In England, he might have hoped for a knighthood and the freedom to play a variety of roles; in America, he can be thankful that the barometer of stardom—money and public recognition—is still there. He cannot afford to experiment, although he talks of playing Falstaff or attempting Pinter.

Money and recognition—these two cornerstones of his comic activity—have also changed. Advertisements for potato chips have made more people aware of his face (and burlesque double-take) than ever before. He invented a catchword for the product—"de-lay-cious"—turning his comedy easily from art to marketing. Cab drivers stop their cars to yell, "Bet you can't eat one!"; grandmothers accost him like one of their own to ask if he really eats potato chips. (Taking his cue from Abe Burrow's baseball sketch and "Sawsie Dusties," Lahr usually replies, "Don't eat 'em, they'll kill ya." The public once again goes away satisfied.) These commercials, amounting to work more easily measured in minutes than days, earns him $75,000 a year, far more than a season on Broadway. Financial security, Lahr's *modus vivendi*, has become superfluous in the affluent society. The money he commands is beyond his needs; and yet he still requires a limitless economic horizon. He is proud to have survived and succeeded in this newest facet of show business: the television commercial. But he is perplexed. Does the star system, to whose emotional and economic axioms he has always subscribed, reduce itself to adding "personality" to products? His laughter was meant for people, not merchandise. The paradox has been hard for him to resolve. Even though his commercials are excellent and he has devised many of their comic situations, he is suspicious. "I wonder if these ads have been good for my career? Here's the strange thing, John: after all these years on stage, the biggest success I've ever had is in these trite commercials. It's stupid."

Success, measured by his usual dollars-and-cents standard, confuses him in ways it never did. In the days when playing the Palace was the theatrical zenith, money was synonymous with quality. The struggle was grueling; the reward well earned. Today, Lahr can watch young singers or undisciplined actors project themselves to millions of viewers, earning in a year the security he could never have imagined for himself in a lifetime. "I'm a mercenary," Lahr keeps repeating when the family suggests possible theater ventures. "I'm a mercenary." These words have been his banner and his explanation, but they grow increasingly hollow, even to him. Yet he is too old to change; his own financial demands must ultimately limit his talent, just as unwieldy economics have begun to smother Broadway. The theater that created the star can no longer afford him. Who can pay his star's salary plus ten per cent of the gross and still meet the other spiraling costs? Who can convince a man who has spent a lifetime in the theater that the connection between professionalism and money is dubious?

Lahr's adventures in the theater over the last decade are a testament to the society in transition, whose changing tastes mirror the emergence of new values. The shows in which he played reflected not merely the drama of his memorable survival as a clown but also the mischievousness of his materialism. He wanted to work, but only if the price was right. The paradox rests as much with him as American show business. He has given glorious life to the stage; yet recalcitrant commercialism may also have contributed, unwittingly, to its process of decay.

Ironically, Lahr's stage career was sustained into the sixties by *Waiting for Godot,* his only "uncommercial" venture. The play led him to a classical repertoire. The prestige and satisfaction of *Godot* whetted his appetite. At sixty-two, Lahr began to confront the classics—a challenge that led him (in spite of himself) to do more justice to his career than most of America's revered funny-men. His musical-comedy talents had always hinted at insights beyond the play. If he took liberties, his fidelity to the author's intentions gave the masterpieces new life. He did Molière and Shaw on television, and in 1957 he starred in Georges Feydeau's classic French farce, *Hotel Paradiso,* in the part Alec Guinness had created in England. Peter Glenville, who had directed the English production, saw Lahr as a spirit who gave a dimension to farce that Guinness, with his dry wit, could not bring out. *Hotel Paradiso* was a tale of romantic infatuation and confusion that unraveled with the precision of a mathematical equation. To Glenville, a Feydeau farce had the frenetic momentum of a Mack Sennett two-reeler. Lahr's athletic comedy and his maturity fitted the necessities of farce as Glenville outlined them in *Theater Arts Magazine:*

> The play has more in common with art and discipline of the ballet dance and acrobat. It also, of course, has to be illumined by the colors and personality of the actor, the latter has always to keep his eyes on the exact requirements of the scene. Rhythm, accent and timing are more important in farce than personal idiosyncracy no matter how diverting. . . . When a great comedian lends his talents to these requirements, the results should be, in its own genre, a work of art . . .

French farce had gone out of fashion in the same way that low comedy in America gave way to the more sophisticated pretensions of plays with "substance" and "message." Glenville had been attracted to Feydeau precisely for the reasons many audiences spurned him: he spoke to the belly, not the head; he was good-natured and superficial. "He appeals to the child in us." This of course was Lahr's terrain. The clown image, the anti-hero, had its resurgence in postwar American literature, but not on stage. The comedian had either intellectualized his role, like Chaplin, and lost the low-comic spontaneity; or, like Jerry Lewis and Milton Berle, developed into a sloppy, vulgar popularity. Lahr saw in *Hotel Paradiso* a chance to keep his burlesque spirit alive in a new form. He did not realize how far from burlesque farce would take him or how close the vagaries of the genre paralleled comic taste in America, which had dwindled to gracious and tepid archetypes of middle-class life.

If Lahr had never played farce, his artistry contained the dramatic elements the genre demanded. "The main point in classical farce is that the performer should have an enormous seriousness," explains Glenville. "Boniface in 'Paradiso' is not a farce part. It needs expertise, timing, sincerity. Lahr had a wonderful personality for farce. I had always been interested and amused by the underlying gloom of his comedy. His age, his attitude, his natural look toward a formidable woman. He had a pathetic, half-defiant stare toward dominating women, and also a naughty appreciation of the younger ones. This was all given to him. This was his own atmosphere; and it was absolutely right."

The obstacles farce posed to Lahr's comedy came from his theatrical training. He was used to creating laughs and inventing comic moments within a sketch. Farce was more rigorous; the performer had to bind himself to the author's strategy, where (as Glenville points out) "the lines are not merely jokes or even witty. The laughter is in the play's architecture—the momentum and situation."

Having discovered a reality within the drama of the absurd, Lahr was now faced with achieving the stylization necessary for French boulevard comedy. He approached *Hotel Paradiso* like a swimmer, eager for the plunge but fearful of the chill. "Bert had a natural suspicion that these things were not in themselves funny," says Glenville. "Practically every line I had to tell him where the laughs were. I knew that he could get a laugh on his own, but not a relevant laugh within the structure of the play. One had to work very hard never letting him be irrelevantly funny by means of funny faces, funny noises, little comedic details lovely in another context, but not right for *Paradiso*.

I said to him, 'No, Bert, if you do nothing there, just look up innocently and say, "Come in," you'll get an enormous laugh. The audience knows that on the other side of the door is an infuriated wife who you've escaped from. A little innocent look at the door is funnier than a grimace.' He was nervous because I would *never* agree that he could make a funny face where he thought there were going to be enormous passages of silence."

Left to his own devices, Lahr might have turned *Hotel Paradiso* into a Columbia Wheel romp. Glenville pushed him into painful and uncharted areas of humor. He had to concentrate, as in *Waiting for Godot,* on the author's rhythms, not his own. He had to bridle his passion for play. Yet there were moments in Feydeau where the instincts of the author and the burlesque-trained comedian meshed. "He had a wonderful rapport with the audience," says Glenville. "This immediate contact was part of the natural vocabulary of his comedy."

The discipline of adapting to the precise demands of French farce was important to Lahr's development. He could be controlled more easily with a vehicle somewhat alien to him, like *Waiting for Godot;* but in a play whose intention was laughter, it took immense patience and acuteness to steer him away from formula responses. The effect of Glenville's tutelage is seen in Lahr's reactions. "Farce is almost a ballet. You overplay, but with sincerity." Lahr acknowledges the proximity of farce to tragedy, the momentum of random events skirting cruelty for hilarious conclusions.

As he told *Newsweek* before the play opened in New York, "I'm anxious to see how the Feydeau thing goes. For one thing, I prefer situations to gags. In farce, you've got to be real. Outrageous things may be happening, but they're happening to a believable person. The moment you start to clown, the fun is gone. That isn't the rhythm of farce. You just keep going and let the audience play it."

Hotel Paradiso posed another problem for Lahr in terms of simple energy. The play was wildly athletic—and a group sport besides. Wolcott Gibbs referred to the direction as "roughly comparable in intricacy to coaching a football team." As Boniface, the hen-pecked philanderer who seeks out a flea-ridden hotel for his tryst, Lahr had to leap upstairs like a teenager for the telephone, crash through chairs that collapsed as he took a seat, and escape nimbly through the side door. In a fast-moving Broadway revue, his energy carried the momentum of the entire comic situation. In farce, it had to be choreographed to the comparable frenzy of the other actors. Lahr could not simply invent comic movements. Often, gestures had to be superimposed on his comedy to fit the situation. He could not roam the stage. His script indicates how unnatural the discipline of the genre was. Unlike musical-comedy scripts or revue scenes, it is marked in his own hand with reminders of where to stand and what gestures to make. "Take circular out of pocket." "Throw a boot on desk." "Climb on trunk." "Sit on settee."

Angela Lansbury made her first stage appearance in *Hotel Paradiso,* as Angelique, Lahr's wife. She remembers her amazement at watching Lahr work. "Bert had a whole set of things, a *shtick* . . . it was almost as if he were working by numbers which I knew nothing about. He would pick out of the scenes what he considered to be the funniest moment, because in his book that was the point you were aiming for and that was the laugh. Glenville, on the other hand, would say to him, 'Yes . . . but don't you realize that there is an area here which is just as funny although it isn't immediately recognizable to you? Will you work on this area of the scene?' This was confusing to Bert. Working with him from the beginning, one could see it bothered him. He would often mutter to me, 'I don't understand what this is all about.' But he was so open-minded and so trusting. Lahr was in an area where he was on thin ice. He was prepared to be shown."

Glenville's success with Lahr was as immediate as it was complete. Lahr respected the director's knowledge of the theater—Glenville had translated *Hotel Paradiso* and had a successful acting career of his own. "Glenville was a great help to me. If I didn't grasp the meaning, he'd come up and show me. I'm not hard to direct, in fact I welcome direction; I search for knowledge, but not from people I know more than. He knew about acting, writing, play construction. He was thorough. He didn't learn his craft from a book."

By cajoling Lahr and appreciating his additions to the play, Glenville surmounted the immense difficulty the language of farce played on Lahr's loose verbal patterns. In *Waiting for Godot,* Beckett's controlled prose was sparse; its philosophical implications made even those words difficult to speak. In *Hotel Paradiso* the situation was reversed. Language spilled out with insignificant and excessive banality. Lahr liked the vivid phrase, but his comic language functioned at its best when concise and distinctive. As Glenville pointed out in his *Theater Arts* article—

> The characters don't utter witticisms or felicitous phrases but talk
> in the flat, exact tones of the middle-class to which they belong . . .

The onslaught of speech was difficult for Lahr. Angela Lansbury watched him with the lines. "Bert got terribly upset, terribly frustrated, absolutely tied up in knots. It took him weeks to learn the part. He'd walk around like the Mad Hatter repeating, 'I've got to learn it by rote, I've got to learn it by rote. Once I learn it by rote, I can forget about the words!' "

A stage manager was assigned to help him. "In the beginning," recalls Miss Lansbury, "he didn't understand the other areas of realism in farce. Lahr would say, 'What would I want to do *that* for? You mean I do nothing there?' Then Glenville discussed it with him. He finally agreed. 'All right, I'll try it.' You could see it was an education for him; it was like playing Restoration comedy. He was afraid to depend on the words; he thought he had to *do* something. He didn't; he found out . . ."

If Lahr had to contend with dainty fobs and tea sets in *Hotel Paradiso*, the play also provided him with vivid low-comic pleasure of writhing like a skewered fish when a steel drill pierced the wall of his hotel hideaway. Lahr lingered on the tip of that drill like a go-go dancer on a bar, pinioned in strenuous pain and curious pleasure. The image of Lahr shifting his weight with each revolution of the drill is theatrical history in itself. "The serpentine movements were his invention," says Glenville. "Where the actor had to sustain one long sight gag was much easier for him. He loved it; and he understood it. The direction and his instincts were hand-in-hand." Where once Lahr would have caterwauled and mugged, his voice now mounted gradually to his familiar bellow, his face dissolved into a montage of emotions. As Walter Kerr recounted the event, his face exhibited "every shade of terror, mortification, ecstasy, and refined paralysis . . ." In matters of the heart, Lahr was also allowed to indulge his passion for extravagance. Wearing tailored suits and speaking with clipped diction, Lahr was an improbable lover. Given a moment of intense passion with his mistress, Lahr's ardor expressed itself in words that were its denial: "I'm seething with molten lava." The hypocrisy of marital righteousness shines through Lahr's façade of concern when he exclaims, "Treachery, double-eyed treachery." Kerr, in fact, noticed Lahr indulging Everyman's sense of make-believe in the part. "Mr. Lahr looks so happy when he thinks his wife has been kidnapped. You may want to share his bliss."

Glenville had wisely allowed some of Lahr's outrageousness to prevail. He was, after all, a French bourgeois being caught with his pants nearly down. As Harold Clurman pointed out in *The Nation:* "The

New York production [of *Hotel Paradiso*] is louder, faster, closer to burlesque. The changes . . . help our audience which can more readily accept departures from realism when they are unmistakable."

Lahr's memory of the show strictly concerns the reaction to his comedy. "I liked *Hotel Paradiso* very much—the reception was tremendous. The audience screamed."

The audience's delight in seeing Lahr cavort and the burlesque machinery once again greased for action was best expressed by Brooks Atkinson, who ended his review with Mehitabel's words from Don Marquis's *Shinbone Alley:* "Wotthehell, wotthehell, there's a dance in the old dame yet."

Lahr's energy and isolation were apparent to the cast. "Bert was very much alone," explains Angela Lansbury. "He would talk and chat. He loved the camaraderie; but he still was apart, continually worrying. Although the part was physically grueling, I was never conscious of his age. He was like an indestructible man. I always remember him in his dressing room, taking off his jacket, and all he'd have on was his dicky. I thought, my God, how did he keep up his weight."

Lahr was an important tutor for the other actors, although he cannot believe that people learned from him. And yet, years later, when Miss Lansbury sent him a Christmas card reading "To Bert—who has taught me all I know," he saved it for his scrapbook. His presence provided a discipline. "He taught me about the craft of comedy," says Miss Lansbury. "He taught me about the signposts and props that hold up a funny situation and how you build it. The rules have to do with movement. I can never forget him. He'd come off stage worrying like a bird dog. He defended and protected those comedy moments which he knew were sure laughs like a soldier with a bayonet. And we learned; none of us ever dreamed of breaking the rules. We learned, therefore, how to get our own laughs. Now, on the stage with *Mame* or Shelagh Delaney's *A Taste of Honey,* if I didn't get a laugh or someone else misses a laugh, I know what to tell them."

For Lahr, the theater world went on long into the night. "They had a whole set of places they went to," says Miss Lansbury. "They moved in a circle of people and places I knew nothing about. Downey's . . . Gallagher's . . . The Stork Club . . . Mildred always wore a mink coat. Suddenly, after a show, you realized that he was a big star."

At home, the star mystique was rarely in evidence. On the surface, its pertinence referred only to Lahr's billing and the politics of getting the right table at "21." Lahr had never been forced to defend the system and he never analyzed it: from the beginning stardom gave him a life he felt could only have been possible in America. The struggle, the diligence, the generosity of reward were all part of something he vaguely understood as the American Way. Everyone who surrounded him—from friends to the hairdresser who arrived monthly to tint his hair brown—acknowledged the same beliefs. If Lahr believed in democracy as an institution, he saw no conflict with the privilege by which his "stardom" insulated and set him apart from the public. People, he knew, respected him for his talent. The money they paid into the box office was a token of their respect. Lahr's attitude about his profession paralleled his feelings about income tax. The more he could make, the more he deserved. Once during a family debate about the caliber of Broadway and our desire to see him perform in outstanding plays, Lahr put a decisive end to the discussion with a capsule summary of his philosophy: "Put me in a jock strap, and if I entertain people for two hours—it's a good show. I'm not an artist, I'm in business. Let a hundred thousand people hate my show; if it's a hit, that's all I care about."

Angela Lansbury and the cast of *Hotel Paradiso* tolerated Lahr's attitude with the same kindness his family did. "He was very conscious of his star status and the very special attention he received. He's one of the old guard. They don't make them like that any more. There are no men coming up like Bert. Bert is one of the last of that special group of American performers. I think they deserve the star treatment; and one can't help but give them first place consideration."

Although *Hotel Paradiso* boasted a popular star, good notices, subtle direction, it could not withstand the prospect of a hot New York summer and public taste. It closed in early June. Lahr's post-mortem on the play reflects the sad dilemma of burlesque farce, which not even his mastery could overcome. "Farce has nothing to say, no special significance. The audience roars with laughter; but when they leave the theater, there is nothing to think about. They've tried other farces since *Paradiso;* none of them have succeeded. They're too contrived. The only way it could hold up would be as a novelty in repertory."

Lahr's first summer in repertory (1960) attested to his conviction that low comedy could exist only as a novelty. Touring with the American Shakespeare Festival, he took the parts of Bottom in *A Midsummer Night's Dream* and Autolycus in *The Winter's Tale* (which was later dropped for economic reasons). Other comedians had tried the classics: Bobby Clark took a running stab at Restoration comedy; Jack Pearl once played Lear. However, Lahr was the most successful clown to adapt to the classics (and perhaps the only person to win the "Best Shakespearean Actor of the Year Award" without any knowledge of Shakespeare's writings or his tradition). Lahr's low comedy found an outlet in Shakespeare that commercial theater denied. Just as Shakespeare's famous clowns Tarleton and Kemp gave way gradually to more subdued clowning, so laughter in America, to be tolerated, had been forced to mind its manners.

Lahr interpreted Shakespeare as an Elizabethan Billy K. Wells. "My idea of Mr. Shakespeare is this: when he wrote for comedians— he wrote for low, low comedians. He wrote for dialecticians from different parts of England, the way a writer today would caricature a Southern or a Brooklyn accent." As if Shakespeare's bawdy good humor were not enough, Lahr sometimes suspected Shakespeare of supporting the same star system that spawned the twentieth-century clowns. "I wonder if there was a star system in those days? Was there? Shakespeare had a stock company, and he used to write for the different personalities. The reason there seems to have been something like a star system is that, if you read his plays, there are a lot of parts in them that are very important: he took care of his people. Autolycus, for instance, isn't important to the story-telling, but is brought in around the edges. It seems to me that Shakespeare's construction indicates that he was saying to himself, 'We've got this Will Kemp under contract—we've got to write something for him.' "

Lahr had his troubles with Shakespeare. The language confused him; and the songs were even more difficult. After the first day of rehearsal, he confided to a reporter, "I'm not worried. But those songs! Well, this is the first time I've done them on my feet and the damn lyrics. I'll get them. They don't make sense. 'Doxie in the dale,' 'the pug in the teeth' or whatever it is. I don't even know the words yet."

Lahr loved playing Bottom, especially the hilarious performance the dim-witted weaver gives in his role as Pyramus. (Later, Lahr would draft a scenario for a musical comedy based on Bottom, allowing him to improvise Shakespeare and play the comedy scenes as written but under commercial conditions.) Bottom's self-importance and his blundering had their equivalent in Lahr's burlesque drunken cop. Lahr understood the character immediately, playing the part as if he never knew the joke. He had learned from *Godot* and *Paradiso* that legitimacy added to the fun. "I played it serious. I was bumbling through it all. I was overdramatic. I did it as legitimate as I knew how. I don't think there was anything *different* in playing Bottom." He had a personal idea of Bottom's predicament.

> Bottom is a—a layman, an artisan. He's a weaver who portrays ninety per cent of the people of the world, with an ego, an exhibitionistic complex—we all have. You talk to anybody, they'll either say I've wanted to be an actor, my daughter is gonna be an actress. I think that's a natural trait, and it must have been in that time too, they had amateur groups that were bumblers . . . And that's the main comedy vein of this thing, but I think it's basically a story of love. Even the laymen, the artisans, they have a love for the Duke and they want to do something for him. But it's travesty, it's burlesque . . .
> *Actors Talk About Acting*

Lahr was conscious of Bottom's responses toward others as much as his *faux pas*. "The laughter was mostly an attitude, a reaction to Thisbe, to the court audience when they were making fun of me. They'd laugh at me. I'd get angry. I always wanted to get off, leave the stage. Some of them would hold me back. I'd always complain to Quince in pantomime what they were doing to me, that they were so bad . . ."

Lahr proudly claimed that he never changed a word of Shakespeare's text ("there are a lot of people out front, devotees, who know the play better than you do, and if you change the text they resent it"). But he added his own touches to Bottom's disastrous denouement as Pyramus. He was able to move the role from travesty to something more human and complex—a situation approaching satire.

When a wardrobe mistress offered to taper Bottom's outfit for him, Lahr got an idea, from which he fashioned the rest of his performance. "I had them make a special belt which I had fixed so that the dagger I wore in the scene really held up the belt. When I took the dagger and stabbed myself, I did a death scene with my pants falling down." He added an extra fillip by trying to wriggle back into the pants like a child catching up with a hula hoop. Lahr also managed to get sufficiently annoyed at Thisbe as they spoke through the wall that he stuck his fingers in her eyes. "It was one of the biggest laughing scenes I've ever done."

Lahr's buffoonery shared much with the Shakespearean wildness. As a clown he had always carried his exploration of sounds and gestures beyond the demands of ordinary speech. These flights of spontaneity related to Shakespearean tradition, and made it easy for him to adapt to Bottom's style, even if it sometimes was incomprehensible to drama critics.

Interviewer: You say that you put gnong, gnong, gnong here in the role of Bottom because you felt it fitted. Yet you may change it—why?

Lahr: You see, the reason I may change it is this. I don't think that Shakespeare, when he wrote this, ever figured a fella would do that. I understand that whoever played Bottom made noises like a donkey or some sound that conveyed that it was braying. . . . I will let the audience decide . . . They're liable to say what the hell is he putting that in here for.

Interviewer: Have you made a study of all sounds of animals?

Lahr: No, no. I've made a study of nothing.

Interviewer: You just neighed like a horse.

Lahr: Well, you hear a horse, you hear a horse! I did it one day, and it sounded all right. I never neighed like a horse before.

Actors Talk About Acting

Even though repertory added prestige to his career, he was not anxious to carry on work in the classics. "They've asked me to do Falstaff and the gravedigger in *Hamlet* at Stratford. I thought Falstaff was too much of a departure at my age, too much of a challenge. I just didn't want to work that hard. I'm a perfectionist, when I go into a thing, I work hard. Falstaff would be a tremendous job."

But the reviews from his Shakespeare tour are mounted on a placard in his bedroom; and his success made him something of a Shakespearean scholar at the Lambs Club. Complaining about material, yet spurning the classics; fretting over money, but looking upon repertory work as the last resort ("I guess if I needed to eat, I'd do it"), Lahr's intentions are contradicted by his instincts for theatrical excellence.

Why does he balk? His comedy has awed critics and been catered to by America's theatrical talent—but he refuses to see himself as a creator. In his eyes, he is a craftsman, in as mundane an enterprise as his father's upholstery business. Repertory theater raises an idea of work for which he has neither the social conscience nor the youthful zest. Can comedy be taught? Can actors learn from something as private as Lahr's personal movements? People have told him "yes"; he is flattered by their confidence, but cynical of the outcome. In his experience, theatrical history is made by individuals. His theater training conceived the stage as an individual vehicle, not a group sport. He resists anything that hints at idealism. "Will you stop this artistic stuff!" he says, in one of his many final statements on the subject. "I know my business. Okay, so maybe it would be more satisfying to do *Waiting for Godot* off-Broadway or join the APA. But you can't pay your rent with a bag of satisfaction, can you?" His infuriating materialism is contradicted by another insecurity. "You've already sold me to the repertory. What makes you think they'd want me? They haven't asked me."

Repertory theater may offer the possibility for change in the performing arts, but Lahr cannot understand the necessity for it. His eyes can only see the last testaments of old-world "quality." Mansions have given way to skyscrapers; theater people are now "intellectuals." Comedy, as he knew it, has gone out of vogue, its present practitioners self-conscious and limited; actors are overpraised and undertrained. Even the nature of entertainment has taken a turn for the worse in his eyes. Where once songs had sheen and polish, they are now jagged with social protest and statement that offend his sense of simple diversion. Movies (mostly foreign) astound him with their frankness. ("Why, I've seen everything there is to see on the screen. Nothing's left to the imagination.") He sees decadence in the present without understanding the injustices of the past. "Once, when I was up in Poole's buying shoes (I think they were seventy dollars then, now they're a hundred and thirty) an old lady said something I'll never forget. She told me, 'Young man, the one thing this generation has lost is a sense of *quality*.' And you know, she was right."

Lahr cannot see the quality in repertory or the importance of his participation in it. Sitting in front of his television, shaking his head in disgust at the headlines, he moves away from the world. He dreams of getting away from the city he can never leave, of learning Spanish in order to live cheaply in Majorca or getting a cottage on an inland Florida waterway so he can fish and breathe "good air," returning to New York when jobs come up. His voice rises when he contemplates his vision. He points, without looking into anyone's eyes, toward the world he fears. "Filth! Rape! Beatniks! . . . That's what we have today in everything. In our movies, on our stages, in our society. What is it? Can you tell me? It can't be a reaction to the War, that's been over nearly twenty years."

Lahr's final bout with the classics was in 1966, when he played Pisthetairos in Aristophanes' *The Birds* in the first (and last) Ypsilanti Greek Theater Festival in Michigan, a curious repertory venture that spent a half million dollars to revive ancient literature and to lure stars to participate in the event. For Lahr, the part (as well as the price) was right. He was receiving thirty-five hundred dollars a week for four performances, a car, and free hotel accomodations. A similar contract had been arranged for Dame Judith Anderson (Lahr refers to her ambiguously as "The Dame"), who was starring in Aeschylus' *Oresteia*. The repertory intention reflected the usual regional confusion between cultural excellence and booster spirit. By committing itself to the star system necessary to attract tourists to the region, the Festival unwittingly initiated the economics of inevitable destruction. Before the plays even opened, the Festival had run out of funds; it was forced to solicit its operating costs of thirty-nine thousand dollars each week during its four-month engagement.

When *The New York Times* announced Lahr's adventure, it was not hard to see the proximity of Aristophanes' intention to Lahr's obsessions.

> The character Mr. Lahr will play is sick of bureaucracy, high prices, and taxes. He wants to leave a war-exhausted country to live in Cloud-Cuckoo Land (a sort of Utopia situation between gods and men), where he can live in peace.

If the impulse of Greek comedy was to thumb one's nose at authority, Lahr had an instinctive sympathy with the political anarchy Aristophanes was suggesting to Athens in the fifth century B.C. The Greek comic theater had resembled a musical revue, with songs and dancing. Its comedians had been given free rein in the festivities, with the ultimate effect being more theatrical than literary. Lahr responded to Aristophanes' free-wheeling format; Aristophanic humor, like Lahr's, came from a conservative impulse that was skeptical of change. As he admitted to *Newsweek:* "I never knew Aristophanes was a writer of comedy . . . I did this stuff in burlesque. His stuff is all such fun and satire—of religion, legislators, avarice, war. He was a reformer, even more than Dickens—that's what I think in my unerudite way."

Lahr was in for more surprises. The director, Alexis Solomos, who had made his reputation directing Greek comedy, sent assistants to block Lahr's show, a Greek custom that confounded the American star. The score to *The Birds* was not available until two weeks before opening. But most ludicrous of all, the translation on which Lahr had accepted the job (Walter Kerr's) was changed on arrival because the director, heeding the advice of a Michigan classics professor, had chosen the William Arrowsmith version. In all this confusion, the American star system and the repertory idea locked horns.

Lahr found the translation unactable, hollow instead of sensuous, antique where it should have been current. "It was stilted and dull. It wasn't funny; there weren't any jokes in it. I understand that in Greek comedy the comedian was supposed to take charge and do anything he wanted in the play." With this vague historical mandate, Lahr instituted his own changes. In one speech Pisthetairos bemoans the many degradations to the bird kingdom, one of which is being served as food. Arrowsmith translated the Greek:

> And then you're taken, they sell you
> as tiny hors d'oeuvres for a lunch
> And you're not even sold alone
> but lumped and bought by the bunch.

Lahr cut out everything in the stanza but the most visceral response— to eating. His rewrites are more playful and vivid:

> They hunt and kill you when they can.
> And if that isn't enough, they fling you
> in a dish, throw sauce in your face, and
> call you a casserole, a fricassee,
> a la cacciatore . . .

In Lahr's mouth, the word "fricassee" becomes as scurrilous a blasphemy as "zounds."

The impulse to make the classics contemporary has become fashionable over the years. If Lahr rewrote in order to perform the work, he ran into conflicts with Aristophanes' outspokenness. Lahr, who loved the vulgar, balked at blatant use of it. "Some of the lines in the translation are salacious; and I thought they would offend the audience. There's such a thing as doing double entendre cleverly. You couldn't say 'shit' or 'fart' and do it subtly, could you? I had to say other things. Ruby Dee played the goddess Iris, and one of my lines to her was, 'You sail my way again and I'll lay my course up your beautiful legs; and believe me, you'll be one flabbergasted goddess when you feel the triple ram of this old hulk.' Having a following of children through *The Wizard of Oz* and the commercials, I thought it would hurt my career, so I refused to do it. The director insisted that I speak the lines. Well, I did it for one performance in our first preview. Every time I said these words, you could feel a natural tenseness and absolute silence in the audience. No laughter—nothing. The next day, the Ypsilanti paper came out and said the play was not only vulgar but totally unacceptable to the audience in Ypsilanti, which I knew it would be. It was a church-going community, and I was almost sure that, if these words weren't deleted, the ministers would go to their pulpits and preach against it. I had no recourse but to call Equity."

Suddenly the defender of public morals, Lahr wanted to expurgate the text. His role of censor got national attention; but his censorship was tenuous. His tomcat's leer mocked his official statements to the contrary. What he really wanted was to eliminate vulgarity without wit. But he was at home with innuendo when defying the audience and speaking, as Aristophanes' henchman, back at the critics.

> Every bird will take to the air and cover you
> With the vilest vituperation.

For a man who balked at obscenity on stage, his biggest laugh came when Pisthetairos and his crony watch a female bird being hotly pursued by a male. When the crony inquired about the species of her lover, Lahr replied, "That must be her husband—the horny pecker."

Lahr thought of leaving the production instead of making a tedious and painful stand about it. Mildred, writing from his trailer dressing room adjacent to the ball field, confided —

> I really feel for your father. He is having great difficulty with the words. I'm afraid to say anything for fear he'll quit. I think this is important for his career.

An Equity ruling assured Lahr's stay at Ypsilanti. They said that while the director had artistic control of the production, Lahr did not have to say anything he did not think proper for the stage. The news was leaked to the press; and Lahr became the topic of controversy.

The most vociferous attack come from John Ciardi of *Saturday Review,* who, although he had not read Arrowsmith's stage translation or seen the production, skewered Lahr for hiding his career behind children. Arrowsmith was a renowned Greek scholar; and in tampering with academic truth, Lahr raised invective as well as eyebrows. "The obscenity wasn't funny," says Lahr. "It was against all the basics of theater—which is enjoyment. I wanted to make the audience laugh—

which I did. If I hadn't rewritten that translation and played it the way it was—audiences would have walked out." Ciardi saw things differently, offended by Lahr's claim that the language was "not fit for children" and anxious to point out that vulgarity, violence, and sexuality were swallowed wholesale by adolescents with every television hour.

> No, Mr. Lahr, it won't work. If your psyche feels uneasy about the vocabulary of Aristophanic gusto, that of course is understandable. . . . You don't know me, Mr. Lahr, and I can't reasonably ask you to take my word for the essential Greek of it. But I know you do know Arrowsmith and I know he will bear me out. If you really want to know something about Greek theater, ask him. And if you don't want to know about it, what are you doing in it . . . I know you mean well—or I'm willing to pretend I believe so—but I insist on believing Aristophanes meant better . . .
>
> August 13, 1966

Lahr was protecting his audience, but also himself. He was not a moralist, although his laughter burlesqued human values. He lived for an audience's response and in fear of its silence. Critics, like Ciardi, argued in the name of poetry, but Lahr was trying to keep alive the comic intention on stage. Lahr's freedom, his comic ad libs, were in the Aristophanic tradition. As Robert Corrigan points out in his essay on Aristophanes—

> Like our late George S. Kaufman, or more recently Bob Hope, Aristophanes was a master of the phraseology and attitude of the wisecrack. But the basic strategy of the wisecrack is to keep the audience with you.

Lahr knew he could not hold an audience's good spirits with vulgarity; he also realized that Greek mythology and politics were dusty footnotes to contemporary life. He appended his assortment of modernisms. When Ruby Dee made a spectacular "flying" entrance, Lahr put her in place, exclaiming, "You interplanetary Peter Pan." When a two-man horse cantered in, Lahr topped the gag, saying, "Ye Gods, it's Pegasus." He sang the "Road to Mandalay," relying on his vibrato "m's" to carry to the back of the ball park; and he stumbled hilariously over ancient Greek names ("Agamem-nem-nem")—with the same droll simplicity he spelled them out phonetically in his script. He dismissed poet and priest as ruler of Cloud-Cuckoo Land with blows from an inflated bladder; and his cop act echoed through his retorts to a finely plumed female who strutted by—"Great Zeus, what a hunk of stuff!" Occasionally, he was forced to comment on the planes that droned over the stadium or the weather, which interrupted many afternoons in the amphitheater. After one thunderstorm, which left the stage looking like an aerial photograph of the Great Lakes, Lahr entered and, noticing the puddles, observed, "This is the biggest birdbath in the world."

Lahr's performance was Aristophanic even if the production was not. The music was reduced to the clarion call of a burlesque trumpet; the dances were cut, at the last minute, by the director. Yet Lahr's performance had a fullness that compensated for a cast not completely professional and an enterprise that never made up its mind whether it was opting for Broadway or repertory. The London *Times* was, perhaps, the most judicious appraiser of the performance, commenting that *The Birds* offered "the spectacle of Lahr in spirited but unequal combat with literature."

The spectacle had a humor and special integrity for his family, who watched him work in temperatures that mounted to 100° on the open stage. The man who slumped in his dressing-room chair during intermission with a thermometer in his mouth, worrying about his health, the audience, the New York Mets, his children's seats, took surprising charge of himself on stage. The performance discovered dimensions of energy that the audience saw only as carefree delight.

He loped off stage like a startled cow—ungainly and cumbersome, trying to remain inconspicuous in his old age. At the end of the play—his nose reddened like a burlesque top banana, his back decorated with flimsy feathers—his movements recalled many evenings in other roles and the fantasies he had tried to tell us as children. The conviction of his playing expressed an understanding beyond the words he knew for it. His face was wrinkled like an apple too long in the sun; his head festooned with a hat that made him look like a Jewish cockatoo. He rode haughtily astride a chariot, his eyebrows at self-important right angles to his eyes. He won the Queen; he flourished the thunderbolt; and for two hours, at least, he ruled the world with a hellion's gaiety. The key to the city of Ypsilanti (and his salary) never seemed as substantial as his playing or the enjoyment he created.

Ypsilanti proved that low-comic humor, as a specialty, could pass for satire but not substitute for it. Critics would praise Lahr's artistry while bemoaning the tameness of the adaptation. Lahr, predictably, pointed to the box-office receipts, where *The Birds* outgrossed *Oresteia*.

He had helped the festival acquire international attention in its first year; but his salary foreshadowed the inevitable extinction of such classical junkets for the future. He had managed, at seventy, to turn a sure disaster into an enjoyable evening. But it was a fatuous and finally self-destructive battle, a fight he waged often during the decade to maintain his own sense of theater for audiences whose view of the world had been changed by mass media. Ypsilanti was a personal success. But the Festival had been drained of funds, its intention being impossible to fulfill under Ypsilanti's self-imposed circumstances.

Television absorbed the comedy sketch, emasculating much of its verve and poignancy. Isolated in hot studios, usually cut off from any audience by a clutter of cables, cameras, and arc lights, the comedian was forced into an electronic vacuum. Deprived of the live response that is so necessary to comic invention, the comedy routines were more often hollow than hilarious. If comedians found television lucrative, they also faced a faster demise through overexposure. Lahr worried about appearing too often on television. In burlesque, *What's the Idea* played years without repeating a theater; now, one Ed Sullivan performance limited the sketch to a single airing every eighteen months. Lahr appeared approximately four times a year on the Sullivan show, a variety entertainment that sustained his old revue routines. New material was expensive, and immediately consumed. Although Lahr considered a television comedy series (and even made a pilot film for it), he was not enthusiastic about the project. He felt there was little challenge to television; but it paid the bills. In the mid-fifties he had done good work on *Omnibus,* a cultural television event long defunct, high-brow and well-intentioned. Lahr played in Molière's *School for Wives* and Shaw's *Androcles and the Lion* and also narrated an *Omnibus* reminiscence written by S. J. Perelman on the delights of burlesque. But quality television was rare; and Lahr considered himself lucky when he had high-caliber material. His last major performance was as Hucklebee, the obstreperous father, in *The Fantasticks* on the Hallmark Hall of Fame, a show that allowed him to sing and grimace within a more relevant framework than a network spectacular. But comedy itself had been changed by the television camera.

With the comic image shrunk to twenty-one inches on the screen, the force and outrageousness of laughter was depleted. The mechanism of buffoonery—the body, the antics, even the prankish texture of language—was limited to the clumsy scope of the camera's eye and the censor's ear. The static quality of television developed a different emphasis in humor. Lahr watched the rise of another (and to his mind, lesser) form of comedy during the late fifties and early sixties. Mort Sahl, Shelley Berman, Mike Nichols and Elaine May were stand-up comedians who brought laughter back to a satire of ideas. Their wit was verbal and eminently suited to a medium that is most comfortable when focusing on static figures.

The new monologues were analytic and political. The laughter of the late fifties acknowledged a nation dubious of power; a middle-class life that brought its special deadening after-effects. There was no longer the wonder and generosity in the humor that had filled Lahr's burlesque intentions, but rather an incisive questioning of societal and human foibles. The new comedians talked with a candor and argot that sometimes violated Lahr's sense of stage decorum. He could never flagellate an audience with the corrosive honesty of a Lenny Bruce or tread thin political ice like Mort Sahl. Lahr's comic vision evolved with movement within a situation; theirs had a more cerebral point of view. Lahr was not verbal about life, nor could he be quiet on stage. Sadly, the comic sketch—no matter how talented—had a style and regularity on television that tended to meld the good with the bad. Many of Lahr's famous sketches were unsuitable for the medium either because they were similar to those performed by network stars (sometimes stolen from Lahr's repertoire) or too high-spirited for an invisible audience.

Lahr returned to Broadway in 1959, not with the classics, but in the familiar format of the revue. The effect of television on its content was obvious. *The Girls Against the Boys* intended to cater to both the Broadway audience and the new television tastes. Lahr teamed with Nancy Walker, another favorite of Broadway *aficianados*. The cast was complemented by two recruits from television—Dick Van Dyke and Shelley Berman. Lahr admits the show was a mistake. "It wasn't our fault—little Nancy's or mine—we had very little help. But what we heard at the start, how it was explained to us, looked exciting."

In theory the show attempted to parlay two types of comic trends, but in practice managed to cancel each of them out. Devoted to the idea of pleasure, the revue floundered because, with the changes of taste, it was not quite sure how to please. Lahr felt at home with the revue and its intentions; the prestige of the classics never provided the appeal of a revue sketch's laughter. Nancy Walker was second only to Bea Lillie in his admiration. Her body, blunted like a thumb, her face as chiseled as a figure off a Greek frieze—she was an effective foil for Lahr. In the show, she performed her stumpy ballet impressions as well as parodying, with Lahr, the fashion of rock 'n roll. By pairing Lahr and Walker, the revue evoked, without realizing it, a hint of theatrical nostalgia and self-congratulation.

The theme of the battle between the sexes for a revue was so worn that only something which acknowledged the peculiarities of contemporary thinking from Wilhelm Reich to Simone de Beauvoir could have provided exciting, fresh terrain. *The Girls Against the Boys* did not. While Walter Kerr emphasized a "softness" in the fun machine ("a musical revue, by heaven, is no place for sentiment"), one scene between Lahr and Miss Walker was memorable for its bone-honest focus on the hatreds of marriage and its secret dependencies. The sketch, "Hostility" (see Appendix 7), takes place in a slovenly one-room tenement. Miss Walker is discovered giving herself a pedicure, cotton threaded through the toes of both feet. Lahr enters wearing a construction helmet and a frown. The wolf-faced wife confronts her meatball husband. His disgusted grunts match her gorgon's glower. They proceed to ritual combat, living out their hatred with silent infighting: slamming tables, eating noisily, clattering dishes. He wants to be served as Master; instead, he is treated as cavalierly as a dog. The house is in a perennial state of siege. Finally, Lahr and Walker retire to their Murphy bed. Lahr undresses and, half asleep, flops under the covers; Miss Walker fidgets daintily with her housecoat. The final and only dialogue ensues:

Nancy: Eddie, Eddie.
Lahr: (Grunts.)
Nancy: You forgot something.
(Lahr kisses her.)
(Blackout)

Sentiment rarely crept into Lahr's comedy. He wanted the audience to feel sympathy for him as a performer, but the characters he created were never emotional toward the world. The cop, the woodsman, the baritone, the near-sighted eye doctor, the baseball player were all creations for the musical revue. Their appeal rested on the inability of the character to understand his egotism and his idiosyncracies. The humor lay in this lack of self-awareness. Sentiment came when the characters began to understand what they were about.

On opening night, the family was in the audience and the spirit of nostalgia—even to the young—was unmistakable. At the end of the performance, Lahr in tuxedo and Miss Walker in evening dress sang a jaunty old-fashioned duet. When they took their bows, my father looked down at the audience to the fourth row, where we were sitting. It was the only time he acknowledged us from the stage. There was a thrill for us in that gesture.

"Hostility" could not salvage *The Girls Against the Boys*. The show lasted two weeks—a victim of material neither contemporary nor incisive.

In his next show, S. J. Perelman's *The Beauty Part* (1962), Lahr embodied satire pertinent to the contemporary society. In it, Perelman, who had sent the Marx Brothers through a series of merry escapades and who admired Lahr as the "last of the great clowns," satirized the emerging middle-class preoccupation with culture. Perelman created a series of loosely connected vignettes in which the eager son of a rich garbage-disposal manufacturer marches into the world to meet culture in all its arenas. Voltaire had sent Candide to test his ideals against the world in much the same spirit.

Perelman claims that the play was born when an elevator operator, recognizing him as the famous *New Yorker* satirist, confided, "I'm having trouble with my second act." He set about creating a play from a few of his New York short stories, using his special ear for the hilarious dead word and his precise eye for the dishonest. As a playwright, Perelman once defined his growing understanding of the craft, an explanation with special pertinence to his appreciation of Lahr. "A playwright is a tailor—he has to fit the pants to a man who will stand in front of a triple mirror. The actor has to get up and withstand the scorn." Writing for Groucho, Perelman had learned the vicissitudes of the comic mind; Lahr was a different experience. "Groucho was distrustful of me because he thought I was too literary. We had constant fights about this subject. 'Oh yes,' he'd say, 'I like it, but what about the barber in Peru?' This was a fear of his—that the barber in Peru, Indiana, wouldn't understand the literary references. But with Bert Lahr, for some happy reason, my material attained some kind of secondary value. He was able to take what I wrote and interpret it perfectly."

Lahr portrayed five of Perelman's gargoyles, from a lady editor to the omnivorous agent-type whom Lahr knew so well. Perelman's fascination with cultural consumption had correlatives in Lahr's frame of reference. His children, growing into maturity, had surprised him. His dream of financial security for them was contradicted by their cultural interests. His daughter had become a sculptress, creating forms that astounded his sense of proportion. ("What's that? You mean that's a woman? That's no woman I've ever seen!") His son showed an interest in writing. ("Do it in your spare time.") Lahr himself had contemplated taking up painting—a pastime he later acquired, turning out lions to satisfy public demand. ("Of course, I'm not as good as Cagney. I need technique. Tonight, I'll try a flower. You think I could get money for these? No kidding!")

The predicaments of the characters were as familiar as the general cultural boom. He understood the forces of greed and ego that whittled at their hearts. His favorite part was Harry Hubris, a conniving theatrical agent, a subject on which he was as outspoken on stage as off it. The judge, Herman Rinderbrust, appealed to him because he confirmed Lahr's worst suspicions about the legal system and the undermining of law and order. ("Some thug kills a guy and runs into a house. He could have enough dope to turn on Pittsburgh; but the police have to knock first and state their business. What is this, Amy Vanderbilt?") The fine points of justice escape him, but his reaction to the fraudulent judge mugging in front of TV cameras is genuine. Even Nelson Smedley, a character frozen in paranoia about a vague Communism, brushed with Lahr's life. No comedian should ever be held to his political beliefs; but Lahr had been enlisted for good causes and bad. He rarely discriminated, justifying his appearance to testify as a character witness on behalf of Senator Joe McCarthy's right-hand man, Roy Cohn, in a suit brought by the attorney general's office in 1964 this way: "Well, I followed Cardinal Spellman."

The rest of Perelman's cultural brigands were as humorous as the ones created for Lahr to portray. Perelman spared few targets. A book publisher and lecturer, whose company—Charnel House—specialized in big movie sales and promotion hokum left little doubt as to Perelman's prototype. Emmett Stagg, the publisher, is quick to acknowledge his real-life identity. In a phone call for the purpose of luring a potential novelist (writing the story of the Civil War "as seen through the eyes of a Creole call girl") into his establishment, Stagg confides:

> Harry, I've got a book. No, I'm not going to let you read it. I'm just going to tell you one thing. (Chuckles.) It'll be a tidal wave, and I'm letting you in on my surfboard. You've got first crack at the movie rights for three hundred G's.

Perelman could skewer Establishment celebrity in a line. As Emmett Stagg says, "In the aristocracy of success, there are no strangers." Perelman also lowered his sights on foundations and the art sponsored by philanthropic money. A sculptress, played with tight-lipped ferocity by Charlotte Rae, creates objects in Castile soap on a Proctor & Gamble Fellowship. The hand of commerce sullies every aspect of the arts: a Mondrian painting turns into a bar; an action painter sells out to Hollywood for a percentage of the gross; an art collector buys her paintings so "they don't clash with the drapes." Even Milo Weatherwax, Perelman's lecherous millionaire, shared with Lahr the vacant prestige of sending a son to Yale. But unlike Perelman's character, Lahr never knew what year of college his son was in.

When *The Beauty Part* tried out in Bucks County during the summer of 1961, it was apparent to Lahr that he had finally found a vehicle that cuffed the ears of his audience without bludgeoning them. The show needed reworking, but Lahr had complete faith in Perelman, the only living satirist who could bring tears of laughter to him on the printed page. Even before Lahr went into full rehearsal, he was telling the press: "This is the funniest material I've ever had." When Jane and I hitchhiked to Bucks County to see the show and camped in the producer's corn field, my father joined us, eating hamburgers and telling us how to build a better fire. The fact that he took time off from work was significant to us; the image of him staring into the flames, his arm around Jane, his tweed rehearsal cap pushed to the back of his head, is memorable for its sense of quiet confidence.

Perelman and Lahr seemed an unlikely team. I remember them sitting in a coffee shop across from the Shubert Theater in New Haven when the play began its pre-Broadway tryouts in 1962. They confronted each other in avid discussion. Perelman, with brush mustache and wire-rimmed glasses, fitted the image of a dry littérateur, or a well-preened buyer for Sotheby's. Small and quiet, he spoke carefully, with a hint of hardness in his voice. Perelman accepted Lahr's suggestions and his worry with stoic kindness. Perelman's mind, like his choice of clothes, was careful and stylized. Whatever his emotions, his image to the world was one of aloof propriety. Their rapport was immediate. In private, the civilized veneer of that relationship was sometimes questioned. "He's rough. He's rough. He wanted every line to stay just the way he wrote it. Finally, Noel Willman, the director, told him before we came into New York that some of them had to be changed."

In New Haven, Perelman stayed close to the theater while Lahr took small tours of the Yale campus. From his Taft Hotel suite he photographed New Haven. He had paid his son's tuition; and now the property was his too. His own education had been a failure. But staring out at the campus he could see his accomplishment. He had brought his family a long way from the desolate possibilities of Yorkville. Yale was as stylized as his English shoes. He liked its customs, and its quaintness.

Serenaded by the Whiffenpoofs at Mory's or standing on the steps of the library, culture and "the top dollar" seemed hand in hand. He had opened many shows in New Haven, but never ventured inside the campus. Now, professors stopped him on the street; students from an academic world he could never imagine asked for his autograph. His work had created all these opportunities; the institution seemed to exist as a suave and polished reminder of his labor. Yet the ultimate joke and pathos about Yale, as for Perelman's Harry Hubris, was that the institution was valued as a commodity. Hubris, pointing to young Lance's university letter-sweater says, "Back to the 'Y' and take a cold shower." Lahr's work was a business that generations with more leisure and opportunity might study as art. But, like Hubris, he saw himself as a product, and the world as a marketplace where the gaudiest object earned the highest bid.

The show had a great many difficulties on the road: it was uneven, wordy, and, for Lahr, precariously political. The play's final gesture was money flung in the audience's face—as venomous a satiric statement as Broadway entertainment has ever seen. Milo Weatherwax, the millionaire patron, entered carrying a bassinet.

> Yes, I'll fess up to same, hardened cynic though I am. (Clears his throat) Friends, this little bundle of happiness is everybody's joy. We must cherish it—share it with us, won't you?

In New Haven, people rushed up front to grab it. The moment was the culmination of Perelman's intellectual disdain. Lahr's munificence brought laughter and indulged his private fantasies, while, at the same time, disturbing him. "I said things out there that were strongly against my politics. I didn't agree with many of Perelman's comments, but the man is adept with absurdities. He makes people laugh. I don't think the actor should voice his own opinions on stage. I don't think it's very important that I understand everything or give my views."

Because Perelman turned burlesque situations to literate ends, Lahr referred to *The Beauty Part* as "egghead" entertainment. He was secretly suspicious, but there was a barometer by which Perelman could tell Lahr's sentiments. "He wore a cap at rehearsals, and when he became genuinely devoted to a comic suggestion, he would automatically turn it around like an old automobile racer." In New Haven, many of Perelman's characters, like the woman editor—Hyacinth Beddoes Laffoon—were fleshed out. "I wrote the thing about Fleur Cowles, but by the time Bert translated it, it wasn't campy or at all offensive. I meant it to be offensive in another sense. Many comedians would have set your teeth on edge. Lahr didn't. He was portraying an old bitch there, a domineering old woman who kept knocking off the heads of her assistants."

The sketch, according to Noel Willman, began brilliantly but didn't go anywhere; the weight of responsibility fell to Lahr. "He had wonderful ideas about it. He'd do something and one would say, 'Bert, that's marvelous!' He'd stammer, 'What did I do?' You'd think he really did not know and you'd wonder how to get him to do it again. This happened several times. There was one moment when he came around from behind his desk and sat on it. He's discussing a magazine idea:

> A naked girl tied to a bed post and a chimpanzee brandishing a whip. No more punch than a seed catalogue.

"Bert used to do a thing there that was marvelously observed and imaginative. It had something to do with the way women with a choker necklace would suddenly free their necks from them. That didn't come from comedy, it came from acting. It was difficult to tell him that. He would get alarmed because he couldn't be quite sure what you wanted. You'd try and get him to do it again. I'd say, 'No Bert, that's not what you did before.' He'd say, 'Show me, show me.' He would try and do it, but it wouldn't happen. Because you would go at him, he would then go off in tangents and suddenly do things which were too extreme, too much, often vulgar. Bert had exquisite taste; it was when he tried to intellectualize, like remembering something he had done, that he went wrong. The same was true of his suggestions. The lines he would go

home and think about were invariably no good. If he suddenly improvised a line in rehearsal or performance it was invariably marvelous."

At times, Perelman's ear for pompous verbiage had just the right
meter for Lahr's nasal, baritone voice. When Milo enters to female
squeals off stage, he says to his wife:

> Now, look here, Octavia, I just had to give our French maid a
> severe dressing down . . .

However, Lahr had difficulty with some of Perelman's convoluted
literary cadences. Perelman's combination of hifalutin English and
Yiddish jargon could keep Lahr's exuberance from taking control.
When Lance discovers to his chagrin, that his fortune comes from
garbage, Milo replies:

> Steady on, lad. After all, think of the millions which, were it not
> for our kindly ministrations, their homes would be a welter of
> chicken bones, fruit peels, and rancid yogurt.

Perelman struggled to adapt his most baroque rhythms to Lahr's vocal
range. The tension was healthy but frustrating. Perelman's language
took on an economy and dramatic impact it sometimes lacked on the
printed page.

The play was well received in New Haven, but ran aground in the
second act, unable to build to a proper explosive conclusion. Despite
these worries, Lahr never was more confident of his material. *The
Beauty Part* was his first comedy to venture so blatantly into the area
of political statement. He felt a kind of creative danger in the play.
He was also playing five different roles, most of them departures from
his usual rogues' gallery. On the closing night in New Haven, I watched
him rush to catch the midnight milk train to New York. Talking over
his shoulder, his make-up still on, his valise trailing half a shirt sleeve
—I was overwhelmed by my father's swelling energy, the hope that
buttressed the hard work ahead in Philadelphia and New York.

In Philadelphia, Perelman was faced with the problem of creating
a scene, adding vinegar to a section of the second act that dwindled to
sentiment. Borrowing the setting—a hothouse—from the Raymond
Chandler fiction he admired, Perelman conceived the Nelson Smedley
sketch in which Lahr was an aged and cantankerous redbaiter, obsessed by the threat of imminent invasion. "When I read it to Bert,"
says Perelman, "I thought he was a little frightened at first. He thought

that this was too political. He said to me, 'Wait a minute, couldn't somebody think that this sketch was a defense of Communism?' I said, 'Don't be ridiculous. As a matter of fact, everyone is so fed up with redbaiting that we might have some success with it.' I asked him to try it. He was wary, but we went ahead. The minute the laughs began to roll back I could see that Bert would never part with the thing. He took what was pretty wild stuff and gave it an extra dimension."

Lahr's improvisations were especially important in the Smedley sketch. "The basic scene was Perelman's invention," explains Noel Willman. "When Bert read this, I was enchanted with him saying to me, 'Noel, now listen, you have to help me with this because I've never played an old man before.' I was terribly charmed, but doubly so when he proceeded to give one of the most stunning performances of an old man that has ever been given. In rehearsal, Lahr would suddenly take lines and change them, often to Perelman's rage. If you examine the sketch, there is less Perelman wit, less Perelman rococo. It is much simpler, closer to a burlesque sketch. There are two reasons for this. First of all, Sid did not have time to polish it; secondly, Lahr gave it this frenzied objective quality. When we began, the sketch had a lot of plot. By the time Bert had finished with rehearsals, we had cut it to the minimum plot line. I thought it was an amusing idea when Sid sat down to write it. I had no idea it was going to be the best thing in the show."

The Beauty Part opened on the brink of the 1963 newspaper strike. Although the critics received it warmly, publicity was drastically limited. In Broadway vernacular, it was a "laughing show." "I sat there and watched people laugh and roll until tears came down their cheeks and they held their sides" was the testament of one critic. But the serious target of the laughter, the well-aimed barbs at America's cultural pretenders, was surprisingly new to Broadway entertainment. It confused some observers, who, while enjoying themselves, were quick to dismiss the play as a cartoon or draw the facile parallel between Perelman as literary satirist and playwright. The social questions raised by the play were almost forgotten by critics who found the laughter more easy to describe than cultural hypocrisy. As Robert Brustein pointed out in *The New Republic,* "The middle-class spectator, whatever his private affections, does not usually like to see money stroked in public." Broadway was, perhaps, the wrong location to launch a debate about democracy and culture. But Perelman as a satirist wanted to bring his vision into the enemy camp. With Lahr as a vehicle of exchange, he had a fine chance to infiltrate middle-class imaginations. Perelman was bold enough to place the show in front of the audience it was about. This was a moralist's tactic, as well as the instincts of a commercial writer. Lahr assured the good spirits and theatrical clarity; but the newspaper strike prevented *The Beauty Part* from reaching the audience it deserved.

The Beauty Part was the most original script Lahr received in a decade. Its quick demise deprived Broadway of a theatrical satirist of immense potential and a comic performance of stunning range. Lahr's sadness about the show's closing did not intervene in his commercial considerations. Perelman wrote him frequently urging him to consent to a London production, where Perelman reigned as the King of American humorists, and where Lahr had never tested his talent. Lahr refused. "They just couldn't pay my price." In 1966, when he was finally promised a salary that would have made him the highest-paid performer ever on the English stage (five hundred pounds a week), he agreed to perform it, only to have the opportunity fizzle. As a consequence, a fine show bowed to the demands of commercial theater.

Where was Lahr's stage future? At sixty-eight, the critics confirmed his significance to American theater history and their allegiance to him. When he weighed public enthusiasm against his theatrical prospects, he was faced with laughable conclusions. His way of working and the content of his comedy could not find a form to suit evolving theatrical tastes. The abrupt closing of *The Beauty Part* had shocked him, although he seemed outwardly resigned. He was too old a trouper not to know the theatrical facts of life. Times change, people change, even a comedian's ear numbs to acclaim. But unlike many of his comic colleagues, Lahr's career had not faltered, nor had his popularity plummeted. The public maintained him as a comic star and applauded his efforts. His comedy demanded a scope and popularity commensurate with that stardom. The revue format proved to be hollow; and satire had not won wide audience appeal. The term "commercial" saturated his imagination like cigar smoke—inescapable and faintly odious. His last Broadway venture would return to the formula of his early commercial success—the book musical, the first he had done since *Du Barry* (1939), when the word "book" was closer to betting than story line.

Lahr appeared in two versions of *Foxy*, a musical adaption of Ben Jonson's *Volpone*. The first took him to the Yukon in the summer of

1962; he did a revised version on Broadway in 1964, after *The Beauty Part* closed.

The original play is a masterpiece of comic construction in which a rich, wily old man (Volpone) feigns sickness and with the help of his henchman plays greed against greed to dupe the parasites who want to inherit part of his fortune. Besides the potential of the updated material, Lahr could go fishing in western Canada, where the show was being subsidized by the Canadian government for playing Dawson City, Yukon Territory. *Volpone,* in its adaptation, was set in a Gold Rush background, offering Lahr yet another chance to manipulate those essentials of low comedy—disguise, false dignity, avarice, and lust. To Ben Jonson, the appeal of his scoundrels lay in the delight and energy they brought to their machinations. Lahr's scheming was no less obsessive than Volpone's.

For a man nearing seventy, the trip to the Yukon was a physical risk. The journey was one day's travel by plane, but ten days by Lahr's route of train, bus, and boat. He packed his medicines, his fishing tackle, his rabbit's foot. He kept his new camera handy (he took a thousand pictures of the Yukon, two hundred of them of cloud formations). He traveled in the Grand Tradition of a super star of the thirties. According to *The New York Times* (which printed a map of the $7,500 trek) "it was one of the most esoteric, expensive and complex itineraries in the history of show business." Lahr never thought of it as a "first"; this was simply the only way he could do the show.

There were many surprises during the eight-week run, not the least of which was Dawson City itself. *Foxy* was intended to lure tourists into the territory. To Lahr, Dawson City was a fossil from a grim, cold past. The shacks on the outskirts were dilapidated and gray with decay. The "tourist attraction" looked like a ghost town; even the freshly painted stores on the main street could not hide the chilled hollowness of the surroundings. Lahr photographed everything on that first day —registering his amazement and apprehension: the gravel road that had jostled him for fifty miles from Whitehorse to Dawson City; storefront signs reading: MILK 75¢ a QUART; the midnight sun that gave the evening the same jagged beauty as the days.

Dawson City was a town of physical extremes: violent colors and blanched, hard earth; rushing streams and arid, granite-faced mountains. Lahr recalled it with fondness. The townsfolk had warmed to the actors, inviting them to brunches and dinner parties. The actors themselves were bound together in a common experience; and Lahr, replaying his film slides of that time, would be touched by the birthday party they gave him—recalling at once the countryside and camaraderie, the price of tomatoes flown daily into the town, and the Indians who stared at his antics from the front rows. In the Yukon, he had panned for gold, fished, and observed, with clinical precision, cirrus cloud formations.

The play was intended to reopen the city as a resort, but Lahr immediately saw the drawback. There were seven hundred people in the town, half of them Indians. There was only one road. The only convenient way to get to Dawson City was to fly from Fairbanks, Alaska. Lahr, an inveterate box-office watcher, tabulated the result. Weekends were the only days the four hundred-seat playhouse would be full. Although the grand premiere brought Canadian officials and Bea Lillie to Dawson City, tourists were not willing to make the pilgrimage. Many a performance would play to an empty house; and Lahr's city clowning was lost on faces cracked from facing into the wind.

In the theater, Lahr found himself with variables he had never considered. The old star came up against a new breed of actor who shared few of his traditions or concepts of the stage. The "book musical" was still as clumsy and simplified as it had been twenty years before; the audience had changed more drastically than their stage entertainment. When Lahr applied his axioms of comedy, forcing attention back toward himself, he could still dominate the stage, but this very power ultimately dispelled the musical's total force. Lahr spoke with fifty years of experience—and he began to realize that nobody in *Foxy* shared those insights or understood him; they had come from another generation—one that never geared itself to the demands of his comedy. The director, Robert Lewis, could not help Lahr; his suggestions and his unwillingness to allow him to improvise reinforced the fact that Lahr was on his own. Lewis, a director responsible for such Broadway standards as *Teahouse of the August Moon, Brigadoon,* and *Jamaica,* did not know how to cope with Lahr. Ring Lardner, Jr., and Ian McLellan Hunter had never written a Broadway musical; yet in their first play they wanted to retain both the theme of *Volpone* and their lines exactly as they had written them. The show was not social satire; written with Lahr in mind, it was a farcical entertainment that encompassed his broad, loose playing. The problem was simple. Without Lahr's laughter, the show had very little to offer—a mediocre book, fair songs, and choreography that rarely kicked an original leg. His laughter and his improvisations gave it a chance; and yet the authors bridled him with language that was not funny and scenes that did not build to a comic climax.

Lahr raged with a venom he usually reserved for liberals. "I'm Bert Lahr. Bert Lahr . . . Don't try to be funny. You be real. I'll be funny," he'd call down to the authors. His reactions were accepted by most of the cast, but not by Larry Blyden, his co-star, who was one of his greatest admirers. Blyden, a young, talented actor, understood Lahr, but talked back to him. Friction was inevitable: Blyden was arguing as much for an understanding of modern theater as for himself. There were no answers to the debate, but his position was one that could not be rebutted on rational grounds, but simply on the irrational credo of The Laugh.

"The authors were stubborn," recalls Blyden. "They indulged Bert in all the things he must not be indulged in: hogging of time, temper tantrums, willfulness, trying to dictate everything to be done in his own self-interest. On the other hand, they never once allowed him to be brilliant. There was no other actor alive who could do what Lahr could on stage. They wouldn't have it. He would say things to them in analyzing a scene that would be so perceptive and so precise that there was no arguing with him. Sometimes, if they'd have listened to him, I would have been hurt in the writing, sometimes he might have been injured (although I doubt it, because Bert is never injured by anything he suggests). But certainly the scene would have worked better. They had their little idea of what was theatrical and what was honest; and they were all wrong. They also refused to admit that when Bert came out there and crossed his eyes, and did the first ridiculous, outlandish take, that that's the kind of play they had . . ."

Lahr's tantrums were frequent; he would argue and apologize and try to begin again, only to run up against the same conflict. He could harangue for hours, with decibels of invective that had their dramatic effect. Blyden recalls that Lahr "created an atmosphere so that people would do anything for him just to continue. It was one of his techniques." Blyden refused to accept this temperament, which—right or wrong—denied problems other than its own. "Every time he does that," Blyden told Lewis, "then I'm going to do it! And I did. We didn't rehearse at all. They would let him take time out for things that weren't important. Had they acquiesced where he was right and disciplined him where he was wrong (because he's a fair man), things would have been easier. He had no faith in the writers or in the director. They weren't as good as he was; he knew better, he just knew better. You'd leave rehearsal, and you'd be bleeding at what they'd done to him. If I was bleeding, I thought, God, what he must be going through. He would go home and work on his lines all evening. He was the first one there in the morning and the last one out at night. . . .

"Bert's characterizations are broad as hell and drawn very much from life. His sense of what somebody would do at any given moment is astounding. He has the guts of a burglar; he'll try something even when his instincts are off. And you'll die with it; it will be horrible. Then, he'll unload it. A lot of the time he would try to clown around in the early stage of *Foxy*. The clowning would bomb. It was a little repulsive actually, but he knew that, and he never did it again. His instincts took him there, and he tried it. Sometimes he would abandon the play completely for a funny line. He came up with dozens. They get laughs; God knows, they get laughs, but in a sense that is abandoning the play; the action is arrested to accommodate the laugh—that is an anachronism. The reality of that time, the people in that specific situation are forgotten. In addition, the life on the stage stops. Bert likes it to be still anyway, because that's his period, that's his day. Bert wants everything around him immobile—with as little life as possible. People are envisioned almost as posts for Bert—who are set in different places and given cues. He then is free to move among those posts, relating everything directly to the audience as he moves. So he has fixed objects who throw him lines which he can then clown on and react to. Life, then, ceases. I objected because I think there's a better way; I think it's better for him, too. Live people dealing with each other in a better way. He doesn't think so. He came up in a school of butchers. They were killers, those guys. You can't expect anyone who started at fifteen and is now seventy to change. People are props. He said to me, 'Well, in this sketch we should do so and so . . .' Well, it is not a sketch. It's a book musical. There are scenes connected to each other. In a sketch you go from one laugh to another, then blackout. In his mind *Foxy* was a sketch . . ."

On stage, Blyden could understand how the feeling of vulnerability Lahr created was part of his own insecurity and yet made his comedy bear down on the audience. "You want to go up there and pinch him on that cheek because you think, 'Oh that poor old soul—he's not going to get through this alive.' The circumstances are killing him. He gets desperate. He's the last of his line. He'll make a face or think of another line. And he'll put it in, and you can all be hanged. Take *The Beauty Part*, when he says, 'You may meet resistance to your concept of what's clean and straight and fine, but if you do, just cram it down their throats.' That's huge. There's not another actor around who can do that. He says, 'Cram-it-down-their-throats' with the anger and the hatred in those little eyes; and it's being done by the most vulnerable man in the world. Or *Hotel Paradiso* is another case, when he gets the drill in his behind. Almost any other comedian would have gotten his laugh and moved away from the drill. Bert knew to stay right there. He knew. He also thinks in terms of routines within a scene. He knows that certain things can throw off a little routine: 'the-screw-in-the-ass,' the 'cram-it-down-their-throats-routine,' the 'tapdancing-to-get-away-routine.' He thinks in terms of getting the absolute maximum out of a moment. But he also knows, after having been around 180 years, when to quit. There's nobody around who knows it."

Blyden was a careful, critical observer. Lahr was perplexed about Blyden's aloofness. In his own mind, Blyden's criticism could be explained by his youth. He was a stripling to comic acting. "If a fella is just a dramatic actor and goes into a musical play, he is astounded, perhaps, by the deportment of some of the actors," Lahr philosophizes. "You go down front; you talk to an audience. Where in a dramatic play you cannot do that. You've got to look at one another and play perfectly legitimate." In a play about Machiavellian manipulation like *Foxy*, the need for dramatic moments, for scheming, and even for confrontation ("looking at one another") was perhaps more important. The differences were glaring; and Lahr, who played a master conniver, suspected a plot. He summoned Blyden to his dressing room.

"I think you're trying to hurt me out there. I think you're trying to kill laughs and I don't trust you."

"I won't continue a conversation on a false premise."

"Look, Larry, I'm not a suspicious guy."

"Bert, you are suspicious."

"No, I'm not."

"Look, Bert, you came up in this school, and you assume that since everybody in that school did that, everybody is *still* doing it. But you've got to realize that you're the only guy *alive* from *that* school of comedy. Nobody around here can do it; nobody here would do it, and nobody here knows *how* to do it!"

"Give me an example."

Blyden mentioned a few incidents. Lahr nodded. From that moment, Blyden recalls, "we never had any trouble." But Lahr's differences with the director were not resolved. Every suggestion, every elaboration was met with the same response: "I'll have to ask the boys." The writers stood their ground; and Lahr felt straight-jacketed through the entire eight-week stint. After two months he was glad to conclude the engagement. He planned to end the summer fishing on Lake Louise. When he arrived there, exhausted and disappointed from the grueling summer tryout, he fell ill for ten days. He never saw the lake or opened his tackle box. The fever could not be diagnosed; it was the first of the serious attacks. Back in New York, he seemed resigned to the fact that *Foxy* was not untapped gold. *The Beauty Part* was available; and *Foxy* still needed a great deal of work.

During 1963, Lahr heard that Billy Rose was interested in acquiring *Foxy*. Despite his unhappy dealings with Rose in the past, Lahr was willing to rationalize anything. "I know Rose is a pretty tough guy; he'll keep these writers in line. He's for the comedian; he's for the show." When Rose dropped out of the picture, Lahr decided to abandon the idea of *Foxy* too. "I saw it was going to be very uncomfortable."

After *The Beauty Part* closed, Robert Whitehead, the original producer of *Foxy* and the man who had sent it to the Yukon, came to see Lahr at his apartment. He was taking over the directorship of Lincoln Center and could not, by contract, do other commercial shows. Lahr told Whitehead: "I think I'm going to have a lot of trouble with these guys, they think they've written Ibsen's *A Doll's House*. I'll help your show, Bob. If I say the wrong thing, I have good enough taste to admit I'm wrong. If we need help, Bob, will you give it to us?" Whitehead not only agreed to help but also informed him that David Merrick was willing to produce the show. Lahr, facing a new season with a daughter in college and a son at Oxford and no other offers, signed the contract.

The only letter my father ever wrote me had reference to *Foxy*. "I begin rehearsals for *Foxy* tomorrow. Let's pray it's a hit." After so much anxiety he was going out on the road again, his hopes having won out over his experience. He trusted Merrick's success, although he'd never seen one of the many shows the producer had mounted. Johnny Mercer, the lyricist, was, in his estimation a pro, and could be counted on continually for good songs. The situation in *Volpone* could be made to work; and despite the oppressive conditions, he was willing to wager his talent against recalcitrant management. Was he still funny? Were his instincts still true? Was Bert Lahr an idea from the past, a name whose talent was a fiction? He strolled in his room after one of his seizures of fever, taking his temperature every quarter of an hour, feeling his pulse, wondering about his legs, his heart, the mysterious ague that rose (he was certain) from his kidneys or his gall bladder or his liver.

He needed confirmation of his talent. *Foxy* represented that challenge; and what he was praying for was not only the cash on hand, but the renewal of that energy and skill that had made people laugh for half a century.

His responses were not difficult to understand for anyone who had watched him as carefully as Blyden. "Bert needs three things. One: he needs to be loved. Two: a thing he needs a little more than that is to be served. Three: he needs to be acclaimed. He doesn't need to love; but he needs to receive it. Laughter is that. Bert comes from a hungry time. When they laughed you were going to eat; when they didn't, you starved. But now, I don't think he knows that. If they're not laughing, he panics. There's nothing vicious in it or greedy or selfish; they are conditions of his life. He had terrible things happen in his life; and yet, he has succeeded and become Bert Lahr by making people laugh."

The first day of rehearsals shattered the hopes of the previous day's letter. Foxy, impersonating an English Lord, was to make his entrance into the Yukon saloon, and, observing the bar and nude painting behind it, say, "How far out." Lahr changed the entrance to "Mmm—how very Wedgewood," and topped it with an observation about the picture, "Mm—Whistler's sister." The lines—which would bring howls from the audience and be mentioned in nearly every review—were contested by the authors.

"Why don't you use 'far out'?"

"Because it isn't funny." When they protested again, Lahr stalked off the stage and called Merrick. Nothing had changed.

Merrick pacified him; but Lahr still had to contend with an unfunny script and adamant authors. At one point, Foxy had to reply to a woman "If you don't mind my saying so, madame, ha-ha-ha." "It was gorgeous the way he hated that line," recalls Blyden. This sent the authors scurrying backstage to admonish him, "You put in an extra 'ha.'" Lahr ordered them from his dressing room. "It got me so goddamn mad I couldn't control myself." Later in the evening, he relented and apologized. But they could not find funny lines when Lahr asked for them, and he was forced to rely on his own resources. "Finally, I just said the hell with them—and that accounted for all the big laughs in the show." When Foxy wheeled his sled on stage and handed the Eskimos a bag of gold, Lahr had to say, "Here, buy yourself a couple of fishhooks." To Lahr the language had no verve, the comic idea was too small for laughter. He reworked it to read, "Here, buy yourself some chocolate-covered blubber." "Don't you think that in rehearsal they came to my dressing room and wanted me to change it back."

For three weeks on the road, no new scenes were written. "The nucleus was there," Lahr claims. "Lardner and Hunter did write some funny situations, but they were obvious sight things." When Lahr asked for a laugh line it was not forthcoming; when he saw a flaw in the construction, it was not mended. Storming across the stage, he kept repeating, "Where's the captain? I'm used to having a captain like Ziegfeld or White or Hopkins."

There was another side of the coin. Lahr knew where to find the laughter; but it always had to relate to him. At one point, Foxy is chasing a girl who, on discovering he's rich, turns track and pursues him, saying, "Play me like a harp." Blyden recalls the problem with such a funny line. "Bert would tell the writers do this, do that. It was guaranteed funny. Jesus, you could smell it. On the other hand, a girl was getting a big laugh in the scene saying 'play me like a harp.' It topped him. He did everything in his power to kill her laugh. In fact, he said to her, 'Honey, I'm sorry I'm going to have to kill that laugh.' Then, he put in another line for himself: 'Yeah, but I got a sore pinky.' Finally, he figured if he waited, and let it hit, then said his line—he would top it. But had he not topped it, he would have killed it."

Lahr was at odds with the play. For the comedy to be successful, he had to get laughs; but his way of getting them hurt the development of the play. The writers had not produced good material, but they were given the added onus of serving Lahr's special demands. "Bert has to enter with the entire stage still and looking at him," says Blyden. "He has to have the biggest laugh in the scene; and he has to have the last line of the scene, and the biggest line that ends it. He has to have that; and he knows how to create an atmosphere in which the audience looks at him because he gives them the big ones. He conditions the audience to look at him because that's where the humor is. If you get a big laugh, it's okay; but he must have one to top that. He must. Otherwise, he's going to be hungry; and he's going to be fifteen and nobody's going to love him; and he's going to be looking for a job . . . I don't think he knows it, but he gets like that.

"He made them throw out the ending because he said he couldn't finish it. A curious thing happened to the play then, because the relationships got all jumbled. There was one section of the show that I had to be in charge of because I was the schemer. Now in order to do that,

I had to take the stage to give some directions to scheme. And yet, he didn't want me to do that because he was on. And when he's on, he wants charge of that stage. He wasn't sneaky. He said to me, 'Look, kid, I'm making them throw out the end of the show, because I'm not strong at the finish, and I gotta be strong at the finish. If they end the show the way it is, it's going to be your show. It's not going to be your show, it's going to be mine.' Direct quote. Verbatim. Never forgot it. It was a thought I'd never heard expressed in the theater. It takes your breath away. By becoming completely his show, *Foxy* was damaged."

Lahr questioned himself during the tryout. His little jokes reflected his worry. Could he still carry a part? Could he learn lines any more? Was he getting senile? The difficulty of getting anything done on the production made him wonder. Was this going to be his last show? His anxiety was genuine and shared by the cast, who realized that *Foxy*'s success rested on his shoulders. Even in his tantrums, there was a sense of theatrical tradition. Turning to Blyden, who shared Lahr's disgust with the director and writers, he said, "I may go down, kid, but if I go down, it's going to be with champions. I'm not going down like a bum." He wanted to quit the show; but fears much deeper than those of success kept him at it. "He survived it," Blyden says. "He took the bit in his teeth and ran. Because he's Bert Lahr, he got away with it. No one else could have."

On February second, two letters arrived at Lahr's dressing room. The first, from Johnny Mercer, acknowledged Lahr's effort in a show uncertain of its future:

> Dear Bert—
> . . . This is the first time I've ever seen a performer do my material better than I meant it. Usually we're happy with 75% or 80% of what we would like—but you find laughs where the laughs aren't even there! You're just marvelous and I love you.

The second letter was from David Merrick's office. Merrick, with nine other shows on Broadway and two on the road in 1964, was rarely present to oversee his last $420,000 production. Jerome Robbins had been dispatched to Detroit to help; but the writers effectively prevented any outside tinkering. The accountants indicated the show was in trouble; and no one needed to remind Merrick of the production problems. *Foxy* needed new sets, new songs, a tighter script. With too many other products on the market, *Foxy* was an unnecessary burden.

Merrick's green envelope informed Lahr that *Foxy* would close in Detroit on Saturday evening, February 8.

Two days later, Merrick changed his mind when investors threatened to sue to keep the show open. He dealt away part of his producing responsibilities to Billy Rose. The next week *Foxy* came to New York. On opening night, Lahr received a note from Merrick: "So proud to be presenting you at last." This was not rhetoric; Merrick had become postwar Broadway's producing legend; and Lahr was perhaps the only theatrical commodity that linked two eras. Merrick disliked the show, but Lahr's talent was something he could appreciate.

The show was a personal triumph for Lahr. The critics were never more lavish in their praise. But in their ebullience over Lahr was a curious hint of the paradox: he was a monument in the face of disaster. *The New York Times* began its review:

> If you admire Bert Lahr and it's un-American not to, you know—"Foxy" is for you . . . It [Foxy] does not fret over refinements of plot and characterization, but it wears its crudities with a grin and has delightful professional gusto. And can more be asked for in this vale of crises than to have Bert Lahr back on stage, mugging shamelessly or being as delicate as a viscount at an unexpectedly rowdy lawn party?

The review, like every other statement about the play, attested to Lahr's position in the theater; it also pointed out the curiously old-fashioned form of *Foxy*. The enjoyment was primarily Lahr's doing; and the structure bore his fingerprints too.

But *Foxy* raised an important question about book musicals. The inability to support their talent forced performers back to a careerist attitude. As a result, the biggest Broadway musicals—*Hello, Dolly!*, *Fiddler on the Roof*—became star showcases.

Without new material, Lahr, like so many other stars, had to settle for *tours de force*. With Lahr, the pointed pinky, the mock effeminacy were hilarious traits that audiences had been viewing for nearly fifty years, but now they demanded more.

Blyden's dissent had predicted Lahr's reception and also the stalemate that lay behind it. "Bert honestly believed that if he came off well in the show, it would work. That's not true. An audience wouldn't come to see just that. They had to know they were coming to see a whopping big show. They've seen Bert be great. Now, they're more interested in seeing Barbra Streisand, they're interested in the new ones. The reviews were bad for the show, great for Lahr. For *Foxy* to be good, everyone else had to score. That meant they had to score when he was on. When he wasn't on, it was pretty deadly. There was a time when theater could have worked that way; but, unfortunately, that time is gone."

However, Blyden learned by competing with an old pro. "Bert found a huge laugh for me in the show. I would never have thought of it. He said it to me on stage. The audience is out there—sixteen hundred of them. He whispered "After the next line, say 'umlaut.' So I said 'umlaut,' and the audience screamed. Then he bumped the laugh further by reacting to it. I never would have thought of it. Who thinks of saying 'umlaut' in conversation for God's sake? He does. He thinks funny. One day he came up to me. 'You're saying "Oh" in front of a line. Don't say "Oh"—you'll get a bigger laugh.' So I took it out; and I got a bigger laugh."

Blyden began to understand when Lahr was going to improvise and how to stay with him. "I could feel him when he was going someplace. I didn't know where he was going. He'd go a step at a time; and I would try and go with him. Every now and then, I'd blow it; and he'd be *livid* with me. And then he'd get over it. He gets mad on stage. And when *he* misses a big one, he'll get the most disgusted look on his face and say, 'Well, I blew that one.' He broke himself up on stage. Sometimes, when he gets mad, he'll quit. He's finished until the next scene."

Blyden, forced to play fast and loose, developed routines for Lahr to follow. "One day on stage I said, 'I'm going to try and follow you, you try and get away.' Lahr replied, 'Do anything you want.' The game of tag began and the audience howled. Lahr chuckled under his breath, 'That's good, kid, thanks.' "

Foxy's reviews were strong enough to sustain a run. To a constant theatergoer like Walter Kerr, Lahr's gestures had a poignancy beyond the outcome of the show.

In any case, the spectacle of Mr. Lahr calling "halloo" to the Grim Reaper is a frightfully moving one . . . and as I watched him reveling . . . I sometimes yearned for that kind of free association musical in which you could really black out a scene as Lahr does when a hard-drinking miner passes out at his funeral. Mr. Lahr leaps from his repose and struggles to get the sodden fellow up, primly explaining, "I'm taking this drunk off the whisky, and putting him on the bier!" There is nobility, and a delicate sense of just how outrageously a bad high pun ought to be, in that.

Blyden's memories notwithstanding, Lahr was not the only focus of critical praise. Magazines lauded the show as well as its star. (*Time:* "The whole show is as cheerful as any show ought to be which rejoices in the presence of the funniest man left alive.") Many shows since *Foxy* have lasted on reviews much skimpier, and without the prospect of a summer World's Fair.

But *Foxy*, which had struggled so long to get to Broadway, found itself strangled by a management problem. *Hello, Dolly!* had opened a few weeks before, and the Merrick office, stung with delight over its popular success, had little interest in promoting the last of its flock. The poster for *Foxy* remained unframed or mounted on Merrick's wall for a long time after the opening. As one member of the office recalled, "Even if *Foxy* had been a great show, nobody would have cared." The management maintains that there were no theater parties for *Foxy* and no "hit feeling" about the show. Lahr felt differently. "It's a wonder we played as long as we did with the treatment Merrick gave us."

Foxy closed after eighty-five performances. When the final curtain fell at the Ziegfeld Theater, the house was full. The audience gave Lahr a standing ovation. In the dressing room, Mildred raged, ready to storm Merrick's office in hand-to-hand combat with the dragon of Broadway. Lahr, like a bartered bride, seemed more resigned. "We could have made it, if the producer cared. He had money for advertising he never used." The Merrick office would offer as many reasons for failure as there could have been for success. The theater was in the wrong district, they claimed. Set apart from Broadway, it could not do any street business. All-time greats, they added, do not sell tickets.

The Ziegfeld Theater had been one of Lahr's earliest memories of Broadway; and now he wondered if it would be one of his last. He could still make people laugh, but what was the commercial appeal of his laughter? In 1932, he alone could sustain a mediocre show when the top price was $5.50 and the galleries could be filled for $.75.

Lahr could still marshal the energy and an enthusiastic following, as his reviews indicated. However, the best ticket was $11.40 and a balcony seat more than the price of a movie. His fans—the ones who recognized him on the street or wrote for his autographed picture— could not afford the price. Merrick's distrust of his product and his unwillingness to market it reflected a planned obsolescence built into the machinery of Broadway. The star's commercial value rested, in part, on his past; and yet, each show forced him, like detergent, to be "new" or "improved" without changing the actual content of the commodity. Lahr's comedy was not obsolete; the format was. Having survived so many changes of taste, Lahr had reached a point where it was no longer a matter of taste, but of the comic material reflecting the emotional, intellectual tenor of the society. As a merchandizer, Merrick knew the value of brand names as clearly as Lahr; but he refused to experiment with the potential. Lahr was both the victim and perpetrator of that attitude.

George White, Lahr reminded himself, never would have treated him that way; nor would Ziegfeld or even Hopkins. The theater was crueler to its performers now; the producer was not so much a man of theater as a man of the marketplace.

"The next time I do a show," he told Blyden, "I don't want all the responsibility." Had he learned from *Foxy?* Blyden and Lahr's family hoped so. "He may not believe it. I really can't see Bert being anything but the focal point of the show. For Bert's own sake, he's got to realize that if somebody else—man, woman, dog, goat, and the whole play work—he's better off. But you can't ignore him; you can't deny him."

Three years later, Lahr stood by the Ziegfeld Theater while a demolition team crashed into its dome and television newsmen prodded him for recollections. Not a nostalgic moment or a teary one—but rather an incomprehensible erasure of a theatrical era already vague in his mind. On television his face was now familiar—associated with a product more substantial than the laughter that sold it and made it a brand name. The Ziegfeld had epitomized the spectacular, grand design of an earlier entertainment in which the clown's blackout bits were usually larger than life rather than reduced (as now) to sixty-second miniatures. The generic term for the Ziegfeld type of amusement had passed to advertising as well—"commercial."

Foxy was not forgotten. In May of 1964, Lahr received the Tony Award for the best musical star actor. A small silver disc, the award gave him more satisfaction than any other accolade. Broadway was honoring its own past. The *Herald Tribune* reported—

Despite the sweep by "Dolly," the biggest most prolonged applause of the evening was reserved for the beloved veteran of the comedy stage, Bert Lahr . . .

As he left the American Theater Wing after the ceremonies, a wino emerged from the shadows. Lahr bowed his head and shied away. The man came closer. His hand was outstretched; his eyes riveted on Lahr's face. He held out a dollar.

"Here, Bert," he said. "And thanks."

DAD

RESTING ON HIS CHAISE LOUNGE IN HIS DIOR BATHROBE, BERT LAHR IS an imposing patriarch. His wife brings him sweetmeats and his glasses; his children sneak him salted nuts (bad for his gall bladder) and report their news, which he cannot decide is good or bad. From his reclining position, my father dispenses his mandates and misgivings. Slow to speak, he sees himself as a quiet ruler, the most observed of all observers. When impelled to action, he is a master of innuendo.

"Bert, will you call Jane and tell her to come home for dinner."

Lahr casts aside his Afghan and resolutely folds his glasses over the Sunday crossword puzzle. He stalks to the phone and dials.

"Hello, may I speak to . . . uh . . . is . . . uh . . ."

"Jane!" Mildred yells from her dressing table.

"Is Jane there? . . . Well, would you tell her to come home. Dinner is ready, and I'm hungry."

A ruler can sometimes forget his subjects, and Bert Lahr is not infallible. He has introduced me to his Players Club cronies: "I'd like you to meet my son, Herbert." When I remind him that I'm "John" not "Herbert," he corrects himself and continues, only to phone his first son long distance and announce, "Good to hear your voice, John."

Friends, who have come to the house regularly over a decade, marvel when he emerges from his bedroom and greets them by their right names. But even my father, whose home is a benevolent dictatorship, understands the political havoc such slips of the tongue can cause. When he appeared on the Joey Bishop night-time discussion show in California, he reminisced about vaudeville and Mercedes but forgot Mildred and the children in New York. Mildred watched the performance at home with clenched teeth. At the end of the show, Bishop interrupted his sign-off message to wave frantically at the camera. "Bert wants to say hello to his wife, Mildred."

At dinner, he enters to music provided either by his hi-fi system or his collection of tapes, both equally mischievous to handle, and both the private property of Bert Lahr. With the family seated and the food steaming on the table, he is still bent over the hi-fi.

"Can you hear it, Mildred?"

Mother stares despairingly at the ceiling as the music tumbles out in decibels that make the water glasses shake.

"Yes—that's fine, Bert. Come to the table."

The music, as we have matured, has become more subdued; but the memories of ragout and radio news, Mantovanni and jellied madrilène still linger. When he leaves the table (as he does five minutes before the rest of us have finished), he totters to his room where he immediately cuts off the music. Dinner is officially over.

From the seat at the head of the table, he has demanded and received the special privilege of watching football games on his portable television set while the family concentrates on their buttered peas. He has arranged a tape recorder under the table and then baited Mildred about the food ("You call this meat? This is petrified wood!") until, to our delight, Mildred informed him just how he could dispose of it. There have been moments when he has gone into a bravura imitation of an opera singer and done the "Shimmy Shawabble" to show Jane that the twist was a burlesque invention. While lecturing us sternly about manners, he has mistaken his tie for a napkin.

He protects his small pleasures with the adamance of a divine right. He discovered the cigar in his seventy-first year with as much enthusiasm as the Manhattan Indians took to firewater. He keeps a box in his drawer; and each time he opens one, Mildred shrinks like a slug held up to a hot flame.

"They make me vomit." "They make me nauseous." "They make me really sick to my stomach." Gasping for air, she leaves the room. Surrounded by the blue-gray halo of cigar smoke, Lahr puffs on. Mildred's persistence and his peculiar sense of responsibility evolve a kind of compromise. If she begins to gag, Lahr moves his armchair close to the air conditioner, holding the cigar into the artificial breeze. The air bellows the smoke into the room, although Lahr inhales contentedly, assured that the currents are taking the smoke into the street. If Mildred continues to complain or if the smoke makes it difficult for even him to breathe, he retires to the bathroom where he finishes his Perfecto in peace.

The family knows he will tire of cigars, just as he grew weary of stereo tapes, Japanese television sets, and painting. These are pastimes, small pleasures to take his mind off work—or the lack of it. He indulges his interests without a thought of being judged. He speaks cryptically about something as if talking to himself and then falls back into an active silence. At his easel, he interests himself in his paints. He experiments with the canvas by turning out a dozen pictures of the same lion and signing each to give to his friends. He displays them on the large bedroom breakfront—pulling out drawers to prop them up. He ponders them like Jackson Pollock before an empty canvas.

"I think I'll paint one looking out over his paws with his body drooping down. I think I'll paint him with tears in his eyes."

"Bert, you don't want a sad lion," cautions Mildred.

"That's how I see him—with tears in his eyes."

To his children, Lahr is a friendly absence, a man who, induced to reveal himself, is at once humble and childishly stubborn, concerned and curiously aloof. Lahr can greet Mildred at the door in beret and smock: or chase her, yelping, into the bathroom threatening to take her picture with a Polaroid camera. He is conscious of having given his family the best of possibilities—but whatever these advantages are, he seems to know only by rumor. When he appeared at Jane's school to receive a report on his daughter, he listened quietly with the three-pieced somberness of the rest of the fathers. After the report, Lahr confided to a teacher, "This is an innovation for Spence, isn't it?" "Mr. Lahr, Jane's been at *Dalton* for two years."

He never knew what grade we were in; he dismissed good marks with bad ("I never got more than a C in my life, just so long as you pass I don't care"). And after bemoaning the cost of private education for as many years as he'd paid for it, his presence at graduations and other official ceremonies was now infamous. He missed as many as he made. At Jane's graduation from Bennett College, he sat through the stodgy ceremony eating an ice-cream cone. At Yale, where the students convene at their colleges, Lahr snuck behind the elm trees in Branford to photograph his son receiving a B.A. The eyes of two hundred parents were glued to him as he tiptoed behind the tree and waited with his camera. When I finally approached the rostrum, he dropped his camera. The crowd moaned in unison as if he'd fumbled on the one-yard line.

Always long-suffering at public gatherings, Lahr has been forced to
go against his principles of nonintervention for the sake of Dr. Spock's
vision of family harmony. He gave a graduation address marking my
matriculation from sixth to seventh grades at Riverdale Country Day
School. When he arrived, he was rushed into the Lower School corridors, notes in hand. "I've never been more nervous," he confided to
Mildred. He told us to concentrate during the summer "on hitting the
ball a country mile, and catching a fish," and a few other things he'd
never done at that age. He appeared at only one official sports event
and left just as his ten-year-old son was intercepting a pass against a
bunch of oversized orphans. His only comment was "Why couldn't
you have done it sooner?"

Bert Lahr has even traveled into the wilderness to observe his offspring at play. He was paying for the kind of air, leisure, and careful
handling he had missed. He looked on with some amazement at tents,
mosquito netting, and an organized schedule of activities more like
the Army than fun. He came to a camp council fire, gazing glassy-eyed
at his daughter, who sat cross-legged in an Indian headdress chanting
the invocation: ". . . Oh, firemaker, light now our council fire so that
we may have light, so that we may have warmth, so that we may sit in
council tonight." My father listened to the words, standing shivering
and cornered by night bugs. "I finally sat down at the campfire and
told the kids all about Indians. What do *I* know about Indians?" Besieged by campers, urged on by eager entertainment directors who
insisted on greeting him and sending him off with a roundelay, Lahr
could rarely muster the enthusiasm for the frontier spirit. Sometimes,
it amused him. He watched a squat camper take aim at an archery
target and then hit a bull's-eye three stands away. Flushed with excitement, she turned to Lahr and announced, "I wasn't even trying." He
tried to cover up his guffaw by asking her a question. "What do you
want to be when you grow up?"

"A horse."

Coming back to New York, he pointed to a fire hydrant. "That was
my summer camp."

He once came to my aid and answered a sixth-grade essay question
on "Why I would like to be an Eskimo." He felt it was a foolish exercise but it was the first A he ever received in school. Only once was I
summoned to his room for a discussion about sex. He began by saying,
"John, sex is beautiful . . ." He tried to elaborate, but never finished

the sentence. Fumbling for words, he concluded the discussion abruptly, "It's beautiful . . . now get to bed."

What does he think of his children? We are never certain. He can storm out of a room announcing, "All right, I'm off you." Like milk and eggs, children go off; and Lahr has been known to ban them from court for as long as a week. He rarely assesses us to our face—he is vaguely proud; but, worried about the security of our futures, he remains silent. He bares his emotion as nervously as a grandmother showing a bit of leg. "They'll forget us, Mildred." His suspicions of betrayal are unfounded but ever-present. He will shuffle into Jane's room when she is out and look at her work. Her interest in demonology and astrology amuses him. "Come home," he told her on the phone, "We need a fourth at the ouija board." When confronted with his ebullient, beautiful daughter he does not always know what to say, except that she inherited his nose—as big an onus as assuming the national debt.

"So you think I look better?" he asks Jane.

"I think you look beautiful, Bertram."

"Aw, shut up," he says, with a wrinkled stage grimace that means love. When I began to write articles about the theater, my father looked on with apprehension. For an actor to spawn a drama-critic son held as much potential disappointment as giving birth to a Cyclops—the latter perhaps being more far-sighted than a critic. "Don't be like Winchell, John. Be honest!" After his dictum on criticism, he retired to his bedroom and worried about his son in private. The telephone would ring in my apartment with a lobbyist's sense of timing. Once, he called me as I was about to review a splendid revival of *Annie Get Your Gun.* "John, I'm glad I caught you. I was thinking . . . don't pan Merman's age." When I wrote a piece disputing Walter Kerr about the nature of criticism, he called me into his bedroom with the article in hand. "This is very well written, John; but Walter Kerr is the dean of critics now. He's been very nice to me."

After six months he began to trust my judgment, and when I was published in a magazine that cost him $1.25 at the newstands, his faith was confirmed. He gave me scripts to read as potential vehicles for him. "This is very deep, very abstract. I don't know what it means"; or "This could be built up. It's commercial, don't you think?" Was he proud? Was he dissatisfied? No one knew. Sometimes he would read the articles as if scanning the want ads and at other times he would lavish more attention on them. When I handed him an article on Harold Pinter, he took it, with paternal tact, to peruse in the bath-

room. It began with a Pinter letter on Samuel Beckett and brought
Lahr hobbling out of the bathroom, swathed in his robe and with his
underpants around his ankles. "What are you, Allen Ginsberg or something?" When I explained that the language was not mine but Pinter's,
he looked again and ambled back to read in pacified silence.

When he found out that I was teaching drama at Hunter College,
his fears of his son languishing in the abyss of bankruptcy were
assuaged.

"What do they pay?"

"It comes to thirteen dollars a class."

"Hey, that's not bad. Let's see. If you could teach six or eight classes
a day—you'd be in business."

He balked when I asked him to come to a class. "I'm not a scholar,
John: I wouldn't want to talk. We'll see." But he did attend a lecture
on *Waiting for Godot,* sneaking into the crowded Park Avenue building. He sat meekly in the back; but when I asked him questions about
performing *Godot* he warmed to the enterprise. He enjoyed recount-
ing his interpretation. At the end of the class, the students clustered
around him, not to get his autograph but asking him to elaborate his
ideas. He had sat, with Mildred, for an hour and a half. It was the first
time he'd been in a classroom in a half century. He did not leave in
the middle claiming an appointment with his agent or an extenuating
rehearsal. He never said he liked the class; but his presence was a tacit
nod of approval. After his visit, he always referred to my course as
"Elizabethan drama." Had he listened? He had, at least, been present.
Through family silences, he would inquire during the year what I was
teaching. When I tried to explain Ben Jonson's *Alchemist,* the words
would echo off him.

"Bert, why don't you listen to him?"

"Whaddya mean, listen. I am listening!"

"How can you listen when you're not looking?"

"I can listen: 'Ben Jonson's *Alchemist* . . .'" Shared moments are
regurgitated in fragments of understanding. Teaching has an aura of
respectability in his eyes that criticism can never have. The names of
ancient plays have the weight of mystery and scholarly concern. He
calls excitedly on the phone to announce he too has a chance to teach.

"John, listen to this." He reads the letter slowly. "Any kind of
course or, perhaps, direct a school production. . . . Thirty-five hundred
dollars a semester. . . . Your title would be Adjunct Professor of
Drama. . . ."

"That's fantastic, Pop."

"Yeah, but I don't know anything about drama. All I know is how to do it. I can't articulate. Maybe I'll see if they could use you."

"Don't be silly—give it a try."

"It's too much work; and anyway, what could I tell them."

"I think you could show them a lot—maybe do some scenes and point out comic tricks . . ."

"Well, we'll see . . ."

"Congratulations, Professor."

When I call him "professor" he chuckles. He is genuinely amused —Bert Lahr a professor. Perhaps there is less to this academic world than meets the eye. He hangs up, laughing at a world that must certainly be crazy. Universities want him as visiting professor! Museums write for costumes and clothes whose only value for two decades were to cover his pale skin. People he's never heard of write claiming to be distant relatives and requesting money. Everyone is willing to listen, he reminds us, except his children. "They'll never listen, Mildred; they're stubborn," he mutters to himself. "Don't get mad at me for saying this, John. Believe me, it's for your own good. When a man goes on stage and he's well dressed, he's got seventy per cent of the audience licked. They give you immediate respect. If you notice me (what am I looking for—a woman?) I've got a clean shirt on every day, my pants are pressed, my shoes—you could see your face in them. And there's such a thing as cologne . . ."

From his closet he brings out a sweater. "But Bert, I gave you that for Christmas." And shoe trees. "Keep the shoe trees. Here, when you buy new shoes, you can use these." And his assortment of ties. ("You like them. Take one. Take two. Say, Mildred, whatever happened to that white Italian tie I got in Florida.") He starts foraging through his closet. "I'll find it, Bert. Let me look." In his random generosity, he has even tried to pawn off presents *I* had given him the previous years—a fishing knife, an indoor putting green. Invitations to dinner are handed out with warnings—"Your father says to dress nicely." He expects, one imagines, that a hoary version of the Ancient Mariner will sit down at his dinner table. Style is threatened at every turn. "Everything's filth and vulgarity. Always the cheap angle. I walk along the street today and what do I see? Lots of kids with beards and girls with skirts up to their knees . . . What is it? Where has the taste gone? Now your sister brought a nice boy up to see me. He was quiet, and very intelligent, but he was dressed like you. You don't take baths, you stink. I once said to Jay C. Flippen, who had an aversion to water like you, 'You know they're going to have to take you to the hospital to break your socks off.' What is it with you kids? Ugh!"

A picture of Jane and me as infants now hangs in a cameo over the fireplace—cherubs framed in suitable baroque gilt. Memories of taking us to the Stork Club in our Easter outfits bring tears to parental eyes. But as adults, my father can never be sure what he's got. A son who is more interested in ideas than making money; a daughter who creates objects she doesn't feel like selling. "You kids think you know everything. Well, we're no idiots, you know. Experience counts for something." In anger as well as illness, Lahr's face spills over its posturing into grotesque laughter. He shouts; he pouts; his nostrils flair wide like a gorilla's. He shoves his finger in the air to unleash a barrage of words from the ether, only to mispronounce them. His son the free-lance writer smiles kindly at his suggestions, but won't take them. "I've got an idea for you. Get pictures of menus from all over the country and reproduce them with menus of today. Talk about how prices have changed. The Free Lunch Era." For days, he asked me to type up a special document. Finally, he took me into the bedroom and confided, "John, I want you to write this up for me and make a copy so I can send it to myself. I've got an idea for a hot dog parlor—you know. Every kind of hot dog, bratwurst, weiners . . . every kind. I want to call it the 'Dog House.' " Bert Lahr, the Industrial Magnate, the landowner of twenty-five thousand acres of useless grazing land in New Mexico he's never seen, is captivated by the quick killing and disturbed that his offspring don't yearn for the "fast buck." He can claim one of the most original ice-cream inventions since the popsicle. While in *Du Barry* he got Betty Grable and Lana Turner to endorse his ice-cream venture called "Tits on a Stick." "We wanted Jane Russell too," he smiles like the man who nearly broke the bank at Monte Carlo.

In a family debate, he once admitted, "Kids—I could take them or leave them." But, as father and patriarch, he is undeniably *there.* As his mood goes, so goes the spirit of the house. If he is hungry, we eat; if he is tired, we are quiet; if he is angry, we get out of the way. We can never know when his interest will be raised or when he will call on us for information. During one family fishing trip, Jane and I argued and discussed *Beowulf* at great length. We often bemoaned the difficulties in translating the "whales road," and Grendel in her "fen-fastness." Two weeks after the discussion, I received a long-distance call from Dad, who was still in Canada. "Hello, John, listen . . . Did Chaucer write *Beowulf?*" When I answered assuredly "No," he cupped his hands over the phone and I could hear him saying, "See, I told you he didn't. That's five bucks."

In another discussion, on neurosis and art, Dad maintained that there was no relation.

"What about Van Gogh?" my sister began passionately. "A lot of mad guys created but they didn't know what they were doing."

Lahr sat back patiently. Jane continued.

"What about that brilliantly beautiful ear of Van Gogh's? You know what he did with it? You know? He cut it off, put it in a box and left it at his mistress' door. That's beautiful. That's insane. That's brilliant."

"That's your sister!" he added and left the table.

Even for his family, Lahr is encountered as an event—something apart from the every-day and yet merging with it. His words, spoken in uncompleted sentences or spilling out in paragraphs, can only be remembered as vivid fragments. His face, which stamps itself so memorably on the eye at each meeting, blurs into more general outlines. The special situations that reveal him are frozen moments from diary jottings—lifted from the expanse of silences.

My father sits in the boat scanning the shoreline. He has been up since six, casting from the dock, slamming doors on tiptoe, and supervising a bass breakfast. The sun is already high, the lake calm—a good fishing day. His blue sneakers squeak on the wood. Everything is packed—water, two tackle boxes, four fishing poles, his beer and sandwiches, an extra can of gasoline for the outboard motor. He is taking his children fishing. The visor of his fishing cap is turned backwards on his head. He looks more like a baseball catcher than a guide. He dabs cold cream on his nose, tells Jane not to move about so much in front, and pushes off for a day on the water.

Jane has been practicing her casting on land. She has fished with mother, brother, guide, but never with father, for long hours of stalking his prey are part of the fun. Jane likes to poke her fishing rod in the water and watch the ripples, talk to the fish, and play guessing games with the woods. She looks at the birds and the trees sprawled in the water like bony hands. She daydreams.

MARK SHAW

In *Hotel Paradiso* (1957)

Overleaf
Portrait (c. 1957)

In *Foxy* (1964)

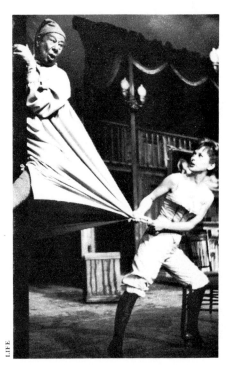

Crawling up the proscenium in *Foxy*

With Nancy Walker in "Hostility" (1959)

As Nelson Smedley in
The Beauty Part

As Hyacinth Beddoes Laffoon in
The Beauty Part (1962)

As Judge Herman J. Rinderbrust with David Doyle
in *The Beauty Part*

Final gesture of *The Beauty Part*

Fishing with *Field & Stream*
editor A. J. McLain

As Pisthetairos with Mildred in
The Birds, Ypsilanti Greek Theater
Festival (1966)

An advertising pose

With daughter Jane

JOHN COCHRAN

DICK RICHARDS

With Mildred at *Time* banquet honoring cover stories

Overleaf
Waiting for rehearsal (1962)

An unlikely Chingachgook, Dad aims the boat down the lake, pointing out turtles slithering off logs and looking for fish breaking water. He shouts above the motor's hum and points to the equipment. We can't hear him, so he settles back on the throttle, steering the boat into a quiet pool. Then he helps prepare the fishing gear. He is surprisingly generous with his equipment. He puts his glasses on to tie the leaders and bites off extra line. The glasses slide down his nose. Jane suspects pike because of the lily pads; father assures her that this is bass water, pointing to the rocky shoreline. He tells us, as he does each trip, that the art of casting is in the wrist, and that if we catch a fish we must keep the tip of our poles high. Jane, eager to show her prowess, makes the first cast. Captivated by its unsuspected arc, Jane watches the lure crash against the rocky promontory and cling to a bush twenty feet above. Lahr looks away for a moment, and then tries to help her.

"See if you can't get it out—pull lightly."

Jane, heaving like a tuna fisherman, snaps the lure free and sends it careening directly over her head into the water behind her. She is afraid to look at her father's tired eyes; her line lies in serpentine knots on the water.

"Reel it in, Jane. Reel it in."

She dips her pole in the water as she cranks the reel.

"Keep your tip up." She raises the pole.

"Hey, I've got a fish."

Dad grabs the line and tugs on it like the Indian guide who usually accompanies him.

"Bottom," he says, sighing.

"I knew I'd get a fish on the first cast."

"Bottom. Jane, do as I say. Keep your pole straight; and let me free the line."

He reaches out to tug it, and a fish breaks the water. Jane reels furiously, her pole dipping in the water and then flailing the air.

Lahr helps it in the boat; and Jane squeals as he takes the hook out of its mouth. A pike.

The fishing is slow; at the end of an hour we have only netted two. Jane, dangling her lure in the water to watch its movement, attracted a bass right under the boat. My father is anxious to move.

We begin to cast along a wooded cove. "There'll be some big ones in here," Jane announces. Sunken logs make the maneuvering hazardous, but my father is after The Big One. The motor inches us along while we cast. A fish swirls as my lure hits the water and then leaps high in the air.

"That's gotta be a six-pounder," Dad says leaning toward the action. The fish jumps again, and on the second leap spits out the lure.

Dad is intent. "Jane, give me your rod."

Dad makes a cast, but with his hand off the motor the boat angles in toward the logs.

"Jane, all you have to do is hold the handle like this. We don't want to go very fast. But when I tell you to move—then do it. Not now. Let me cast back in there." They change places and Dad trips over his tackle box.

He takes aim and sends a long cast into still, deep water. He reels in slowly.

"They're in here. We know they're in here."

He casts again; and suddenly his reel begins to hum. A fish—and a big one.

Dad's head stiffens, his nose points out like a bloodhound; the tip of his rod shoots high into the air.

"Uh—huh! This is a beaut!"

We catch a glimpse of a large pike. From the boat it could be as large as twenty pounds. But, with all the excitement we are moving, again, into the logs.

"Steer the boat clear of the logs, Jane . . . I don't want to lose him in the logs. Turn the throttle."

Jane turns the throttle—the wrong way. The boat suddenly jolts into reverse at a fantastic speed; and Dad sprawls on his back at the bottom of the boat, the fish being yanked behind. Jane tries to adjust the motor; but before she can shut it off, we are already rammed against the shore. When Dad recovers his pole, the line is broken.

We return home four hours early, in tired silence . . . Dad at the helm.

"I smell, I really smell."

Dad is sick again. The fevers began in 1962 and come unexpectedly; no doctor can explain them. They can last from two days to ten. They leave him frustrated and furious, and the family exhausted.

"Don't come near—I really stink. The doctor won't let me take a bath. I can't stand myself. Phew—this is terrible . . .!"

In bed, with the covers pulled up to his chin, he stares at the ceiling, his nostrils elevated above the sheets, like a hippo in water. He clears his throat, but continues staring. He fumbles for the thermometer, shakes it, and sticks it in his mouth.

The doctor has been to see him. Another doctor. He is so demanding that they get tired of coming. When they don't discover anything but send him a big bill, he fires them like baseball managers. The doctor stays with Dad an hour, but refuses to give him penicillin. As Mother is showing him to the door, Dad pushes himself on his side with a low grunt.

"Get me the telephone book, John—I want to find a doctor." He looks for a minute and then becomes interested in the perspiration that lathers his forehead. He grabs the towel around his neck and wipes his face as if he'd just come off a tennis court. He reaches for the thermometer again and crams it in his mouth. Three minutes later, he is squinting down his glasses, "Tsk, tsk—102."

He gets up to go to the bathroom. His hair—what is left of it—is uncombed and damp. He looks like a newborn bird. He wobbles on his feet and I try to help him into the bathrobe. He never wears pajama bottoms and suddenly realizes there are women present. He searches for a loin cloth and ends up hiding behind me as he eases into the robe. When I touch his arm, I can feel the bone. What fat there is hangs loosely to one side. He walks carefully toward the bathroom muttering, "Those goddamned nuts, I should never have eaten them."

When he comes back to bed, he shrinks with cold, holding his hands to his chest like an old lady.

"It's freezing in here. Turn on the heat." The room is very warm. His face is grizzled and beaten. He sinks back with his eyes shut— pained and hoping and afraid.

He scares me. He has lost weight since his illness. He is convinced it's cancer; but when we point out that he has not eaten regularly in five weeks, he takes heart. "That's right. If you don't eat, how can you gain weight." He has a job, and he must keep working. He can get up out of a sickbed and do a scene. In front of the camera, he is vivacious and agile. But at home it is a different story. Is this how it will end— rubbing his nose to keep from crying, sitting nervous and petulant? There is no rage, not even a howl. In bed, he is frozen in fear, pulled up into a fist of bone and flaccid skin. He is suddenly shrunk to a size less than human—he sits motionless, graceless, grinding his teeth in frustration.

Came to see Dad; his temperature was down.

"You know what I'd like—some soup. What kind have we got?"

I brought in six varieties. He chose chicken noodle.

"But I can't eat the noodles—strain them out."

He was lying in the chaise longue when I brought it to him. I wrapped a napkin around his neck and put the tray on his lap. He took a spoonful and spluttered like a motorboat, the soup spraying the room.

"There's salt in this. You know I can't have anything with salt in it."

He's getting better.

"Well, we're going to find out what this is once and for all," he says.

Dad is going to Mt. Sinai Hospital for observation.

When we arrive, mother meets us in front of his bedroom marked "Mr. Smith." "He keeps telling me I read my lines wrong. I can't do anything right. But the nurse who met us wanted to have him go up in a wheelchair. Imagine Bert Lahr going up in a wheelchair."

His presence in the hospital is supposed to be secret; but nurses send him notes and doctors bring their teams of interns to meet him. He tries to be sociable. He can't understand the people around him. The young doctors, looking very serious, gaze at him—while the head physician pokes his liver and asks him questions. When they take him for observation, he has to be lowered onto a stretcher. With a white sheet around him and strapped to the stretcher, Lahr looks like a roped calf. His stomach rises in a hillock between the straps.

"Everything will be okay, Pop."

"Yeah, well, I'm an orthodox coward . . ."

They wheel him down pale green hallways.

A week of testing reveals nothing. The doctors come, examine his charts, and leave. Each time after they exit, he whispers, "They're all charlatans—every damn one of them. Maybe country doctors are dedicated . . ." He takes his temperature.

"Well, what is it?"

"Parker '51."

"I think I've got a temperature. I feel like I'm getting the chills."

Mother sighs. Dad watches for a fever behind every rumble in his stomach.

"Oh, Bert—I'll bet you haven't got a fever."

"Whaddya mean, I'm a walking thermometer."

"I'll say you are! You never take it out of your mouth."

"Wanna bet?"

"Five dollars."

Dad takes out five dollars and holds it toward mother.

"I don't have five dollars, but my word is my bond." She writes out an I.O.U. and hands it to him.

"What is that," Dad laughs. "A piece of paper. She's trying to con me. 'My word is my bond.' "

"Take your temperature."

We wait as my father puts the thermometer in his mouth and watches the clock. He takes it out after three minutes and holds it up to the light. Turning back to Mother, he announces, "It's normal—you win."

"That's the easiest fiver I've ever made."

"I guess I didn't keep it in long enough."

He returns to his desk and tries again—this time he waits twenty minutes.

"I'm all mental since that illness. I've got a complex. Turn off those Christmas carols, they make me sad. The boys at the club think so too."

Dad surveys the Christmas tree and his family sitting around with the presents. He has never gotten up early with his family to open them. His presents are stacked in a neat pile for his arrival. He begins ripping at the carefully wrapped gifts.

"Toilet water, socks—that's all I get." He laughs and looks toward Mother, raising his eyebrows to show he's teasing her.

He goes inside and brings out a sweater.

"Bert, that was my Christmas present to you!" Mildred says.

"I have three sweaters—a pink one, a yellow one, and one in blue. Try this on, John. Let's see how it looks."

He buttons the cardigan on me and stands back to judge.

"Hey, it doesn't look bad. You keep it. Feel that material. That's one hundred per cent wool. It would cost you forty dollars in the stores."

"$62.50," says Mildred.

The news of an English production of *The Beauty Part* reached Dad today. He was excited, and got out of his bed—another fever—to call S. J. Perelman. He tried to hide his illness.

"Hello, S. J., this is B. L."

He talked excitedly, and after the conversation confided, "He's a tough one. Never wants to chop a line. I think he's got confidence in me now though . . ."

This will be his first time on the English stage. There have been many days of waiting; but Lester has just confirmed the deal, although no papers have been signed. "At this point, John, I don't care if I go or don't go." But the apartment looks like a campaign headquarters. The trunks are open and on Jane's bed things are being laid out in profusion: his tails, top hat, two hair pieces, a portfolio of sketches in case there are TV shots, extra batteries for his radio, his walking cap, two pairs of ankle-length boots that he had made in Spain at four times their actual value, pictures of the family, good-luck charms . . .

He is happier now. After so many days of indecision and waiting. Moving Bert Lahr to England is like moving a sideshow.

"Did you call Cele?"

"No."

"Write that down so I can remember to do it." Then he writes the memo himself. Mother laughs. Despite his efforts at consideration, she will have to make the calls, check for the limousine, and probably make sure he gets his card to enter the Garrick Club—a social event he has been looking forward to with pride.

He rolls some cellophane in his right hand and relaxes in the chair. The television is off. He is thinking, smiling, pondering. So many things to do. He is warming to the part.

"Some awfully funny lines in that script . . . Do they understand the word 'scratch'? What should I use. How about 'lolly'? Does that mean the same thing. You know it's kind of low class around there."

"Yes."

"Write that in the script, Mildred—lolly."

"I hope they like it over there. Tynan is a big fan of mine; and

S. J. Perelman, well, the Marx Brothers' movies have made him some kind of saint. I just hope we go over. Knock on wood." He raps the table.

"Now, when I get there, I can't spend too much time going places. This is a tough show. I'll need to rest. I saw Maurice [Chevalier] today, he said they'd love me over there. I hope so. And even Maurice, he's seventy-nine, said to me, 'Bert, I'm fine but I have to rest between shows now.' You should see him, not a wrinkle on his face" (touching his skin). "Now, I just have to rest and watch my weight. No nuts. If I can make some friends over there . . . If I can just make some friends. People annoy me; and I just stay away. I can tell when somebody really likes me—like Maurice—well, then I'll approach them. Now your mother, she likes everybody.

"Let's do the lines. I know my first scene already. Let's do it, Mildred."

Mother puts down her sewing and wearily holds up her Samuel French copy of the play. "Take it from Hyacinth Laffoon . . ."

Dad interrupts the reading. "Do they know Barry Goldwater over there? How about *Lolita?* Do they know what *golem* is? Well, we'll have to change that; but S. J. will think of something."

Lahr stops again. "I'll have to find another word for 'bomb.' I think 'stink' is better."

When we tell him that "bomb" means "success" in England, he adds with the conviction of a Jesuit, "Yes, I'll have to change that line."

Sitting in the chair, he toys with the gestures of Hyacinth Laffoon. His eyebrows point heavenward, he preens himself. His pursed lips become an expression of her fastidiousness. He squints, his shoulders jostle to and fro like a woman getting comfortable in her girdle.

He misses a word and his hand reaches up to his forehead. His index finger rubs against it as if it were cushioning a pool cue. He repeats the line trying to find the right intonation. Finally, he has had enough.

"I'm getting paid the most money that any American comedian has ever earned over there—550 pounds a week. They're letting me take it out because I'm giving work to a lot of English people."

He won't listen about the English tax structure, which will take nineteen of every twenty shillings he earns. We tell him about the English theaters, how the public supports its theater, how cheap the seats are in comparison to Broadway prices. He worries for a moment about the tight money squeeze in England. Would it affect his show?

Looking up from the script on his desk, he adds—"We'll certainly miss you kids."

The trunks have been on the docks for a week; but the English producers delay sending Dad his ticket. On the phone to England, he is politic but adamant. The producers apologize and assure him the fare is in the mail. It never comes. Finally, two weeks after the scheduled departure, his agent calls with news that the show had been canceled. The English producers could not raise the money. They had been stalling. The news came late in the evening, and when we visited the next morning, Dad had already left the house. A bottle of Sherry was set on the living room table, and a blue towel draped over the back of his favorite chair.

Mother said he sat up all night. He mentioned nothing about it that evening.

We go with him to the Ed Sullivan show. He's doing his "Cop Act." The television studio is crowded; the lights hang down from the ceiling like stalactites. Technicians scurry in front of the audience getting ready for the eight o'clock show. Above the stage are four large screens. The audience can see the action better from the screens because a labyrinth of wires and cameras clutters the stage. Sullivan comes before the show. "Look kids, we've got the Dave Clark Five on tonight. Now I don't mind if you carry on when they come out, but remember there are other stars on the bill." He disappears behind a screen. The lights come up; the technicians flap cue cards toward Sullivan and ready the first act a few feet from where he announces what is on the program. He forgets to mention Dad, who is last on the bill.

We know the cop act by heart. Watching above on the screens, the camera loses his motion in close-ups. Dad has to rush through the sketch because the show is running late. He can't wait for responses. The audience laughs; but they know the joke almost as well as they know the face. On stage, the atmosphere is cramped and antiseptic; linoleum floors, white light, the audience stacked up on raked seats in front of the performing area.

After the performance, we sit with Dad while he packs his equipment—one policeman's hat, one blank revolver, and a badge. We mention that Sullivan didn't announce him; he is surprised. "Oh, this guy's like that. You never know. We're all absentminded." He keeps his make-up on. On the way out, he stops to thank Sullivan. People cluster around; and my father notices a young girl standing to the side of them.

"Little girl—miss—did you want my autograph?"

She hands him a pad, hesitating a moment to look at his face. He continues toward the elevator, where he recognizes one of the show's producers.

"Hello, Cy." The man is wearing sunglasses and a diamond ring on his little finger.

"Another one in the can, Bert. Eighteen years. Fifty-two weeks. Oi."

"That's a fortnight, isn't it?" smiles my father.

When we walk out into the cold evening air, the children rush screaming toward him. His pen won't write. "Just put an X," says one girl, anxious to catch the Dave Clark Five.

At home, he is perplexed about Sullivan's omission. "Well, that's the way he is. We're good friends. Maybe he just forgot. He does that."

"Bert, you weren't even billed—it's disgusting . . ."

He calls his agent. No answer: taking his magnifying glass he inspects the television listings. Mildred is right.

"Well, I got the booking last week. At my age, I'm in this business for the money," he adds, taking off his shirt so that his gut dips over his belt. "Anyway, who cares?"

He rarely attends public occasions; but tonight the family is going to a gala premiere of a grade-B movie, *Cast a Giant Shadow*. As we pull up, a policeman tells the chauffeur, "11:30, driver." People are cordoned off from the opening; they strain to see the faces. A man stands on top of the television truck spotting the famous people as they enter and positioning the television crew.

"There's Bert Lahr. Bert Lahr. Dolly in, for chrissake! Dolly in. Keep it coming . . ."

Hands reach out pulling him toward the white light of the TV cameras.

The camera light is merciless. It makes Dad look old; it uncovers blemishes on female faces usually well disguised by make-up. The television announcer standing smooth and dinner-jacketed calls my father to the podium. We try to listen to what he is saying; but with the screaming and the bustling television cameramen, his voice fades out. He talks with his hands in his pocket. He seems relaxed, uncaring, smiling wanly his professional smile. He pushes his way inside. Radio newsmen clutch at him as he walks slowly past. They are young and eager. As they talk, their eyes flash toward the lobby doors for the next celebrity. They talk to him with a professional nonchalance. They thrust the microphone up to his mouth, asking him the first question that comes to their mind. They know nothing about him; they don't care. There is no understanding, simply business.

"Will you please not block the aisles! Please go to your seats."

The usher approaches my mother. "Lady, will you please get out of the way."

"I'm waiting for my husband."

"All right, lady, will you please step aside." He tries to push her.

Another woman squirms past, clearing space for herself with a pointed elbow. "I don't care, George, I just want to take one look . . ."

Dad comes toward us; but a Marine sergeant begins his patter. "It's Bert Lahr, ladies and gentlemen, Bert Lahr. How are you, Bert?"

"Fine."

"Those commercials of yours are just the greatest."

"Yes, I was just saying to one of the other networks, after all these years in the business these commercials have finally made me known." (He doesn't really want to say that.) It is what the public wants to hear and what they expect. It saddens him. He doesn't look at the Marine, who pushes closer to him.

"Do you have something to say to our boys overseas?" He moves the microphone under Dad's nose. "I'm sure the boys abroad would love to hear something from one of America's most famous comedians, a man who has made them laugh since they were kids . . ."

Dad thinks for a while. The Marine is insistent.

"Well—hello."

The sergeant waits for more, then rattles on. "I snuck in last night and saw the picture. *Cast a Giant Shadow,* and Bert, believe me, it casts a great glow over this great country. It makes you proud to be . . ."

There is a sudden surge of new arrivals. Elbows shoot over Dad's ear. He cannot even turn to see who is pushing him. The Marine loses his guest and searches into the mass of perfumed faces for someone new, talking continuously into the microphone.

As we take our seats, no one is looking toward the screen. They are gazing around for famous faces, glancing at the show of diamonds and fall dresses. A woman in a sequined evening dress walks stealthily behind my father. Dad doesn't see her. She is wearing a heavy diamond ring on the outside of her gloved index finger. She reaches into her purse and pulls out a small camera. She lurches at Dad, snapping his picture just as he looks up at the sudden movement.

After the movie, there is another crush to get out. There will be a banquet at the Hilton, where he will be introduced and photographed. He will see old faces and columnist friends. Perhaps he will have a good time. The pattern is always repeated.

As he leaves the movie theater, he tries to look inconspicuous. A little girl passes with her mother. "Look mommie—there's the potato chip!"

He glances at her and lowers his head through the crowd.

They haven't spoken in two days. It began when Mother asked Dad to stop taking his temperature every five minutes.

"There's a lot of things that you do which annoy me!" he said, and for forty-eight hours they have not uttered a word to one another.

Jane called to ask me to mediate. She tried to talk to him, but he sat like a Buddha with his back to Mother. "My temperature's up. I have to take my white pills. Where are they? Your mother's a nag . . . nag . . . nag!" Jane began to laugh. Now Dad isn't talking to her either.

Tonight, we sent them a one-word telegram: TALK.

Mother handed us each envelopes with goodbye letters as she boarded the plane with Dorothy McHugh for Europe. It was the first trip she had ever taken without Dad. At the airport, he was quiet; and even at Mother's melodramatic moment he said nothing.

As he turned away from the observation deck, he was crying. He wiped the tears from his eyes and turned to Frank McHugh.

"They'll miss us."

He quit the Lambs Club today—the second time he's left it. This exit was final. The family is very upset; he's accepting no calls. "I need the Lambs like I need eight nostrils," he keeps saying.

He has asked me down to the club many times—it has always been exciting to see his pictures among the memorabilia on the walls. He was a member when the club could boast the finest performers—W. C.

Fields, Bobby Clark, Bert Wheeler, Will Rogers. He has performed on the stage at the club. They have given him special evenings; and it was here that he read his speech—perhaps the only one he ever wrote himself—celebrating fifty years on the American stage. He was the corresponding secretary who liked to boast, "I'm the only secretary who never corresponded." And there are two Flemish seventeenth-century landscapes donated by him.

He was going to put on the Lamb's Gambol—the annual production that raises money for the club. He enjoyed the idea. He had already lined up stars to perform and had commissioned new song material. Mayor Lindsay had even been contacted to make an appearance. All that effort is canceled. It was nice to see him making plans.

"I'm still Bert Lahr. I've still got a name. I'm still a great comedian. I've got my pride, you know. Doing things behind my back. I wanted to put on a show; they wanted a dais. For chrissake. They elected me Collie, and then they form an executive committee to overrule the things I want. Well, I'm not going down there and be humiliated by a bunch of amateurs. The phone hasn't stopped ringing. They're incensed at the club. They're incensed at what happened to me . . ."

There's no reasoning with him. The memories of the past, his own sense of theatrical tradition evoke no response.

"You want tradition? I belong to a club—the Players Club—that ninety per cent of those guys couldn't get in. What do I do when I go down there, anyway. Talk show business. Cut up a few touches? None of those fellows are my friends. Most of them haven't been in the theater for years."

A telephone call interrupts the discussion. A Lambs Committee is forming in protest. Lahr speaks to the organizer. "It's no use, Lew. Thanks for your letter. Anything to tell them? Yeah—tell them to go fuck themselves."

He hangs up and starts considering his future. "A couple of days a week I'll go down to the Players with Frank McHugh. And I'll take up painting. It'll pass a little time." He stops and looks at the list of performers he had planned. "I would have liked to put on that show."

We're going down to the Players—a long taxi ride from Eighty-fifth Street. Peering out the window of the cab, he sees the Plaza, which brings back the memory of The Mayfair and Billy La Hiff's Tavern. "If they tear down the Plaza that will be it. We'll go to Spain or some nice place. Lester's secretary rented a villa in Greece for five hundred dollars a year. If it's that reasonable, maybe we could go there. All I need is a boat. I'll fish." He shakes his head in disgust and, gazing out the window at new buildings, says, "Will you come and see me if I move out of the city?"

We ride the rest of the way in silence.

Dad's says he's doing a movie; but today he's scheduled for a medical examination for the company's health insurance. It is standard procedure for film companies, he says. There are more small humiliations in old age. He has worried about the examination all week. The last time, his blood pressure went up ten points in the doctor's office.

I wait for his call, but it doesn't come until late that evening.

"How did it go, Dad?"

"Oh, not too well." His voice lowers. "I didn't sleep too well. My blood pressure is up."

"Are they going to insure you?"

"Well, we'll see."

The next morning he calls in a sunny voice to say that things have been "firmed up."

"I met the producer at the Dorset," he reported over the phone. "It's not a great part, but I think I get the sympathy, even though I'm around the edges." He is talking about *The Night They Raided Minsky's*—a film about a type of burlesque he never knew. He hasn't worked for a while; and the script is better than average. He is interested.

"I told him I wouldn't do it unless the part was built up. He wouldn't commit himself. So after lunch, I asked him to take a walk up Fifth Avenue, figuring that people would recognize me. Sure enough, we started walking and people stopped. I could see them saying, 'That's Bert Lahr.' That showed him I was still a drawing card."

He writes out his lines to memorize them. He puts the sheets of paper away in his desk when we arrive. At dinner, he gets mad at himself for not retaining names or missing a key line in his script. "Isn't that terrible. I can't remember things. Yesterday, you know, I took an injection of B-12. Well, I called up the doctor to ask him a question and I forgot. Luckily, I remembered about an hour later. I'm in a hell of a fix. I see people in a restaurant—intimate friends—and their names slip my mind . . ."

"Dad, you were doing that twenty years ago too."

He goes on as if he didn't hear me. "And I don't remember their names. You can't look at them and say, 'Pardon me, what's your name again.' I don't know. I just don't know. When I was young I could look at a script and get it just like that." He snaps his fingers, adding somberly, "Now, it's labor. It's the goddamnedest thing. I can't remember . . . (forgetting) . . . pseudonyms."

"The dog doesn't like me. I pet him. I feed him. I play with him. He won't even come near me."

"It's just that when people are around he hasn't seen for a while, he gets excited," Jane explains.

"Here, Barry. Here Barry."

"Dad, that was our last dog. This one's Merlin."

"What kind of a name is that for a dog—Merlin. Who's Merlin?"

"It was named for Oscar Wilde's grandson—Merlyn Holland."

"You can't call a dog Merlin." He swishes his shoulders like a hairdresser. "Here, Merlin. Here, Merlin. If I walk the dog, I'm not calling him Merlin. Suppose somebody stopped me on the street and asked me what the name of the dog is. How can I say Merlin? I'll call it Toto. Here Toto, here Toto."

Dropped in on Mother and Dad today. Dad was in rare form. "This dog is a pest. Stop it, Merlin! All he wants to do is nip . . . Stop it! . . . Oh . . . Merlin, cut it out!"

We talked about his new movie, and he mentioned my criticism. "When you write the word 'hooker,' it sticks out like a sore thumb, John. Use classical language—'harlot' or 'woman of the streets.'"

I apologized for not visiting more frequently. He tried to listen while patting the dog.

"Don't be silly. You're young and active. We don't expect you to be around all the time. We can't do that. We go out. We come home. We sit—that's our life now . . . Stop that, Merlin! God, this dog's a pest."

A BEGINNING
AND AN END

"During the last decades the interest in professional fasting has markedly diminished. It used to pay very well to stage such great performances under one's own management, but today that is quite Impossible. . . .
. . . Are you still fasting?" asked the overseer. "When on earth do you mean to stop?" "Forgive me, everybody," whispered the hunger artist; only the overseer, who had his ear to the bars, understood him. "Of course," said the overseer, and tapped his forehead with a finger to let attendants know what state the man was in, "we forgive you." "I always wanted you to admire my fasting," said the hungry artist. "We do admire it," said the overseer, affably. "But you shouldn't admire it," said the hungry artist. "Well, then we don't admire it," said the over- seer, "but why shouldn't we admire it?" "Because I have to fast, and I can't help it," said the hungry artist. "What a fellow you are," said the overseer, "and why can't you help it?" "Because," said the hunger artist, lifting his head a little and speaking, with his lips pursed, as if for a kiss, right into the overseer's ear, so that no syllable might be lost, "Because I couldn't find the food I liked. If I had found it, believe me, I should have made no fuss and stuffed myself like you or anyone else. . . ."

Franz Kafka, "The Hunger Artist"

AUGUST 12, 1967. WE ARE GOING ON AN OUTING. DAD IS TAKING ME to the park. We are not visiting Central Park, which is right out- side his apartment, but Carl Schurz Park, six blocks east on the River at Eighty-sixth Street. It is nearly sixty years since he has seen it. We are going by cab because he can't walk very far, and this will be the longest walk he's taken in a week. Our trip will take three quarters of an hour.

As we start for the elevator, I notice Dad is carrying his camera. "I'm gonna take pictures of where I lived."

We get into the cab. He says in his adenoidal tone reserved for headwaiters and cab drivers, "I want to go to Eighty-first and First; then to Eighty-eighth between First and York. Hold your flag, Bill, I want to take a few pictures." He always calls cabbies "Bill," and I look at the real name of the driver: Seymour J. Million, number 4907.

"I'm lookin' at your face," says number 4907. "You're very familiar. You're in the pictchahs?"

Lahr waits for a second. "I've done some pictures."

The cabbie stares into his mirror. "I just can't place the face. You know I had Steve and Eydie in here last week . . . One of your ranks died a while back—Clara Bow."

"I was never in silent pictures. I didn't know her . . ." But Clara Bow isn't so easily dismissed. Dad's eyes stop focusing on the storefront signs and people, and solidify somberly into a quiet thought. Clara Bow has been dead for two years. He didn't know her, but others, many others who represented his theater world, have passed away. Buster Keaton, Spencer Tracy, Sherman Billingsley, Louis Shurr—all dead, all younger than he. Now he prefaces all prospects for the future with a rap on wood saying, "God willing."

The cab comes to a sudden stop, and Lahr peers out at a brownstone walk-up whose first floor is now a Chinese laundry.

"That's where I was born, John. I think it was—let me see. It was the second floor in the back, or was it the first?"

"It was the top floor in the back, Pop."

"Yeah, I guess it was—the top floor in the back."

He slithers out of the cab carefully and slowly, grunting as he pushes himself with his camera—a Japanese model with an instant light meter and automatic lens adjuster—out into the sunlight.

A minute or so later he is back. "Eighty-eighth and York."

"Right down here, John," he points due north on First Avenue. "Right down here, is it on this block?—No. Right *there* is where I went to school." He is pointing to a vacant lot, soon to be covered by a modern apartment building.

He looks at the lot. "I guess it's been torn down."

The façades have changed on First Avenue. "That used to be a candy store, where we'd load up before school. It was called 'Cheap Jack's.' "

We are at Eighty-eighth Street now; and he is pointing in amazement at a corner bar now under Irish management. "That used to be Schmidt's."

We stop in front of another brownstone walk-up with dark green iron lattice work on the doors and an elaborate fire escape that cannot camouflage the building's drab exterior.

"We lived on the first floor in the back." He stares at it from across the street. He has no desire to get nearer, but paces back and forth getting a good angle for his camera shot. Crouching low with his camera propped on the top of a parked Chevrolet, he focuses. The rim of his hat, usually tilted at a rakish angle over his face, is pushed upward like a press photographer's. He takes the picture, and then checks the intricate adjustments to make sure. The building has been recorded; he can file the picture away in the large wooden box of slides he keeps near his desk. He is satisfied; picture taken, mechanism checked—we move on. Grit from the hot summer day irritates his eyes; tears trickle down over the large pouches. He bends his head over the camera to examine the lens. The flesh beneath his chin expands in fine layers like pizza dough.

We have come to see the places of Old New York he has mentioned so often with his family at dinner. We have come here finally to pinpoint the store where, for a nickel, you could carry off a pail of beer and for the same price get a night's entertainment at the nickelodeon. Two blocks east is the park, bordering the river. He has reminisced about swimming the muddy currents and diving from the wooden pylons. He played in the park; he practiced tapdancing before he ever went on the stage. We have come to see all this.

We walk slowly down Eighty-eighth Street. He carries the camera in the crook of his left elbow like a baton. He can still remember the names of the friends he has not seen in sixty years, but not what they looked like.

"Tommy Lark lived right there, and Solly Abrahams lived across the street." He points to the large corner building on York Avenue.

"Now the nickelodeon was around here." He stops to survey the two corner stores. "It could have been that one there, too," he says pointing to a butcher shop on the corner of Eighty-ninth.

"This must be the place," he says, deciding on the butcher shop. "It cost five cents at night, three cents in the daytime. It was run by a contortionist called 'Snakerino.' He dressed in snakeskin and performed between shows. They played silent movies, and there was a piano. We sang along as the pictures flashed on the screen. That's about all I can . . . oh yeah, and they had planks for seats—just wooden planks."

He points to the white traffic line down the center of York Avenue. "They had trolley cars here and right there is where I was hit. I had to have fourteen stitches." He taps his forehead.

"Let me see, I can't remember this street so well, but I know I came here often . . . it's all changed so much. I just can't visualize it . . ."

As we come to the park, he is looking for the ferry slip where he used to dive. He can remember the water and how he hid his clothes behind the rocks and spent hours leaping off the mossy logs, fighting the strong current.

"See, it was over there. It was right where the highway goes, I guess. I remember it used to be right down by the House of Good Shepherd . . . right over there." He stops and smiles. "It was a home for wayward girls. They used to throw us money on a string and ask us to get cigarettes for them . . . Sometimes they used terrible language."

As we walk into the park, he comes to a halt. "Let's stop here. I want to rest a minute." He looks at his legs. He doesn't say anything about them except, occasionally, to recognize their independence from his body by announcing, "Legs!" and then shaking his head in disgust.

We pass Gracie Mansion, the residence of the mayor. It is being repaired so we have to detour around it.

"Now *this* was not here when I lived at Eighty-eighth . . . No, I don't remember this at all."

I lead him back to the front of the house where a tarnished bronze plaque gives its history. "Built in 1799."

A boy, palming a football, yells to his friend who bobs and weaves a few feet ahead of him. "Go out ten and cut to the trash can." He completes it. Lahr watches.

"I was never very good at football. I used to make believe I threw the discus down where the ferry used to be. I mean I really threw it, but it was only a rock, you know."

We continue through the park, looking for the bandstand. He follows slowly. "It was a bandstand. On Sundays, they used to have concerts there . . . I used to practice tapdancing when it was quiet . . ."

I lead him to a large, somnolent plaza at Eighty-sixth Street. An old woman walks abruptly into the space and, without looking around, begins to distribute breadcrumbs from a large paper bag. The wind expands the baggy calico sleeve of her dress like a buzzard's wing.

"This must be it, Pop."

He glances around. "It wasn't here. It couldn't have been here. There was kind of a gazebo, you know . . ." He scans the circumference of the park. "Well, then, I guess it's all gone. It's pretty here *now*."

We walk out of the park, glancing at the beautiful bit of old New York that has been turned into fashionable townhouses at Eighty-sixth Street, Henderson Place. "It all used to be pretty bad in this section here. Not quite middle class, except for these houses on the river. Let me see, who lived here? I used to know him when I was a kid. I think his name was . . . he passed away later on . . ."

The Eighty-fourth Street baths are our next stop. Dad doesn't expect them to be there, but he turns the corner anyway. He wants to make sure.

But when we approach the spot there are only luxury apartment buildings. He looks eagerly for the baths where he swam all day for fifteen cents.

"No. They've built this place up. It's not here. It used to be right here. Geez, I haven't any picture of what was." We gaze at the Triborough Bridge, strung like a massive skein of wool against the full blue sky. He points to the island, which still remains. "That's Blackwell's Island." He turns around unexpectedly and starts back toward Eighty-sixth Street.

He begins to mutter to himself, "Frankie . . . Frankie . . . Frankie . . . Frankie?"

"What did you say, Pop?"

"I'm trying to think of his name, the kid I used to know here."

We pass the plaza again. The old woman now stands in animated conversation with some pigeons. They are pecking at her outstretched hands for breadcrumbs. A group of people have collected.

"How about that for a picture?"

"Yeah, I'm going to take it." The professional photographer's hauteur. He has already planned the shot. He cocks his camera and takes aim, poised like a skeet shooter with his weight on his front foot. He squints and focuses on the woman who is too involved with her birds to notice him. But the people watching begin to look away from the birds and concentrate on the familiar face. They don't interrupt; they just stare. He takes one shot, but a bird flies across the old woman's face. Not satisfied, he tries another angle.

"Got it that time." He ambles toward the cab stand with his camera strung like a St. Bernard's flask around his neck. A park attendant who has been watching him follows behind us. Dad pretends not to notice.

"Say, Mister?"

There is no reply.

"Is that Bert Lahr?" he says quietly, moving next to him.

Dad turns slowly and gradually begins to smile.

"I was born in Yorkville too, Bert. My old man was always talking about how he used to know you when you lived around here."

The park attendant extends his hand. "How are you, sir," Dad says, shaking it and noticing the drab gray park uniform.

We walk on. "Do you remember 'Schneider's Miracle,' John? I wore a costume just like that." He is tired now and he walks slowly. He squints at his camera before putting it back in the leather case. He examines it closely again, and then suddenly looks up in fierce disgust.

"For chrissake, I forgot to put the camera on automatic. I'll have to take all the pictures again."

Maybe, he says, he'll do it next week. Maybe he will never do it. We hail a cab. As he bends inside, he groans to himself, "Aaaaah! if I could only walk . . ."

Back at the apartment, a script of *Minsky's* has been delivered and placed, businesslike, at the center of his desk. Near it are his radio, the dictionary, and a fly swatter imported from the kitchen. He sits silently at his desk.

Mother pulls me aside to ask if I've sent Dad a birthday card. To-morrow he will be seventy-two; and I've forgotten.

When I come back to the room to see him, he is still at his desk preparing to read the movie.

"Hey, Pop, what do you want for your birthday?"

He doesn't answer.

"What can I get you?"

"Save your money, John. I don't want any more birthdays. It's sort of stupid, don't you think. What are you celebrating. Like Beckett says, a child is born and immediately he's dying. It's stupid."

A fly strafes his head and Lahr pans around the room looking for it. He puts on his glasses and reaches for the fly swatter as the pest lands on his dictionary. Raising the swatter slowly, he comes down on the book with a butcher's menace. The fly glides with infuriating ease to the other side of the desk.

"The son-of-a-bitch! He's been hit before."

He turns on the color television, a golf tournament. He adjusts the portable set on his desk for the baseball game, and fits the ear-phones in place. The radio plays Jerome Kern.

He laughs at the script. I say something, but there is no answer.

"I think I'll go home, Pop. Thanks for the walk."

I kiss him on the top of his bald head. It is beaded with summer sweat and smelling like the inside of a baseball glove.

Richard Avedon's picture of him as Estragon bears down on me as I leave the room. In it, my father's hands are pressed to his chest with a novitiate's urgency; his face swollen with a nameless, punishing despair.

"See 'ya, Pop."

Without looking up he mumbles, "Okay, kid."

I shut the door quietly. He is silent: sitting surrounded by noises and the flickering images of television. He is waiting.

Avedon's photograph evokes Estragon's words—Dad's words—"Don't touch me! Don't question me! Don't speak to me! Stay with me!"

EPILOGUE

BERT LAHR DIED IN THE EARLY MORNING OF DECEMBER 4, 1967. Two weeks before, he had returned home at two a.m., chilled and feverish, from the damp studio where *The Night They Raided Minsky's* was being filmed. Ordinarily, a man of his age and reputation would not have had to perform that late into the night, but he had waived that proviso in his contract because of his trust in the producer and his need to work. The newspapers reported the cause of death as pneumonia; but he succumbed to cancer, a disease he feared but never knew he had.

For the few days that he teetered on the brink of consciousness the family was with him—talking, listening to his demands, concentrating on muffled words. He told me for God's sake to get a new suit of clothes because they knew him in this hospital; he mentioned his project to update *A Midsummer Night's Dream,* which he wanted E. Y. Harburg and Harold Arlen to write for him. He kept imagining he was still at work. "Mildred," he said, "why aren't my clothes laid out, I've got a seven o'clock call."

I heard him singing in bed. The nurse thought he was calling for help, but bending over him, she saw he was doing an old routine. The words were inaudible, but the rhythm was musical comedy. His last word, whispered two days before a quiet death, was "hurt."

At the end, they had to strap his hands, which kept jutting out in illness, as they had vigorously in life. He clutched at the air—hopeful and bewildered.

Many praised his art. Editorials throughout the nation mourned his death: his leering humanity had become a part of America's heritage. In an age of uniformity, Bert Lahr remained unique. His voice never lost its range; his statement never lost its hard truth. He told us about the limitations of the body, about the isolation and humble beauty of the soul.

He made a most gorgeous fuss.

He made us laugh, until, at times, we cried.

APPENDICES

APPENDIX 1

"The New Teacher," a Kid Act

Based on the Avon Comedy Four by
Joe Smith and Charlie Dale (c. 1900)

The Kid Act reflected the good-humored anarchy and vague frustration of an immigrant New York population. The dialects and stereotypes are taken off the streets and put on the stage. Obstreperous students bait the overbearing, incompetent teacher. Bert Lahr grew up in such conditions; his own truncated schooling bore the scars of the nation's indifference to its poor. The Nine Crazy Kids based their act on this prototype of urban farce.

Teacher: I've just received a message from my brudder asking me to come down and take charge of de schoolroom vhile he's layin' home sick in bed. He says dere are a lot of nice boys and girls. I must see who dey are. (He takes the cow bell from the table, goes to the door, and rings it. Enter Reginald Redstocking.) That must be vun of de girls. Do you belong to de classroom here?

Reginald: I should say I do.

Teacher: Why are you so late this morning?

Reginald: I had to stay at home this morning to do some knitting for my mother.

Teacher: Vot vas you knitting?—notting. Vhere are de rest of de children dat belong her vit you?

Reginald: Down in the yard playing pinochle.

Teacher: Vell, I'm going down to catch dem! You stay here and practice your singing lesson. (Teacher exits; Reginald sings "Sunbonnet." Teacher enters. Sharkey leaves seat and begins to shadowbox.)

Isador: Teacher! Look out for him! He's a Young Kipper. He's a fast boy.

Teacher: I'll slow him up! I suppose you boys don't know what I am?

Chorus: WE DON'T KNOW AND WE DON'T CARE. (Reginald pulls out a pea-shooter and shoots a pea in Teacher's face. Teacher slaps his hand over his eye.)

Teacher: Cut dat out! I'm no shooting gallery! Now, I will call out the roll.

Isador: (Reaches in pocket, pulls out a roll, and hands it to Teacher.)

Teacher: Vat's dat?

Isador: You asked for a roll, and here's de roll. It's a bagel. Tomorrow I'll bring you a pineapple.

Teacher: QUIET. I'm calling de rolls! Your name is in de book! And dose dat

I hear, say "here," and dose vot are not here, say "absent." **Now!** Reginald Redstocking?

Reginald: I'm not here.

Teacher: Can't you see yourself sitting down? John L. Fitz-Corbett Sharkey?

Sharkey: I'll be back in a minute.

Teacher: I don't care if you never come back. Isador Fitzpatrick?

Isador: I couldn't come today.

Teacher: By golly, no vunder my brudder is sick. The foist lesson vill be in geography.

Reginald: Teacher! I know him.

Teacher: You know who?

Reginald: George Graphy. He used to come and keep company with my sister.

Teacher: I'm speaking about geography. The name's in the book. Isador! Name me two of de largest oceans in de world.

Isador: The Atlantic and Pacific.

Teacher: No sir! Dat's a tea company. I said de two largest oceans in de world. O-X-Y-G-E-N. Oceans.

Isador: Oh, you mean an notion.

Teacher: Yes.

Isador: (Pointing to his forehead) In mine head, I got it an notion.

Teacher: (Hitting Isador over the head with a rattan stick) Vot did you say you got?

Isador: Now I got it—a headache.

Teacher: Dat's better! Speaking about oceans—Reginald! Name me two of de largest islands in the Pacific Ocean.

Reginald: Hawaii, Teacher.

Teacher: I'm pretty well t'ank you.

Isador: How's your brother?

Teacher: He's feeling pretty well, t'ank you.

Isador: Give him my regards.

Teacher: T'ank you. Sharkey—you tell us two of de principal oceans in de world.

Sharkey: How are you, Teacher?

Teacher: None of your business! Isador, you tell me.

Isador: How do you do?

Teacher: Stick out your hand.

(Isador sticks out his hand and Teacher hits him over the head.) How do you feel?

Isador: Ah! Fudge!

Teacher: Pooh!

Isador: Pooh! Pooh! On you.

Teacher: QUIET! The lesson is spellink!

Chorus: I-N-K. Ink!

Teacher: Who said anything about ink?

Sharkey: You spell "ink."

Teacher: I said spellink is de lesson. Not you should spell "ink." Reginald, spell de void "delight."

Reginald: D-e-l

Sharkey: D-e-l

Isador: Deal—

Teacher: Ve are not playing cards here. Reginald! Spell de void "delight."

Reginald: D-e-l-i-g-h-t. Delight! There!

Teacher: Correct! Sharkey! Do you know vot de void delight means?

Sharkey: To get tickled to deat'.

Teacher: Somebody should do dat to you. Isador! Stand up! Now make me a statement wit de void "delight."

Isador: De wind blew in de window nad blew out de light.

(Teacher grabs the rattan stick and runs after Isador, who scurries around the classroom. Isador grabs a book from Teacher's desk as he runs by it, and Sharkey gets up to protect him, standing in front of Teacher, who yells at Isador, "Put down de school." Isador slams book on Teacher's head.)

Teacher: And dat's enough of dat lesson!

Reginald: Oh, glory!

Teacher: (Imitating Reginald) Oh, Halleluljah! De next lesson is hysterics. Sharkey—vhere was Abraham Lincoln born?

Sharkey: Abraham Lincoln was born in a log cabin he helped build himself.

Teacher: Isador. Vhere was de Declaration of Independence signed?

Isador: On de bottom!

Teacher: Reginald! Who was de fadder of our country?

Reginald: George Washington.

Teacher: And de mudder?

Reginald: Mary Christmas.

Teacher: Vot vas Daniel Webster, Reginald?

Reginald: Daniel Webster was a well-read man.

Teacher: Fine. Isador! Vot is a well-read man?

Isador: A healthy Indian.

Teacher: The next lesson is recitations. Reginald! Recite!

Reginald: Anything in particular?

(Isador and Sharkey take spitballs out of their desks as Teacher glances at the audience, holding them ready to let fly as Reginald recites.)

Reginald: (Reciting) Oh, the snow . . .

(As Reginald recites the poem, both Sharkey and Isador hit Teacher with spitballs.)

Teacher: (Jumping angrily up and down) Please, don't aggravation me! Reginald! Continue.

Reginald: (Continuing) Oh, the snow! The beautiful snow,
　　　　　　Once I was as pure as the beautiful snow . . .

Isador: But he fell in the mud.

Teacher: Sharkey, now you recite.

Sharkey: Johnny O'Farrell sat down on a barrel
The barrel was loaded
And so was O'Farrell
The barrel exploded
Farewell, O'Farrell.

Teacher: You should die de same way, Shakespeare. Isador! You recite now.

Isador: Poor little Fido,
Poor little pup
Drinks his milk
From a Chinese cup.
Poor little pup
He'll stand on his hind legs
If you'll hold the front ones up.

Teacher: De last lesson is arithmetic. I want you boy to multiply at de same time from one to a hundred. Commence! (He uses the rattan stick like a baton.)

Chorus: One and one is two; two and two is four; four and four is eight; eight and eight is sixteen; sixteen and sixteen is thirty-two; thirty-two and thirty-two is sixty-four; sixty-four and sixty-four is . . . La-la-la-la-la-la-la-la-la.

(They all start to sing and dance, with the teacher joining in the mayhem.)

(Curtain)

APPENDIX 2

"Flugel Street"
by Billy K. Wells (c. 1918)

Billy K. Wells, who launched Bert Lahr in burlesque, was one of the few who wrote specifically for that medium. His "Flugel Street" is a classic bit. Like so much burlesque humor, it contrasts the violence, ignorance, and inequities of city life with the comic character who is made the butt of the situation by his stubborn opposition to everything around him. The sketch was written as the labor movement was beginning to widen in America; ironically it foreshadows Lahr's later hostility toward theatrical unions.

Lahr: (Enters, stares at audience, then talks to the orchestra.) If I ask you a answer, will you question me? Can you play the Irish reel? (The orchestra plays in unison. One player is off key.) No, no, that ain't it. (The music is struck up again. The same discord prevails.) C'mmon. Stop. I said Irish. (Finally, the music is played correctly.) That's it. That's it. (After four bars, the cornet wails loudly out of tune. Looking into the pit, Lahr barks at the players.) Vhat's the matter, you sick? No, you ain't sick. You're dead, but you're too lazy to close your eyes. Don't you know you ain't got no business to . . . (He gives a Bronx cheer.) . . . in there? Now, don't do that no more.

Cornet player: Don't tell it to me. Tell it to the boss.

Lahr: Vell, I'll tell it to you 'cause I'm the boss.

Bandleader: Say, stop picking on that man.

Lahr: Vell, did you see vat he did? He went like that. (He blows another Bronx cheer.)

Bandleader: Well, leave him alone. If you pick at him, you pick at me and the rest of the boys, and we don't stand for that.

Lahr: I don't care whether you stand for it or not he ain't got no business to . . . (produces another Bronx cheer) in here and that's all.

Bandleader: Well, we'll make you care. We belong to the same union, and we don't stand for it.

Lahr: Vell, I don't care for you and your union somehow, any place, or anywhere. I'll take care of us. You mind your business.

	(The straightman enters from the left. He comes up to Lahr and taps him on the shoulder.)
Lahr:	Come in.
Straightman:	Just a moment. I want to speak to this gentleman here. (He points to the bandleader in the pit.)
Lahr:	Vell, I want to speak to this gentleman here. (He points to the cornet player.)
Straightman:	Well, I want to speak to this gentleman here. (He speaks louder and points again to the bandleader.)
Lahr:	Vell, I'm going to speak to this gentleman first!
Straightman:	I'd like to see you. (He glares fiercely at Lahr.)
Lahr:	Hell. (He walks away.)
Straightman:	Now, don't you do that again. (Turns quickly.)
Lahr:	That was camouflaged. I'm teaching him how to play that thing.
Straightman:	You're trying to teach *him* (pointing to the player) how to play that instrument. (He laughs.) Why, my boy, you can't teach him how to play that. Why, he has played that instrument for the last twenty years. Come on. (He pushes Lahr.) Come on, get off this street. Get off this street before someone comes along and picks you up and puts you in an ashcan. (He stalks away.)
Lahr:	Then the street will be clean. (To player) See, he likes you. He likes you more than he likes me, but through me he is coaxing a bump on your eye and through him you're going to get a bush on your eye, and I'm going to bust you. (He moves toward player.)
Straightman:	(Rushing at Lahr and pushing him away) Oh no you won't. No you won't. You won't bust anyone around here. Now you keep quiet for just a minute. Just one minute.
Lahr:	Fifty-eight, fifty-nine, sixty. (He lunges at the player.)
Straightman:	(Moving toward Lahr again and pushing him away) Now see here, you. If you don't keep quiet, I'm going to put a sign on your eye "closed for the season."
Lahr:	Can I open next season? (To player) See, you're the cause of this. You look good and intelligent and all that, but you don't seem to realize that you're sitting in a good position for me to kick your front teeth out. (Turns to straightman) Boy, I'm gettin' tough. Gettin' touououououough!!
Straightman:	You only think you're getting tough.
Lahr:	Well, I'll take him outside and fight him ten rounds and spot him six. (To audience) You saw me come out and ask for the Irish reel. Everybody gave it to me and was going along nice and sweetly and he had to (make noise) . . . in there. I didn't mind the way he jazzed, but the way he jazzed.
Straightman:	(To bandleader) What's the matter?
Bandleader:	Why, the big stiff said unions are no good.
Straightman:	Well, what are you going to do about it?
Bandleader:	We're going to quit.

Straightman:	Quit? That's the spirit exactly. That's the idea. (Orchestra leaves the pit.) Now listen, fellers, when you get outside wait for him and if you kill him, it will be all right.
Lahr:	Do you think *I'll* be there?
Straightman:	Yes, you'll be there, and there'll be a pair of black horses driving right ahead of you.
Lahr:	Oh! I'm going to be a jockey!
Straightman:	It'll be your last ride!
Lahr:	I'll win that.
Straightman:	Ah, bah! Ladies and gentlemen, did you ever see the way these men stick together! That's what I call unionism. One for all and all for one. (Turns to Lahr) Do you know what they are going to do? They're going to quit.
Lahr:	No, they ain't.
Straightman:	Well, what are they going to do?
Lahr:	Go downstairs and play pinochle.
Straightman:	What right have you got to come out here and argue with those men?
Lahr:	I didn't argue with them. He went (makes a Bronx cheer) like that.
Straightman:	(Moving center stage) Ladies and gentlemen: If we had more men like these in this world this would be a different country. Just look back twenty-five years ago. What did the laboring man of this country have to work for? Why, he had to work for the small, measly sum of eight, ten, twelve cents an hour. Now, why did he have to do that? Because there were no unions in those days. But look at that same man today. Why, he's getting seventy cents, eighty, ninety cents, one dollar an hour. And that is what unionism has done. Most people are under the impression that a union is filled with socialistic ideas. But that is not so. All that a union man asks are his rights, and he being one of the principal leaders of this great nation today. Why, he's entitled to such. Why, only yesterday I was reading in one of our leading newspapers where the packing house employees of Omaha, Nebraska, had won their strike. Now, they could never have won their strike had it not been for the unions. Look all over the U.S. today. Look in your own homes, town factories. You don't find any more small children there. No. Why? Because the unions won't stand for it. That's why I say all of us, everyone of us, should thank that wonderful organization, the American Federation of Labor! (He turns to Lahr.) And you (slaps him on the chest) have the nerve to come out here and argue with these men!
Lahr:	I didn't argue with them. They went like that . . . (He produces a Bronx cheer.)
Straightman:	Do you wear any union clothes?
Lahr:	I got a union suit on.
Straightman:	Have you got a union label in that hat (taking Lahr's hat off his head) ?
Lahr:	Yes.

Straightman: Where?

Lahr: There—six and a half.

(The straightman punches his hand through the hat and throws it down and stomps on it. Then he walks away, as Lahr is left on stage looking forlornly at his hat. He moves to pick it up, and then drops it cowering in fear at the straightman's words.)

Straightman: Put that down. Leave that alone.

(He walks two steps toward center stage as Lahr tries to pick the hat up. Then he turns around.)

Don't touch that. A union man! Why you're nothing but a scab. A fine union man you are. You don't even know where Western Union is. (He walks off stage right.)

Lahr: (Looking at his hat) You're a scab, do you hear me? A scab!

Straightman: (Entering loudly) Begone.

(Lahr drops hat and runs to the left of the stage, putting his coat above his head to protect himself. He shivers in fear.)

Begone, you Alabama crap-shooting meat hound you. Back to the wilds of Africa from whence you came. Back with your ancestors, where you can hang by your tail and throw coconuts at the rest of the monkeys. Begone I say. Begone. (He exits right.)

Lahr: (Slowly lowering the coat from above his head) Did he went? Hat, I think he ruined you. (He picks up the hat and stares through it.) But I can see through it all now. But don't get mad at me, I didn't do it, and it wouldn't have happened if he didn't . . . (makes Bronx cheer noise) . . . in there.

(Lahr puts on the hat. A man enters from the left wearing a straw hat. He sees Lahr gesticulating with his hat and mimics him.)

Lahr: (Turning to the man) What do you know about a union? (The man begins to speak, but is cut short.) You don't know nothing, that's why—because! Now you see that. (Lahr points to the man, who stands center stage.) If there was more like that there wouldn't be so many. Just look back twenty-five years ago. Look what a working man had to do. He had to work for a living. Does he do it now? No. He has the woman working for him. Look in all your beautiful homes nowadays. You don't see any more little children. No. Why? Because the unions won't stand for it. Why, only yesterday I was reading in today's paper. What did I see? You don't know, and if you did, you couldn't tell me. That's why I say all of us, every one of us, we should all thank that wonderful organization, the American Express Company. They can take your trunk and you never get it and when you get it, you don't need it. Ah! (Lahr takes the man's hat.) Got a union label in yours? (He crushes the hat over his knee.) Begone. Begone, you Alabama crap-shooting meat hound. Back to Africa. Back where you can get a tail. You're a fine union man. Vhy, you don't even know where the Union Station is!

Man: Can you beat that!

Lahr: Hey, I bet you don't even have a union suit. (Lahr reaches toward the man and yanks at his pants, which fall to the floor. The man stands in his long underwear. Lahr does a doubletake, turning to the audience in bewilderment, yelling, "Gnong, gnong, gnong!")
(*Blackout*)

APPENDIX 3

"Beach Babies" (c. 1924)

The afterpiece was a bright, concise comic sketch that sent the patrons away satisfied. It usually brought the biggest attractions of the evening back for a final vaudeville turn. Although this piece was embellished by Lahr, it was written by Little Jeanie and her agent, and is typical of the makeshift quality of vaudeville and burlesque creation.

The stage set is a bathing tent on left, and on right, a bench with a newspaper. Girl comes out of tent in her bathing suit and walks across stage and off. Child (Jeanie) comes on and sees tent—steals clothes and goes off. Comedian (Lahr) comes on and Straightman enters also.

Lahr: (To Straightman) Hello there. Where, where are you going?

Straightman: I'm going fishing—Do you know where I can get some fish?

Lahr: Sure, walk down a block and turn to your right—there's a fish market there.

Straightman: I don't want to buy any fish. I want to catch them.

Lahr: Oh. You want to catch some fish?

Straightman: Why don't you come along?

Lahr: No, I'll stay here and catch myself some dears.

Straightman: Deer hunting? On a seashore? Is that a new sport?

Lahr: New sport? Why dear hunting is one of the oldest of seaside sports.

Straightman: Say, do you mean d-e-e-r-s?

Lahr: No, I mean d-e-a-r-s.

Straightman: Oh, I got you—chasing the chickens again. Well, I don't know about that sport.

Lahr: I know, that's why you're going fishing.

Straightman: What! Well, lots of luck and goodbye.

Girl: (Enters and silently flirts with Lahr. She trips.) Oh, that was my foot.

Lahr: Yes. I know it wasn't mine.
(Girl goes into tent.)

Lahr: Well, it looks like the hunting season is now open. (Girl takes off bathing suit and throws it out.)

Lahr: (Picks it up.) Empty. I never did care for these things empty. I think I'll take it down to the drug store and have it filled.
(Girl starts screaming.)

Girl: Oh me! Oh my! What the—ooh!

Lahr: A lady in distress. I must look into this.
(Lahr starts to go into tent.)

(Sticks her head out.) Oh, you mustn't come in here.

Oh—I thought you were in trouble.

I am. Someone has stolen all my clothes.

Isn't that nice?

What?

I mean, it happened to me twice.

Can't you help me—Where is my bathing suit?

(Sees suit and kicks it out of sight.) Bathing suit? Oh yes, where is it? (He offers pants, hat.)

Oh, that won't do. Can't you find me something else?

I am sorry, miss, but I'm a stranger in town. You better come out and help me look for it.

Oh, but I can't come out like this!

That's all right with me.

But I haven't got a thing on.

Neither have I—where shall we go!

Oh, stop fooling, I must have something to wear.

(Looks around and finds a newspaper on bench.) The very thing—a newspaper.

A newspaper! Why, how?

Wrap it around you like an apron. You can see how it looks on me. (Puts it on and walks across the stage, giving back to audience.)

Do you think it will be all right?

Why, it's just the thing for the hot weather.

Thank you. (Goes back into tent, then comes out again.) Yoohoo, I won't be long.

Don't worry. I'll wait.

(Lahr sits down on bench. Jeanie comes on.)

Hello!

Goodbye.

Hello, my name is Jeanie—what's yours?

Santa Claus.

Hello, hey! Why don't you say Hello?

Don't bother me, little girl.

What are you doing? Waiting?

No. I'm not waiting.

Who are you waiting for?

I'm not waiting for anybody.

Well, how long are you going to wait?

Will you go away—you don't have to wait any longer.

You're my Daddy, aren't you?

I hope not.

Why don't you want to be my Daddy?

No, I don't want to be your Daddy.

Well, whose Daddy do you want to be then?

I don't want to be anybody's Daddy—Can't you see I've got some things on my mind?

Jeanie:	What's the matter, are you in love?
Lahr:	No—I'm not in love. Come back in fifteen years and I'll talk business with you.
Jeanie:	Nobody loves you?
Lahr:	No—Nobody loves me.
Jeanie:	Well, I love you. (Falls over him.)
Lahr:	Listen, little girl—Go ask that man where the tide goes when it goes out.
Jeanie:	All right—Goodbye!
	(Girl comes out of tent with newspaper dress on.)
Girl:	Well—How do you like it?
Lahr:	Oh! It's ripping!
Girl:	Oh! Where?
Lahr:	No, no—I mean it's swell, it's a pipping.
Girl:	Don't you think it's too long?
Lahr:	Well, yes, but we'll fix that. (He tears off a strip.) How's that?
Girl:	That's better, but it's a little too plain.
Lahr:	Plain? Say do you like scallops?
Girl:	Yes.
	(Lahr tears scallops.)
Lahr:	Is that better?
Girl:	Oh no, I don't like that at all.
Lahr:	Say, I can't keep this up all day. (Tears another strip.) How's that?
Girl:	Oh, that's better.
	(Jeanie comes between them.)
Jeanie:	Is this her?
Lahr:	Is this who?
Jeanie:	The one you had on your mind?
Lahr:	Oh, isn't she cute? (Takes Jeanie off stage. She comes back.) As I was saying— (Jeanie is between them.)
Girl:	Who is this child?
Lahr:	I don't know, never saw her before.
Jeanie:	Oh, he knows me, he's my Daddy!
Girl:	Daddy! Is she your child?
Lahr:	Oh, no, she's joking. Come here, little girl, here's a red dime, go out and get yourself some rough on rat lozenges.
Jeanie:	Thank you—goodbye (going off). I'll be right back and give you some of my candy.
Lahr:	Won't you sit down?
Girl:	I can't sit down.
Lahr:	Why? Did you hurt yourself someplace?
Girl:	No, I'm afraid I'll tear my dress.
Lahr:	Oh, that's all right, we'll buy another.
	(They sit down; Jeanie comes on crying.)
Jeanie:	Booo Hooo (etc.)
Lahr:	What's the matter, honey?
Girl:	What did you do to her?

Lahr:	She looked at me and started to cry.
Girl:	Well, you must have done something to her or she wouldn't be crying that way.
Lahr:	Come here, what's the matter?
Jeanie:	I lost my dime.
Lahr:	How cute—she lost my dime. Never mind, I'll give you another. (Lahr looks for dimes, but he hasn't got any.)
Lahr:	Go on, I'll owe you one.
Jeanie:	No, I want it now.
Lahr:	Here, here's a white one.
Jeanie:	I don't want a white one; I want a red one.
Lahr:	Well—tomorrow I'll give you a blue one.
Jeanie:	Thank you, Daddy.
Lahr:	Don't call me Daddy.
Jeanie:	All right, Daddy.
Lahr:	I'm not your Daddy.
Jeanie:	Goodbye, Daddy!
Lahr:	Goodbye, try and get yourself run over, dear. (To Girl) Nice weather we're having.
Girl:	Yes, but I hope it doesn't rain.
Lahr:	Rain—I hope we don't have a wind storm. Let's look at the weather report. Ah! here it is, fair weather with gradually rising temperature. (pause) Can I depend on that?
Girl:	You must not believe everything you see in a newspaper.
Lahr:	But I believe everything I see in this newspaper. (Makes a pass at Girl.)
Girl:	Oh, don't—someone might see us.
Jeanie:	Oh yes! I can see you. (Lahr puts Jeanie between legs.)
Lahr:	As I was saying— (Woman enters.)
Woman:	I beg your pardon, have you seen a little girl around here?
Lahr:	(To Girl) I beg your pardon, have you seen . . . Oh, no. (To Woman) Please, lady, don't bother me.
Woman:	My baby, my baby, I've lost my baby.
Lahr:	That's too bad—I've lost plenty of them, but you don't see me bragging about it.
Jeanie:	Yoohoo—can't find me.
Woman:	Oh! There you are, come to Mother, Mother's little lamb.
Lahr:	Lamb—if that's a lamb, I'll never eat lamb again.
Woman:	So you were hiding my child?
Lahr:	Hiding your child! Why, we were trying to get rid of her.
Jeanie:	He gave me money to buy candy.
Woman:	Oh, you were stealing my baby.
Lahr:	Stealing, I'll give her a thing or two Lady——Pooh! Pooh.
Woman:	You can't get out of it this way, I know what you are, you are a couple of kidnappers.

Girl:	Kidnappers, why the very idea. (Starts arguing.) (A fight takes place. Jeanie kicks Lahr, Woman tears dress off Girl. Girl runs into tent.)
Woman:	You ought to be ashamed of yourself, stealing children at your age.
Girl:	We don't want your child.
Lahr:	No, we have our own.
Girl:	What!
Lahr:	No, I mean, if we want them, we'll have them.
Woman:	Come here, we'll not talk to these crooks.
Lahr:	Crooks! Say, I'll have my lawyer write you a letter.
Girl:	There are my clothes!
Lahr:	So you're the Jessie Jimmy.
Woman:	Come, dear, here are your clothes.
Girl:	Thank you.
Straightman:	(Straightman comes on with some fish.) Say, look what I caught, isn't that a beauty!
Lahr:	Beauty. Why, you should see what I caught.
Straightman:	What?
Lahr:	The most beautiful girl you ever laid eyes on—ooh! Come here, I'll introduce you to her.
Straightman:	Maybe she has a girl friend.
Lahr:	Miss—may I introduce a friend of—
Girl:	Ooh!
Straightman:	Why you darn fool—that's my wife. (*Blackout*)

APPENDIX 4

"Chin Up"

From Life Begins at 8:40 (*1934*)

by David Freedman

This sketch, by one of the most successful comedy writers of the period, represents the more sophisticated comedy Bert Lahr was attempting in the mid-thirties. In it, controlled tone, limited gesture, and sparse language were Lahr's comic resources. The opportunity to burlesque upper-class attitudes delighted Lahr; he was to have similar opportunities later in *Du Barry Was a Lady* and *The Beauty Part*.

A drawing room. Well furnished. Richard enters, looking dour.

Pater:	Not well.
Richard:	What is it?
Pater:	Gambling debt.
Richard:	Gambling debt?
Pater:	Can't pay it, broke.
Richard:	Borrow?
Pater:	Can't borrow, no credit.
Richard:	One thing to do.
Pater:	Right. Honor of family.
Richard:	Other way out?
Pater:	Not sporting.
Richard:	Right, stout fellow.
Pater:	Got a bit here?
Richard:	Poison?
Pater:	Right.
	(Butler enters with glass on tray.)
Richard:	Here you are.
Pater:	Thanks.
	(Butler exits; Pater raises glass.)
	Give you the Duchess.
Richard:	How jolly.
	(Pater drinks.)
Richard:	Does it hurt?
Pater:	Rawther.
Richard:	Well, chin up.
Pater:	Chin up.
Richard:	Stiff upper lip.

Richard: Honor of family.
Pater: (Prone) Honor of family. Cheerio, my boy. (Head drops.)
Richard: Cheerio, Pater. (Glances at watch.) Must dress.
   (Starts to go, but there is a knock on door.)
   Come.
   (Agatha enters.)
   Hello, Agatha.
Agatha: Hello, Dick.
Richard: Chin up, Agatha . . . (indicates) . . . the pater.
Agatha: (Looks at body.) Passed out?
Richard: Passed *away*. Gambling debt.
Agatha: Too bad.
Richard: Right.
Agatha: Dick.
Richard: Yes, Agatha.
Agatha: Our wedding anniversary.
Richard: Right.
Agatha: Something to tell you.
Richard: Right.
Agatha: Other man.
Richard: (Walks over to her.) You?
Agatha: Right.
Richard: Not faithful?
Agatha: Not faithful.
Richard: Rotten business.
Agatha: Putrid.
Richard: One thing to do.
Agatha: Poison?
   (Butler enters.)
Richard: Right.
Agatha: Got any?
   (Butler at her elbow, poison on tray.)
Richard: Here you are.
Agatha: Thanks. (Takes glass. Butler exits. She raises glass.) To the Duchess.
   (Drinks.)
Richard: How jolly. Does it hurt?
Agatha: Rather.
Richard: Too bad . . . well, chin up.
Agatha: Chin up.
Richard: Stiff upper lip. Honor of family.
Agatha: Honor of family . . . Cheerio, Dick. (She expires.)
Richard: Cheerio, Agatha. (Looks at watch.) Must dress.
   (Starts to walk left. Knock on door.)
   Come.
Mater: (Entering) Richard, my boy.
Richard: Mater.
Mater: Yes—

Richard: The pater—dead. (Indicates.)
Mater: (Looks at bodies.) Right—and Agatha.
Richard: And Agatha.
Mater: Beastly.
Richard: Right.
Mater: Chin up.
Richard: Chin up—stiff upper lip.
Mater: Right.
          (Richard starts to go.)
          Richard.
Richard: Not well?
Mater: Perfectly well—something to tell you.
Richard: Right. (Pause) Difficult?
Mater: Terribly difficult.
Richard: Right.
Mater: You.
Richard: Yes?
Richard: Not legitimate?
Mater: Not legitimate.
Richard: Bastard?
Mater: Quite.
Richard: (reeling) Chin up.
Mater: Chin up.
Richard: (Regaining precarious restraint) Stiff upper lip.
          Honor of family.
Richard: (Stands erect.) And you?
          (Butler enters.)
Mater: One thing to do.
Richard: Right.
Mater: (Sees Butler at elbow.) This it?
Richard: Rather.
Mater: Thanks. (Raises tumbler.) To the—
Richard: Duchess.

APPENDIX 5

"If I Were King of the Forest" from The Wizard of Oz *(1939)*
Lyrics by E. Y. Harburg, music by Harold Arlen.

The comic lyrics of E. Y. Harburg were written with a careful understanding of Lahr's personality. "If I Were King of the Forest" sports impossible rhymes ("elephant/cellophant") and funny vowel sounds ("gen*u*flect") that Lahr could elongate and make outrageous. In this song, the character of Bert Lahr, his film role, and the world of fantasy are adroitly combined.

Lion: If I were king of the forest,*
          Not queen, not duke, not prince,
          My regal robes of the forest
          Would be satin, not cotton, not chintz.
          I'd command each thing,
          Be it fish or fowl,
          With a regal woof,
          And a royal growl.
          As I'd click my heel
          All the trees would kneel
          And the mountains bow
          And the bulls kow-tow
          And the sparrows would take wing,
          If I, if I were king.

          Each rabbit would show respect to me,
          The chipmunks genuflect to me,
          Tho' my tail would lash
          I would show compash
          For ev'ry underling,
          If I, if I were king.
          Just king.

Dorothy, Tin Man, and Scarecrow:
          Each rabbit would show respect to him,
          The chipmunks genuflect to him,
          His wife would be Queen of the May.

Lion: I'd be monarch of all I survey,
          Monarch of all I survey.
          Mahahahahahahahahah—ah—narch of all I survey.

* Copyright 1938 (Renewed), 1968 Metro-Goldwyn-Mayer Inc.

Dorothy:	Your Majesty, if you were king,
	You'd not be afraid of anything.
Lion:	Not nobody, not nohow.
Scarecrow:	Not even a rhinoceros?
Lion:	Imposserous.
Tin Man:	How about a hippopotamus?
Lion:	I'd thrash him from
	His top to his bottomamus.
Scarecrow:	Supposin' you met an elephant?
Lion:	I'd wrap him up in cellophant.
Dorothy:	What if it were a brontosaurus?
Lion:	I'd show him who's king of the forest.
All:	But how? . . . How?
Lion:	How? Courage!

        What makes a king out of a slave?
           Courage.
        What makes the flag on the mast to wave?
           Courage.
        What makes the elephant charge his tusk,
        In the misty mist or the dusky dusk,
        What makes the muskrat guard his musk?
           Courage.
        What makes the Sphinx the seventh wonder?
           Courage . . . Courage.
        What makes the dawn come up like thunder?
           Courage.
        What makes the Hottentot so hot,
        What puts the "ape" in apricot,
        What have they got that I ain't got?

All:	Courage!
Lion:	For courage is the thing of kings,
	With courage I'll be king of kings,
	And all year round
	I'd be hailed and crowned
	By every living thing.
	'f I, 'f I, 'f I, 'f I, were king . . .
	If I—Iffffff-I—were KING.

377

APPENDIX 6

The Baseball Sketch (*1951*)

By *Abe Burrows*. From Two on the Aisle,
a *revue by Betty Comden, Adolph Green, and Jule Styne.*
Directed by *Abe Burrows.*

The Baseball Sketch is one of the first Broadway comedy bits about television. Abe Burrows originally wrote it as a vehicle for himself, but he revised the sketch to emphasize the ballplayer (Lahr), not the announcer. For the Baseball Sketch, Lahr wore a New York Giants uniform (his favorite team), complete with baseball spikes. As a long-time friend of many ballplayers, he enjoyed the chance to wear the outfit and spoof the national pastime.

The sketch began with a TV announcer sitting at a table with a microphone and scripts, unconscious of the television camera pointed toward him. He is bored. Suddenly a light goes on.

Announcer: (Very sharp) Good evening, sports fans everywhere . . . (music in and out) Yes, sports fans, this is Bill Burns. Your old sportscaster bringing you highlights and spotlights from the world of sports on the spot. This program is . . . spontaneous and unrehearsed. These sportscasts are telecast to you through the courtesy of our sponsors, the makers of Sawsie Dusties, the cereal that gives you that quick extra energy. And now, friends, for our guest tonight. Sawsie Dusties is proud our guest on tonight's parade of sports stars and sports fans, here's a real old timer . . . a great ballplayer and a great man.
(Lahr belatedly comes out in uniform from stage right. The lights get him. He squints.)

Lahr: (Crosses to the front of table, backside to camera) Now, NOW?

Announcer: . . . Lefty Hogan, hiya Lefty . . . Sit right here, Lefty.

Lahr: (Trying to look happy) Hi ya, Buster.

Announcer: Well, Lefty, say hello to our TV audience.
(Lefty waves to camera.)

Announcer: Now, Lefty, tell the folks—how long have you been donning those spiked shoes?

Lahr: Huh?
(Announcer repeats.)

Lahr: (Crosses legs, looks at shoes.) Well, I've had these shoes about two, three years.

APPENDIX 6

Announcer: How long have you played big league baseball?
Lahr: Huh?
Announcer: How long have you played big league baseball?
Lahr: Well let's see now . . . I started in 1920 and this is . . . 'bout fourteen, fifteen years.
Announcer: If you started in 1920, that would make it more than twice as long as that.
Lahr: Well, I ain't counting the time the other side was batting.
Announcer: Well, you were a great symbol of American sport all these years . . . and you're still a great pitcher.
Lahr: No, I'm a coach—been a coach for ten years.
Announcer: Oh, of course—what with covering sports I never get a chance to see a game. (Chuckles; Lahr imitates him.) Of course you're a coach . . . and a coach is very valuable. Eeerr—exactly what does a coach do?
Lahr: (Doing a double-take) Well, I try to learn the young players all my experiences just like they was once teached to me.
Announcer: Where did you first play baseball?
Lahr: At college.
Announcer: You went to college?
Lahr: Sure I went. Do I look like a diseducated guy? . . . I played college football, basketball, and baseball . . . I went to college for six years.
Announcer: Why six years?
Lahr: I had a contract . . . so like I said I played college football, basketball, baseball . . .
Announcer: And finally, Lefty, you became a professional—you had to. You had to because of that deep love you possessed for this great sport! Because of that you wouldn't rest until you became part of this beloved game.
Lahr: No, I wanted to make some dough.
Announcer: Magnificent sportsman that you are . . . and what a great pitcher you were. Tell me, Lefty, after being so great, what made you decide to take off your armor and cease to do active battle on the field of honor with the other knights of baseball?
Lahr: I never played night baseball . . . only daytime.
Announcer: No, I mean why did you quit pitching?
Lahr: Whyn't you say so. You talk like a umpire. Well, why I quit pitching was I hurt my hand . . . busted it . . . couldn't pitch no more . . .
Announcer: Hurt your hand in the service of the great game! Ah, but you went down in action. Tell me, Lefty, how'd it happen, this tragedy of a great athlete?
Lahr: Well, it was back in 1948 . . . I was pitching against the Red Sox . . . and in the first inning I got a tough break.
Announcer: What was it?
Lahr: They made nine runs. I never missed a bat. So anyway . . .
Announcer: But you had hurt your hand.
Lahr: No! No—I didn't hurt my hand . . . so anyway, in the second inning I was a little better—they only made six runs. But still the manager turned me out, anyway.

Announcer: But all the time your pitching hand was hurt and sportsman and gentleman that you are you made no mention of it.

Lahr: No, my hand was all right . . . so then later I got dressed and went home and when I came in the door, my wife said, "Well, they certainly made a bum out of you today." So, I socked her and busted my hand.

Announcer: Broke it defending your reputation as a pitcher . . . tell me one more thing, Lefty. What advice would you give to young boys who are eager to become future ballplayers?

Lahr: Well—I'd tell 'em—

Announcer: What would you tell these future diamond greats?

Lahr: Well, I'd—

Announcer: What yesterday has to say to today.

Lahr: Well—

Announcer: What's your advice to these young, young kids?

Lahr: (Exasperated) They'll be old men before I get to tell 'em. (Stops.) Now what was the question?

Announcer: What's your advice to these young kids?

Lahr: Well, I'd say they should practice a lot . . . work hard . . . stay away from girls . . . live clean lives . . . don't take baths—that softens up their hands . . . eat good healthy meals . . .

Announcer: Now, that's what I wanted to hear you say.

Lahr: It is?

Announcer: Yessiree—ladies and gentlemen, those meals are mighty important. Especially breakfast. Now tell me, Lefty, what's your favorite breakfast?

Lahr: Pizza.

Announcer: And what do you take for that quick, extra energy?

Lahr: A hook 'a rye.

Announcer: What a grand sense of humor . . . but, seriously, Lefty, now that it's almost time to go, how about those Sawsie Dusties?

Lahr: How about what? (squinting quizzically)

Announcer: Sawsie Dusties—you remember, you were going to tell the young folks something about them.

Lahr: Oh yeah, now I remember, Buster. Now, kids, listen.

Announcer: That's right, Lefty. Tell the kids about those great Sawsie Dusties.

Lahr: Well, listen—

Announcer: Tell them about that quick extra energy.

Lahr: When you go to the grocery—

Announcer: Tell them about Sawsie Dusties' rich, tangy goodness.

Lahr: —buy some—

Announcer: Tell them what's the most important thing to remember about Sawsie Dusties.

Lahr: (Glaring at the camera disgustedly) Don't eat 'em—THEY'LL KILL YA! (*Blackout*)

APPENDIX 7

"Hostility"

By Arnold B. Horwitt and Aaron Ruben.
Directed by Aaron Ruben. From
The Girls Against the Boys (1959)

This sketch stressed Lahr's gestures, not his words, his ability to exist in a state of frenzied hilarity without having to deliver jokes about it. Lahr enjoyed the scene because he played against Nancy Walker and because silent family rage was something he knew from his childhood and his own adult temper tantrums. Because the scene relies so completely on movement and reaction within small areas of intensity, it fitted the scope of television and became a popular routine.

Lahr enters. He wears a construction worker's helmet and outfit. Also heavy work shoes. Carries metal lunch pail. Lahr comes in obviously angry. Slams the door behind him. Nancy ignores him. He opens and slams door again; she still ignores him. He glares at her from door area. She doesn't look up. Then he glares at lunch pail. He crosses to kitchen table, puts lunch pail on it. He angrily opens it and holds up a large sandwich, which has one bite out of it. He glares at sandwich and at her. Then strides to garbage container and vehemently slams sandwich in. No reaction from Nancy. He clangs the lid of the garbage can several times. Looks again to see if he has gotten a rise out of her. Nancy still intent on nails. Peeved, he takes off blue work shirt. He goes to hook on door on which her blouse hangs. Drops blouse on floor and hangs his shirt and helmet on hook.

Lahr crosses to sink to wash. Clangs lid of garbage pail again. Starts to turn on water, notices dishes in sink. Lifts out moderate pile, throws her a look. Reaches in and removes second, king-sized, pile of dishes. He turns on water, reaches for soap. No soap. Noisily bangs open and shut cabinet drawers looking for soap. Nancy resignedly rises and hobbles over on her heels to a cabinet he's overlooked, takes enormous box of Vel out. Lahr holds out his hand and she pours soap powder in it, then puts box back in cabinet. Quick turn back to each other.

Lahr washes energetically, making blubbery seal sounds. She grimaces in silent anguish. She sees her blouse on the floor. She crosses to the door, picks up her blouse, takes his shirt off hook and puts her blouse back on it. Lahr has finished washing and is blindly looking for a towel. She crosses to him and thrusts his shirt at him. Thinking it's a towel, he dries his face on it. He looks at it, realizes what she's done, is furious, and throws it on the floor. She ignores all this.

He now goes to cabinet, takes out bottle of rye and large brandy snifter. Fills it to top and drinks noisily. During this Nancy tenses herself to survive the nightly

381

ritual. After downing booze, he exhales voluptuously in her direction. She fans herself as fumes envelope her. He puts the bottle back in cabinet.

Lahr now goes to table. Nancy intent on her toes. Lahr turns in his chair and makes noisy chomping sounds. She continues pedicure. Finally, he takes knife and hammers noisily on plate. She ignores this as she carefully fans toes with newspaper. Lahr abandons hammering, comes over, watches with rising but suppressed fury. Finally attempts to stomp on her foot, which she quickly withdraws. She slips into her mules and rises as they glower at each other. Still glowering, they do a turn around each other. Then she trudges over to stove to start dinner. He registers satisfaction at his victory, sits on sofa, and starts to read newspaper.

Nancy begins preparing dinner with vehement movements that reflect her fury. She sets timer, lights oven, and lights burner under tea kettle. Lahr starts to laugh at something in newspaper. She looks at him; he sees her and stops. She looks at Lahr, then at garbage can. Goes to garbage can and gets sandwich out. She crosses to table, gets knife, and cuts off piece of sandwich with bite out of it, wraps rest of sandwich in wax paper and puts it back in lunch pail. Takes lunch pail up to ice-box, looking at Lahr all the while, and puts it in icebox. She takes a vegetable from icebox, goes to sink and turns on faucet to rinse it. Tap is turned so it makes annoying coughing sound. She crosses back to icebox and opens it, looks for something, oblivious to faucet racket, which is beginning to annoy Lahr. He looks up from paper wondering when the hell she is going to turn it off. Seeing she has no intention of stopping it, he leaps up, tears over to the sink, and with an angry gesture, turns it off. He starts back to sofa, but a look comes over his face as he realizes Nancy is bending over. He goes to kick her just as she straightens up. They glare at each other. She realizes his hand is resting on icebox, so she deliberately shuts door on it. He gives her a withering look as he returns to sofa and newspaper. Nancy has gone to table. She gets a serving spoon from drawer and goes up to stove. No sooner does Lahr get comfortable again when the whistling kettle starts. He starts reacting to this and again Nancy goes about her duties ignoring the whistle.

He rises in fury, rushes to stove, and turns off burner under kettle. As he turns away to go back to sofa, she turns burner back on so that kettle gives one final whistle.

Nancy goes to stove and opens oven door. Cloud of black smoke pours forth. She takes out casserole and puts it on table. Goes to sink and gets sugar and cream. Lahr sniffs, stalks over to table to inspect this mess. She stirs it. Just as he's about to sit down she slops some food on his plate. Then delicately spoons some on her own plate. As Lahr sits at the table, still sniffing in disbelief, she takes the casserole back to the stove, and gets two bottles of beer from the icebox. She brings them to the table.

Lahr holds his nose and tries to eat, then covers his eyes and tries to eat, then gives up and starts to take a bite as Nancy comes to his side and pulls out enormous drawer to get bottle opener. She closes drawer, leaving him two feet from table. She opens the beer. He pushes his chair back to table.

Lahr takes a forkful of food, reacts in dismay and disbelief, and takes a huge gulp of beer to wash it down. He shakes lots of salt into it, then lots of pepper, then lots of both together. Tastes again, then matter-of-factly picks up plate, opens door to hall, whistles for dog. He holds plate down, pantomimes urging dog to eat, is rejected, and trudges back to table resignedly, where Nancy is eating away.

Lahr sits down and reaches for bread basket, discovers it is empty. Turns it upside down (for her benefit). Raps it on table. She suddenly gets up. Fetches long, large loaf of rye bread. Takes it to table just as he is about to eat again, pulls open drawer, forcing him back. She gets bread knife out of drawer, puts knife and bread on table, goes back to her chair and resumes eating, while Lahr is all this time struggling to close drawer. Finally, in a rage, he slams drawer in so hard it goes out the other end and pokes Nancy in stomach.

Lahr returns to table, and Nancy goes to stove and gets coffee pot, gets cups. Lahr pushes his plate aside, leans back and starts tooth-sucking noise. On first hearing, Nancy freezes. She brings coffee pot to table as he orchestrates tooth-sucking. She is standing behind him, visibly restraining herself from pouring it on him. She places his coffee cup in front of him. He does one last tooth-sucking at her. She pours him coffee, then herself, leaves coffee pot on table and sits down. Lahr puts sugar in his coffee. Then he pours cream, stirs. Then rises, goes to sink, and pours out coffee. As Nancy sips her coffee, Lahr crosses to sofa, doing several last tooth-suckings at her behind her back. He sits, starts taking off shoes, accompanied by loud groans. He drops the first shoe with loud thud. Then he takes off second shoe and quietly places it on floor. Nancy has been waiting for the second shoe noise, looks over, sees shoe on floor, does "take" with coffee cup. Lahr yawns prodigiously, scratches self, groans, coughs, stretches out on sofa and snores. Nancy has finished her coffee and commences clearing the table. She slams down chair near him, piles dishes together, and rattles them loudly as she takes them to sink. She pushes table aside, bumps it up and down a few times, pushes other chair aside, rattles table again, and starts for bed. She stops, comes back and bangs table a few more times. She goes to the alcove in the back wall and lets down Murphy bed with a loud thump. This jars Lahr sufficiently awake to noisily stumble across to bed in half sleep. He lets trousers drop and steps out of them as he crosses. He flops in bed and is fast asleep.

Nancy has taken off housecoat and is now in a slip. She turns out the lights and gets in bed beside him. They both lie still, the only sound that of Lahr snoring. Finally, after a pause she speaks:

Nancy: Eddie. Eddie.

Lahr: (Grunts.)

Nancy: You forgot something.

     (Lahr kisses her.)

     (*Blackout*)

INDEX

INDEX

INDEX

About the Author

The youngest recipient of the George Jean Nathan Award for Dramatic Criticism, John Lahr is the author of a biography of the English playwright Joe Orton, *Prick Up Your Ears*, and a critical study, *Coward: The Playwright*. His novels are *The Autograph Hound* and *Hot to Trot*. He has been the literary manager of the Tyrone Guthrie Theatre in Minneapolis and of the Vivian Beaumont Theater at Lincoln Center in New York.

Mr. Lahr now lives in London, where he writes a monthly theatre column for *New Society*. His latest collection of essays, *Automatic Vaudeville*, will be published in 1984.

A Note on the Type

This book was set on the Linotype in Baskerville, a fac-
simile of the type designed in 1754 by John Baskerville,
a writing master of Birmingham, England. This type was
one of the forerunners of the "modern" style of type faces.
The Linotype copy was cut under the supervision of George
W. Jones of London.